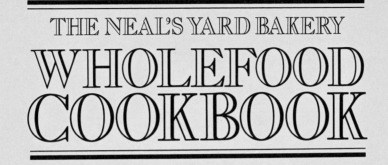

THE NEAL'S YARD BAKERY
WHOLEFOOD COOKBOOK

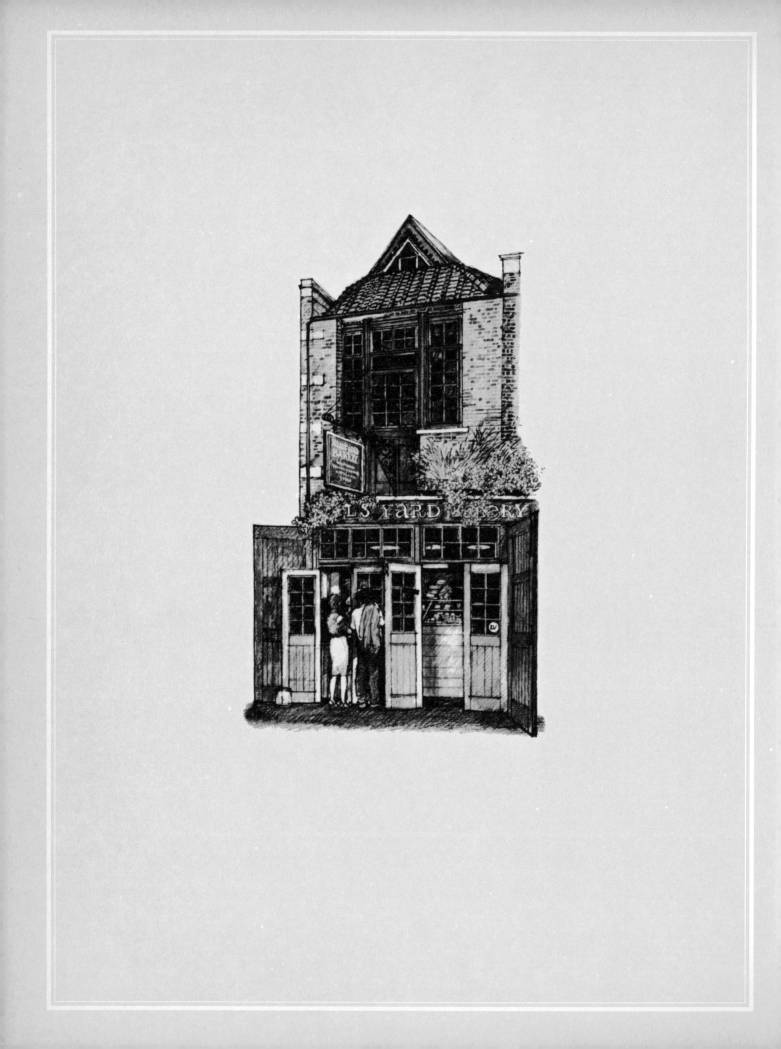

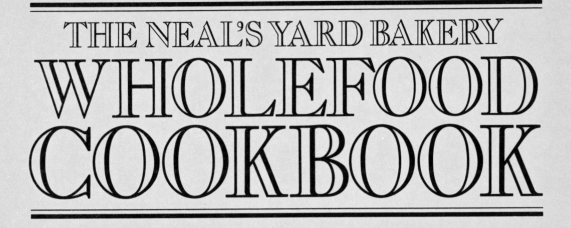

THE NEAL'S YARD BAKERY
WHOLEFOOD
COOKBOOK

Rachel Haigh

Salem
House

SALEM HOUSE PUBLISHERS
TOPSFIELD, MASSACHUSETTS

Editorial Director Pamela Norris
Editors Beverly LeBlanc, Joanna Lorenz, Miren Lopategui
Art Director Roger Bristow
Designers Jane Warring, Tessa Richardson-Jones

Photography by Geoff Dann
Illustrations by Eric Thomas, Robert Micklewright,
David Ashby and Vanessa Luff
Stylist Sue Brown

First published in Great Britain in 1986 by
Dorling Kindersley Publishers Limited,
9 Henrietta Street, London WC2E 8PS

First published in the United States by
Salem House Publishers, 1987,
462 Boston Street, Topsfield, MA 01983

Library of Congress Cataloging-in-Publication Data

Haigh, Rachel, 1952-
  The Neal's Yard wholefood cookbook.

  Includes index.
  1. Cookery (Natural foods).   2. Food, Natural.
3. Neal's Yard Bakery (London, England).   I. Title.
II. Title: Wholefood cookbook.
TX 741.H34   1987   641.5′637   86-22062
ISBN 0-88162-271-0

The publishers would like to thank the Controller of
Her Majesty's Stationery Office for permission to
reproduce some of the nutritional information in the
charts from The Composition of Foods and The
Supplementary Booklet Immigrant Foods.

The publishers would like to thank Jimmy Tsao, Josephine
and staff for all their help, and would also like to thank the
following for the loan of some of the items which appear in
the photographs of this book: Neal Street East, 5 Neal Street,
London; David Mellor, 26 James Street, London;
Elizabeth David, 46 Bourne Street, London.

Typeset by Chambers Wallace Ltd, London
Printed and bound in Italy by Lego
Reproduced in Singapore

CONTENTS

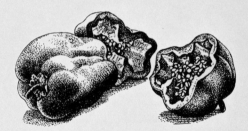

PREFACE

This book is based on the extensive experience of the Neal's Yard Bakery Co-operative in preparing, cooking and selling whole foods.

Neal's Yard is a small triangular area in Covent Garden in London, surrounded by high Victorian warehouse buildings, which were formerly part of London's main wholesale fruit and vegetable market. What makes Neal's Yard remarkable are the distinctive and original businesses which occupy these buildings.

Narrow alleyways lead into the Yard, which is full of plants and bustling activity. Situated along two sides of the triangle are the businesses: The Dairy, Flour Mill, Bakery, Apothecary, Soup and Salad Bar, Organic Fruit and Vegetable Shop and Alternative Therapy Rooms. The Neal's Yard Wholefood Warehouse is situated at the entrance to one of the alleyways.

The Yard was started by Nicolas Saunders, who bought the semi-derelict buildings in the mid-seventies and set up the original Neal's Yard Warehouse. He actively encouraged and helped others to start up most of the businesses now operating in the Yard. These businesses are in fact quite separate, although compatible with Nicolas Saunders' original aim of providing in one area both natural health care and a complete range of whole foods.

The Neal's Yard Bakery Co-operative incorporates the Flour Mill, Bakery and Restaurant in Neal's Yard and the Wholefood Warehouse in Portobello Road in West London. The Co-operative specializes in the sale of high quality whole foods and the business itself is organized along unconventional lines. The Bakery was set up in 1978 by Clare Taylor with a group of her friends and former workmates, and it was formally registered as a co-operative in 1980. In 1981 it bought the Neal's Yard Flour Mill and in 1983 opened its own wholefood warehouse in Portobello Road. Each member of the Co-operative shares in the ownership of the business and takes an equal part in all its operations. This means that all jobs are shared, from bread making and serving customers to administration and management decisions.

This book is the result of countless requests from customers for whole food information and for the recipes from the restaurant. Many of the dishes served daily at the Bakery Restaurant are included and there is also a wide range of other dishes, reflecting the diversity of modern vegetarian cooking. All the recipes have been scaled down to a quantity suitable for domestic use and have been carefully tested for accuracy. The first part of the book is a detailed reference section, providing invaluable information on whole foods.

As people are becoming more and more aware of the importance of whole foods in a balanced diet, there is increasing curiosity about the food we eat: Where it comes from, how it is grown, what processing (if any) is needed for its production and the different ways in which it can be prepared and presented. It is hoped that this book will succeed in answering most of these questions.

The information and recipes in this book were collated by Rachel Haigh, a founder member of the Neal's Yard Bakery Co-operative. Simon Blackley, also a founder member, contributed the sections on grains and flours.

INTRODUCTION

Why eat whole foods?

Whole foods, or natural foods, are foods which have not been over-refined or -processed, which have not been subjected to chemicals and which do not contain harmful additives.

As a result of modern technology, the concept of eating foods in a whole, natural state has been seriously eroded. We can now eat banana-flavored desserts which contain no bananas, buy fruit which is large and glossy as a result of chemical nutrients and chickens which have been artificially fattened by the use of hormones. We can also keep naturally perishable foodstuffs for weeks without danger of mold or decay and separate out the very heart of a kernel of wheat. These are remarkable scientific and technological advances, but what is happening to the nutritional value of the foods themselves?

The economic pressures of large-scale agriculture have led to the increasing use, particularly in the "developed" world, of a wide range of chemicals. Drugs are added to animal feed, artificial fertilizers are added to the soil and herbicides, insecticides and fungicides are sprayed over crops. It has been widely claimed that this has greatly increased yields. Aerial crop-spraying with weedkillers, for example, is clearly more efficient and economic than the traditional, labor-intensive method of walking the field and plucking out the weeds by hand. However, the costs of these chemicals both in terms of the environment and of human health are only now beginning to be appreciated.

Many of the chemicals are poisonous in large quantities. Some, such as DDT, have already been banned in many countries. Others, such as inorganic nitrate (used as a fertilizer), are still used in high concentrations. The use of these chemical fertilizers is addictive, so that the fertilizers used now, for instance, often need to be 20 times stronger than 5 years previously. This can result in total depletion of the soil and pollution of ground water and streams. Herbicides and pesticides get into the food chain and end up on our plates, along with the other chemicals left in or on the foods themselves.

The long-term dangers of eating foods grown with the help of chemicals may not be fully understood, but it is widely accepted that there is a connection between modern agricultural practices and the recent increase in degenerative and debilitative diseases. There is no doubt that wherever possible it is safer to eat whole foods made from organically grown plants.

Another source of chemicals in the modern diet is processed and refined food. Food additives now include flavorings, preservatives, stabilizers, antioxidants, sweeteners, colorants and bleaching agents. Although natural additives have been used in food for centuries, as many as 3,000 additives are now available to food manufacturers, many derived from chemicals.

Since 1951, the consumption of food additives has more than doubled, and it has been documented that the average adult living in a Western society currently consumes about 4 pounds of additives a year. Although many additives are now tested before use, their long-term effects are unknown. The evidence increasingly suggests that these foreign substances in the body may cause many modern diseases. Not only can additives affect the foods to which they are added, and therefore the nutritional value of those foods, they can also be harmful in cumulative quantities.

By incorporating whole foods in your diet, the cumulative dangers of additives are avoided or lessened, and, because true whole foods have not had anything removed during processing, most if not all of their nutritional value is retained.

Types of whole food diet

A whole food diet is not necessarily vegetarian, and could include meat, poultry and fish reared without the aid of chemicals. Organic butchers exist who will supply meat that they claim has been reared naturally and killed in a humane manner. Some people on a whole food diet will not eat meat or poultry, but will eat fish with an otherwise vegetarian diet.

Vegetarian (Lacto vegetarian)
The recipes in this book (and those served at the Neal's Yard Bakery Restaurant) are based on vegetarian whole foods. Meat, poultry and fish are excluded; dairy products, eggs and honey are included.

Vegan
A vegan diet is totally vegetarian, and no animal products are consumed. This means that dairy products such as cheese, milk and yogurt are excluded, as are eggs and honey. Vegan recipes in this book are indicated by the symbol ⓥ.

Gluten-free
Gluten is a sticky protein contained in the starchy part of some grains. In recent years medical research has indicated that some allergies may be attributable to gluten consumption. In these cases a gluten-free diet is recommended. Grains and flours which do not contain gluten are maize, rice, millet, buckwheat, chickpea and soy. Gluten-free recipes in this book are indicated by the symbol ⒼⒻ.

A balanced diet

A correct balance of proteins, fats, carbohydrates, fibers, vitamins and minerals is essential for a healthy diet. As a general rule, you should try to eat at least twice as much carbohydrate as protein, keep your sugar and fat intake to a minimum (particularly saturated fats, see p. 45) and cut down on salt. Fiber is also essential for the healthy functioning of the digestive system, although it is not actually digested and absorbed. This means eating mainly cereals, beans, vegetables and fruit, and cutting down on animal fats, sugar and salt.

NUTRIENTS	FUNCTION IN BODY	EFFECT OF DEFICIENCY
Proteins	Essential for formation, growth and repair of all body cells, and for the functioning of the enzymes, hormones and antibodies which regulate and control our bodies. Proteins are made up of amino acids. There are about 20 amino acids, 8 of which are present in protein-containing foods. The rest are synthesized by the body from these 8. Foods which contain all of the 8 essential amino acids are called complete proteins; foods which contain only a few are called incomplete proteins.	Usually coupled with starvation. The body wastes away and metabolic processes decrease.
Fats	These are needed for energy and to form layers of protective tissue in the body. The fat-soluble vitamins A, D, E and K are stored in this fatty tissue. Fats can be saturated or unsaturated, the former containing cholesterol (see p. 45).	Excess is more common than deficiency. Too much fat, particularly saturated, can lead to obesity and heart disease.
Carbohydrates	The body's major source of energy, made up of sugars, starch and fiber. They are also needed to metabolize proteins for body tissue repair, and to run the central nervous system. Unrefined carbohydrates (i.e. grains) are nutritious, but refined carbohydrates (i.e. white sugar) offer only "empty" calories.	Listlessness, fatigue and nausea. Excess refined carbohydrates are stored as fat in the body, and can lead to tooth decay, high blood pressure, heart disease and diabetes.
Fiber	Not a nutrient, but essential for the elimination of waste material and toxins in the body. Fiber adds bulk to food, and exercises the jaw muscles.	Has been linked to chronic and debilitating diseases of the digestive tract and, possibly, the circulatory system.
Vitamins	Usually needed in minute quantities, but nonetheless essential for healthy functioning of the body. Water-soluble vitamins (the B group and C) need to be taken regularly as they cannot be stored in the body for long; fat-soluble vitamins (A, D, E and K) last longer.	
A *(retinol)*	Helps in cell differentiation. Also needed for healthy skin and mucous membranes, and for good night vision.	Softening of bones and teeth, dry skin and night blindness.
B *group*	The major function of all the B vitamins is to break down food into simple sugar molecules for energy and to form new red blood cells. They are also important for the functioning of the brain, nervous and circulatory systems and for healthy hair, skin, eyes and liver. B vitamins work best in conjunction with each other.	
B$_1$ *(thiamine)*	Breaks down carbohydrates for energy. Assists the functioning of brain, nerves and muscles.	Constipation and abdominal pains, and, in extreme cases, beri-beri.
B$_2$ *(riboflavin)*	Breaks down fats, carbohydrates and proteins for energy. Easily destroyed by light.	Mouth and throat infections and eye fatigue. Common in non-milk drinkers.
B$_3$ *(niacin)*	Breaks down fats, carbohydrates and proteins for energy.	Digestive disorders, sore, swollen tongue and failure to grow in children.
B$_6$ *(pyridoxine)*	Breaks down proteins into amino acids for the formation of red blood cells and hormones.	Anemia, nervous disorders and fatigue.
B$_{12}$ *(cobalamin)*	Essential for forming red blood cells and for synthesizing RNA and DNA. Also essential for healthy nerves. Vitamin B$_{12}$ can be found in dairy products but is rare in vegetable foodstuffs, so vegans should take a supplement.	Rare but can result in serious anemia.

NUTRIENTS	FUNCTION IN BODY	EFFECT OF DEFICIENCY
Folic acid	Also a B vitamin. Used in formation of RNA and DNA, and in breakdown of proteins into amino acids. Important in early pregnancy.	Poor growth, gastro-intestinal problems and anemia.
C *(ascorbic acid)*	Essential for formation of antibodies and for healing and aiding recovery. Helps form collagen, needed for the body's connective tissue. Also needed for absorbing iron and for producing hemoglobin and epinephrine.	Bleeding gums, poor teeth, low resistance to disease and slow healing.
D *(calciferol)*	Needed to absorb and regulate calcium and phosphorus, and for strong bones, teeth and gums. Can be absorbed from sunlight as well as food.	Softening of the bones and rickets.
E *(tocopherol)*	Protects vitamin A and unsaturated fatty acids in the body from harmful oxidation. Assists in healing.	Rare, but can lead to muscular wasting, and abnormal fat deposits and red blood cells.
K *(phytomenadione)*	Essential for blood clotting.	Rare, but can lead to internal and external bleeding.
Minerals	These are necessary for cell growth and repair and regulation of the body. Macro-minerals (calcium, phosphorus, magnesium, sodium, potassium and chloride) are needed in quantities of 100 mg or more a day, and micro-minerals, or trace elements (iron, iodine and zinc) are needed in quantities of only a few mg or less a day. A balance of minerals is very important, as they often work in conjunction with each other. For instance, sodium and potassium work together, as do calcium, phosphorus and magnesium. Taking single mineral supplements can upset this balance, so it is best to obtain them from a varied diet of whole foods.	
Calcium	Essential for forming bones and teeth, and for maintenance of muscular contractions, nerve impulses and blood clotting. It should be balanced with phosphorus and magnesium.	Muscular problems, fragile bones and tooth decay. Can also lead to insomnia and nervous exhaustion.
Chloride	Needed with sodium and potassium for regulation of body fluid. Helps in formation of gastric juices in stomach for digestion of proteins.	Can lead to imbalance of sodium in body.
Iodine	Needed to form two hormones in the thyroid gland which regulate energy metabolism and protein synthesis.	Can lead to goiter, a swelling of the neck, and also obesity and listlessness.
Iron	Essential for forming hemoglobin in red blood cells, which transport oxygen from the lungs to all cells in the body. Should be balanced with a trace of copper and vitamin C for correct functioning.	Deficiency is common, and can lead to anemia and fatigue.
Magnesium	Important, with calcium and phosphorus, for the functioning of the skeletal and nervous systems.	Muscular weakness and delerium.
Phosphorus	Works with calcium for healthy bones and teeth, and also assists in the body's release of energy. Should be balanced with calcium and magnesium.	Excess is more common.
Potassium	Closely linked to sodium in regulation of body fluids, particularly in the muscle cells and blood.	Can lead to impaired neuro-muscular functioning and even heart attacks.
Sodium	Regulates the body's fluid balance and monitors the passage of nutrients into, and waste out of, the cells. Must be balanced with potassium.	Excess is more common, causing fluid retention and high blood pressure.
Zinc	Important for growth and repair of tissues, protein synthesis and the body's defence system. Should be balanced with iron and copper.	Fatigue, low resistance to infection and stunted sexual maturity.

Planning a whole food vegetarian diet

All of the body's nutritional requirements can be met in a whole food vegetarian diet. The basic food values of each type of whole food are described below, and there is a simple chart to show the best proportions of these foods to take as part of your general intake. Detailed nutritional charts are given in the information section of this book, showing the recommended daily allowances of the major nutrients and the corresponding quantities contained in the various whole foods.

Grains, beans, nuts and seeds

Grains and beans are the most important part of a whole food vegetarian diet as they are rich in protein, carbohydrates, vitamins (especially the B group), minerals and fiber. When sprouted, they are a particularly good source of vitamins, especially C. It is a mistake to see grains and beans as just stodgy carbohydrates. Carbohydrates are necessary for the processing of other foods and will only be fattening if the body's overall calorific intake is too high. Nuts and seeds do have a high calorific value, being rich in fats and oils, but they are also full of proteins, vitamins and minerals.

Grains, beans, nuts and seeds are the best sources of protein in the plant kingdom. The important point to remember is that their proteins complement each other. Meat, poultry and fish supply us with what is sometimes called complete or first-class protein. This means they contain all the amino acids which the body needs to synthesize protein in the body. Grains, beans, nut and seeds provide incomplete or second-class protein, which contains just some of these amino acids. However, the various amino acids present in these plant whole foods can be combined so that they add up to a complete protein. For instance, the combination of grains and dried beans, grains and nuts, grains and seeds, or milk with any of these, will give a complete protein. Soybeans are in fact complete proteins and need no other food in this respect.

Vegetables

Vegetables form an important part of a whole food vegetarian diet because of the many vitamins, minerals and essential fiber they provide. They are generally low in calories. Dark green, leafy vegetables are the most nutritious, and are particularly important for those not eating dairy products because of their calcium and vitamin B_2 (riboflavin) content.

Take care not to overcook vegetables, especially those high in the water-soluble vitamins B and C. Steaming or light stir-frying is probably the best method of cooking, but because heat, water and even oxygen destroys many of the vitamins, be sure to include some raw vegetables in your diet.

Fruit

Fruit is high in some vitamins, minerals, carbohydrates (in the form of glucose and fructose, or fruit sugar) and fiber. It can have a high calorific value, especially dried fruit, but is low in fats. Most fruits are high in vitamin C, especially citrus fruit. Yellow- and orange-skinned fruits are also often high in vitamin A. All fruits contain dietary fiber in the cell walls and skins, dried fruit containing most of all.

Fruit's natural sweetness makes it an ideal snack food for children, but because some fruit is acidic and high in fiber it can cause upset stomachs and should be eaten in moderation.

Seaweeds

Seaweeds form a useful part of a whole food vegetarian diet as they are high in protein, vitamins and minerals, particularly calcium, potassium, sodium, iodine and iron. They contain the elusive vitamin B_{12}, seldom found in plant substances and essential in small quantities. Seaweed is therefore of particular importance if you are following a vegan diet.

Dairy produce and non-dairy alternatives

In nutritional terms, one of the most important nutrients that dairy products and eggs can offer a vegetarian is vitamin B_{12}, mainly found in meat products. The protein found in dairy products and eggs is of animal origin, and therefore complete. They also contain vitamin B_2 and calcium.

Eggs, particularly the yolks, are a very nourishing food. However, they are high in cholesterol and for that reason should be eaten in moderation. All dairy products contain saturated fats and cholesterol to some degree, which is why your consumption should be limited. Many non-dairy substitutes are available, such as vegetable margarine and soy milk, which are of nutritional value and free of saturated fat.

Naturally processed products

Naturally processed products are included in a whole food diet because they are obtained from whole foods in a natural way without the use of chemicals, retaining most if not all of the nutritional value. Soybean products such as tofu, tempeh and miso have processed the soybean into a form much easier to use and cook, and are exceptionally high in protein, iron, calcium and B vitamins, as well as being low in fats and cholesterol. Yeast extracts are also a valuable supplement to the diet. Oils, if cold-pressed, are high in nutrients and unsaturated fats; sweeteners such as honey, if unrefined, are useful nutritional alternatives to refined sugar. There is no "recommended amount" of naturally processed products as they vary so much in their nutritional content, but a selection will provide valuable protein, vitamins and minerals.

The recommended balance

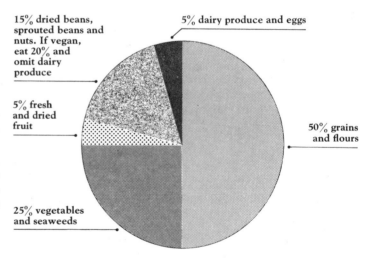

15% dried beans, sprouted beans and nuts. If vegan, eat 20% and omit dairy produce

5% dairy produce and eggs

5% fresh and dried fruit

50% grains and flours

25% vegetables and seaweeds

If you follow these general guidelines for a balanced diet and include an interesting variety of the available whole foods, you will discover a nutritious, delicious and often exciting way of eating which will have long-reaching benefits. Do remember, however, that if you are planning a major change of diet it is best to change gradually. Do not alter your way of eating overnight, as your system will doubtless object.

The first part of this book is a complete guide to the different kinds of whole foods, including basic preparation and cooking directions. Page references to actual recipes are given, as specific examples of the delicious ways in which the whole foods can be used. The second part of the book contains over 200 attractive and nutritious recipes made with whole foods, many from the Neal's Yard Bakery Restaurant.

GRAINS

BARLEY
Pot barley ☐
Pearled barley
Barley flakes ☐
BUCKWHEAT
Whole raw buckwheat ☐
Roasted buckwheat ☐
Buckwheat spaghetti
CORN OR MAIZE
Corn-on-the-cob ☐
Popcorn ☐
Polenta ☐

MILLET
Whole millet ☐
Millet flakes ☐
OATS
Oat groats ☐
Steel-cut oats ☐
Old-fashioned oats ☐
Oat flakes
Oat bran and germ
RICE
Brown rice ☐
White rice ☐

Rice flakes ☐
Wild rice ☐
RYE
Whole rye berries ☐
Cracked rye
Rye flakes ☐
SAGO AND TAPIOCA
SOY
Soy flakes
Soy grits
Soy bran

WHEAT (Common wheat)
Whole wheat ☐
Cracked wheat ☐
Bulgur or bulgur wheat
Wheat flakes ☐
Malted wheat
Wheat bran
Wheat germ
WHEAT (Durum wheat)
Semolina
Pasta
Couscous

☐ Pictured opposite page 16

The grains described in this section include cereal and non-cereal grains. Cereals are cultivated members of the grass family: they are, in descending order of world grain production, common wheat and durum wheat, rice, maize, millet and sorghum, barley, oats and rye. Today's cereal crops are by far the most important plant food available, and provide the staple diet for the majority of the world's population. They are abundant in the carbohydrates which our bodies convert into energy, and when used unrefined they are also a rich source of protein, fiber and essential minerals and vitamins. The non-cereals buckwheat, sago, tapioca and soy have also been included in this section because of their similar usage.

Grain products

All cereal grains can be cooked and eaten whole, but most are processed before being prepared as food. This section will describe the various processed products which are available. Individual grains and their products are listed on pages 12-15.

The diagram below shows the different parts of a typical cereal grain. It is a seed, and has three main parts. The *bran* is the outer protective layer; the *endosperm* is the white starchy part which forms the bulk of the grain, providing a storehouse of food for the seed when it starts to grow. The *germ* is the wheat embryo, the point from which new growth starts. By weight, about 85 per cent of the grain is endosperm, 12 per cent is bran and 3 per cent is germ. Different grain products use all or part of the grain; those which use the unrefined grain without removing any part have the greatest food value.

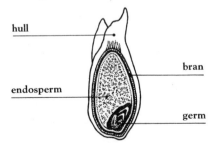

hull

bran

endosperm

germ

Whole grains

Most cereal grains have an indigestible *hull* or husk around them, which must be removed before they can be processed further for use as human food. The only grains which do not have a hull are wheat, rye and maize; these are known as naked or free-threshing grains.

Whole cereal grains are an extremely useful food as, being unrefined, they retain all the nutritional value of the bran and germ. They are delicious cooked and eaten whole, either as a dish on their own or in stews and salads.

Flakes

Flakes are made by flattening whole grains between rollers, making them easier to cook and more easily digestible when eaten raw, for instance in granola. In addition, flakes are often lightly precooked, either by toasting or steaming.

In most cases, nothing is removed in the flaking process, so the flakes retain the full food value of the whole grain. However, be careful not to confuse genuine cereal flakes with some commercial brands of breakfast cereal, which are often highly processed and refined products with little nutritional value.

Cracked grains

These are cut or broken pieces of cereal grain. As with flakes, they are more easily cooked than whole grains and are often used in oatmeal, stews and breads. Perhaps the most widely known products in this category are bulgur and couscous, both of which are precooked, although this is not the case with all cracked grains. Some cracked grain products are genuine whole foods, others are partially refined.

Meals and flours

Meals and flours represent the next stage of processing. Details of milling processes and the different kinds of flours available are given in the chapter on Flours (see p. 16).

Bran and germ

Bran and germ are discarded by-products in the manufacture of white flour. For years they have been used to make animal feed, but more recently they have been promoted as health foods. Wheat bran and germ are the most commonly available, but oat bran and germ, and rice bran and germ (sometimes known as rice polishings) can also be found.

Bran and germ do contain valuable elements of the grain, but their health-giving properties should not be over-estimated. They are not in themselves whole foods, and are of less value when taken in this form than when eaten as part of the whole grain or as part of food made from unrefined whole wheat flour.

Malted grains

Cereal grains, in particular barley and wheat, are grown not only for use as food but also for malting. In the malting process, grains are first steeped in water to stimulate germination, when the grain's carbohydrates are converted into sugars to boost new growth. Just before the first shoot appears, when the sugar level (maltose) is at its highest, the process is stopped by kiln-drying. Malted grains are usually then milled and mixed with water to make a sweet mash, which is fermented for beer and liquor production or used for preparing malt extract.

Malted wheat grains are available in some whole food stores. They make a sweet and nutty addition to whole-grain bread or can be used on granola as a healthy alternative to sugar.

Storage

Heat, moisture and light are three of the primary causes of deterioration in any foodstuff. Cereal grains are no exception, and are best stored in a cool dry pantry or cellar or on kitchen shelves positioned as far away as possible from your stove, and away from direct light if you can.

The action of oxygen is the fourth major cause of deteriora-tion. Whole grains stored in the right conditions can remain usable for many years, and should certainly stay fresh for a year or two in a kitchen shelf. But loss of flavor and nutritional value begins as soon as the grain is broken open during milling, so store flakes, cracked grains and flours in airtight containers. Grain products should be used within 3-6 months.

Note: Each grain is listed alphabetically, and describes the forms in which it is available in order of refinement, from the whole unprocessed grain to the more highly processed product. The flours milled from each grain are dealt with separately in the chapter on Flours (see p. 16).

GRAINS AND THEIR PRODUCTS Per 4 oz	Water	Protein	Fat	Carbohydrate	Fiber	Vitamin A	Vitamin B$_1$	Vitamin B$_2$	Vitamin B$_3$	Vitamin B$_6$	Vitamin B$_{12}$	Vitamin C	Vitamin D	Vitamin E	Folic acid	Iron	Calcium	Magnesium	Sodium	Potassium	Phosphorus	Zinc
	g	g	g	g	g	µg	mg	mg	mg	mg	µg	mg	µg	mg	µg	mg	mg	mg	mg	mg	mg	mg
Recommended daily allowance	N	80M 60W	N	N	25-30	750	1.5	1.5	18	1.5	3	30	2.5	8	200	12	500	250	2500	2500	500	15
Barley – pot (whole)	14	10.5	2.1	69.3	4	0	0.31	0.1	7.8	0.25	0	0	0	N	50	6	50	91	4	562	N	2.3
– pearled	11	7.9	1.7	83.6	6.5	0	0.05	0.12	2.5	0.22	0	0	0	0.2	20	0.7	10	20	3	120	210	2
Buckwheat – whole	11	11.7	2.4	72.9	9.9	0	0.6	N	4.4	N	0	0	N	N	N	3.9	114	N	N	448	282	N
–spaghetti	14	10.8	1.8	73	0.4	0	0.2	0.08	1.2	N	0	0	N	N	N	5	30	N	700	N	210	N
Corn – popcorn	N	0.36	0.1	2	0.04	N	N	Tr	Tr	Tr	0	0	N	N	N	0.08	0.4	N	N	N	68	N
Millet – whole	12	9.9	2.9	72.9	3.2	0	0.73	0.38	2.3	N	0	0	N	N	N	6.8	20	162	N	430	311	N
Oats – whole	13	13	5.4	66.1	10.6	0	0.3	0.1	1.5	N	0	0	N	N	N	4.6	55	N	10	N	320	N
– rolled	8	14.2	7.4	68.2	1.2	0	0.6	0.14	1	0.1	0	0	N	N	N	4.5	53	N	2	352	405	N
Rice – brown	12	7.5	1.9	77.4	4.2	0	0.59	0.07	5.3	0.5	0	0	0	N	49	1.4	10	112	3	250	221	1.8
– basmati	11	7.4	0.5	79.8	N	0	N	N	N	N	0	0	0	N	N	1.3	19	N	N	N	N	N
– white	12	6.5	1	86.8	2.4	0	0.08	0.03	1.5	0.3	0	0	0	0.3	29	0.5	4	13	6	110	100	1.3
– flakes	13	6.6	1.2	77.5	0	0	0.21	0.05	4	0.44	0	0	0	N	8	20	N	N	N	N	N
– wild	N	12	0.6	60	0.8	0	0.36	0.5	4.9	N	0	0	N	N	N	3.4	15	N	5.5	175	270	N
Rye – whole	11	9.4	1	77.9	0.4	0	0.15	0.07	0.6	N	0	0	N	N	N	1.1	22	N	1	156	185	N
Sago	13	0.2	0.2	94	N	0	Tr	Tr	Tr	Tr	0	0	N	Tr	Tr	1.2	10	3	3	5	29	N
Tapioca	12	0.4	0.1	95	N	0	Tr	Tr	Tr	Tr	0	0	N	Tr	Tr	0.3	8	2	4	20	30	N
Soy	N	26	14	25	3.7	60	0.8	0.23	1.7	0.6	0	0	N	N	N	6.5	172	N	4	1300	425	N
Wheat (common) – whole	13	14	2.2	69.1	2.3	0	0.59	0.12	4.3	0.4	0	0	N	N	N	3.1	36	N	3	370	383	N
– cracked	N	8	1.6	55	1.9	0	0.33	0.08	2.7	N	0	0	N	N	N	2.5	33	N	1	N	310	N
– flakes	N	4.9	1	38.2	1.11	0	0.18	0.59	2.05	N	0	0	N	N	N	1	18.2	N	1.17	188	170	N
– bulgur	N	10	N	65	1.5	0	0.24	0.12	3.8	0.19	0	0	N	N	N	3.1	25	N	N	N	290	N
– bran	8	14	5.5	26.8	44	0	0.89	0.36	29.6	1.38	0	0	0	1.6	130	12.9	110	520	28	1160	1200	16.2
– germ	N	26.5	17.8	76	4	0	1.45	0.61	5.8	0.93	0	0	N	*	62	10	118	300	4	1000	1840	N
Wheat (durum) – semolina	14	10.7	1.8	77.5	N	0	0.1	0.02	0.7	0.15	0	0	0	Tr	25	1	18	32	12	170	110	N
– pasta	11	11.7	6.2	76.1	5.7	0	0.37	0.04	4.8	N	0	0	0	N	18	1.5	23	47	2	230	N	1.5

KEY
All whole foods are uncooked unless otherwise stated. Some whole foods may not be included in the chart, as there is currently no nutritional data available.
g: grams   **mg:** milligrams   **µg:** micrograms   **N:** no available data   **Tr:** trace   **M:** adult men   **W:** adult women.   The recommended daily allowances are averages and vary depending on age, occupation and metabolism.   Figures in bold type indicate the whole food with the highest level of nutrient.   **✻** Exact figure unknown but thought to be very high.

Barley

Barley originated in the East. It has a short growing season and is suitable for cultivation in a wider range of climatic areas than other cereals. In ancient times barley was more important than wheat as a human food, but today it is grown mainly for animal feed and for malting. It is high in vitamin B$_3$.

Pot (whole grain) barley

Barley grains grow encased in a tough hull, which must be removed before the grain can be used as human food. Pot barley has been scoured to remove this hull, but it does retain some of the bran. Cooked on its own it makes a pleasant change from rice, potatoes or pasta. Alternatively, add to stews, soups or broths.

Basic cooking method (Serves 3-4).
1 cup pot barley
3 cups water
Wash the grains and put in a saucepan with the water. Bring to a boil, cover and simmer for about 45 minutes until the barley is tender and all the liquid is absorbed. Add a little more water if necessary, or boil off excess liquid by removing the lid of the pan for the last few minutes of cooking.

If you are adding uncooked pot barley to other ingredients, remember that it will need at least 45 minutes of steady cooking but that after 60 minutes it will start to turn mushy, and will absorb three times its volume of liquid.

Recipe: Barley, Fruit & Vegetable Pollo (see p. 99).

Pearled barley

The more refined pearled barley is pot barley which has been polished, like white rice, to remove all the bran. Its nutritional value is therefore diminished. Pearled barley is usually added to soups.

Barley flakes

Barley flakes are made by flattening grains from which the hulls have been removed. They are usually lightly toasted, and can either be eaten raw in a cereal or cooked to make a barley oatmeal-style dish.

Recipe: Basic Muesli (see p. 69).

Buckwheat

Despite its name, buckwheat is not a true cereal but a member of the plant family which also includes rhubarb, sorrel and dock, a common weed. Probably originating from China, its major producing areas are the USA, Canada, France and parts of eastern Europe.

Whole raw buckwheat

Whole hulled kernels of buckwheat are a dark greenish-pink color. The basic dish of boiled buckwheat, sometimes called *kasha*, is made from roasted kernels. The unroasted kernels can be used, but they are best cooked with other ingredients, as in a casserole. Buckwheat has a strong, woody flavor, and needs to be complemented by other strong flavors.

Basic cooking method (Serves 3-4)
1 cup whole raw buckwheat
5 tbsp melted butter or oil
2½ cups water

To roast the buckwheat, sauté it in the butter or oil in a saucepan over medium heat. Keep turning until the grains turn an even brown. Add the water to the roasted buckwheat, bring to a boil, turn down the heat, cover the pan and simmer for 15-20 minutes. Remove the lid for the last few minutes of cooking to boil off any excess liquid. The kernels should have swollen and burst.

Recipe: Unroasted Buckwheat Casserole (see p. 117).

Roasted buckwheat

Kernels of roasted buckwheat have the same distinctive shape as the raw ones, but are a darker, reddish-brown color. To cook them, omit the roasting stage of the cooking method above and simply boil the kernels as directed in about three times their own volume of water.

Recipe: Buckwheat & Coconut Salad (see p. 90).

Buckwheat spaghetti

Not all buckwheat spaghetti is made entirely from buckwheat flour. Often it is made from a mixture of wheat and buckwheat, so if you want gluten-free noodles, check that you are getting 100% buckwheat spaghetti. The noodles are a dark gray color, and although they are cooked in the same way as ordinary pasta, they have a stronger flavor.

Recipe: Buckwheat Spaghetti with Mushrooms, Dill & Sour Cream (see p. 102).

Corn (Mealie or Maize)

The maize plant is the largest of the cereals, often reaching a height of over 10 feet. Originating in Mexico, it is now an important crop in tropical and sub-tropical areas throughout the world.

The kernels of corn grow in tightly packed rows on an ear or "cob," each plant producing one or two ripe ears 6-8 inches long. There are many varieties of maize, but the main types are dent corn, which is dried and ground into meal, popcorn, fresh corn-on-the-cob and those grown for animal feed. The commonest types produce white or yellow kernels, but there are also red, purple and even black-seeded varieties.

Corn-on-the-cob

This is the whole ear or cob of maize, to be cooked and eaten as soon as it is ripe. In season, fresh corn-on-the-cob makes a delicious meal. For basic preparation and cooking, see page 28.

Popcorn

Popping corn comes from hard-kernel varieties of maize. Partially dried, the moisture that remains in the kernels expands and "pops" them when they are heated.

Basic cooking method (Makes 4 cups)
½ cup popping corn
1 tbsp oil

It is best to pop corn in a heavy-bottomed saucepan with a lid. Lightly brush the bottom of the pan with oil and heat it almost to burning point before adding a layer of corn, one kernel thick. Cover with the lid and shake the pan over a high heat until it is all popped.

Polenta

Polenta is similar to cornmeal (see p. 18), but it usually has a fine, granular texture more like semolina than ordinary flour. Polenta is an Italian word, and in parts of Italy the dish made from it (also called polenta) is as common as pasta. Like pasta, polenta can be served hot with just about any sauce. Alternatively, it can be served as fried or broiled strips.

Basic cooking method (Serves 4)
5 cups water
1 tsp salt
1 cup polenta

Put the water in a saucepan, add the salt and bring to a rolling boil. Gradually shake in the polenta, stirring constantly with a whisk. When all the polenta has been added, reduce the heat to the lowest possible setting and simmer very gently for about 45 minutes, stirring regularly so it does not stick.

Either eat as a hot, very thick oatmeal-style dish, or allow to cool before cutting into strips which can then be broiled or fried.

Recipe: Polenta Pudding with Seasonal Fruit (see p. 128).

Millet

Native to Asia, millet is probably the least familiar of the cereal grains to the West. Tropical millets, of which sorghum is one, are cultivated in the arid tropics, tolerating poor soils and drought conditions which no other crop could survive. Most varieties have exceptional keeping qualities, making them a valuable reserve against times of famine in many parts of Africa, India and Pakistan.

The most widely cultivated of the temperate millets is common millet. It is high in iron and B vitamins and is gluten-free.

Whole millet

Millet has the smallest kernels of any of the cereals. They grow enclosed in outer hulls, which must be removed before the kernels can be eaten. Hulled millet kernels are tiny, round and hard and are usually pale yellow.

Cooked millet has a clean, delicate flavor and light texture that make it particularly appetizing in hot weather. It should not be combined with strongly flavored foods as its flavor can easily be overwhelmed. Serve hot with steamed or stir-fried vegetables or allow to cool and use in salads.

Basic cooking method (Serves 4)
a knob of butter
1 cup whole millet kernels
3 cups water

Melt the butter in a saucepan, add the millet and stir over a medium heat for 2-3 minutes until some of the kernels begin to crack open. Use just enough butter to coat the kernels lightly. Add the water, bring to a boil and then turn the heat right down, cover the pan and simmer without stirring for 40-45 minutes. The kernels should burst open and fluff out, and all the water should be absorbed. Add a little extra water if the pan goes dry before the millet is cooked, or remove the lid for the last few minutes to boil off any excess liquid.

Millet may also be baked in the oven as a sweet pudding. Cook it exactly like Rice Pudding (see p. 130), except that millet may need slightly more liquid.

Recipe: Millet Casserole (see p. 108).

Millet flakes

Flaked millet, the whole hulled kernel flattened between rollers, can be cooked or eaten raw as part of a gluten-free muesli.

Recipe: Gluten-Free Muesli (see p. 70).

Oats

Oats, native to central Europe, are an important cereal of the temperate zones. They are distinguishable from wheat and barley by their open, spreading seed head. The kernels are easily digestible with a rich, creamy flavor.

In the USA, oatmeal means the cooked breakfast cereal known in the UK as porridge. In Britain, "oatmeal" is used to denote raw oats milled to various degrees of coarseness, as distinct from rolled oats or oat flakes, which are oat kernels flattened between rollers to make them quicker to cook.

Oat groats

Oat groats are the whole oat kernels, with only the hulls removed. They are usually pale yellow in color, long and thin with a smooth, shiny surface. Like other cereal grains they may be boiled and eaten whole, but they are more commonly used after being processed into one of the forms described below.

Steel-cut oats (Cracked)

Steel-cut oats are made by chopping up whole oat groats, each kernel being cut into three or four pieces. When cooked it produces a coarser oatmeal than quick-cooking, taking longer to cook but having a rather fuller flavor, which some people prefer.

Recipe: Steel-Cut Oatmeal (see p. 71).

Old-fashioned oats

Old-fashioned oats are partially cooked in steam before being flattened between rollers, greatly reducing the eventual cooking time needed. These are made from oat groats and make a fairly coarse oatmeal.

These can be eaten raw in the Swiss cereal muesli, or toasted with oil and honey or malt extract to make the crunchy breakfast cereal known as granola (see pp. 68-69). They are also widely used in cookies.

Recipe: Basic Oatmeal (see p. 70).

Quick-cooking oats

These oats are made by flattening the cut pieces of oat grain known as steel-cut oats (see previous page). They consist therefore of smaller, finer pieces than old-fashioned oats, and cook more quickly, giving a smoother oatmeal. Like old-fashioned oats, they have usually been partially cooked in steam before going through the rollers.

Commercial brands of instant oatmeal, which may have been precooked for longer and rolled more thinly to reduce cooking time to a minimum, tend to be a good deal more expensive than the quick-cooking oats available in whole food or health stores.

Quick-cooking oats can be used in cookies and flapjacks, and as a decorative topping on the crust of whole wheat bread.

Recipe: Oat & Raisin Cookies (see p. 143).

Oat bran and germ

The bran and germ of the oat kernel is a fine brown powder which can be made into a quick and nourishing gruel or thin oatmeal and then flavored with a little puréed fruit or vegetables. This gruel is suitable for babies from about 9 months on. Oat bran and germ can also be sprinkled over savory dishes.

Rice

Rice is one of the world's two most important food crops, the other being wheat. Rice originated in Asia and is now grown throughout the humid tropical and sub-tropical regions. India and China are the largest producers, though rice is also widely grown in the USA and Italy.

Rice is a good source of starch, although it contains less protein than other cereals. There are many varieties of rice, but they fall into the basic categories of short-grain and long-grain. Short-grain rice has a softer, stickier texture and is often used in Japanese and Chinese cooking. Long-grain rice has dry, separate grains and is often used in Indian cooking. The choice is really a matter of personal preference. Long-grain rice usually takes longer to cook.

The practice of refining the grains of rice by polishing or "pearling" them removes the bran and germ to leave a smooth white grain. This has led to diseases such as beri-beri in areas where people have had little other than white rice to eat. Unpolished brown rice is widely available, and some whole food stores also stock rice that has been organically grown.

Brown rice

Simple boiled brown rice makes a delicious accompaniment to almost any savory dish. Rice is often badly cooked; but if you use the following method the rice will be tender but firm with a delicate flavor that does not need to be helped by a lot of salt.

Rice can be served hot with any savory dish. Nutritionally, it makes a particularly good combination with lentils, beans or peas.

Basic cooking method (Serves 3-4)
1 cup brown rice
2 cups water
a little salt

Wash the rice and put it with the water in a saucepan. Bring to a boil over a medium heat. When the water starts to boil, reduce the heat so that it is barely simmering and then leave the pan as tightly covered as possible to cook. Do *not* stir the rice, because stirring breaks up the grains and releases a starchy substance which will gather at the bottom of the pan, stick and burn.

Forty minutes after it has come to a boil, all the liquid should have been absorbed and the rice should be almost cooked. If not, add more water or boil off the excess as necessary. Remove the pan from the heat and allow to stand, covered, for at least 5 minutes before serving. (The rice will continue to cook during this time.)

It is better to wait until the rice is cooked before seasoning it with salt. You can flavor rice during cooking with herbs, or color it with saffron. A similar yellow color can be achieved with turmeric, but this gives the rice a rather muddy taste. Alternatively, add a few whole coriander seeds during cooking.

The directions given here are for short-grain brown rice. Long-grain will take about 5-10 minutes longer to cook, and may require a little more water.

Recipe: Rice Pudding (see p. 130).

White rice

White rice lacks the flavor and texture of brown rice, as well as much of the nutritional value. If you do wish to use it, try to find a good quality rice that has not been over-polished, such as Basmati. Remember that the more "instant" a commercial brand of rice claims to be, the less flavor and goodness it is likely to have, and that it may even have been bleached.

Rice flakes

Rice flakes are made from either brown or white rice and are usually toasted before being flattened between rollers. They may be cooked to make a hot rice breakfast cereal or used as part of a gluten-free muesli.

Recipe: Gluten-Free Muesli (see p. 70).

Wild rice

This wild grass, not in fact a true rice at all, is native to the Great Lakes area of North America where it is still traditionally hand harvested by Native Americans. The difficulty of harvesting wild rice makes it very expensive, but it is thought to be rich in vitamins and particularly rich in proteins. It has a subtle, slightly "nutty" flavor.

Rye

Rye is a hardy cereal, tolerating cold climates and poor soils. Native to Southwest Asia, it is now an important food crop in northern and eastern Europe and in some areas of Russia. It is also grown in the USA and Canada, where it is used mainly in the production of rye whiskey. Rye is the only cereal other than wheat that contains enough gluten to be suitable for making leavened bread, although it is usually mixed with wheat flour. It is particularly high in B vitamins, potassium and magnesium.

Whole rye berries

Rye berries are thin and long, with a greenish-gray color and a distinctive, slightly bitter flavor.

Cooked rye berries make a good addition to a thick vegetable soup or stew, combining particularly well with sweet root vegetables such as carrots or parsnips. Rye is also fairly easy to sprout (see p. 23).

Basic cooking method (Serves 4)
1 cup whole rye berries
3 cups water

Wash the rye thoroughly before adding it to the water in a saucepan. Bring to a boil, reduce the heat, cover the pan and simmer for about 45 minutes. The berries should have started to burst. Drain through a strainer.

Recipe: Rye & Vegetable Broth (see p. 78).

Cracked rye (Kibbled rye)

Cracked rye, produced in the same way as cracked wheat, is used mainly in the making of heavy, coarse breads popular in northern and eastern Europe.

Recipe: Soak a spoonful overnight and add to Basic Whole Wheat Bread (see p. 149).

Rye flakes

Rye flakes are whole rye berries that have been flattened and lightly toasted. They will add a pleasant tangy flavor to a granola.

Recipe: Granola 1 (see p. 68).

Sago and tapioca

Sago and tapioca are not derived from cereals, but are used in a similar way to many cereal products. Sago is a granular product, prepared from the starchy pith of the sago palm. Tapioca, similar in appearance to sago although usually consisting of smaller granules, is prepared from the starch of the cassava root. Both products may be used to make the sweet puddings which bear their names. Nutritionally, their value is strictly limited as they consist exclusively of carbohydrate.

Recipe: Apricot & Orange Sago Cream (see p. 121).

Soy

Soy is not a cereal crop but a legume, a member of the family that includes all the beans, lentils and peas. The soy products listed in this section are included because of their similar usage to many cereal products. Whole soybeans and other soy products, such as miso, tamari and tofu, are dealt with elsewhere (see pp. 50 and 51 respectively).

Soybean flakes

Soy flakes are made by toasting and then flattening whole soybeans. They can be cooked into a hot breakfast cereal or baked in cookies and crumbles.

Soy grits

Soy grits are crushed and cooked soybeans. They can be used in any dish to replace whole soybeans, for example in pasties, pies and bean loaves, and will take far less time to cook.

Recipe: Soy & Oat Cereal (see p. 71).

Soy bran

This is the coarse outer layer of the soybean, milled into small flakes. Like wheat bran, it may be sprinkled on breakfast cereals or added in small quantities to just about any dish to provide extra dietary fiber, although this should not be necessary for anyone already basing their diet on whole foods.

Recipe: Gluten-Free Muesli (see p. 70).

Wheat (Common wheat)

Wheat was first brought under cultivation 10,000 years ago in Mesopotamia. Although there are many varieties of wheat, there are two main types: durum wheat, from which we get pasta products, semolina and couscous; and common or bread wheat, which is grown predominantly to be milled into flour for baking. Together, they constitute the most important food for over a third of the world's population.

Common wheat can be grown over a wide climactic range, but is most successfully cultivated in the temperate zones, including the UK. The main areas of production are the great wheat belts of North America.

Whole wheat kernels

Wheat kernels are a beautiful golden color, with a marked crease along one side. Because wheat does not need to be hulled, the bran remains intact and its valuable vitamins, fats, minerals and fiber are retained. When cooked, the outer layer of bran bursts slightly to reveal the puffy white of the grain. Cooked whole wheat has a pleasant chewy texture (making it a good vegetarian food for meat-eaters) and a rich, slightly sweet flavor. Whole wheat kernels with the hull removed are called *berries*.

Uncooked wheat kernels can be added to slow-cooking casseroles, and they combine well with certain beans, for example flageolet and pinto. Wheat kernels that have been partially cooked or soaked overnight can be added to whole wheat dough for an extra chewy loaf. Cooked wheat kernels can be served on their own with a knob of butter as an alternative to rice or potatoes, or cold to give body to a green salad.

Basic cooking method (Serves 2-3)
1 cup whole wheat kernels
4 cups water
Wash the kernels before adding them to the water in a saucepan. Bring to a boil, cover and simmer for about 1 hour, until the grains begin to burst open. Drain through a strainer. The cooking time may be reduced by soaking the kernels for 6-12 hours beforehand.

Cracked wheat (Kibbled wheat)

Cracked wheat consists of coarse pieces of whole wheat kernel, cut by steel blades (like steel-cut oatmeal) or roughly milled. It cooks more quickly than whole wheat kernels although less quickly than bulgur.

Recipe: Soak a spoonful overnight and add to Basic Whole Wheat Bread (see p. 149).

Bulgur or bulgur wheat (Burghul)

Bulgur is a more refined version of cracked wheat, and has been steamed and dried before being cracked. Some of the bran is lost in this process, giving uncooked bulgur a pale, sandy color. When cooked, bulgur swells to a fluffy texture similar in appearance to couscous, but it is heavier than couscous and has more flavor. It comes in varying degrees of coarseness.

Basic cooking method (Serves 3-4)
1 tbsp olive oil
1 cup bulgur
2½ cups water or vegetable broth
Heat the oil in a saucepan, add the bulgur and stir for a minute or two over a high heat. Use just enough oil to moisten the bulgur slightly. Add the liquid and bring to a fast boil. Stir for 1 minute; then turn down the heat, cover the pan and simmer for a further 10 minutes; at this stage most of the liquid should have been absorbed. Coarse grades of bulgur may need to simmer for a little longer, so add some water if the pan becomes dry.

Take the pan off the heat and keep in a warm place for 10-20 minutes (a 250°F oven is ideal). Before serving, fluff up the bulgur with a fork and season to taste.

Recipe: Tabouleh (see p. 95).

Wheat flakes

Wheat flakes are whole wheat kernels flattened between rollers, and are usually lightly toasted. They can be eaten raw as a breakfast cereal or cooked like jumbo rolled oats to make a coarse wheat oatmeal.

Malted wheat

Malted wheat kernels (see p. 11) are slightly larger and darker in color than ordinary wheat. A scattering of these sweet, nutty grains will liven up a bowl of granola, or they can be added to bread dough.

Recipe: Add a spoonful to Basic Whole Wheat Bread (see p. 149).

Wheat bran

Unprocessed coarse wheat bran consists of small, dark brown flakes. Bran is a useful source of fiber for those whose diet consists largely of refined foods, though extra fiber is unnecessary for anyone already eating a whole food diet. A little bran may be sprinkled on breakfast cereal or added to savory dishes.

Many commercial brands of bran cereal are made by grinding the bran very finely and then mixing it with water, and often sugar, into a paste which is then shaped and toasted. Bran in this form has been shown to produce almost no improvement in digestive health.

Recipe: Bran Muffins (see p. 137).

Wheat germ

The bulk of wheat protein is contained in the germ, and it is also rich in vitamin E. Separated wheat germ can be eaten raw as a cereal, mixed with hot milk for a thick, nourishing drink, cooked as an oatmeal or simply used to enrich breads and cakes.

It is still better to eat wheat germ in an unseparated form, in the whole kernels or freshly milled whole wheat flour.

Recipe: Granola 2 (see p. 69).

Wheat (Durum wheat)

Durum wheat produces a large kernel with a lower gluten content than common wheat. It thrives in dry conditions and is widely grown throughout the Mediterranean region, as well as in parts of North America, India and Russia.

Semolina

Semolina is produced from the endosperm, the starchy part of the kernel. Semolina pudding is usually made from refined semolina, but unrefined 100% whole wheat semolina milled from durum wheat can now be found in some stores. It does make a very easy sweet or savory pudding, ideal for convalescents and babies of 12 months and older. It can also be used to make whole wheat pasta.

Basic cooking method (Serves 3)
a knob of butter
½ cup whole wheat semolina
2½ cups milk or other liquid
Melt the butter in a saucepan over a low heat and stir in the semolina; there should be just enough butter to coat all the semolina. Add the liquid a little at a time, stirring continuously with a beater to avoid lumps. When all the liquid has been added, cover the pan and simmer over a very low heat for 5 minutes, stirring occasionally.

You can use all milk to make this semolina, or you can use a proportion of fruit or vegetable juice. The exact amount of liquid will depend on how thick you like semolina.

Recipe: Crustless Cheesecake (see p. 124).

Pasta

Pasta is made from durum wheat semolina. Until recently only pasta made from refined semolina was available, but now whole wheat pasta made from unrefined semolina can be found. Dried pasta is made from semolina, salt and water; fresh pasta has eggs added. Both come in many shapes and sizes, and can be eaten with many sauces.

Basic cooking method
Pasta should be completely immersed in boiling salted water and cooked for 5-15 minutes, depending on the type (see the directions on the package for the exact times). Fresh pasta will take less time to cook, about 5 minutes. When the pasta is *al dente* (with a slight firmness to the bite) or cooked to your liking, drain it thoroughly and toss in a little butter or olive oil to prevent the strands sticking.

Recipe: Macaroni & Cheese (see p. 108).

Couscous

Couscous is made by steaming, drying and cracking kernels of durum wheat. Though similar to bulgur, it is a more refined product and has a paler, creamier color before cooking and a lighter texture and taste when cooked. It comes from the Mediterranean countries of North Africa, where it is an important food.

Couscous makes an ideal summer dish served with a stew of seasonal vegetables, as it is light but filling. It can also be made into delicious puddings and cakes.

Basic cooking method (Serves 3)
1 tbsp oil
1 cup couscous
a little salt (optional)
2 cups water
Heat the oil in a saucepan. Add the couscous and toss in the hot oil for 2-3 minutes; there should be just enough oil to lightly coat all the particles of couscous. Season with a little salt if you wish, add the water and bring to a fast boil. Stir until the bulk of the water is absorbed, and then remove the pan from the heat, cover and leave in a warm place for 10 minutes (a low oven, 225°F, is ideal). Fluff up with a fork before serving.

Recipe: Couscous Cake (see p. 141).

FLOURS

All-purpose flour	Durum flour	potato starch
Barley flour	Masa harina	Rice flour
Bread flour	Maslin	Rye flour
Buckwheat flour	Millet flour	Self rising flour
Cake flour	Oat flour	Soy flour
Chickpea flour	Pastry flour	Whole wheat flour
Cornmeal	Potato flour or	

"Meal" means anything that has been milled or ground. Meals are sometimes understood to be coarser products than flours, but for general purposes the two words are interchangeable. Whole wheat flour, for example, is flour that has not been sieved or otherwise refined.

Types of wheat
Hundreds of varieties of wheat are grown in America but they each belong to one of five classes, based on if the grain is hard or soft (see p. 17), the kernel color and time of planting.

The five American classes are: hard red winter, hard red spring, soft red winter, white and durum. The hard wheats are best for bread baking and the soft wheats are better for general baking, such as cakes and cookies. Durum wheat is used to make semolina and pasta.

Methods of milling flour
Even before cereals were cultivated as crops, early man had probably learnt to crush the kernels of wild grasses between stones to make meal. This meal was mixed with water and cooked as a hot cereal or bread, and was found to be far more palatable and digestible than the whole kernels. Later, wind and water mills worked on the same principle of stone-crushing the kernels, although using a different source of power.

The small mill in Neal's Yard uses a traditional design, similar to that of wind and water mills. Kernels are introduced between a fixed stone and a moving or "traveling" stone, where it is cut by the rough surfaces to emerge as flour around the edge. This, and only this, is true stoneground whole wheat flour: nothing has been added and nothing has been taken out. If you have ever eaten bread baked with flour freshly milled in this way, you will probably agree that there is nothing like it.

The sieving or "bolting" of stoneground whole wheat flour to remove some of the bran and so produce a lighter, paler flour has been practiced for thousands of years, and there are fine, delicate pastries which can only be made using sieved flours. However, the steel roller mills which now produce by far the greatest proportion of all wheat flour refine the flour still further, removing all the bran and germ and leaving only the starchy part behind.

In steel roller milling, the separation of the bran and the germ from the endosperm is an integral part of the mechanical process. The grains are sliced open and the white, starchy endosperm is scooped out and pulverized between as many as thirty sets of high speed steel rollers into the finest white flour. The bran and germ have been removed. Whole wheat flour produced by the steel rolling process is inferior to that produced by the stoneground method, because so much of the grain's delicate nutrients are destroyed by the severity of the steel rolling. Adding bran and germ afterward cannot adequately compensate this loss. If you buy whole wheat flour at Neal's Yard in London, it will be labeled "Whole meal."

Why whole wheat is better
White flour uses only the starchy part of the grain, the endosperm. It contains neither the bran, a source of fiber and vitamins, nor the germ, rich in minerals and vitamins, particularly vitamin E. Whole wheat flour contains all the nutrients of the whole kernel, and is also free from additives such as bleaching agents. (An additive sometimes used in whole wheat bread is vitamin C, used to aerate the dough and help it to rise; whole wheat flour has a weaker gluten content than all-purpose flour, for example, so breads made with it may be lower and have a coarser texture.)

Whole wheat flour is a major source of dietary fiber, considered essential to good health and the proper functioning of our digestive system. The increase in degenerative diseases over the past hundred years has been directly linked to the increasing refinement of our food, and in particular to the use of white bread. Most nutritional experts seem to agree that the single most beneficial change to the modern Western diet would be for each household to increase its consumption of bread, and to switch from white to whole wheat bread. (Other excellent sources of fiber are unrefined grains, vegetables and fresh fruit.)

Whole wheat flour
Whole wheat flour describes any 100% flour, that is, flour milled from the whole of the grain and from which nothing has been added or removed. It could refer to flour milled from any grain, i.e. whole wheat flour, whole berry rye flour or whole grain barley flour.

Flour enriching
Highly-refined white flours, such as all-purpose, self rising and bread, are labeled on the bag as being "enriched." This means the manufacturer has synthetically replaced the B-complex vitamins and minerals removed during the milling process. Whole wheat flour is not enriched because the bran and germ of the kernel are not removed during milling, so the flour still contains all its natural goodness.

Flour enrichment began in the 1940s when nutritionists discovered almost one-third of the population was on the borderline of being undernourished. Across the country, shoppers were overwhelmingly buying larger quantities of highly-refined, soft textured white bread rather than the coarser breads made from whole wheat flour. Studies indicated low-income families were suffering the most from nutrition deficiency and a large part of their daily diets consisted of low-cost white bread.

In 1941, the first enrichment programs started, adding the missing B-complex vitamins thiamine, niacin and riboflavin. Today's levels of enrichment are the same as those adopted in 1943. Iron and, only recently, calcium are also added.

Commercially-enriched flour has the same or higher levels of thiamine, niacin and riboflavin as whole wheat flour. Whole

Popcorn (see p. 13) is a dried variety of corn.

Polenta (see p. 13) is a granular type of cornmeal.

Corn-on-the-Cob (see p. 13) is the whole ear, eaten fresh as a vegetable.

Whole wheat (see p. 15).

Cracked wheat (see p. 15) is broken whole wheat.

Wheat flakes (see p. 15) are flattened grains.

Whole rye berries (see p. 14).

Rye flakes (see p. 14) are flattened whole rye berries.

Oat groats (see p. 13).

Steel-cut oats (see p. 13) are milled oat groats.

Old-fashioned oats (see p. 13) are rolled oats.

Pot barley (see p. 12).

Barley flakes (see p. 13) are flattened pot barley.

Whole millet (see p. 13).

Millet flakes (see p. 13) are flattened whole millet.

Brown rice (see p. 14).

Wild rice (see p. 14) is actually a water grass.

Rice flakes (see p. 14) are flattened, toasted rice.

Whole buckwheat (see p. 13).

Roasted buckwheat (see p. 13) is the roasted whole kernels.

Dried Beans, Peas & Lentils (See p. 20)

Pinto beans (see p. 22) lose their speckles when cooked.

Black kidney beans (see p. 21) are similar to red.　**Red kidney beans** (see p. 22) are tender and sweet.

Black-eyed peas (see p. 21) have a creamy-smooth taste.

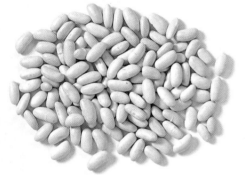

Cannellini beans (see p. 21) have a good firm texture.

Soybeans (see p. 22) are very nutritious and have a variety of uses.　**Black soybeans** are similar in taste and use to the yellow.

Lima beans (see p. 22) have a rich floury taste.

Ful medames (see p. 21) are good eaten like a vegetable.

Mung beans (see p. 22) are usually skinless, as here.

Adzuki beans (see p. 21) can be red or black.

Flageolet beans (see p. 21) have a delicate flavor.

Yellow split peas (see p. 22).
Green split peas (see p. 22).　**Marrowfat peas** (see p. 22).

Chickpeas (see p. 21) have a distinctive, nutty taste.

Split red lentils (see p. 22).
Brown lentils (see p. 22).　　**Green lentils** (see p. 22).

wheat flour, however, does contain higher levels of sodium, calcium, phosphorus and potassium.

Federal law does not require flour enrichment, however, 30 states and Puerto Rico require white flour and bread to be enriched.

Flour bleaching

Bags of white flour are labeled "bleached" or "unbleached," terms covered by Food and Drug Administration regulations.

Unbleached flour still has the bran and germ removed, but other than enrichment (see above), it does not contain any chemical additives. Unbleached flour is slightly higher in protein, making it better for bread baking if white flour is being used alone or mixed with whole wheat. Baked goods made with unbleached flour will have a creamier-colored texture than if bleached flour is used.

Bleached flour, however, contains chemical bleaching and/or maturing agents. Bleaching agents are used to whiten flour but do not have any effect on the baking properties. Maturing agents, on the other hand, do not whiten flour but instead oxidate it so the general baking characteristics are improved.

Flour bleaching was adopted after the public developed its taste for fine-textured baked goods made from white flour. Freshly-milled white flour does not make good baked goods. Yet, if it is left to stand for several months, a natural oxidation occurs in the flour and it becomes whiter with a finer texture. Chemical bleaching speeds up this process.

Flour strength

The "strength" of a flour is a measure of its gluten content. Gluten is a form of protein, a sticky substance of great elasticity contained in the starchy part of the grain. Wheat contains the most gluten, rye rather less. Maize, rice, millet and the non-cereals buckwheat, chickpea, soybeans, potato, sago and tapioca are all entirely gluten-free.

When flour is mixed with water and yeast in bread making the gluten in the flour forms "strands" which trap bubbles of carbon dioxide given off by the fermenting yeast. This gives an aerated, elastic dough which rises well and means that the loaf will hold together when sliced.

Hard flours contain 10-14 per cent gluten; soft flours contain 7-10 per cent gluten. Only wheat and rye flour contain enough gluten to make yeasted bread. Of the wheat flours, white flour is harder than whole wheat flour because it has had all the bran and germ (which contain no gluten) removed.

The harder wheats are valued by commercial millers and bakers for their high gluten content, which gives lighter, higher loaves, but the softer types are widely acknowledged to have the best flavor. The harder wheats come mainly from the USA and Canada and the softer types come mainly from Europe, including the UK, and Australia.

Hard flours are generally used for bread and for puff piecrust pastries. Soft flours are good for sauces, cakes, dough and cookies, giving them a soft, melt-in-the-mouth texture.

The gluten in a flour can be affected by the handling it is given and also by other ingredients. Heavy kneading and working of a dough will actually make the gluten more elastic, and therefore stronger, as will adding salt or an acidic ingredient such as lemon juice. Gentle handling of a mixture will help keep the gluten content soft, as will the addition of sugar or fat. This is why many cakes and sweet or fruit breads do not rise as much as bread made from strong wheat flour.

Storage

As with grains, heat, moisture and light are the main causes of deterioration in flour. Use airtight containers and store away from direct heat or light. A cool, dry pantry or cellar is ideal. Whole wheat flour is best stored in the refrigerator or freezer, this is because it contains all the wheat germ which contains fat. The fat content makes it more susceptible to spoilage.

Stoneground whole wheat flour is best used as freshly milled as possible. If you can, buy only the quantity you need for the next month or two. All flour with a high gluten content should be used within two months for best results. There are a few small mills, including the Neal's Yard Flour Mill in London, where it is possible to buy really fresh flour. Alternatively, you may wish to consider buying a domestic hand or electric stone-grinding mill, so that you can grind your own.

Measuring flour

The most accurate way to measure flour is to dip the measuring cup or spoon into the flour, remove a heaping measure and then level off with the straight edge of a knife or spatula. Do not tap the measuring cup on the counter unless the recipe specifically calls for a "packed" measure. Whole wheat flour is measured the same as white flour. Whole wheat flour is not sold presifted but it should not be sifted because that would remove the small wheat kernel particles.

FLOURS Per 4 oz	Water	Protein	Fat	Carbohydrate	Fiber	Vitamin A	Vitamin B₁	Vitamin B₂	Vitamin B₃	Vitamin B₆	Vitamin B₁₂	Vitamin C	Vitamin D	Vitamin E	Folic acid	Iron	Calcium	Magnesium	Sodium	Potassium	Phosphorus	Zinc
	g	g	g	g	g	µg	mg	mg	mg	mg	µg	mg	µg	mg	µg	mg	mg	mg	mg	mg	mg	mg
Recommended daily allowance	N	80M 60W	N	N	25-30	750	1.5	1.5	18	1.5	3	30	2.5	8	200	12	500	250	2500	2500	500	15
Buckwheat flour	N	4.8	1	28.1	1	0	0.22	0.06	1.8	0.22	0	0	N	N	N	1.8	N	N	N	N	120	N
Cornmeal	12	9.3	3.3	71.5	N	**25**	0.3	0.08	1.8	N	0	3	N	N	N	4.2	17	N	1	284	N	N
Millet flour	13	5.8	1.7	75.4	N	0	0.68	0.19	2.8	N	0	0	N	N	N	N	40	N	21	365	N	N
Oat flour	9	12.4	**8.7**	72.8	7	0	0.5	0.1	1	0.12	0	0	0	0.8	60	4.1	55	110	33	370	380	**3**
Potato flour	N	8.8	0.88	**88**	1.7	Tr	0.45	0.15	3.7	Tr	0	**20.6**	N	N	N	**18.8**	36	N	37	1706	194	N
Rice flour	12	6.4	0.8	80.4	N	0	0.1	0.05	2.1	N	0	0	0	N	N	1.9	24	N	5	241	N	N
Rye flour	**15**	8.2	2	75.9	N	0	0.4	0.22	1	0.35	0	0	0	0.8	78	2.7	32	92	1	410	360	2.8
Soy flour	7	**36.8**	7.2	28.2	**11.9**	N	**0.75**	**0.36**	2.4	**0.57**	0	0	0	N	N	6.9	210	**240**	1	**1660**	**640**	N
Wheat flours – all-purpose	13	9.8	1.2	80.1	3.4	0	0.33	0.02	2	0.15	0	0	0	Tr	22	2.4	150	20	2	140	110	0.7
– self-rising	13	9.3	1.2	77.5	3.7	0	0.28	0.02	1.5	0.15	0	0	0	Tr	19	2.6	**350**	42	**350**	170	510	0.6
– bread	**15**	11.3	1.2	74.8	3	0	0.31	0.03	2	0.15	0	0	0	Tr	31	2.2	140	36	3	130	130	0.9
– whole wheat	14	13.2	2	65.8	9.6	0	0.46	0.08	**5.6**	0.5	0	0	0	1	57	4	35	140	3	360	340	**3**

KEY
All whole foods are uncooked unless otherwise stated. Some whole foods may not be included in the chart, as there is currently no nutritional data available.
g: grams **mg:** milligrams **µg:** micrograms **N:** no available data **Tr:** trace **M:** adult men **W:** adult women. The recommended daily allowances are averages and vary depending on age, occupation and metabolism. Figures in bold type indicate the whole food with the highest level of nutrient.

All-purpose flour

This is a highly-refined white flour that is a combination of hard and soft wheats and frequently used for most household baking. During the milling process, the bran and germ are removed so this flour is made from the endosperm part of the wheat kernel. It is usually sold enriched (see p. 16) and bleached or unbleached (see p. 17).

In most recipes whole wheat flour can be substituted for all-purpose but sometimes additional liquid is needed.

Barley flour
(Barley meal)

Barley flour is milled from pot barley. Because some of the bran is removed along with the hull it has a rather pale color. Barley has a very low gluten content, making it unsuitable for use in leavened doughs unless combined with wheat flour, but it can be used in cookies and cakes or to make a delicious unleavened barley bread.

Barley flour is suitable for people who are allergic to whole wheat flour, or have difficulty digesting whole wheat products.
Recipe: Dervish Barley Bread (see p. 152).

Bread flour

Bread flour is not stoneground. The bran and germ have been removed not by sieving but by the steel roller milling process, described on page 16. Most white flour has been bleached, so try to find a supplier of unbleached bread flour if you can. Slightly creamy in color, unbleached flour will produce a less anemic bread than white flour, with a good yellow-gold crust.

The all-purpose flours available in any grocery or supermarket are generally used for breadmaking. It is better, however, to buy a bread flour which not only makes good white bread but can also be used for rolls and coffee-cakes, and for thickening gravies and sauces. Adding a small proportion of bread flour to whole wheat flour in breadmaking increases the strength of the dough, as the bread flour releases its gluten quickly.

Some commercial bread flour has had potassium bromate added, which is a maturing agent. Potassium bromate is added to high-protein flours and helps produce baked goods with better volume and crumb structure. If it has been added, manufacturers are required by federal law to label the package "Bromated."

Buckwheat flour

Buckwheat flour, milled from whole raw buckwheat, is gray in color, darker even than whole wheat rye flour. Buckwheat contains no gluten, so the flour is not suitable on its own for making yeasted bread. Delicious buckwheat pancakes can be made, however, using either buckwheat flour on its own or a mixture of buckwheat flour and wheat flour.

Buckwheat flour is particularly useful to those on gluten-free diets. Undiluted, its flavor is likely to be too strong for most people, but a little will add a pleasant bite to cakes and cookies made with other flours.
Recipe: Buckwheat Crêpes with Tomato Sauce (see p. 101).

Cake flour

Low in gluten, this is a very finely-ground flour suitable for making soft-textured cakes. It is a specialty flour not readily available.

Chickpea flour
(Gram/Besun flour)

Gram is the Indian word for any dried bean, whether lentils, peas or beans. Gram flour is most commonly milled from whole chickpeas. It is widely used in Indian cookery, made into samosas and bhajis and mixed with whole wheat flour to make chapatis. It is also used for thickening sauces, to which it gives a pleasant, nutty flavor. Like all the pulses, chickpeas contain no gluten.

If your local health food store or supermarket doesn't stock chickpea flour, try an Italian delicatessen.
Recipe: Onion Bhajis with Yogurt Sauce (see p. 86).

Cornmeal
(Maize/Mealie meal)

Cornmeal is available in various degrees of coarseness and is usually a strong yellow color. This is 100% cornmeal, preferably stoneground. Do not confuse it with the much paler meal sometimes available, from which the germ has been removed and which therefore has little food value and a very thin flavor, or with the highly refined cornstarch sold as a thickening agent. Avoid purchasing any cornmeal with "degerminated" on the label; this is the version with the germ removed to increase shelf-life.

Corn contains no gluten at all, so cornmeal is not suitable for making yeasted bread unless combined with wheat flour. But it may be used on its own or mixed with other flours to make an enormous range of soda breads, soups, muffins, cakes, pancakes and dumplings. It may also be cooked as a hot cereal, and is a very pleasant alternative to oatmeal. The method is shown below.

Serve hot, like oatmeal, with milk or cream. When cold, it may be cut into slices, fried in a little butter and served with honey or jam for a delicious "next day" breakfast.
Basic cooking method (Serves 4)
1 cup cornmeal
3 cups cold water
a little salt

Mix the cornmeal with about one-third of the cold water. Put the rest of the water in a saucepan, add a little salt and bring to a boil. Stir in the mixture of meal and water, using a beater to prevent lumps forming. Stir continuously over a medium heat until a thick oatmeal consistency is reached. Remove the pan from the heat, cover and leave to stand for 5 minutes before serving.

As with oatmeal, any left over can be cooled and stored overnight in the refrigerator, where it will set firm.

Recipe: Use instead of chickpea flour in Tomato Soup (see p. 79).

Durum flour

Durum is the hardest wheat, so this flour has a high gluten content. It is used primarily to make pasta.

Masa harina

This is Mexican cornmeal (maize flour) which has been treated with lime, and is used to make tortillas. A tortilla dough is made from masa harina, water and salt. Balls of the dough are flattened into rounds and then fried in a hot, ungreased griddle.

Maslin

Maslin means mixed, and usually refers to a mixture of rye and wheat. In the past, rye and wheat were often sown together as a mixed crop, and the resulting mixture of grains was milled and then baked as maslin bread, which was the common bread in England for hundreds of years.

Millet flour

Millet contains no gluten, so millet flour is not suitable on its own for making yeasted bread. Because its delicate flavor is easily swamped, it is best not mixed with other flours, but it can be used instead of oat flour or cornmeal to make muffins and pancakes. It can also be cooked like semolina into an easy pudding.

Recipe: Rhubarb & Banana Crumble (see p. 129).

Oat flour

This fine oat flour is the main ingredient of traditional Scottish bannocks and oatcakes, cooked on a griddle above an open flame. It has a very low gluten content, so its use in the baking of leavened bread is limited, but a small proportion of fine oat flour (up to a quarter) added to whole wheat flour gives a rich, moist bread with a good flavor and excellent nutritional value.

A half-and-half mixture of fine oat flour and whole wheat flour makes delicious sweet muffins and wonderful crêpes. (For crêpes, allow the mixed batter to stand for at least 1 hour before using.)

Recipe: Dervish Barley Bread (see p. 152).

Pastry flour

Available in whole wheat as well as white, this flour is made from all soft wheat so it is ideal for baked goods with a crumbly texture, such as piecrusts and cookies. It is not suitable for making bread or anything from a batter. Although finely ground, it is not as fine as cake flour (see above). Because it is made from soft wheat, pastry flour is low in protein.

Potato flour or potato starch
(Farina)

Potato flour is not in any sense a whole food, but it deserves mention because of its value, especially in gluten-free diets, as a thickener. It can be mixed with an ordinary wheat flour to make potato bread or potato biscuits, although a far better flavor and food value can be achieved by using freshly cooked and mashed whole potatoes instead.

It is the coarsely ground endosperm of hard wheat and often used in breakfast cereals.

Recipe: Cheesecake (see p. 122).

Rice flour

Refined rice flour is used in commercial catering as a non-stick dusting for breads and pastries and as a thickening agent. However, 100 % rice flour milled from whole brown rice is far better value as a food. Rice is totally gluten-free, so rice flour cannot be used to make ordinary yeasted bread loaves, but it can be used to make a variety of gluten-free cakes, cookies and crêpes. It can also be cooked in a pan with milk or water, like whole wheat semolina (see p. 15).

Look for rice flour in health-food stores or the imported food section of larger supermarkets.

Rye flour

Rye flour may be either 100 % whole wheat or white. White rye flour, from which most or all of the bran has been removed, has of course less flavor and a lower food value. Whole wheat rye flour is darker than whole wheat flour, with a distinctive gray color. Its strong flavor makes it most suitable for bread, though in central Europe it is also used for cookies and gingerbread, as well as for the well-known Scandinavian crispbreads.

Rye contains less gluten than wheat, so rye bread always tends to be heavier than an equivalent wheat bread. The greater the proportion of rye flour used, the denser the bread is likely to be. For this reason, most rye bread contains at least half wheat flour.

If you do use only whole wheat rye flour, do not expect your bread to be very much darker than whole wheat bread. The European *schwarzbrod* or black rye bread contains molasses, coffee, chocolate or other colorings, and is in fact often made from white rye flour. Some brands of rye flour sold in supermarkets are labeled "medium," refering to the color, not the texture.

Recipe: Rye Bread (see p. 154).

Self rising flour

This is all-purpose flour with salt and levening agents added, eliminating the need to add baking powder and salt to recipes.

Soy flour
(Soybean flour/Soya flour)

Soy flour is made by partially cooking soybeans and grinding them into a creamy yellow-colored flour. Rich in protein like all soy products, it can be used to enrich whole wheat bread and cakes, giving them a full, creamy flavor.

As with all the dried beans, soybeans do not contain any gluten, so soy flour may be used for gluten-free cakes. For yeasted breads, it should be used in combination with wheat. Soy flour can also be used in cakes, puddings, pastries and cookies. Mixed to a cream with water it makes a good substitute for egg glaze.

Recipe: Apple, Soy & Almond Pudding (see p. 120).

Whole wheat flour

Whole wheat flour is simply milled wheat kernels with nothing removed. It is naturally rich in B-complex vitamins, fat, protein, vitamin E, and contains more trace minerals and dietary fiber than highly-refined white flours. Whole wheat flour is a light golden brown, and close inspection should reveal the dark particles of bran and yellow flecks of germ which give it its color.

Supermarket whole wheat flours are usually about the same grade of fineness. At larger health food stores, however, it is available with different degrees of coarseness. At Neal's Yard Bakery, a fairly coarse whole wheat flour is used to make all the bread, pita breads and pizzas, and a finer whole wheat flour is used for all the cakes, cookies, biscuits, pastries and croissants.

There are, in fact, very few baked goods that cannot be made successfully using whole wheat flour. Whole wheat breads and cakes are not, of course, as light as those made with white flour, but they are not as pallid or bland in appearance or taste.

For somone starting a whole food diet and not used to the generally heavier textures of baked goods made with all whole wheat flour, begin by baking with half whole wheat and half all-purpose flours; gradually change the proportions to all whole wheat.

When first beginning to bake with whole wheat flour, remember it has greater absorbency than white flour so extra liquid may be necessary.

Graham flour is another name occasionally used for whole wheat flour. It is named after Rev. Sylvester Graham (1794-1851), an early advocate of nutrition and healthy home baking. Although cook books from the last century often included recipes for graham flour it is not widely available today:

Recipe: Basic Whole Wheat Bread (see p. 149).

DRIED BEANS, PEAS & LENTILS

Adzuki beans ☐
Black-eyed peas ☐
Black kidney beans ☐
Cannellini beans ☐
Chickpeas ☐

Fava beans ☐
Flageolet beans ☐
Ful medames ☐
Kidney beans ☐
Lentils ☐

Lima beans ☐
Marrowfat peas ☐
Mung beans ☐
Navy beans
Pinto beans ☐

Soybeans ☐
Split peas ☐

☐ Pictured opposite page 17

Dried beans, peas and lentils are the seeds of pod-bearing leguminous plants. Some are eaten fresh, such as green peas, green beans and runner beans; most are eaten dried.

For thousands of years fresh seeds, peas and beans have been dried and stored. Many poorer cultures still rely on dried beans for their survival, especially during times of drought and crop failure. Beans have sometimes been regarded as a poor man's food, but in these days of growing food shortages and increased nutritional awareness their true value is recognised.

The growing cycle for most beans is about three months. The majority prefer a warm, temperate climate, although hardier strains do grow successfully in colder northern areas. Because of their durable nature, dried beans, peas and lentils are not subjected to additives, a rare phenomenon in this day and age. But do rinse and sort them through before you soak and cook them, because it is common to find small twigs, pods and stones that have not been removed.

Nutritional value
Dried beans, peas and lentils are highly nutritious, containing protein, vitamins, minerals and fiber. They are particularly high in vitamins B_1 and B_2, iron and potassium, and also contain very little fat. Dried beans form a vital part of a whole food vegetarian diet.

The protein which beans contain is incomplete, that is, it contains only a certain number of the amino acids needed to make up a complete protein (see p. 8). To make up a complete protein, beans can be combined with either one or all of the follows: grains, nuts, seeds or milk. An exception is the soybean, which contains all of the essential amino acids and is therefore a complete protein.

Storage
Once cooked and cooled, beans may be kept for several days in an airtight container in the refrigerator, or frozen (see p. 65). Beans can last for years and still be capable of germinating in the right conditions, as has been proved with legumes excavated from Inca temples and the tombs of the pyramids. However, as with most foods, the fresher they are the better. In general, you should not store beans for more than one year. Buy them in small quantities and store in clean, dry airtight jars. Store away from sunlight, and do not keep in glass jars unless you are going to use them up very quickly.

Soaking
Most beans need soaking and cooking before eating, the exact times varying according to type and age. Beans triple in size when soaked and cooked, so be sure to place them in a sufficiently large bowl or saucepan. Rinse them well and remove any stones or debris. Cover with three times their volume of water and leave to stand for the suggested soaking time (see the chart right). Do not soak for more than 12 hours as the beans may begin to ferment. Lentils and split peas do not need soaking.

Alternatively, to speed up the soaking process, put the beans in a saucepan covered with three times their volume of cold water, bring to a boil and cook for 5 minutes. Remove from the heat and leave to stand for at least 1 hour before cooking.

Cooking
When you have soaked the beans, transfer to a saucepan with their liquid (which will contain vitamins and minerals from the beans) and top up with fresh cold water, if necessary, to cover. Do not add salt during cooking because it will toughen the skins. Cover with a lid and boil gently until cooked. Remove one or two, let cool a little and then taste.

All beans can be cooked this way except kidney beans and soybeans. Red kidney beans sometimes contain a toxic substance on the outer skin which must be removed by vigorous boiling for the first 15 minutes of the cooking time. Soybeans contain a substance called trypsin-inhibitor, which prevents the body from absorbing protein, so they should be boiled vigorously for the first hour. If you are using a pressure cooker, fast boiling will happen automatically.

You can save time by cooking extra beans and refrigerating them once they have cooled. They will keep safely in the refrigerator for 3-4 days in an airtight container. Chickpeas and soybeans should be rinsed daily, however.

Soaking and cooking chart

DRIED BEANS, PEAS AND LENTILS	SOAKING TIME	COOKING TIME	PRESSURE-COOKING TIME
Adzuki beans	3-4 hours	1 hour	15 minutes
Black-eyed peas	8-12 hours	1 hour	15 minutes
Black kidney beans	8-12 hours	1½ hours, boiling vigorously for the first 15 minutes	20 minutes
Cannellini beans	8-12 hours	1½ hours	20 minutes
Chickpeas	8-12 hours	3 hours	40 minutes
Fava beans	8-12 hours	1½ hours	20 minutes
Flageolet beans	8-12 hours	1½ hours	20 minutes
Ful medames	8-12 hours	2 hours	30 minutes
Kidney beans	8-12 hours	1½ hours, boiling vigorously for the first 15 minutes	20 minutes
Lentils: large	none	30 minutes	10 minutes
small	none	20 minutes	10 minutes
Lima beans	8-12 hours	1½ hours	20 minutes
Marrowfat peas	8-12 hours	1 hour	15 minutes
Mung beans	4-8 hours	45 minutes	10 minutes
Navy beans	8-12 hours	1½ hours	20 minutes
Pinto beans	8-12 hours	1½ hours	20 minutes
Soybeans	8-12 hours	4 hours, boiling vigorously for the first hour	50 minutes
Split peas: green	none	30 minutes	10 minutes
yellow	none	30 minutes	10 minutes

DRIED BEANS, PEAS & LENTILS Per 4 oz	Water	Protein	Fat	Carbohydrate	Fiber	Vitamin A	Vitamin B₁	Vitamin B₂	Vitamin B₃	Vitamin B₆	Vitamin B₁₂	Vitamin C	Vitamin D	Vitamin E	Folic acid	Iron	Calcium	Magnesium	Sodium	Potassium	Phosphorus	Zinc
	g	g	g	g	g	µg	mg	mg	mg	mg	µg	mg	µg	mg	µg	mg	mg	mg	mg	mg	mg	mg
Recommended daily allowance	N	80M 60W	N	N	25-30	750	1.5	1.5	18	1.5	3	30	2.5	8	200	12	500	250	2500	2500	500	15
Adzuki beans	**16**	21.5	1.6	58.4	4.3	6	0.5	0.1	2.5	N	0	0	N	N	N	4.8	75	N	7	N	350	N
Black-eyed peas	12	22.7	1.6	56.8	N	10	0.59	0.22	**7.7**	0.48	0	1	0	N	**439**	6.5	110	53	6	688	360	N
Chickpeas	10	20.2	5.7	50	15	190	0.5	0.15	1.5	N	0	**3**	0	N	180	6.4	140	160	40	800	300	N
Fava beans	14	25	1.2	51.8	6	65	0.45	0.19	6	N	0	0	0	N	N	4.2	104	N	8	1123	360	N
Kidney beans	11	22.1	1.7	45	25	Tr	0.54	0.18	2	0.5	0	Tr	0	N	140	6.7	140	180	40	1160	410	2.8
Lentils	12	23.8	1	53.2	11.7	60	0.5	0.2	2	0.6	0	Tr	0	N	35	7.6	39	77	36	670	240	3.1
Lima beans	12	19.1	1.1	49.8	21.6	Tr	0.45	0.13	2.5	0.58	0	0	0	N	110	5.9	85	164	**62**	**1700**	320	2.8
Marrowfat peas	13	21.6	1.3	50	16.7	**250**	0.6	0.3	3	0.13	0	Tr	0	Tr	33	4.7	61	116	38	990	300	3.5
Mung beans	12	22	1	35.6	22	24	0.45	0.2	2	0.5	0	Tr	0	N	140	8	100	170	28	850	330	N
Navy beans	11	21.4	1.6	45.5	**25.4**	Tr	0.45	0.13	0.56	2.5	0	0	0	N	N	6.7	180	180	43	1160	310	2.8
Pinto beans	8	22.9	1.2	**63.7**	4.3	N	0.84	0.21	2.2	0.5	0	N	0	N	N	6.4	135	N	10	984	457	N
Soybeans	10	**34.1**	**17.7**	28.6	N	24	**1.1**	**0.31**	2.2	**0.88**	0	N	0	N	100	**8.4**	226	**265**	5	1677	**554**	N
Split peas	12	22.1	1	56.6	11.9	150	0.7	0.2	3.2	0.13	0	Tr	0	Tr	33	5.4	33	130	38	910	270	**4**

KEY

All whole foods are uncooked unless otherwise stated. Some whole foods may not be included in the chart, as there is currently no nutritional data available. **g**: grams **mg**: milligrams **µg**: micrograms **N**: no available data **Tr**: trace **M**: adult men **W**: adult women. The recommended daily allowances are averages and vary depending on age, occupation and metabolism. Figures in bold type indicate the whole food with the highest level of nutrient.

Adzuki beans
(Aduki/Azuki/Feijoa beans)
These are small dark red or brown beans with a characteristic sweet, nutty flavor and a smooth, creamy texture.

Adzuki beans originated in China and are much favored in Japan where they are known as the "King of beans." They have been used medicinally for many years in China and Japan to treat kidney disorders. Adzuki beans are now grown in Southeast Asia.

Adzuki beans can be used in soups, pâtés, savory and sweet dishes. They may also be sprouted (see p. 23).
Recipe: Adzuki Bean Soup (see p. 72).

Black beans
(Frijoles negros)
These large black-skinned, kidney-shaped beans are part of the huge common bean family which originated in South America. Columbus introduced the family to Europe in the sixteenth century and many varieties evolved. Black kidney beans are now principally grown in Thailand and China, and are extremely popular in the Caribbean. (In fact Chinese "black bean sauce" is usually made from soybeans and not black beans.)

Tender and sweet-tasting, black kidney beans can be used in any recipe requiring red kidney beans, and they are delicious in soups, salads, curries and other savory dishes. See the special cooking directions on page 20.
Recipe: Black Bean Chili (see p. 100).

Black-eyed peas
(Cowpeas/Black-eyed beans)
These small cream-colored beans with black and yellow "eyes" probably originated in Africa, where they can still be found. They reached America via the slave trade in the seventeenth century and were adopted by the Southern farmers. They are now principally grown in California.

Black-eyed peas have a smooth, creamy flavor, and are high in folic acid. They are quick to prepare and blend well with other flavors, and they are delicious in pâtés, casseroles and soups. Black-eyed peas may also be sprouted (see p. 23).
Recipe: Beanburgers (see p. 99).

Cannellini beans
(Fazolia beans)
Cannellini are small, white beans and are in fact part of the large common bean family. They are very popular in Argentina where they were first cultivated, but now they are widely grown and exported from Italy. They have a firm, fluffy texture, even after cooking, and a good savory flavor. Try them in soups, salads and savory dishes.
Recipe: Minestrone (see p. 77).

Chickpeas
(Garbanzos/Bengal gram/Chana dal)
These small golden brown, filbert-shaped beans originated in western Asia and traveled through India and the Middle East to the Mediterranean. There are several varieties, but of the two main types the Middle Eastern chickpea is slightly smaller and darker than the Mediterranean chickpea.

In India chickpeas are called *gram*, and a coarse flour is milled from them to make chapatis, breads and bhajis. In the Middle East chickpeas are used to make hummus and falafal.

Chickpeas are high in fats, vitamin A, vitamin C and folic acid, and their distinctive, nutty flavor is delicious in salads, casseroles and other savory dishes. They may also be sprouted (see p. 23).
Recipe: Hummus (see p. 83).

Fava beans
(Broad/Windsor/Horse beans)
These large, pale brown beans are indigenous to Europe, and were very popular in England during the Middle Ages. They are most often eaten as a fresh vegetable, although the dried beans are extremely popular in southern Europe. The main producers are Spain and Greece. Nutritionally, fava beans contain some protein and are quite high in potassium.
Recipe: Vegetable Pâté (see p. 87).

Flageolet beans
(Green haricot beans)
These pale green, slender beans have a rich, delicate flavor. Part of the common bean family, they are principally grown in France and Italy, where they were first cultivated.

Flageolet beans are eaten fresh as well as dried, and are delicious in salads and savory dishes. They can be sprouted (see p. 23).

Ful medames
(Egyptian/Field/Foul beans)
These are small, round brown beans which need a lot of cooking. Part of the fava bean family, they were first cultivated in the Middle East. They are very popular in the Middle East and Egypt, where they are now principally grown for export.

Ful medames are very good in soups, casseroles, salads and other savory dishes.

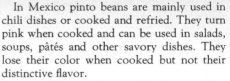

Kidney beans
(Mexican/Chili beans)

These are large, shiny, red kidney-shaped beans with a rich, floury texture. There are a number of varieties with colors ranging from maroon to pinky-red. Kidney beans are a member of the common bean family. They originated in Central America and are now grown principally in America and East Africa.

Kidney beans are very high in fiber and also contain magnesium. They are delicious in soups, casseroles and chili dishes, and are the main ingredient in the traditional Mexican dish *chili con carne*. For specific cooking directions, see page 20.

Recipe: Red Bean Salad (see p. 93).

Lentils
(Dhal/Dal)

These small beans originated in Southeast Asia and spread to Europe via India and the Middle East, where they are still very popular.

There are several varieties of lentil, the most common being the small, red lentil (sometimes sold split), the larger green or continental lentil and the Indian brown lentil, which is a red lentil from which the outer casing has not been removed. Other types which are sometimes available include the yellow lentil, and the Puy lentil from France.

Lentils are particularly high in vitamin B_6. They do not require any soaking and cook quickly. Lentils will cook to a soft, grainy-textured purée, although green and Puy lentils will retain some of their shape. You can use lentils as purées or in soups, bakes, burgers and curries. They can also be sprouted very successfully (see p. 23).

Recipe: Fresh Coriander Dhal (see p. 105).

Lima beans
(Butter/Madagascar beans)

These large creamy-white or pale green beans originated in South America and traveled to Central and North America, Africa and the Far East. A main grower is now Madagascar. They are sometimes called "butter beans" because of their pale, creamy color.

Lima beans are particularly high in sodium and potassium. They have a soft, floury texture and a smooth, succulent flavor and are delicious in salads, pâtés, soups and almost any savory dish, or can be puréed to make smooth, creamy dips. They retain their shape well when cooked.

Recipe: Lima Bean Salad (see p. 90).

Marrowfat peas
(Whole green/Blue peas)

Marrowfat peas are large, gray-green in color and have a floury texture. They belong to the same family as the garden or common pea. All peas were similar in appearance and taste to the marrowfat pea until the sixteenth century, when the sweet green pea we are familiar with today was developed, now the most common variety of fresh pea (see p. 30). They contain more vitamin A than any other dried bean.

Marrowfat peas are mainly grown in northern Europe. They are the main ingredient in "mushy peas," a traditional dish in the North of England. Dried marrowfat peas need long soaking and cooking and are delicious in soups and other savory dishes.

Recipe: Vegetable Pâté (see p. 87).

Mung beans
(Green/Golden gram)

These tiny olive-green beans originated in India but they grew quickly in popularity in the Far East and are now common in most countries from China to southern Indonesia. They are now principally grown in Australia, Thailand and China.

Mung beans are available whole, split and skinned. They are often eaten sprouted and are then known as bean sprouts or bean shoots. You can sprout your own (see p. 23).

Mung beans are high in iron and have a good flavor and creamy texture. They can be used in soups, casseroles and mixed grain dishes.

Recipe: Mung Bean Casserole (see p. 109).

Navy beans
(Boston/Pearl haricot beans)

These small, white beans are in fact a variety of common bean and are principally grown in America. They are the main ingredient in Boston baked beans.

Navy beans are particularly high in fiber. They are light and tasty and can be used in pâtés, soups and other savory dishes.

Recipe: Home-Style Baked Beans (see p. 107).

Pinto beans
(Pink beans)

These medium-sized, speckled brown beans are part of the common bean family and are indigenous to Mexico. They are now grown mainly in the USA. Pinto beans are very high in carbohydrate and also contain a fair amount of vitamin B_1 and phosphorus.

In Mexico pinto beans are mainly used in chili dishes or cooked and refried. They turn pink when cooked and can be used in salads, soups, pâtés and other savory dishes. They lose their color when cooked but not their distinctive flavor.

Recipe: Pinto, Zucchini & Mushroom Bake (see p. 109).

Soybeans
(Soya beans)

These small, round beans originated in China and have been cultivated there for many thousands of years. They are now principally grown in North America and Canada. Soybeans are usually yellow or black but green and red varieties are also grown.

Nutritionally, soybeans contain higher proportions of protein, fats, B vitamins and minerals than any other bean. They contain complete or first-class protein, similar to that found in animal foodstuffs (see p. 8). Soybeans also have a high proportion of unsaturated fatty acids, which contain linoleic acid and lecithin. Both these substances help lower the level of cholesterol in the blood, therefore reducing the risk of hardening and thickening of the arteries and associated heart disease.

Soybeans do take a very long time to soak and cook (for special cooking directions, see p. 20). When cooked, whole soybeans have a firm, nutty flavor and are delicious in salads, risottos, pâtés and other savory dishes. They can also be sprouted (see p. 23).

By-products of the soybean are described later in this book. They are soy flour (see p. 19), soy milk (see p. 47), soy oil (see p. 49), miso (see p. 50) and tamari and shoyu, or soy sauces (see p. 51). Soy grits are soybeans that have been cracked; you can substitute soy grits for soybeans but the texture will be different.

Recipe: Soybean Salad (see p. 93).

Split peas

Split peas are a variety of common pea which have a natural tendency to split when dried and hulled. They may also be steamed and polished. Both yellow and green split peas are available; they are both slightly sweeter than the whole, marrowfat pea.

Split peas need no soaking and cook quickly, but they do not retain their shape when cooked. They make excellent purées and can be used in soups, savory dishes and pâtés.

Recipe: Fresh Coriander Dhal (see p. 105).

SPROUTED GRAINS, BEANS & SEEDS

First accounts of sprouting came from China many thousands of years ago, and the Aztecs and certain native American tribes were also familiar with sprouted grains, beans and seeds. Although sprouted barley was used in Roman times to obtain malt for making beer, and sprouted beans were used by Captain Cook and the crew of the *Endeavour* in the eighteenth century to prevent scurvy, people have been slow to discover their nutritional and medicinal properties, and it is only in recent years that keen interest has developed.

Sprouted grains, seeds and beans are highly nutritious, and can be easily sprouted at home. Commercially produced sprouts are also available from most whole food stores.

Nutritional value

Sprouted grains, beans and seeds are some of the most complete foods available to us, being rich in protein, fats, carbohydrates, fiber, vitamins, minerals and trace elements. They are generally eaten a few days after germination has taken place. At germination, a frenzy of activity occurs inside the previously dormant seed, breaking down the proteins, carbohydrates and oils into far less complex and more digestible amino acids, sugars and fatty acids. Minerals combine with enzymes to become easily assimilated by the body. Vitamins already present in the dormant seed increase dramatically in quantity and vitamin C, not present in unsprouted grains, seeds and beans, is synthesized. The vitamins found in most sprouted grains, beans and seeds are vitamins A, B_1, B_2, B_6, C, D and E.

Soybean sprouts are the most nutritious of all, as they also contain vitamins U and K. Another exceptional sprout is alfalfa, which contains vitamin B_{12}. This essential vitamin is only found in three other plant substances, namely comfrey, seaweeds and fermented soybean products.

What can be sprouted

Most grains, beans and seeds can be sprouted. They must be whole and neither hulled, split, cracked nor roasted. In other words, pearled barley, split peas, cracked wheat or roasted buckwheat will not sprout. It is possible to find whole, untreated grains, beans and seeds in most whole food stores. Do not buy grains or seeds intended for pets, agricultural or horticultural use because they may have been chemically treated.

Not all whole cereal kernels can be sprouted. Wheat, rye and maize kernels can be sprouted successfully (in fact, wheat kernels are one of the easiest and most rewarding to sprout) but other cereal grains grow encased in an indigestible hull (see p. 11). The removal of this hull generally damages the kernels too much for them to be viable for sprouting.

Using sprouts

Sprouted grains, beans and seeds are usually eaten raw in salads and sandwiches, but they can also be used in soups, stir-fries, casseroles and other savory dishes, and can be added to breads. Wheat sprouts are particularly delicious, and fenugreek sprouts have a slightly spicy flavor. Adzuki sprouts have a nutty taste that is good in salads, and alfalfa sprouts make a tasty and nutritious sandwich filling.

Sprouting grains, beans and seeds

If you have a sprouter, follow the manufacturer's directions. Alternatively, you can use a jelly jar:

1 Measure the quantity of seeds you will need. 1 tbsp of dried seeds is about right for a 2 lb jelly jar. The seeds may expand to eight times their original size, so be sure to have enough room for adequate air circulation and swelling. Pick over the seeds to remove any that are damaged or pieces of grit.

2 Soak the seeds for the suggested time (see chart below) in at least three times their volume of cool water, preferably filtered.

3 Drain the seeds. The soaking liquid will contain minerals, sugars and amino acids and can be reserved for soups or sauces. Put the seeds into the jelly jar and stand in a warm, ventilated place out of direct sunlight.

4 All sprouting seeds need rinsing between two and five times a day (see chart below). This removes the toxic wastes produced by the multiplying cells. If the seeds are not rinsed, they will rot. After rinsing be sure to drain well, because excess water will also cause the seeds to deteriorate.

5 Within 2-6 days the sprouts will be ready for harvesting. All sprouts should be eaten within a week of germination. After this time photosynthesis begins to take place and the nutritional value of the sprouts diminishes.

Sprouting mucilaginous seeds

Mustard, cress and radish are mucilanginous seeds. They are unsuitable for sprouting in jars and are best grown as follows:

1 Place a thick layer of paper towels or blotting paper on a saucer and sprinkle the seeds on top.

2 Instead of rinsing, just sprinkle water onto the seeds four or five times a day and keep the paper moist at all times. Do not allow it to dry out or become waterlogged.

3 Harvest when the sprouts are ready (see chart below).

Sprouting chart

GRAINS, SEEDS AND BEANS	SOAKING TIME	RINSING FREQUENCY PER DAY*	HARVESTING TIME
Adzuki beans	12 hours	3	3-6 days
Alfalfa seeds	6 hours	3	3-6 days
Barley grains	12 hours	3	3-4 days
Black-eyed peas	12 hours	3	3-4 days
Buckwheat kernels	12 hours	3	4-5 days
Chickpeas	12 hours	4	5-6 days
Cress seeds	none	5	4-5 days
Dried peas	12 hours	3	3-5 days
Fenugreek seeds	12 hours	3	4-5 days
Flageolet beans	12 hours	3	4-5 days
Lentils	8 hours	3	2-5 days
Millet grains	12 hours	3	2-3 days
Mung beans	12 hours	3	2-6 days
Mustard seeds	none	4	4-5 days
Navy beans	12 hours	3	4-5 days
Pumpkin seeds	12 hours	3	2-4 days
Radish seeds	none	5	4-5 days
Rice	12 hours	3	2-3 days
Rye berries	12 hours	3	3-5 days
Sesame seeds	8 hours	3	3-4 days
Soybeans	10 hours	4	2-6 days
Sunflower seeds	12 hours	3	2-6 days
Wheat kernels	12 hours	3	2-4 days

*Note: Sprouting seeds should ideally be rinsed at least three times a day, but if this is impossible once in the morning and once in the evening will be sufficient.

FRESH VEGETABLES

Artichokes, French ☐
Asparagus ☐
Avocados ☐
Beets
Broccoli ☐
Brussels sprouts
Cabbages
Carrots
Cauliflowers
Celery
Celery root ☐
Chicory ☐

Corn-on-the-cob
Cucumbers
Eggplant ☐
Endive ☐
English runner beans
Fava beans
Fennel ☐
Green beans
Jerusalem artichokes ☐
Kohlrabi ☐
Leeks
Lettuces

Mushrooms
Okra ☐
Olives ☐
Onions
Parsnips
Peas
Peppers ☐
Potatoes
Pumpkins and squashes ☐
Radicchio ☐
Radishes ☐
Rutabago

Salsify/Scorzonera ☐
Sea kale
Spinach
Sweet potatoes ☐
Swiss chard
Tomatoes
Turnips
Watercress
Yams
Zucchini ☐

☐ Pictured opposite page 32

An essential part of the human diet since prehistoric times, the serious cultivation of vegetables began as the early hunter-gatherers gradually relinquished their nomadic lifestyles. Initially farmed in China, the Middle East and South America, many varieties of vegetables were brought to Europe and then North America as a result of conquest and exploration. Today, the production of vegetables for domestic consumption is a major industry in many countries and there is a wide range of both local and imported produce to choose from.

Vegetables play an important role in a whole food diet. Served raw or cooked, they offer a rich variety of attractive colors, textures and flavors to add interest to your diet. They are made up primarily of water (at least 80 per cent of content in many cases); the rest is carbohydrate, protein and fat. They are also a valuable source of fiber, and contain a range of vitamins and minerals. The leafy vegetables tend to be particularly nutritious and you should include at least one serving of these in your daily diet.

Sources

Ideally, vegetables should be organically grown (see p. 7) and eaten straight from your own garden. If this is not possible, you should try to buy organically grown vegetables. These are increasingly available with the growth of public awareness of the danger of chemically grown foods, and can even be found in some supermarkets.

Locally grown produce is also recommended. You should familiarize yourself with the growing seasons of vegetables and make the most of them when they are cheap and plentiful.

Additives

Unless you grow your own or can buy organically grown vegetables (see p. 7), it is probable that many of the vegetables you buy or the soil in which they are grown will have been treated with some sort of chemical spray or pesticide. Since many vegetables are imported it is possible that preservatives or mold inhibitors have been used. The simplest answer is to peel them, but since the most nutritious part of many vegetables is just beneath the skin, this would be a terrible waste. However, a good wash or scrub with a vegetable brush will remove excess chemicals, without removing essential nutrients.

Choosing vegetables

The best quality, freshest vegetables will have the finest flavor and are the most nutritionally sound. When choosing vegetables at your supermarket or local farmers' market, do not be dissuaded from holding them and checking them as necessary to ensure you get good quality produce.

1 Choose firm, undamaged vegetables.
2 Avoid limp, faded or withered vegetables.
3 Avoid vegetables with bruising, soft spots or frostbite.
4 Do not buy more than you need, especially of salad vegetables. These will keep in the refrigerator but are usually best if bought and consumed on the day of purchase.
5 Do not be persuaded always to buy the cheapest: this is often false economy as you may have to throw some away.
6 Do not always assume the bigger the better. Very often the smaller the vegetable, the sweeter and tastier it will be.
7 Make the most of vegetables with a short seasonal availability, such as artichokes, asparagus, peas and beans.

Storage

Most vegetables will keep for a few days in a cool, airy place. An old-fashioned pantry with open ventilation to the outside is ideal for this, or the vegetable compartment of the refrigerator. Wire or plastic vegetable racks are also suitable but make sure that you position them in a cool place and not next to the stove or any other appliance which gives off heat. As a general rule, vegetables to be stored should not be washed, sliced or packed too closely together.

In general, if your lifestyle and budget allow, leave the supplier to worry about storage. Shopping daily or every couple of days means less to struggle home with and hopefully the freshest, best quality vegetables of the day.

If growing your own, pick as required or freeze (see p. 63).

Cooking methods

Ideally, the majority of vegetables require a minimum of cooking if their character, taste and freshness are to be maintained. To prepare, wash well or scrub with a vegetable scrubber and trim or top and tail as required.

Baking

This simple method of cooking vegetables needs little personal attention and leaves the top of the stove free for other food.

Prepare the vegetables by dicing, chopping or slicing as desired. Place in an ovenproof dish with a cover, brush with melted butter or oil, season to taste, cover and bake in a pre-heated oven at 400°F until tender.

This method is suitable for root vegetables and can also be used for soft vegetables such as zucchini, squash and mushrooms. Root vegetables will take about 1-1½ hours to cook and soft vegetables 15-30 minutes, depending on size.

Boiling

Boiling vegetables has become less popular because of the loss of valuable nutrients into the water and the tendency to over-cook. However, it is still a useful cooking method and the vegetable liquid can be used to make soups and sauces.

First prepare the vegetables by trimming, dicing, chopping or slicing as required. Bring a saucepan of water to a boil and add a little salt, if desired. Add the vegetables to the water. Do not use too much water: the vegetables just need to be covered. Cover the pan, return to a boil and simmer until tender.

Most vegetables can be boiled. They are best left whole so that fewer of the nutrients can leak into the water.

Braising

First, prepare the vegetables by dicing, chopping or slicing as desired. Blanch the vegetables by plunging into boiling water for 2-3 minutes. Drain, heat a little vegetable oil or butter in a heavy-bottomed saucepan and lightly brown the vegetables.

Now add ⅔ cup of vegetable broth or water to each 1 pound of prepared vegetables. Cover with a tightly fitting lid and simmer gently until cooked. Remove the vegetables. The liquid can be reduced to make a sauce by rapid boiling, or by thickening with arrowroot or kuzu (see p. 50).

Alternatively, put the blanched vegetables into a covered ovenproof dish with a little hot liquid and cook in a preheated oven at 350°F for 15-20 minutes or until tender.

Braising is particularly suitable for root vegetables, but can also be used for fennel, leeks, celery and red cabbage.

Deep-frying

Make sure you choose a vegetable oil with a high smoke point for deep-frying, such as peanut, sesame or soy oil.

First chop, slice or prepare the vegetables as desired and pat dry to prevent the oil spitting. Heat the oil in a deep, heavy-bottomed saucepan, preferably fitted with a wire net with which to raise or lower the food. Heat to approximately 375°F. To check whether the oil is hot enough, drop in a cube of bread and watch if it browns within 40 seconds.

Lower the prepared vegetables into the hot oil. Fry until tender and crisp and then drain well on paper towels.

Deep-frying is suitable for French fries, onion rings and vegetables coated with batter (Japanese tempura-style).

Pressure-cooking

Vegetables cook extremely quickly in a pressure cooker. Prepare the vegetables or leave whole as desired and follow the manufacturer's directions for cooking times.

Use this method for older, tougher vegetables rather than tender young ones as these can easily overcook.

Shallow-frying or sautéeing

For shallow-frying or sautéeing, first prepare the vegetables by dicing, chopping or slicing. Dry on paper towels.

Heat a little vegetable oil or butter in a heavy-bottomed skillet and add the vegetables. Cook over a high heat for 1-2 minutes, then reduce the heat and cook until tender.

Shallow-frying is suitable for soft vegetables, such as zucchini, tomatoes and eggplant, and also for root vegetables.

Steaming

There are a variety of petal steamers available designed to fit inside a covered saucepan. A colander or strainer will do as well, so long as the saucepan lid fits snugly into the top and the steam from the boiling water does not escape around the sides.

Vegetables may be left whole if small enough, or they can be diced, chopped or sliced as desired. Cover the bottom of the saucepan with 2-3 inches of water and bring to a boil. Add the vegetables in the steamer, cover and steam until tender. Steaming takes a few minutes longer than boiling.

All vegetables can be steamed.

Stir-frying

The tradition of stir-frying or quick-frying comes from the East. A wok (special pan) is best suited for the purpose. Its shallow, rounded shape allows you to use very little oil, yet still have a large surface area to cook in. Be sure to use vegetable oil with a high smoke point, such as peanut, sesame or soy oil.

Dice, chop or slice the vegetables into small pieces. Pat dry. Heat the oil in the wok, and add the vegetables, beginning with the vegetable which needs the longest cooking time. Stir continuously. As soon as the pieces of vegetable are well covered in oil and the flavor is sealed in, push them gently to the sides of the wok and add the next vegetable. In this way you end up with lightly cooked, crisp and nutritious vegetables.

All vegetables can be cooked this way, so long as they are cut into small pieces.

FRESH VEGETABLES Per 4 oz	Water	Protein	Fat	Carbohydrate	Fiber	Vitamin A	Vitamin B₁	Vitamin B₂	Vitamin B₃	Vitamin B₆	Vitamin B₁₂	Vitamin C	Vitamin D	Vitamin E	Folic acid	Iron	Calcium	Magnesium	Sodium	Potassium	Phosphorus	Zinc
	g	g	g	g	g	µg	mg	mg	mg	mg	µg	mg	µg	mg	µg	mg	mg	mg	mg	mg	mg	mg
Recommended daily allowance	N	80M 60W	N	N	25-30	750	1.5	1.5	18	1.5	3	30	2.5	8	200	12	500	250	2500	2500	500	15
Artichokes, French (cooked)	84	1.1	Tr	2.7	0	90	0.07	0.03	0.09	0.07	0	8	0	0	30	0.5	44	27	15	330	40	0
Asparagus	92	3.4	Tr	1.1	1.5	500	0.1	0.08	0.8	0.04	0	20	0	2.5	30	0.9	26	10	2	240	85	0.3
Avocados	69	4.2	22.2	1.8	2	100	0.1	0.1	1	0.42	0	15	N	3.2	66	1.5	15	29	2	400	31	N
Beet	87	1.3	Tr	6	3.1	Tr	0.03	0.05	0.1	0.05	0	6	0	0	90	0.4	25	15	84	300	32	0.4
Broccoli	89	3.3	Tr	2.5	3.6	2500	0.1	0.3	1	0.21	0	110	0	1.3	130	1.5	100	18	12	340	67	0.6
Brussels sprouts	88	4	Tr	2.7	4.2	400	0.1	0.15	0.7	0.28	0	90	0	1	110	0.7	32	19	4	380	65	0.5
Cabbages – Chinese	90	0.9	0.1	2	0.4	110	0.04	0.03	0.5	N	0	19	0	N	N	0.5	32	N	17	190	30	N
– green	90	3.3	Tr	3.3	3.1	300	0.06	0.05	0.3	0.16	0	60	0	0.2	90	0.9	75	20	23	260	68	0.3
– red	90	1.7	Tr	3.5	3.4	20	1.06	0.05	0.3	0.21	0	55	0	0.2	90	0.6	53	17	32	300	32	0.3
– white	90	1.9	Tr	3.8	2.7	Tr	0.06	0.05	0.3	0.16	0	55	0	0.2	26	0.4	44	13	7	280	36	0.3
Carrots	90	0.7	Tr	5.4	2.9	12000	0.06	0.05	0.6	0.15	0	6	0	0.5	15	0.6	48	12	95	220	21	0.4
Cauliflowers	93	1.9	Tr	1.5	2.1	30	0.1	0.1	0.6	0.2	0	0.6	0	0.2	39	0.5	21	14	8	350	45	0.3
Celery	94	0.9	Tr	1.3	1.8	Tr	0.03	0.03	0.3	0.1	0	0.3	0	0.2	12	0.6	52	10	140	280	32	0.1

FRESH VEGETABLES Per 4 oz	Water	Protein	Fat	Carbohydrate	Fiber	Vitamin A	Vitamin B1	Vitamin B2	Vitamin B3	Vitamin B6	Vitamin B12	Vitamin C	Vitamin D	Vitamin E	Folic acid	Iron	Calcium	Magnesium	Sodium	Potassium	Phosphorus	Zinc
	g	g	g	g	g	µg	mg	mg	mg	mg	µg	mg	µg	mg	µg	mg	mg	mg	mg	mg	mg	mg
Recommended daily allowance	N	80M 60W	N	N	25-30	750	1.5	1.5	18	1.5	3	30	2.5	8	200	12	500	250	2500	2500	500	15
Celery root (cooked)	90	1.6	Tr	2	4.9	0	0.04	0.04	0.5	0.1	0	0.5	0	0	0	0.8	47	12	28	400	71	0
Chicory	**96**	0.8	Tr	1.5	0	Tr	0.05	0.05	0.5	0.05	0	0.5	0	0	52	0.7	18	13	7	180	21	0.2
Corn-on-the-cob	65	4.1	2.4	23.7	3.7	240	0.15	0.08	1.8	0.19	0	12	0	0.8	52	1.1	4	47	1	300	130	**1.2**
Cucumbers	**96**	0.6	Tr	1.8	0.4	Tr	0.04	0.04	0.2	0.04	0	0.2	0	Tr	16	0.3	23	9	13	140	24	0.1
Eggplant	93	0.7	Tr	3.1	2.5	Tr	0.05	0.03	0.8	0.08	0	5	0	0	20	0.4	10	10	3	240	12	0
Endive	93	1.8	Tr	1	2.2	2000	0.06	0.1	0.4	0	0	0.4	0	0	**330**	2.8	44	10	10	380	67	0.4
English runner beans	89	2.3	0.2	3.9	2.9	400	0.05	0.1	0.9	0.07	0	20	0	0.2	60	0.8	27	27	2	280	47	0.4
Fava beans	84	4.1	0.6	7.1	4.2	250	0.1	0.04	3	0	0	15	0	Tr	0	1	21	28	20	230	99	0
Green beans (cooked)	**96**	0.8	Tr	1.1	3.2	400	0.04	0.07	0.3	0.06	0	5	0	0.2	28	0.6	39	10	3	100	15	0.3
Jerusalem artichokes (cooked)	80	1.6	Tr	3.2	0	Tr	0.1	Tr	0	0	0	2	0	0.2	0	0.4	30	11	3	420	33	0.1
Kohlrabi	N	2.8	0.2	9	1.6	30	0.1	0.05	0.3	N	0	71	0	N	N	0.5	54	N	10	430	68	N
Leeks	86	1.9	Tr	6	3.1	40	0.1	0.05	0.6	0.25	0	18	0	0.8	0	1.1	63	10	9	310	43	0.1
Lettuces	**96**	1	0.4	1.2	1.5	1000	0.07	0.08	0.3	0.07	0	15	0	0.5	34	0.9	23	8	9	240	27	0.2
Mushrooms	92	1.8	0.6	0	2.5	0	0.1	**0.4**	**4**	0.1	0	3	0	Tr	23	1	3	13	9	470	**140**	0.1
Okra	90	2	Tr	2.3	3.2	90	0.1	0.1	1	0.08	0	25	0	0	0	1	70	**60**	7	190	60	0
Olives (in brine)	77	0.9	11	Tr	4.4	180	Tr	Tr	0.1	N	0	N	0	N	N	1	61	22	**2250**	91	N	N
Onions	93	0.9	Tr	5.2	1.3	0	0.03	0.05	0.2	0.1	0	10	0	Tr	16	0.3	31	8	10	140	30	0.1
Parsnips	83	1.7	Tr	11.3	4	Tr	0.1	0.08	1	0.1	0	15	0	1	67	0.6	55	22	17	340	69	0.1
Peas – fresh	79	**5.8**	0.4	10.6	5.2	300	**0.32**	0.15	2.5	0.16	0	25	0	Tr	N	1.9	15	30	1	340	100	0.7
– frozen	79	**5.8**	0.4	7.2	7.8	300	**0.32**	0.1	2.1	0.1	0	17	0	Tr	78	1.5	33	27	3	190	90	0.9
Peppers – green	94	0.9	0.4	2.2	0.9	200	Tr	0.03	0.7	0.17	0	100	0	0.8	11	0.4	9	11	2	210	25	0.2
– red	94	1	0.2	5	1.3	3300	0.06	0.06	0.4	N	0	**204**	N	N	N	0.4	10	N	N	N	22	N
Potatoes	76	2.1	0.1	20.8	2.1	Tr	0.11	0.04	1.2	0.25	0	15	0	0.1	14	0.5	8	24	7	170	40	0.3
Pumpkins	93	0.6	Tr	3.4	0.5	1500	0.04	0.04	0.4	0.06	0	5	0	Tr	13	0.4	39	8	1	310	19	0.2
Radicchio	**96**	1.6	Tr	Tr	0.8	1840	0.08	0.08	Tr	0.08	0	16	N	N	N	0.08	64	N	8	256	24	N
Radishes	93	1	Tr	2.8	1	Tr	0.04	0.02	0.2	0.1	0	25	0	0	24	1.9	44	11	59	240	27	0.1
Rutabagas	91	1.1	Tr	4.3	2.7	Tr	0.06	0.04	1.2	0.2	0	25	0	0	27	0.4	56	11	52	140	19	N
Salsify (cooked)	81	1.9	Tr	2.8	N	N	0.03	N	N	N	0	4	0	N	N	1.2	60	14	8	180	53	N
Scallions	92	1.6	0.4	4.8	N	890	0.06	0.11	0.5	N	0	29	0	N	N	1.2	43	N	4	178	N	N
Sea kale (cooked)	**96**	1.4	Tr	0.6	1.2	N	0.06	N	N	N	0	18	0	N	N	0.6	48	11	4	50	34	N
Spinach (cooked)	85	5.1	0.5	1.4	6.3	6000	0.07	0.15	0.4	0.18	0	25	0	2	140	4	**600**	59	120	490	93	0.4
Squash	**96**	0.6	Tr	3.7	1.8	30	Tr	Tr	0.3	0.06	0	5	0	Tr	13	0.2	17	12	1	210	20	0.2
Sweet potatoes	70	1.2	0.6	21.5	2.5	4000	0.1	0.06	0.8	0.22	0	25	0	4	52	0.7	22	13	19	320	47	N
Swiss chard	N	3.2	0.4	6	1.2	9400	0.07	0.19	0.7	N	0	28	0	N	N	3.2	130	N	150	560	42	N
Tomatoes	93	0.9	Tr	28	1.5	600	0.06	0.04	0.7	0.11	0	20	0	1.2	28	0.4	13	11	3	290	21	0.2
Turnips	93	0.8	0.3	3.8	2.8	0	0.04	0.05	0.6	0.11	0	20	0			0.4	59	7	58	240	28	N
Watercress	91	2.9	Tr	0.7	3.3	3000	0.1	0.1	0.6	0.13	0	60	0	1	200	1.6	220	17	60	310	52	0.2
Yams	73	2	0.2	**32.4**	4.1	12	0.1	0.03	0.4	N	0	10	0	N	N	0.3	10	40	N	500	40	0.4
Zucchini	N	0.8	Tr	2.5	0.4	210	0.03	0.06	0.6	0.05	0	25	0	N	N	0.3	18	N	0.5	130	19	N

KEY
All whole foods are uncooked unless otherwise stated. Some whole foods may not be included in the chart, as there is currently no nutritional data available. **g:** grams **mg:** milligrams **µg:** micrograms **N:** no available data **Tr:** trace **M:** adult men **W:** adult women. The recommended daily allowances are averages and vary depending on age, occupation and metabolism. Figures in bold type indicate the whole food with the highest level of nutrient.

Artichokes, French (globe)

Artichokes are from a thistle-like plant similar to the *cardoon*, which is indigenous to North Africa. Artichokes are now grown in both America and Europe.

Their delicate flavor and unusual appearance make them a delightful addition to any meal. Choose ones with tightly closed leaves and no sign of browning.

Preparation and cooking
Remove the tough outer leaves. Cut off the thick stems close to the base so that the artichokes will stand up by themselves. Rinse them well and leave upside down to drain. Half fill a large pan with salted water and bring to a boil. Add the artichokes and simmer gently for 30-40 minutes or until one of the outer leaves pulls away easily. Drain.

If you require the hearts, remove the leaves and carefully pull off all the hairy "choke" with your fingers or with a knife. This can be done before or after basic cooking.

Serving suggestion: Warm with melted butter or a Hollandaise sauce, or cold with Mayonnaise (see p. 96).

Asparagus

Asparagus is thought to have originated in the Middle East and found its way to Europe in the late Middle Ages. The most common varieties are green and white.

Asparagus should be eaten as fresh as possible. Look for tight, well formed heads and avoid those with very thin or very thick stalks, or those which are wrinkled and woody.

They are usually eaten as an appetizer, but can also be added to soups, soufflés or quiches. Their delicate flavor can be lost if they are added to highly seasoned or spicy food.

Preparation and cooking
Trim the ends, wash well and tie in bundles of about 8 stalks. Put the bundles, tips up, into a deep saucepan and add sufficient boiling water to cover the stalks but not the tips; these should be covered with foil. Simmer gently for about 10 minutes or until tender. The fresher the asparagus, the less the cooking time required. Eat hot or cold.

Serving suggestion: Warm with melted butter or Hollandaise sauce, or cold with Mayonnaise (see p. 96).

Recipe: Use instead of broccoli in Red Pepper & Broccoli Quiche (see p. 111).

Avocados
(Avocado pears)

Botanically classed as a fruit, avocados are generally used as vegetables. They can be rough and purple-black or smooth and green: the small black variety generally taste best. Choose avocados which yield all over to gentle pressure.

Avocados are usually eaten raw with a vinaigrette dressing but they are also delicious sliced, puréed or cooked in savory dishes.

Preparation and cooking
Cut in half lengthwise and remove the large pit. Peel and slice thinly if required. If preparing in advance, a little lemon juice sprinkled over will prevent browning.

If you are going to use avocado in a cooked dish, add at the very end of cooking and simply warm through before serving.

Serving suggestion: Halved with Italian dressing in the center.

Recipe: Egg & Avocado Mayonnaise Dip (see p. 82).

Beet

Beets are native to the Mediterranean, and are now grown in America and Europe. Both raw and ready-cooked beets can be bought. Ready-cooked beets have often been boiled in a mixture of water and acetic acid and have a strong vinegary taste. Where possible, buy ones that have been cooked in plain water or boil yourself (see below). Being a root vegetable, they store better when raw. Buy firm, small beets if you can. It is also possible to buy pickled beets in jars.

Raw beets can be grated into salads. Cooked beets are delicious served hot on their own, with a sauce or in soups.

Preparation and cooking
Cut off the roots and tops and wash well, taking care not to tear the skin, or the color and flavor will be lost during cooking. Place in a pan of cold, salted water and bring to a boil. Simmer for 40-60 minutes or until tender. Cool a little. Remove the skin, leave whole or slice or dice as required.

Serving suggestion: Cold and chopped with fresh mint in a salad.

Recipe: Potato & Beet Soup (see p. 78).

Broccoli

Broccoli is a variety of cauliflower, and has been grown in Europe for nearly 3,000 years. There are several varieties: white, green, and purple; hearting (rather like a cauliflower) or sprouting. Calabrese is a green sprouting variety. Look for strong stems and heads for the sprouting varieties and closely packed heads for the hearting varieties.

Broccoli can be served as a side vegetable or added to soups, quiches and other savory dishes.

Preparation and cooking
For sprouting broccoli, be sure to cook the leaves and stems as well as the heads. Trim off any tough or fibrous ends from the stems and wash well. Halve the stems and heads lengthwise if they are large. Steam for 6-10 minutes. For hearting broccoli, cook as for cauliflower (see p. 28).

Serving suggestion: With fresh parsley.

Recipe: Red Pepper & Broccoli Quiche (see p. 111).

Brussels sprouts

Brussels sprouts are another sturdy vegetable, well suited to cold climates and frosty nights. Look for small, compact sprouts and avoid those with yellowing leaves.

Preparation and cooking
Wash thoroughly, trim the stem end and peel away the outer leaves. Make a small incision in the bottom of each sprout, then simmer gently in boiling, salted water for 5-6 minutes or steam for 6-10 minutes. Drain well. Alternatively, sauté until tender.

Serving suggestion: Tossed in melted butter with fresh marjoram.

Recipe: Chestnut Roast (see p. 104).

Cabbages

Cabbages have long been grown in Europe, and there are a number of varieties.

Red and white cabbages are round and firmly packed. They are delicious finely shredded in salads, or cooked for a few minutes only so as to retain their crispness.

Savoy cabbage is a beautiful green cabbage with loose wrinkled leaves, whereas the roundhead or common cabbage has smoother leaves. Both these cabbages can be eaten raw or cooked.

Chinese cabbage (sometimes called **pe-tsai**) is similar to romaine lettuce in appearance, tall and elegant with its own distinctive flavor. Another type of Chinese cabbage is **pak-choi**, with broad white stems and dark green leaves. Both can be eaten raw or stir-fried.

Preparation and cooking
Remove any damaged leaves, cut the cabbage down the center and remove the hard core. For salads, wash if necessary and finely shred.

To cook, shred or cut into wedges and put in a large saucepan with a few inches of boiling salted water. Cook for 2-4 minutes with a tightly fitting lid. Remove from the heat and drain well in a colander. Shredded cabbage can also be steamed for 4-6 minutes.

Serving suggestion: Shredded and stir-fried in soy oil and shoyu (see p. 51).

Recipe: Curried Coleslaw (see p. 90).

Carrots

These sweet and easily digestible root vegetables are native to Europe, now cultivated worldwide. They are very nutritious, and their sweet flavor and bright orange color make them an attractive vegetable for young children.

In early spring and summer, baby carrots are sold with their leafy tops which can also be eaten. Main crop carrots are usually larger and coarser. Buy firm, bright carrots.

Preparation and cooking
For early crop or baby carrots, remove the tops and wash well. For salads, young raw carrots can be grated, eaten whole or cut into bite-sized pieces. To cook, steam for about 10-15 minutes until tender but crisp.

Main crop carrots may need a good scrubbing and should be sliced, diced or chopped into similar sized pieces before being boiled for 10-15 minutes or steamed for 20 minutes.

Serving suggestion: Tossed in melted butter and sprinkled with fresh basil.

Recipe: Savory Kombu & Carrots (see p. 112).

Cauliflowers

Cauliflowers are thought to have originated in the Middle East and they reached Europe by the thirteenth century.

Look for cauliflowers with firm heads and crisp green leaves. Eat raw or cooked.

Preparation and cooking
For salads, wash as necessary, trim off the stem and leaves, and break into flowerets.

To cook whole, first cut off the bottom of the stem so that the cauliflower will stand on its own. Trim off any old or broken leaves. Put in a covered saucepan with about 3 inches of boiling salted water. Boil vigorously for 10-15 minutes or until tender but still firm.

Alternatively, cut into small pieces and steam for 4-8 minutes.

Serving suggestion: Cooked with coriander.

Recipe: Cauliflower & Carrots with Spicy Filbert Sauce (see p. 103).

Celery

Celery is native to Europe but is also grown in America. It is low in calories and has negligible nutritional value. However, its crisp lively flavor makes it a delicious addition to salads and it is often used in Chinese dishes, soups or casseroles. Look for crisp, small celery.

Preparation and cooking
To eat raw, wash well and trim off the root and leaf ends. You can reserve the leafy tops for decoration or as a flavoring.

To braise celery, first wash well, remove the leafy tops and cut into medium-sized pieces. If braising on top of the stove, cook gently for about 10 minutes. If braising in an oven, cook for 10-12 minutes. You can also boil celery for 8-10 minutes or steam for 12-15 minutes.

Serving suggestion: With fresh herbs.

Recipe: Sprouty Salad (see p. 94).

Celery root
(Celeriac/knob celery)

Celery root has its origins in the Mediterranean regions of Europe. It looks rather like a turnip and has a taste similar to celery. It can be eaten raw in salads, steamed, boiled or puréed.

Preparation and cooking
For salads, peel off the outer skin if it looks tough and cut into small pieces or grate.

To cook, cut into small pieces and boil for 10-15 minutes or steam until soft, about 15-20 minutes. Celery root can also be braised for 15-20 minutes or stir-fried.

Serving suggestion: Use cooked and puréed in place of mashed potatoes in savory dishes.

Chicory
(Curley endive/British endive)
The beautiful, green curly leaved chicory is a member of the endive family, native to southern Asia or Egypt.

The most popular varieties are the batavian or escarole and the curly or mop-head chicory. Chicory is generally used in salads but can also be sautéed and eaten hot or added to soups and savory dishes. It has a lightly bitter flavor.

Preparation and cooking
For salads, wash well and shred raw or blanched. To blanch, plunge into boiling water for 2-3 minutes. Drain and cool before using.

To cook, saute in a little oil or butter for about 3-5 minutes. Chicory can also be braised.
Serving suggestion: Raw with vinaigrette.
Recipe: Use instead of lettuce in Green Salad with Dill Dressing (see p. 91).

Corn-on-the-cob
(Corn/Maize/Indian corn)
Corn has been cultivated in parts of southern America for many thousands of years. The plants traveled to central and northern America and then to Europe in the sixteenth century.
Buy or pick corn as fresh as possible. Look for shiny, cream-colored cobs surrounded by green leaves with black tassels at the top. The corn can be eaten whole, on the cob, or as kernels. Add hot or cold kernels to savory dishes.
Preparation and cooking
For corn-on-the-cob, remove the outer leaves and silky fibers and trim the stems. Boil in plenty of salted water for 10 minutes or until tender. If the recipe calls for corn kernels, cook as above and then scrape the cob downward with a sharp knife, so that all the corn comes off. Cut close to the cob so that the nutritious germ is not lost.
Serving suggestion: With melted butter, salt and lots of black pepper.
Recipe: Corn & Mushroom Salad (see p. 95).

Cucumbers
Cucumbers originated in India, traveled to Europe and were popular with the Greeks and Romans. The cucumber is the fruit of the plant, picked and eaten in an immature state. There are a number of varieties, ranging from the small ridged cucumber to the long, smooth type. Choose small, smooth cucumbers, because these will be most tender.
Preparation and cooking
For salads, simply wash and slice or cut into the size you desire. There is no need to peel them unless their skins are very tough. If they

are bitter, salt and "bleed" as for eggplants (see p. 27). Be careful to rinse off the salt before using.

To steam, cut into small pieces and cook for about 3 minutes. To sauté, cook in oil or butter for 3-5 minutes.
Serving suggestion: With fresh thyme.
Recipe: Lettuce, Cucumber & Miso Soup (see p. 76).

Eggplant
(Aubergines)
This spectacular purple or white vegetable is probably native to India and traveled via the Middle East to the Mediterranean. It is important in the local cuisines of both regions, and there are many recipes for its use.

When buying, look for firm and shiny skins. The size makes no difference to flavor.

Eggplant is often stuffed and baked or sautéed, or used in ratatouille.
Preparation and cooking
Young fresh eggplant need only be washed and the stems and leaves removed before being sliced and cooked. Older eggplant can taste slightly bitter and contain a great deal of water, but this can be remedied by slicing thickly, sprinkling with salt and leaving to drain or "bleed" for 30 minutes in a colander. Rinse and pat dry before cooking.

Sauté eggplant slices in a little butter or oil over a high heat until lightly browned, about 5 minutes on each side.
Serving suggestion: Seasoned with fresh mint.
Recipe: Stuffed Eggplant with Tomato Sauce (see p. 115).

Endive
(British chicory/Belgian witloof)
Endive probably originated in western Asia. It is grown commercially under layers of straw in order to produce the broad, tightly packed white leaves. It has a slightly bitter taste and is popular in salads.
Preparation and cooking
For use in salads, wash, trim off the bottom and either slice or peel off each leaf separately.

To bake, trim the root end and either leave whole or cut lengthwise down the center. Endive can also be braised, or boiled whole in a very little salted boiling water with a knob of butter for about 20 minutes or until tender.
Serving suggestion: Sprinkled with paprika.
Recipe: Mushroom, Apricot & Endive Salad (see p. 92).

English runner beans
Runner beans are a variety of green bean. They originated in Central America and were probably introduced to Europe during the seventeenth century. They should be eaten as young and fresh as possible. When buying, choose crisp, bright beans.
Preparation and cooking
Wash and top and tail the beans, and pull away the stringy edges if necessary. They can be left whole but are usually sliced diagonally. This can be done with a bean slicer, if available. Cook in boiling water for about 5 minutes or steam for about 10 minutes. Drain well.

Serving suggestion: With butter and sage.
Recipe: Use instead of okra in Summer Okra Casserole (see p. 116).

Fava beans
(Broad/Windsor/Horse beans)
Fava beans originated in the Middle East and have been eaten there and in Europe for thousands of years. They are best eaten young and tender and you should look for small, plump pods. Immature fava bean pods can also be cooked whole, like snow peas (see peas, p. 30).

Fava beans can be used raw or cooked in salads, as a side vegetable, puréed or in savory dishes. They can be eaten dried (see p. 21).
Preparation and cooking
To use raw in salads, split the pods and remove the beans, or just trim if eating whole.

To cook, boil in a little salted water for 10-12 minutes (less for young pods) or until tender. Or, steam for 15-20 minutes.
Serving suggestion: Steamed and tossed in sour cream with fresh parsley, chives or dill.
Recipe: Creamy Fava Bean Soup (see p. 75).

Fennel
(Florence fennel)
This bulbous, pale green and white vegetable with its slight anise flavor originated in Europe, probably in or around Greece.

Choose white or pale green bulbs as dark green fennel may be bitter. Fennel can be eaten raw in salads or braised.
Preparation and cooking
Cut off the tough fibrous stems and trim the bottom. If using raw, slice or chop thinly. If preparing in advance, keep in water with a little lemon juice to prevent browning.

To bake fennel, cut into thin slices, put in an oiled or buttered covered ovenproof dish and cook gently in a 350°F oven for about 30 minutes or until just tender when tested with a fork.

Fennel can also be boiled for 10-12 minutes or steamed for about 10-15 minutes. Be careful not to overcook.
Serving suggestion: With fresh parsley.
Recipe: Fennel & Tomato Salad (see p. 91).

Green beans
(String beans)
Originally from Central America, these beans, as their name suggests, were probably brought to Europe for cultivation by French explorers in the seventeenth century.

The sweet-flavored beans should be bright green, firm and crisp. They are best eaten as a side vegetable, but can also be added to soups, savories and quiches, or cold in salads.
Preparation and cooking
Wash well in cold water and top and tail with a sharp knife. Cut into small slices. To cook, boil for 5-10 minutes or steam for 10-15 minutes or until tender. Drain. If serving cold in salads, rinse in cold water.
Serving suggestion: Warm with a knob of butter and a little grated nutmeg or lemon juice, or cold with vinaigrette.
Recipe: Gado-Gado (see p. 106).

Jerusalem artichokes
(Sunchokes)

Jerusalem artichokes were introduced to Europe from North America early in the seventeenth century. They are not related to the French or globe artichoke.

They have a distinctive, twisted tuberous appearance, and crisp, sweet flesh which is delicious whether eaten raw or cooked. Choose firm artichokes which are smooth.

Preparation and cooking

To eat raw, remove any hard nodules, wash well and cut into similar-sized pieces.

Cook in boiling, salted water for 15 minutes until tender, or steam for about 20 minutes. (A little lemon juice in the cooking water will prevent the artichokes from browning.) They can also be shallow-fried for 10-15 minutes, turning often to prevent sticking. If you need to peel, do so after cooking.

Serving suggestion: With cream and nutmeg.
Recipe: Artichokes & Tomatoes with Basil (see p. 97).

Kohlrabi

This strange-looking vegetable is a member of the cabbage family. It probably originated in Europe and has increased in popularity in recent years. It is high in vitamin C.

Kohlrabi is not the actual root of the plant but a bulbous part of the stem from which the leaves grow out. It can be purple or green, and is best when young, crisp and tender.

Kohlrabi can be eaten raw in salads, cooked as a side vegetable or added to savory dishes. It has a delicate flavor reminiscent of turnips.

Preparation and cooking

Cut off the twiggy stems protruding from the vegetable and wash well. To eat raw, grate or cut into small pieces for salads.

To cook, chop and steam for about 15 minutes until tender, or boil in salted boiling water for 10-15 minutes. Kohlrabi can also be braised and sautéed.

Serving suggestion: With butter and chives.
Recipe: Fresh Vegetable Curry (see p. 106).

Leeks

Leeks are native to Europe and are thick-stemmed cream-colored vegetables with a mild, onion-like flavor. Choose leeks which are small and firm, with crisp tops.

Leeks are often served with a white sauce, but are also delicious in soups, stews and other savory dishes.

Preparation and cooking

Leeks can be very dirty and need thorough washing and cleaning. Trim the root and any tough green parts. Slit down the middle and leave whole or cut into small rings and steam for 5-10 minutes depending on size. It is best not to boil leeks because they lose their flavor and tend to fall apart easily. Leeks can also be braised for about 10-12 minutes.

Serving suggestion: With a white or cheese sauce (see p. 109).
Recipe: Leeks Vinaigrette (see p. 84).

Lettuces

Lettuces have been cultivated for many thousands of years. Probably originating in the Mediterranean region, they were popular with the Greeks, the Romans and the Chinese and can be found worldwide.

There are three main varieties of lettuce: the cabbage (or butterhead) lettuce, the romaine lettuce and the crisphead lettuce. Cabbage lettuces are round with firm hearts and are fairly loosely packed. Romaine lettuces have long leaves and are crisper and sweeter than the other varieties. Crisphead lettuces have tightly packed, solid heads. Iceberg is a popular variety of crisphead lettuce.

Lettuces are generally interchangeable, although the crisp, firm-hearted varieties tend to have more flavor. Lettuces are most commonly used in salads but can also be eaten as a hot vegetable or in chilled soups.

Preparation and cooking

For salads, wash the leaves well in cold water and either leave whole or chop or tear into smaller pieces as desired.

To eat as a hot vegetable, prepare as above and then stir-fry in a little oil or butter for a few seconds only until soft and warmed through. Do not overcook.

Serving suggestion: Raw and chilled with vinaigrette dressing.
Recipe: Lettuce, Cucumber & Miso Soup (see p. 76).

Mushrooms

Wild mushrooms have been prolific in Asia and Europe for many centuries, but it was not until the end of the seventeenth century that cultivated mushrooms appeared in Europe.

Mushrooms are edible fungi. They contain small quantities of valuable nutrients and their subtle flavor and distinctive texture make them a delightful addition to almost any savory dish.

Commercial button mushrooms are related to the larger, flat field mushrooms. The latter are tastier but the button mushrooms are easier to use for salads and garnish. Choose from fresh specimens and eat on the day of purchase if possible. They can be eaten raw or lightly cooked.

Preparation and cooking

Most mushrooms need only to be wiped gently to remove any dirt from their skins. They need not be peeled but you should trim the stem. If they need to be washed, drain well to prevent from becoming soggy. If eating raw, slice, if desired.

Mushrooms can be lightly sautéed, baked or added to casseroles or soups. They need very little cooking, so add toward the end of a savory dish or sauté over a fairly high heat for a few minutes only to seal in the juices. Steam mushrooms for 5-10 minutes or poach in a little salted water for 3-5 minutes.

Serving suggestion: Steamed or baked with crushed garlic and melted butter.
Recipe: Stuffed Baked Mushrooms (see p. 86).

Okra
(Lady's fingers/Gumbo)

Okra originated in Africa, and are widely used in Creole, African, Middle Eastern and Oriental cooking. They are the immature seed pods of the plant and are often used in soups, casseroles or spicy dishes. The pods should be green and firm.

Preparation and cooking

Trim the ends and wash well. Cut into pieces or leave whole as required. To reduce their "slimy" texture, cut in small pieces, sprinkle with salt, leave for 20 minutes to drain in a colander and then rinse off. Sauté for 5-10 minutes (depending on size) or steam gently for 10-15 minutes until tender.

Serving suggestion: Steamed and chilled with vinaigrette.
Recipe: Summer Okra Casserole (see p. 116).

Olives

Olives are the fruit of a tree native to the Mediterranean. There are a number of varieties, but basically they are either black or green. Black olives are fully ripened; green olives are immature. Olives are very rich in oil, and are used for olive oil (see p. 49).

Olives are available whole, pitted or stuffed with almonds, red pepper or pimientos. They are usually sold in oil or brine.

Preparation and cooking

Olives are usually eaten raw as a savory cocktail snack but they can be added to many savory dishes, either whole (pitted) or chopped as required.

Use olives in pizzas, pasta sauces, spicy casseroles and savory tomato dishes. They can also be puréed and added to dips, sauces and even bread.

Recipe: Whole Wheat Pizza (see p. 119).

Onions

Onions originated in Central Asia and spread both eastward and westward to all the major continents. Different varieties are now grown all over the world.

There are many types of onion. They can be white, yellow or red, small or large, round or slender. Some onions can be eaten raw, such as scallions (green onions) or shallots, and all can be used in most savory dishes.

Preparation and cooking

Peel, trim and slice, chop or cut as desired. Whole onions can be boiled for 15-30 minutes, depending on size. Whole or sliced onions can be steamed for 40 or 15 minutes respectively. Sauté sliced onions in a little oil or butter for 5-10 minutes until soft and golden.

For baking, place the unpeeled whole onions on a baking tray and cook in a 300°F oven for 1½-2 hours.

Serving suggestion: With a herb butter.
Recipe: Onion Bhajis with Yogurt Sauce (see p. 86).

Parsnips

Parsnips are native to eastern Europe. They have a sweet and slightly floury taste, and are delicious raw, cooked or puréed. Choose firm, young parsnips which do not have any brown parts.

Preparation and cooking

Cut off the leafy tops and trim the root. Do not peel unless the skin seems very hard. Leave whole, quarter or slice. Steam sliced parsnips for 10-15 minutes until soft, or boil vigorously for 15-20 minutes and mash or purée. Parsnips can be sautéed for 10-15 minutes, or blanched and baked in a 400°F oven for 45-60 minutes.

Serving suggestion: With butter and nutmeg.
Recipe: Sesame Roast Parsnips (see p. 114).

Peas

Peas are native to the Middle East. During the sixteenth or seventeenth centuries the sweet green shelling peas we are familiar with today were developed.

Most peas today are frozen or canned and fresh peas have a short season. Home-grown garden peas are best of all, so pick them when they are small and sweet (petit pois) as they can become rather tough and floury if left too long. Snow peas (sugar peas or mange tout) are another variety. These immature peas are eaten with their pods and are crisp and sweet.

Fresh peas can be puréed, added to soups, casseroles, salads and other savory dishes.

Preparation and cooking

First shell the peas, discarding any that are discolored or damaged: about 1 pound of podded peas gives about ½ pound of shelled peas. Wash and put in a saucepan with the minimum amount of salted boiling water. Boil for 2-10 minutes, depending on the size and freshness of the peas. Drain well. Peas can also be steamed for 3-8 minutes.

For snow peas, first top and tail, then stir-fry in a small amount of butter or oil for a minute or so and serve immediately.

Serving suggestion: Tossed in a little butter with fresh mint.
Recipe: Pineapple Salad (see p. 92).

Peppers

Peppers are indigenous to South America and the West Indies, but they traveled to Europe in the sixteenth century and are now grown extensively in the southern Mediterranean.

There are many types of pepper, varying in shape, taste and color. They can be red, green or yellow, square or heart-shaped and mild or pungent in taste. The larger, sweet-tasting varieties (bell peppers, pimientos and pepperons) are delicious raw in salads or cooked in savory dishes. For the smaller, extremely hot chili peppers, see the entry on page 57.

Buy firm, glossy peppers. Red, green and yellow are more or less the same, although the red peppers tend to be sweeter.

Preparation and cooking

Slice off the stem end and remove the seeds and core. Leave whole or slice as required.

To cook, steam whole peppers for 10-15 minutes, or slice and sauté or stir-fry in a little oil or butter for 5-10 minutes.

To stuff peppers, prepare as above and fill with your choice of stuffing. Bake for about ¾-1 hour in a 300°F oven.

Serving suggestion: With a little marjoram.
Recipe: Ratatouille (see p. 110).

Potatoes

Indigenous to South America, potatoes arrived in Europe in the seventeenth century. Many varieties of potato are available.

When buying potatoes in bulk, store in a cool place away from the light, to prevent them from turning green or sprouting. New potatoes should be eaten fresh and not stored. Potatoes should be firm and blemish-free.

Preparation and cooking

To cook new potatoes, first wash well, taking care not to damage the skins. Boil in lightly salted water for as short a time as possible, about 10 minutes. For older, main crop potatoes, cook in one of the following ways:

Boiled potatoes. Scrub well. If large, halve or quarter. Put into a saucepan of cold water and bring to a boil. Add salt and simmer gently for 15-20 minutes, or until cooked. Drain well, season and add a knob of butter.

Steamed potatoes. Scrub thoroughly, cut the potatoes into similar-sized pieces and steam until cooked, about 25-30 minutes.

Roast potatoes. Wash and cut into similar-sized pieces. Do not peel or the valuable nutrients just under the skins will be lost. Put in a saucepan, pour boiling water over and simmer for 10 minutes. Drain and pat dry. Heat some vegetable oil in a roasting pan in a 400°F oven until hot. Take the pan out of the oven, carefully add the potatoes and baste them evenly. Return to the top shelf of the oven and roast for about 45-55 minutes or until golden brown, turning the potatoes over once or twice, and basting occasionally.

Baked potatoes. This is one of the most nutritious and delicious ways to eat potatoes. Preheat the oven to 425°F. Wash, dry and prick the potato skins to prevent splitting. Bake in the center of the oven for 1-1½ hours.

Serving suggestion: With grated cheese.
Recipe: Gado-Gado (see p. 106).

Pumpkins and squashes

This large vegetable family probably originated in Central and South America and quickly spread to America and Canada. During the late sixteenth and seventeenth centuries, visitors to the New World returned to Europe with squashes and pumpkins. Of the many varieties now grown, the most common are summer and winter squashes and the American pumpkin.

All squashes and pumpkins have a delicate, watery flavor. They can be eaten as a light side vegetable, stuffed or even, in the case of the pumpkin, used in sweet dishes such as the traditional pumpkin pie.

Preparation and cooking

If the pumpkin or squash is young enough, the skin can be cooked and eaten. If it is too old, peel first. Halve or slice into rings as required and scoop out the seeds.

Steam or sauté in small pieces for about 5-10 minutes or until just tender.

To stuff a pumpkin or squash, cut in half lengthwise and remove the pith and seeds, leaving about 1 inch of flesh. Fill with your choice of stuffing and bake in a 350°F oven for about 30 minutes until cooked and tender.

Serving suggestions: With herbs and butter.

Radicchio
(Radicchio rosso)

Radicchio is another form of endive. Its exciting red color makes it a welcome addition to any salad. Prepare and use as for endive (see p. 28).

Radishes

Radishes are relatives of the cabbage family and are native to southern Asia. They are thought to be one of the oldest cultivated vegetables in the world. They grow well in almost any climate and their crisp texture, bright pink-red color and peppery flavor make them a pleasant addition to any salad. White, yellow and black radishes can also be found. Look for firm, blemish-free specimens. Radish seeds may be sprouted (see p. 23).

Preparation and cooking

Top and tail radishes and wash well. Cut into rings or small pieces if desired. Radishes are usually eaten raw, but can be steamed for 5-10 minutes, according to size. They can also be sliced and stir-fried.

Serving suggestion: With butter and chives.
Recipe: Red Bean Salad (see p. 93).

Rutabaga
(Swedes)

Rutabagas originated in northern Europe, where they were a major food before the advent of the potato, and grow best in cold climates.

Normally the round yellow-orange root is the part that is used, although the green leafy tops are more nutritious.

Look for small, unblemished specimens. Rutabaga can be boiled and mashed, served on top of casseroles, or added to soups and savory dishes.

Preparation and cooking

Scrub well but do not peel unless the skin is particularly tough or damaged. Cut into even pieces or slices and boil for 15-20 minutes or steam for 20-25 minutes or until tender. Drain well before serving.

Serving suggestion: Mashed with a little butter and grated nutmeg.
Recipe: Rutabaga & Orange Pie (see p. 116).

Salsify/Scorzonera

Salsify originated in Europe and still grows wild in southern Europe and southern Asia. It has long, white, bitter-tasting roots, and is very similar to the fibrous roots of wild endive. It is also known as oyster plant.

Scorzonera is related to salsify, and has a similar appearance but is black-skinned and has more tiny root fibers growing out of the main fiber. It is sometimes known as black salsify or viper's grass.

Both can be used for soups, salads, as a cooked vegetable or added to savory dishes.

Preparation and cooking

Cut off the tiny roots from the main fiber. Top and tail and wash very well. For salads, grate and sprinkle with a little lemon juice if desired.

Cook in boiling salted water for about 20

minutes or until tender. Salsify can also be steamed (about 30 minutes) or sautéed in a little butter or oil for about 20-25 minutes until tender.

Serving suggestion: With a little cumin.

Sea kale

Indigenous to western Europe, sea kale has long, thick white stems and small, dark green, wrinkled leaves. It is actually a herb of the mustard family, but is eaten as a vegetable.

Sea kale has a pleasant, nutty flavor and can be used raw, steamed or sautéed.

Preparation and cooking
Wash well and cut into pieces.

To cook, sauté or steam for 3-5 minutes only, so that it remains crisp. Overcooking sea kale can make it rather tough and the flavor is diminished.

Serving suggestion: Sautéed in a little butter or oil with garlic.

Recipe: Use to replace Swiss chard in Stir-Fried Swiss Chard & Mushrooms (see p. 115).

Spinach

Spinach is thought to have originated in Persia, and had been brought by the Moors to Europe by the tenth century. It is one of the most nutritious vegetables, being rich in iron, calcium and magnesium.

Young spinach can be eaten raw in salads and older spinach cooked as a vegetable or served in soups, quiches and other savory dishes. Look for firm, green leaves. Spinach shrinks when cooked, to about one-third or one-quarter of the original volume.

Preparation and cooking
For salads, first wash extremely well. Remove coarse stems as necessary. Chop or tear into small pieces.

To cook, first trim any tough stems and then wash and rinse well. Put straight into a large saucepan with a little salt but no added water and cook gently until the leaves are soft, about 8-10 minutes. Drain well.

Serving suggestion: With a little nutmeg.

Recipe: Nori & Spinach Rolls (see p. 85).

Sweet potatoes

The exact origin of the sweet potato is uncertain. Columbus brought them to Europe from America, but they were already cultivated in parts of Asia at this time. They feature in many Creole and South American dishes.

Despite the name, sweet potatoes are not related to the potato but have similarities both in looks and usage. Beneath the yellow or pink-brown skin the starchy interior can be pale yellow or bright orange; the light colored centered ones are called sweet potatoes, and the moister, brighter colored centered ones are called yams (see right). Sweet potatoes are drier than yams.

Preparation and cooking
To bake, choose sweet potatoes of a similar size or cut into similar-sized pieces. Wrap in aluminum foil if you wish. Put on a baking tray and cook in a 425°F oven for about 1½ hours or until cooked.

To boil or steam sweet potatoes, wash well but do not peel unless the skin is very tough.

Cut into small pieces and either boil in salted boiling water for 15-20 minutes or steam for 20-25 minutes until very soft. To make a purée, put in a blender with a little butter or oil and seasoning and blend until smooth.

Serving suggestion: Puréed with a little ginger or nutmeg.

Recipe: Caribbean Stew (see p. 102).

Swiss chard
(Chard/Sea kale beet)

This vegetable comes from central and eastern Europe. Other varieties include rhubarb chard and spinach beet, which taste like spinach. Swiss chard has dark green wrinkled leaves which surround strong white stems. It is highly nutritious, although, as with spinach (see p. 31), you need to buy a large amount as it decreases in size when you cook it.

Preparation and cooking
Wash the leaves well and trim the stems. If the stems are very thick, cut out and chop into small pieces. Steam for 8-10 minutes.

Serving suggestion: Tossed in butter.

Recipe: Stir-Fried Swiss Chard & Mushrooms (see p. 115).

Tomatoes

Tomatoes originated in South America and were introduced to southern Europe in the sixteenth century. They are in fact botanically classed as fruit but are used in savory dishes.

There are many varieties to choose from, with differing shapes and sizes. Choose firm, blemish-free specimens, which should not be too dark in color.

Although tomatoes are not especially nutritious, their bright color stimulates the appetite and their pleasant flavor blends well with many other vegetables. They can be eaten raw or cooked in soups, purées, sauces and other savory dishes.

Preparation and cooking
For salads, wash and leave whole, halve, quarter or slice into rings as required.

For use in hot dishes, tomatoes are often first peeled by pouring boiling water over them and leaving for about 15 minutes. The skins should then peel away easily.

Tomatoes can be halved and broiled for 3-4 minutes or baked whole. To bake, cut 2 slits crosswise in the top to prevent bursting and bake for 10 minutes in a 350°F preheated oven.

Serving suggestion: With fresh basil.

Recipe: Buckwheat Crêpes with Tomato Sauce (see p. 101).

Turnips

Turnips are an ancient northern European vegetable, and were a major food before the arrival of the potato from South America.

The edible part is the swollen root, normally round and white with a little pink or

green coloring around the base. They have a crisp, bitter flavor. As with rutabagas, the greens or flowered turnip tops are far more nutritious than the roots and can be cooked as a leaf vegetable.

Turnips can be eaten raw but are usually cooked in curries, savory dishes and soups. Young baby turnips are particularly tender and best for eating raw.

Preparation and cooking
Cut off the root and leafy tops and wash well. For salads, chop or grate as required.

Cook baby turnips whole in boiling salted water for 10-15 minutes. For main crop turnips, cut into similar-sized pieces and boil for 10-15 minutes or steam for about 15-20 minutes or until tender. To cook the green tops, cut off any fibrous stems, wash well, break into pieces and steam for 5-10 minutes until tender.

Serving suggestion: Boiled and puréed as an alternative to mashed potato.

Recipe: Use instead of parsnip in Fresh Vegetable Curry (see p. 106).

Watercress

Watercress is a member of the mustard family and has grown wild for thousands of years. It is extremely high in fiber and vitamin C. Watercress can be used raw in salads, as a garnish, or cooked in coups and savory dishes. Avoid wilting, discolored specimens.

Preparation and cooking
For salads, simply cut off the roots, wash well and chop or tear into bite-sized pieces.

To cook, prepare as above and sauté gently for 3-5 minutes.

Serving suggestion With orange vinaigrette.

Recipe: Cream of Watercress Soup (see p. 74).

Yams

Yams are native to the Orient, and are now also grown in the tropical regions of America. A large tuberous root, yams have a bright orange center and are actually the moist variety of sweet potato.

Peel and then prepare as for sweet potatoes.

Serving suggestion: Baked in slices with orange juice and brown sugar.

Recipe: Use instead of sweet potatoes in Caribbean Stew (see p. 102).

Zucchini
(Italian squash)

Zucchini are a miniature variety of squash, picked and eaten in an immature state. They are dark green in color and can be long and cylindrical or round in shape. Choose small zucchini as these have less tough skins.

Zucchini can be eaten raw in salads, sautéed or steamed.

Preparation and cooking
For use in salads, trim the ends, wash well and either grate or slice finely. Do not peel.

To sauté or steam zucchini, first wash and leave whole or slice thinly. Sauté sliced zucchini in a little butter for 5-8 minutes, or steam for 4-6 minutes until just tender.

Serving suggestion: With fresh thyme.

Recipe: Rutabaga & Orange Pie (see p. 116).

FRESH FRUIT

Apples ☐
Apricots
Bananas ☐
Blackberries
Blueberries
Boysenberries
Cherries ☐
Clementines ☐
Cranberries ☐
Currants
Damsons
Dates ☐

Figs
Gooseberries
Grapefruit ☐
Grapes ☐
Greengages
Guavas ☐
Kiwifruit ☐
Kumquats ☐
Lemons ☐
Limes ☐
Litchis
Loganberries

Mangoes ☐
Mangosteens
Melons ☐
Mulberries
Nectarines
Oranges ☐
Papayas ☐
Passion fruit ☐
Peaches ☐
Pears ☐
Persimmons
Pineapples ☐

Plums
Pomegranates ☐
Rambutans
Raspberries
Rhubarb
Satsumas
Strawberries
Tangerines
Ugli .

☐ Pictured opposite page 33

There is evidence of the cultivation of fruit as long as 8,000 years ago; centuries of exploration, conquest and trade have ensured the development of indigenous produce and the introduction of non-native fruit in many parts of the world. Today, many varieties of fruit are available, local and imported.

As with vegetables, fresh fruits are an important component of a whole food diet. They offer an attractive choice of colors, flavors and textures and are nutritionally important. Most fruits are valuable sources of vitamin C and carbohydrate in the form of natural sugars (fructose). They also contain dietary fiber as well as other vitamins and minerals (see the nutritional chart on page 33). Best eaten raw, fruit can also be cooked in a variety of ways. Use as a snack, as a substitute for desserts, with grains or yogurt for breakfast, in salads, cakes or pies, or extract the juices for a healthy drink (see p. 61).

Sources
Try to use local organically grown produce (see p. 7) rather than imported fruit wherever possible and make maximum use of the fruit in season.

Additives
Unless you grow your own fruit or have a good organic supplier, it is likely that most of the fruit you buy will have been treated with pesticides. In general, a thorough scrub and/or wash should be sufficient to remove additives. Apples and pears in particular have firm skins which can withstand many sprays without the underlying flesh being affected. However, with babies and young children, it may be wise to peel fruit.

Citrus fruit for export is also treated with antifungal and antibacterial preservatives, as well as glazing and sealing agents, which can cause allergic reactions and irritations. Always wash in warm soapy water and rinse well, especially when the recipe calls for the rind of a fruit.

Choosing fruit
Look for a healthy color and avoid withered, damaged or discolored specimens. When choosing firm fruit check for bruising and soft spots. Pit fruit should be firm but yielding. For berry and other soft fruit, avoid baskets stained with juice and check that the underneath fruit is not crushed or moldy.

Storage
Soft fruit deteriorates rapidly and is best purchased on the day required or stored overnight in the refrigerator. Apples, the harder varieties of pears and citrus fruit can be bought in larger quantities and will last for some time in a cool, dry, well-ventilated place. Exotic fruit is best consumed within a few days of ripening: a slightly unripe mango, melon or papaya will ripen in a few days if put in a warm place. Most fruit can be frozen (see p. 65).

Cooking methods
In general, fruit is at its best when eaten raw. However, rhubarb, damsons, tart apples, and damaged, overripe or unripe fruit (particularly gooseberries, plums and apricots) benefit from being cooked.

Stewing or poaching
Slice or chop the fruit as required. Heat a little water (filtered if possible) in a heavy-bottomed saucepan and sweeten if liked. Flavor with lemon rind, cinnamon or a little ground nutmeg. Add the fruit to the boiling water and simmer gently until tender. Small pieces of fruit will cook very quickly (about 4 minutes) but allow longer for whole fruit. Test with a skewer or sharp knife to see if they are cooked.

This method is suitable for apples, pears, gooseberries, cherries, blackberries, plums, Damsons, apricots, peaches, nectarines and rhubarb. You can also poach dried fruit, after initial soaking.

Puréeing
Stew or poach the fruit (see above) and cool. Drain off most of the liquid, remove any pits and purée the fruit in a blender or food processor. Alternatively, push the fruit through a metal strainer with a wooden spoon. Sweeten as required, either with sugar or a natural sweetener such as honey.

This method is suitable for all fruit which can be stewed or poached (see above). However, ripe soft fruit such as strawberries and raspberries can be puréed raw. Just press through a strainer or purée in a blender or food processor.

Baking
This method is suitable for firm fruit such as tart apples, some varieties of pears, peaches and nectarines.

For apples and pears, remove the core and fill with dried fruit, flavored with cinnamon or ground cloves. Slit the peel in a ring about half-way down with a sharp knife, to prevent bursting. Place in a shallow baking dish and bake at 400°F until tender. This will take 30-50 minutes. Serve the baked apples hot or cold.

For peaches and nectarines, remove the pits and cut into halves. The indentations can be filled with a sweet stuffing of your choice, if desired. Bake as above for 20-30 minutes or until tender.

Fresh Vegetables (See p. 24)

Squash (see p. 30) can be baked plain or stuffed.

Zucchini (see p. 31) can be eaten raw in salads or cooked in a number of ways.

Peppers (see p. 30) can be white, green, red or yellow in color.

Hokkaido is an orangy-red variety of squash (see p. 30).

Okra (see p. 29) are the immature seed pods of a plant, eaten whole.

Radicchio (see p. 30) is a salad vegetable with a sharp, fresh taste.

Fennel (see p. 28) has a slightly aniseed flavor.

Avocados (see p. 27) can be green, as here, or purply-black in color.

Eggplant (see p. 28) are rich and smoky.

Olives (see p. 29) can be green or black, depending on their age when picked.

Chicory (see p. 28) has a sharp taste, good in salads.

Endive (see p. 28) has a slightly bitter taste, and can be eaten raw or cooked.

Artichokes (see p. 26) are popular as an appetizer.

Asparagus (see pp. 26-7) has a delicate, subtle flavor.

Broccoli (see p. 27) can be sprouting and green, as here, or hearting and purple.

Radishes (see p. 30) are usually red in color, but black can also be found.

Sweet potatoes (see p. 31) are orange-fleshed.

Celery roots (see pp. 27-8) taste similar to celery.

Kohlrabi (see p. 29) can vary in shape and be purple or green.

Jerusalem artichokes (see p. 29) have crisp, sweet flesh with a slightly nut-like flavor.

Scorzonera (see p. 30) is a type of salsify and has a similar bitter flavor.

Fresh Fruit (See p. 32)

Watermelons (see p. 36) can be ridged or smooth.

Melons (see p. 36) are available in a variety of flavors and colors.

Pomegranates (see p. 37) contain delicious red seeds.

Passion fruit (see p. 36) are full of juicy, tangy seeds.

Dates (see p. 34) are rich, sticky and nutritious.

Pineapples (see p. 37) have golden-yellow flesh, sweet and yet slightly sharp.

Fresh Fruit grapes image

Grapes (see p. 35) can be blue or green, and have a lovely delicate flavor.

Kiwi (see p. 35) have a slightly tart flavor.

Guavas (see p. 35) are soft-fleshed and very aromatic.

Papayas (see p. 36) have pinky-orange, juicy flesh and a distinctive aroma.

Mangoes (see p. 36) have a lovely scent and soft, almost slippery flesh.

Bananas (see p. 34) are a nutritious, filling fruit.

Lemons (see p. 35) are used for their sharp, acidic taste and fresh aroma.

Limes (see p. 35) are used in the same way as lemons.

Peaches (see p. 36) have velvety skin, which varies in color, and soft flesh.

Cherries (see p. 34) can be red or black.

Grapefruit (see p. 35) can vary in color and in sweetness.

The **sweet orange** (see p. 36).

Clementines (see p. 34) are sweet-tasting citrus fruit.

Cranberries (see p. 34) are acid, so are not eaten raw.

Bramley cooking apple (see p. 33).

There are many varieties of **pear** (see p. 36).

Apples (see p. 33) vary greatly in their sweetness, color and uses.

FRESH FRUIT Per 4 oz	Water	Protein	Fat	Carbohydrate	Fiber	Vitamin A	Vitamin B₁	Vitamin B₂	Vitamin B₃	Vitamin B₆	Vitamin B₁₂	Vitamin C	Vitamin D	Vitamin E	Folic acid	Iron	Calcium	Magnesium	Sodium	Potassium	Phosphorus	Zinc
	g	g	g	g	g	µg	mg	mg	mg	mg	µg	mg	µg	mg	µg	mg	mg	mg	mg	mg	mg	mg
Recommended daily allowance	N	80M 60W	N	N	25-30	750	1.5	1.5	18	1.5	3	30	2.5	8	200	12	500	250	2500	2500	500	15
Apples – tart	86	0.3	Tr	9.6	2.4	30	0.04	0.02	0.1	0.03	0	15	0	0.2	5	0.3	4	3	2	120	16	0.1
– dessert	65	0.2	Tr	9.2	1.5	23	0.03	0.02	0.1	0.02	0	2	0	0.2	4	0.2	3	4	2	92	6	0.1
Apricots	87	0.6	Tr	6.7	2.1	1500	0.04	0.05	0.6	0.07	0	7	0	N	5	0.4	17	12	Tr	320	21	0.1
Bananas – eating	71	1.1	0.3	19.2	3.4	200	0.04	0.07	0.6	**0.51**	0	10	0	0.2	22	0.4	7	**42**	1	350	28	0.2
– cooking (plantains)	67	1	0.2	28.3	5.8	60	0.05	0.05	0.7	0.5	0	20	0	N	16	0.5	7	33	1	350	35	0.1
Blackberries	82	1.3	Tr	6.4	7.3	100	0.03	0.04	0.4	0.05	0	20	0	**3.5**	N	0.9	63	30	4	210	24	N
Blueberries	85	0.6	Tr	14.3	N	130	0.02	0.02	0.4	0.06	0	22	0	N	6	0.7	10	2	1	65	9	0.1
Cherries	82	0.6	Tr	11.9	1.7	120	0.05	0.07	0.3	0.05	0	5	0	0.1	8	0.4	16	10	3	280	17	0.1
Cranberries	87	0.4	Tr	3.5	1.1	20	0.03	0.02	0.1	0.04	0	12	0	N	2	1.1	15	8	2	120	11	N
Currants – black	77	0.9	Tr	6.6	8.7	200	0.03	0.06	0.3	0.08	0	200	0	1	N	1.3	60	17	3	370	43	N
– red	83	1.1	Tr	4.4	8.2	70	0.04	0.06	0.1	0.05	0	40	0	0.1	N	1.2	36	13	2	280	30	N
– white	83	1.3	Tr	5.6	6.8	Tr	0.04	0.06	0.1	0.05	0	40	0	0.1	N	0.9	22	13	2	290	28	N
Damsons	76	0.5	Tr	9.6	4.1	220	0.1	0.03	0.3	0.05	0	3	0	0.7	3	0.4	24	11	2	290	16	0.1
Dates	23	2.2	0.5	**72.9**	8.7	50	0.09	**0.1**	2.2	N	0	0	0	N	N	**3**	59	N	1	**648**	**63**	N
Figs	85	1.4	Tr	9.5	2.5	500	0.06	0.05	0.4	0.11	0	2	0	N	N	0.4	34	20	2	270	32	0.3
Gooseberries	90	1.1	Tr	3.4	3.2	180	0.04	0.03	0.3	0.02	0	40	0	0.4	N	0.4	28	7	2	210	34	0.1
Grapes	76	0.6	Tr	15.3	0.9	Tr	0.04	0.02	0.3	0.1	0	4	0	N	6	0.3	18	6	2	240	21	0.1
Grapefruit	91	0.6	Tr	5.3	0.6	Tr	0.05	0.02	0.2	0.03	0	40	0	0.3	12	0.3	17	10	1	230	16	0.1
Greengages	78	0.8	Tr	11.8	2.6	N	0.05	0.03	0.4	0.05	0	3	0	0.8	3	0.4	17	8	1	310	23	0.1
Guavas	83	0.8	0.6	9.4	N	168	0.05	0.05	1.2	N	0	**242**	0	N	N	0.9	23	13	4	289	N	N
Kumquats	81	0.9	0.1	17.1	3.7	600	0.08	**0.1**	N	N	0	36	0	N	N	0.4	63	N	7	236	23	N
Lemons	85	0.8	Tr	3.2	5.2	Tr	0.05	0.04	0.2	0.11	0	80	0	N	N	0.4	**110**	12	6	160	21	0.1
Limes	91	0.5	**2.4**	5.6	N	10	0.03	0.02	0.1	0	0	46	0	0	N	Tr	13	N	2	82	0	N
Litchis	82	0.9	Tr	16	0.5	Tr	0.04	0.04	0.3	N	0	40	0	N	N	0.5	8	10	3	170	35	N
Loganberries	85	1.1	Tr	3.4	6.2	80	0.02	0.03	0.4	0.06	0	35	0	0.3	N	1.4	35	25	3	260	24	N
Mangoes	83	0.5	Tr	15.3	1.5	1200	0.03	0.04	0.3	N	0	30	0	N	N	0.5	10	18	7	190	13	N
Melons – cantaloupe	94	1	Tr	5.3	1	**2000**	0.05	0.03	0.5	0.07	0	25	0	0.1	30	0.8	19	20	14	320	30	0.1
– honeydew	94	0.6	Tr	5	0.9	100	0.05	0.03	0.5	0.07	0	25	0	0.1	30	0.2	14	13	20	220	9	0.1
– watermelon	94	0.4	Tr	5.3	N	20	0.02	0.02	0.2	0.07	0	5	0	0.1	3	0.3	5	11	4	120	8	0.1
Mulberries	85	1.3	Tr	8.1	1.7	Tr	0.05	0.04	0.4	0.05	0	10	0	N	N	1.6	36	15	2	260	48	N
Nectarines	80	0.9	Tr	12.4	2.4	500	0.02	0.05	1	0.02	0	8	0	N	5	0.5	4	13	9	270	24	0.1
Oranges	86	0.8	Tr	8.5	2	50	**0.1**	0.03	0.2	0.06	0	50	0	0.2	**37**	0.3	41	13	3	200	24	0.2
Papayas	87	0.5	0.1	11.3	N	710	0.03	0.05	0.4	N	0	73	0	0	1	0.7	24	8	4	221	0	**0.4**
Passion fruit	73	**2.8**	Tr	6.2	**15.9**	10	Tr	**0.1**	1.9	N	0	20	0	N	N	1.1	16	39	**28**	350	N	N
Peaches	86	0.6	Tr	9.1	1.4	500	0.02	0.05	1	0.02	0	8	0	N	3	0.4	5	8	3	260	19	0.1
Pears	83	0.3	Tr	10.6	2.3	10	0.03	0.03	0.2	0.02	0	3	0	Tr	11	0.2	8	7	2	130	10	0.1
Persimmons	64	0.8	0.4	33.5	1.5	N	N	N	N	N	0	66	0	N	N	2.5	9	N	1	310	26	N
Pineapples	84	0.5	Tr	11.6	1.2	60	0.08	0.02	0.2	0.09	0	25	0	N	11	0.4	12	17	2	250	8	0.1
Plums, dessert	84	0.6	Tr	9.6	2.1	220	0.05	0.03	0.5	0.05	0	3	0	0.7	3	0.4	11	7	2	190	16	Tr
Pomegranates	80	1	0.6	16.6	N	0	0.07	0.01	0.3	0	0	7	0	0	N	0.7	13	12	1	379	0	N
Raspberries	83	0.9	Tr	5.6	7.4	80	0.02	0.03	0.4	0.06	0	25	0	0.3	N	1.2	41	22	3	220	29	N
Rhubarb (cooked)	**95**	0.6	Tr	0.9	2.4	55	Tr	0.03	0.3	0.02	0	8	0	0.2	4	0.4	93	13	2	400	19	N
Strawberries	89	0.6	Tr	6.2	2.2	30	0.02	0.03	0.4	0.06	0	60	0	0.2	20	0.7	22	12	2	160	23	0.1
Tangerines	87	0.9	Tr	8	1.9	100	0.07	0.02	0.2	0.07	0	30	0	N	21	0.3	42	11	2	160	17	0.1

KEY
All whole foods are uncooked unless otherwise stated. Some whole foods may not be included in the chart, as there is currently no nutritional data available.
g: grams **mg**: milligrams **µg**: micrograms **N**: no available data **Tr**: trace **M**: adult men **W**: adult women. The recommended daily allowances are averages and vary depending on age, occupation and metabolism. Figures in bold type indicate the whole food with the highest level of nutrient.

Apples

Apples originated in the Middle East and are now commercially grown in most countries with a temperate climate. There are over 2,000 varieties, both tart and dessert.

To eat raw or for use in salads, choose a dessert apple: Cortland, Golden Delicious, McIntosh, Newtown Pippin, Winesap, Red Delicious and Granny Smith. There may be other local varieties available. For stewing, baking or puréeing, use a tart apple: Golden Delicious, Rhode Island Greening and Yellow Transparent. If flavor and shape are important, as in pies and dessert, use a dessert apple rather than a tart apple.

Apples can be used in soups, salads, savory dishes, puddings, cakes, pickles, jellies, chutneys and for juices. They are also available dried (see p. 39).

Preparation and cooking

Wash the apples and peel if desired. Core and cut into quarters or slices as required. If not using immediately, brush with a little lemon juice to prevent browning. Stew, purée or bake whole.
Recipe: Apple, Soy & Almond Pudding (see p. 120).

Apricots

These gorgeous yellow-orange fruits originated in China and are now widely available. There are several varieties.

Look for apricots with a good color and no bruises. If they are ripe, they should yield evenly to pressure. However, most imported apricots are picked unripe before shipping. If you buy unripe apricots, leave on a windowsill or shelf at room temperature for a few days; fully ripe apricots should be refrigerated.

Apricots can be eaten raw or cooked. Use in soups, salads, savory dishes, puddings, cakes, jellies, pickles, chutneys or for fresh juice. Apricots are also available dried (see p. 39).
Preparation and cooking

Wash and remove the peel if desired by pouring boiling water over the fruit and leaving to stand for 10 minutes. The peel should then come off easily. Cut in half and remove the pit. Leave halved or slice as desired. Brush with a little lemon juice to prevent browning.

To cook, either stew or purée.
Recipe: Mushroom, Apricot & Endive Salad (see p. 92).

Bananas

Bananas originated in the Tropics. There are many varieties and they are generally available all year around.

There are two main types, for cooking and to eat raw. Eating bananas are usually bright yellow. Look for firm fruit without black patches which indicate bruising. Black speckles do not mean that the fruit is bad but it will probably need to be eaten fairly soon.

Bananas for cooking, or plantains, are larger, usually green in color and should not be eaten raw. They are used in many Caribbean and African dishes. Bananas are also available dried (see p. 39).
Preparation and cooking

Peel off the outer peel and use as required. Brush with a little lemon juice to prevent browning. If using in a fruit salad, add just before serving. Cooking and eating bananas can also be baked whole or sliced and fried.
Recipe: Baked Bananas with Yogurt Sauce (see p. 121).

Blackberries
(Bramble)

This northern European plant still grows successfully wild, in what remains of the dwindling rural hedgerow. It is also grown commercially in America. Look for plump, glossy, fresh fruit.

Blackberries combine well with apples, as in traditional apple and blackberry pie, but they are also delicious eaten raw or cooked in cakes and pies, puddings and soufflés, or made into jams and jellies.

Preparation

Wash the blackberries carefully in a colander. Drain and remove any imperfect fruit. Serve raw with a little sweetener and/or cream or yogurt.
Recipe: Use instead of raspberries in Red Currant & Raspberry Summer Pudding (see p. 129).

Blueberries

Although northern European in origin, blueberries are mainly grown commercially in America. The smaller bilberry can be used in the same way.

Choose firm, undamaged fruit and eat raw or use in puddings, cakes, jams and jellies.
Preparation and cooking

Wash and drain thoroughly in a colander and serve raw with a little sweetener and/or cream or yogurt as desired.

To cook, simmer gently in a little water for 5-10 minutes until tender. They do not contain many pips so do not need to be sieved.
Recipe: Use instead of apricots in Hunza Cream (see p. 125).

Boysenberries

Developed in California, these are similar to large raspberries or loganberries.

Look for firm, undamaged fruit, and eat on the day of purchase or store in a refrigerator. Prepare and use as for raspberries.
Recipe: Fresh Fruit Tart (see p. 125).

Cherries

Middle Eastern in origin, cherries are grown commercially in America and many European countries. There are basically two types of cherry, bitter and sweet. The bitter, dark-skinned cherries such as Morello are used mainly for cooking and jam-making. Sweet cherries can vary in color from pale yellow to deep purple-red. Bing cherries are deep red and very plump. Look for glossy fruit which yield to gentle pressure and eat on day of purchase or store in a refrigerator. Use in salads, desserts, cakes and jams.
Preparation and cooking

Raw cherries should be washed and stemmed before eating. To cook, boil gently for 5-10 minutes in a little water. Set aside to cool. Remove the pits by cutting into the center of each cherry with a sharp knife or use a special cherry pitter.
Recipe: Cherry Pie (see p. 123).

Clementines

Clementines are a cross between a sweet orange and a tangerine. They are fairly small, loose-skinned, orange-red fruit. They are very sweet and contain virtually no seeds.

Look for firm, heavy fruit without soft or brown spots. As with all citrus fruit, they may be stored at room temperature or in a refrigerator and will usually last for about 10 days. Eat on their own, or in sweet and savory salads, desserts and cakes.
Preparation

Remove the skins and break the flesh into natural segments. Clementine skins are fairly thin and they do not have much pith.

Cranberries

Although European in origin, cranberries are mainly grown commercially in America and Finland. They are too tart to eat raw and are usually made into cranberry sauce or jellies. You very seldom find them fresh but many stores stock frozen cranberries.
Preparation and cooking

Wash fresh cranberries in a colander and drain well and simmer in a little water for 5-10 minutes until tender. For most sauces and jellies, straining the fruit is necessary. If using frozen cranberries, thaw as directed on the package and use as desired.
Recipe: Use instead of gooseberries in Gooseberry Fool (see p. 125).

Currants

Currants may be red, black or white. They are very tart and are usually not eaten raw but made into desserts, pies, jams, jellies or juices. Look for plump, evenly colored fruit.
Preparation and cooking

Currants grow in thick clusters on little stems. Each currant must be removed from its stem before cooking. Wash and drain well in a colander, and simmer in a little water until tender or use as desired. Dried currants, available at supermarkets, are really dried grapes.
Recipe: Red Currant & Raspberry Summer Pudding (see p. 129).

Damsons

Damsons are a type of sour plum, dark purple in color. Because of their tart flavor, they are generally used for cooking. Choose fresh-looking fruit which yield all over under gentle pressure. Use in puddings, jams and jellies.
Preparation and cooking

Wash thoroughly and simmer gently for 10 minutes in a little water. Remove from heat and allow to cool. Halve, remove the pits and then purée or use as desired.
Recipe: Use instead of prunes in Prune & Raspberry Whip (see p. 128).

Dates

The fruit of the date palm, dates are native to the northern Persian Gulf. They are cultivated in the USA, Algeria and Tunisia.

The small oblong fruit are usually golden or dark brown, with a shiny, sticky skin, and a long narrow pit inside the fibrous flesh. Eat raw on their own or in salads, or cooked in puddings. (For dried dates, see p. 39).
Preparation

Wash fresh dates and remove the pits. Eat raw or use as required.
Recipe: Use instead of apricots in Sprouty Salad (see p. 94).

Figs

Figs are indigenous to Syria, Turkey and India. Fresh figs can be green or purple, and there are over 700 varieties. Look for even-colored fruit which yield evenly under gentle pressure. Fresh figs are extremely delicate.

A perfectly ripe fresh fig is best eaten and savored on its own. Slightly unripe figs may be steamed or poached as a dessert or used in cakes, jams, chutneys or pickles.

Figs are also available dried (see p. 39) and are often roasted and made into a caffeine-free coffee substitute (see p. 61).

Preparation and cooking

Fresh figs need only be washed carefully before eating. To cook slightly unripe figs, steam or poach in a little water for 5-10 minutes until tender.

Recipe: Add to Exotic Fruit Salad (see p. 132).

Gooseberries

Gooseberries are in fact a member of the currant family. They have a short summer season, often lasting only a few weeks. Choose firm undamaged fruit. The large, plump yellow varieties are often sweet enough to eat raw, but the smaller green ones need to be cooked. Use raw in fruit salads or cooked in cakes, desserts, jams and pickles.

Preparation and cooking

Wash the raw fruit well and top and tail with scissors or a sharp knife before eating. To cook, wash, top and tail and then simmer in a little water for 5-10 minutes until tender. Gooseberries have many pips so strain, if desired.

Recipe: Gooseberry Fool (see p. 125).

Grapefruit

Grapefruit are one of the largest members of the citrus family and originated in the West Indies. They may have white or pink flesh: white grapefruit are good for making juice; the pink-fleshed varieties are generally sweeter and may be eaten like an orange.

Look for even-colored heavy fruit, which are juicier. Use raw in salads and as appetizers, or cook in cakes, desserts or marmalades. Grapefruit halves can also be broiled or baked.

Preparation

Pink grapefruit may be peeled and eaten like an orange. To prepare a grapefruit, cut in half and cut inside the edge with a grapefruit or sharp knife to free the flesh from the skin. Carefully cut between the segments, freeing the flesh from the dividing membranes.

Recipe: Citrus Cocktail (see p. 81).

Grapes

Grapes probably originated in western Asia. They can be red, deep blue or green and are grown commercially in many parts of the world, both as dessert grapes and for making wine.

Common varieties are the Tokay, ruby seedless, Flame and queen (reds), Thompson seedless, Perlette seedless, Italia, calmeria and almeria (greens) and exotic and ribier (deep blues).

Look for plump, fresh grapes, which are firmly attached to their stems. Grapes are often dried for raisins, currants and golden raisins (see p. 39).

Preparation

Grapes are usually eaten raw. They have a delicate flavor which can become lost in highly-flavored dishes.

Before eating grapes, wash carefully. If you wish to remove their skins and seeds, cover with boiling water for 30 seconds, drain and peel off the skins. Cut the peeled grapes in half and remove the seeds.

Recipe: Halve, de-seed and add to Exotic Fruit Salad (see p. 132).

Greengages

Greengages are a northern European plum. They are small and greenish-yellow. Look for even-colored fruit which yield all over to gentle pressure. Eat greengages as one would a dessert plum, either raw, stewed or puréed or in puddings, cakes and jams. They are one of the sweetest varieties of plum.

Preparation and cooking

To eat raw, wash well. To cook, put in a saucepan, cover with water and simmer gently until tender, about 10-15 minutes. Leave to cool, halve and remove the pits. Use as required, adding a little sweetener if liked.

Recipe: Use instead of apricots in Apricot & Orange Sago Cream (see p. 121).

Guavas

Guavas are grown in most tropical and subtropical countries, and probably originated in Haiti. Round or pear-shaped, they usually have yellow skins with bright red or pink flesh containing numerous seeds, similar to a tomato. Look for yellow fruit which yield evenly to gentle pressure.

Guavas are perhaps an acquired taste but make a delicious and unusual addition to fresh fruit salads, and can also be used in puddings, cakes and jams.

Preparation

Wash the guava well and cut into quarters. Peel off the skin and eat the flesh and seeds. A little lemon juice sprinkled over will prevent browning.

Recipe: Add to Exotic Fruit Salad (see p. 132).

Kiwi
(Chinese gooseberries)

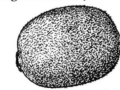

Kiwi originated in China. The outside of the fruit is brown and hairy and inside is bright green flesh surrounding tiny black edible seeds.

Look for undamaged fruit which yield evenly to gentle pressure.

Nutritionally, kiwi are rich in vitamin C. Eat kiwi on their own or add sliced to salads, desserts, cakes and jams. They can also be used as a very attractive garnish for sweet or savory salads.

Preparation

Fresh kiwi should be peeled with a sharp knife before eating. Slice or cut into quarters for a salad. For use as a garnish, slice crosswise or lengthwise as desired.

Recipe: Exotic Fruit Salad (see p. 132).

Kumquats

These tiny citrus fruits, no bigger than an olive, originated in China. Their popularity has grown in Western countries over the past few years, and they are increasingly available.

Look for small, heavy, bright orange fruit, without marks or bruises. The whole fruit is eaten, including the skin, which is usually sweeter than the flesh inside.

Preparation

Wash thoroughly and remove any stems. Use whole, halve or slice thinly as desired.

Recipe: Chop and add to the stuffing in Baked Apples (see p. 121).

Lemons

Lemons originated in India and are now grown in subtropical countries all over the world. They are an extremely versatile fruit and can be used in a large range of dishes, both savory and sweet. Do not forget to make use of the lemon rind or zest, because this can add a wonderful tang to certain dishes. Lemon juice will also prevent fruit and vegetables from browning once they have been cut.

Look for even-colored, heavy fruit without bruises. Avoid shriveled or soft fruit.

Lemons are not suitable for eating raw but the juice and rind can be added to soups, puddings, cakes, jams and pickles. They are also used for garnishes.

Preparation

Cut the lemon in half crosswise and extract the juice with a lemon squeezer or by hand. Lemons are good for garnishing a range of dishes: slice crosswise or cut into wedges or in different directions for a variety of effects. Remove the seeds, if desired.

To obtain lemon rind, wash and dry the fruit and then grate finely, turning the lemon often to avoid the white pith. Alternatively, quarter the lemon and remove the peel in four pieces. Scrape out the pith and slice finely for shredded rind or chop finely as desired.

Recipe: Tabouleh (see p. 95).

Limes

Limes are the tropical equivalent of lemons. Indian in origin, they grow widely in tropical climates. They are smaller than lemons and are vibrant green, turning to yellow at their peak of ripeness. Look for firm, heavy fruit. Prepare and use as for lemons.

Recipe: Tapioca & Lime Soufflés (see p. 131).

Litchis

Chinese in origin, these succulent exotic fruit have a rough, brownish-pink skin and creamy-colored smooth flesh surrounding a large black pit. The flesh has a subtle, delicate taste and fine aroma.

Look for firm heavy fruit, avoiding those with cracked or damaged shells or with a wrinkled appearance.

Preparation
Peel off the outer shell. Eat the flesh immediately or add to fruit salads. The large pit can first be removed with a sharp knife if desired.
Recipe: Add to Exotic Fruit Salad (see p. 132).

Loganberries

Loganberries look like large, dark raspberries and have a similar flavor. They are a cross between a raspberry and a blackberry. Look for firm undamaged fruit. Prepare and use as for raspberries.
Recipe: Use instead of strawberries in Strawberry Mousse (see p. 130).

Mangoes

Mangoes are indigenous to India but are now grown extensively in all tropical countries. There are over 1,000 types of mango tree, and the fruit varies greatly in size and color.

Look for firm, heavy fruit which yield slightly to pressure and are without bruises. Mangoes can be enjoyed on their own or used in fruit salads, cakes, drinks, chutneys, quick breads and jams. Dried mangoes are also available (see p. 39).
Preparation
Mangoes have a large seed in the middle. Cut the fruit lengthwise on one side, as close to the seed as possible. Repeat on the other side of the seed so you have two large slices of flesh which can be peeled off the seed. Scoop the flesh out of the skin with a spoon or cut into smaller pieces as required.
Recipe: Exotic Fruit Salad (see p. 132).

Mangosteens

Mangosteens are Far Eastern fruit and are very seldom found in the West, but should not be missed if available.

The outside of the fruit is a deep purple. Inside the thick, pithy shell is a rich, cream-colored fruit similar in taste and texture to a litchi. Look for heavy, bright fruit and eat by themselves or in fruit salads.
Preparation
Break or cut open the hard outer casing. Segment and eat the creamy flesh, discarding the seeds within. The flesh adheres tightly to the seed(s), so remove as you eat.
Recipe: Add to Exotic Fruit Salad (see p. 132).

Melons

Melons are indigenous to Asia and Africa and there are many different varieties. They have a high water content, low calorific value and a delicate, sweet flavor. Look for firm, heavy fruit without bruises or soft spots and which yield to fingertip pressure around the stem base. Smell the fruit as it may give off a delicate bouquet when ripe.

These are five common melons:

1 Musk melons are the popular melons with the netting skin and bright orange flesh.
2 Cantaloupe are small and round with yellow-green skin and sweet, orange flesh.
3 Honeydew are oval with smooth, whitish skins and sweet green flesh.
4 Ogen are small and round with ribbed striped skins and very sweet yellow or pale green flesh.
5 Watermelons are the largest of the melons and are oval or round with dark green, sometimes striped or mottled skins. The flesh is bright pinky-red and very crisp and sweet, and contains numbers of flat, black seeds.

Melons are often eaten as appetizers, either on their own or filled with other ingredients. They are also delicious in sweet and savory salads.
Preparation
Cut the melon in half lengthwise and scoop out the seeds. Cut into wedges, if desired. Watermelons have seeds throughout the flesh, so pick them out as best as you can. Because melons contain so much water, cut over a large bowl to catch the juice. Use as required.
Recipe: Melon & Tomato Salad (see p. 91).

Mulberries

Mulberries are the fruit of the mulberry tree. There are many varieties but white and black are the most common. They have a distinctive flavor. Prepare and use as for raspberries.
Recipe: Use instead of raspberries in Prune & Raspberry Whip (see p. 128).

Nectarines

Nectarines are Chinese in origin and not a cross between a peach and a plum as many people believe. They are in fact a variety of smooth-skinned peach and the name is probably derived from "nectar," owing to the delicious flavor. The color can vary from yellow to red.

Prepare and use as for peaches.

Oranges

Oranges are probably the most popular citrus fruit. Far Eastern in origin, they are now grown commercially in many subtropical countries. There are hundreds of varieties, which fall into two main groups: bitter for cooking and sweet for eating.

Look for firm, bright, heavy fruit without soft spots or bruises.
Eat oranges by themselves or add to savory and sweet salads, desserts, cakes, jams and marmalades. Orange juice is also delicious on its own or in soups and baked dishes. Orange rind or zest can be added to many sweet and savory dishes. Wash well before grating.
Preparation
Wash and dry the orange. Carefully score the orange with a sharp knife into quarters, taking care not to pierce the flesh. Peel off the skin and pith, segment the flesh or slice into rings.
Recipe: Apricot & Orange Sago Cream (see p. 121).

Papayas
(Pawpaws)

Papayas originated in Central America and

are now abundant in all tropical countries. They vary in size and color, the most common being the yellow-skinned varieties. The flesh is bright pink and contains numerous tiny black seeds, with a sharp, peppery flavor.

Look for papayas without soft spots or bruises and which give under gentle pressure.

Papaya makes a wonderful breakfast alternative to grapefruit or prunes. Use also in salads, puddings and other desserts.
Preparation
Cut the papaya in half lengthwise, scoop out the seeds and discard.

Passion fruit
(Purple granadillas)

Passion fruit are a small knobbly purplish-brown exotic fruit native to Brazil, with a hard shell encasing numerous juicy seeds. They have a very strong tangy flavor which is particularly good in fruit salads and drinks.

Look for firm, heavy fruit with slightly wrinkled skins. Use in puddings, sweet and savory salads, cakes, juices and jams.
Preparation
Cut the fruit in half with a sharp knife. Scoop out the seeds and juice with a teaspoon, and eat raw or use as required. If you do not like the seeds, pass through a strainer.
Recipe: Exotic Fruit Salad (see p. 132).

Peaches

Peaches are probably Chinese in origin, and there are over 2,000 varieties. They have a furry skin and vary from yellow to pinkish-red.

Look for firm heavy fruit without soft spots or bruises which give under gentle pressure.

Peaches are enjoyed on their own, or added to salads, cakes, desserts, jams and chutneys. They are also available dried (see p. 39).
Preparation and cooking
Wash and cut in half with a sharp knife. Remove the pit and use the fruit as required. If you wish to peel the peach, pour over boiling water, leave for 30 seconds, drain off the water and the skins should peel off easily. Brush with a little lemon juice to prevent browning.
Recipe: Peach Custard Tart (see p. 126).

Pears

West African in origin, pears are now grown in most temperate countries. There are over 5,000 varieties.

Look for firm fruit without soft spots or bruising and which yield to gentle pressure at the stalk. Pears can be eaten on their own or used in sweet and savory salads, desserts, cakes, jams and pickles.
Preparation
Wash, core and peel as desired. Eat whole or slice lengthwise. Cut pears may be sprinkled with lemon juice to prevent browning.
Recipe: Peach & Pear Crumble (see p. 127).

Persimmons
(Kaki fruit/Sharon fruit/Date plums)

Persimmons originated in China and Japan and are now grown in many subtropical countries. They resemble large orange tomatoes and have succulent, sweet orange flesh.

Look for heavy, bright fruit without bruising or cracks in the skin. The fruit should yield evenly to gentle pressure. When ripe, persimmons are really quite soft. Do not be persuaded to eat unripe as they contain tannic substances which taste horrible.

Persimmons are best enjoyed on their own or in a fruit salad, but they may be added to desserts and cakes or made into jams and chutneys if desired.

Preparation
The stem of a really ripe persimmon will pull away easily. Having removed the stem, cut the fruit in half and scoop out the flesh. Alternatively, cut into quarters and carefully peel off the skin.

Recipe: Place slices on top of Polenta Pudding with Seasonal Fruit (see p. 128).

Pineapples
Pineapples are one of the most popular exotic fruits. Indigenous to South America, they can be found in almost every tropical country in the world and are generally available all year around.

Look for firm, heavy fruit without soft spots or bruises. They should yield gently to fingertip pressure and may have a pleasant aroma when ripe. Another way of testing for ripeness is to carefully pull a leaf out of the crown. If the leaf comes away easily, the pineapple is probably ready to eat.

Pineapples are delicious on their own or in sweet and savory salads, savory dishes such as risottos, desserts, cakes and jams.

Preparation
There are many ways to cut a pineapple. One of the simplest is to cut the pineapple crosswise in 1-inch slices and then cut off the skin around the edges of each slice. If the core in the middle seems very tough or fibrous, this should also be removed. Take care to remove all the tiny black "eyes" with the skin because they can cause skin irritation in and around the mouth if eaten.

Pineapples may also be cut into wedges or chunks or you can cut a lid off the crown and scoop out the flesh inside. The shell may then be filled with a mixture of fresh fruit, mousse, sherbet or ice cream, or even chopped vegetables for a savory salad.

Recipe: Pineapple Salad (see p. 92).

Plums
Plums are European in origin and are commercially grown in many temperate countries. There are many varieties including both dessert and cooking plums. They can be small or large and vary in color from golden-yellow to green or deep purple.

Look for firm, plump fruit which yield evenly to gentle pressure. Avoid shriveled or extremely soft plums. Dessert plums can be eaten by themselves or added to fruit salads. Both dessert and cooking plums can be used in desserts, cakes and jams.

Preparation and cooking
Dessert plums should be washed, halved and the pits removed. Peel if desired. Cooking plums may be stewed in a little water until tender, about 10-15 minutes. Leave to cool and then carefully remove the skins and pits. Use as required.

Recipe: Add ¼ pound plums to Rice Pudding (see p. 130).

Pomegranates
Pomegranates are indigenous to Iran. Their hard, reddish shells reveal hundreds of bright red, juicy seeds when cut open.

Look for firm, even-colored fruit, the heavier the better, and without bruises.

Pomegranates are eaten raw. The deep red seeds are sucked for their juice and then usually discarded. Pomegranate juice is used as a flavoring, to add to sweet or savory dishes or drinks.

Preparation
Cut a thin slice off the stem end of the pomegranate, cut the fruit into sections and bend back to reveal the juicy red seeds. If you want to extract the juice, press the seeds through a strainer into a bowl.

Rambutans

This delightful Far Eastern exotic fruit is still quite rare in the West. It has a pinkish-red spiky outer casing and cream-colored flesh which resembles a litchi in looks and in flavor.

Choose healthy looking fruit, heavy in weight with a good pinky-red tinge. If very green, they will probably not be ripe. Eat on their own or added to fruit salads.

Preparation
Break open the hairy outer shell. Inside the creamy white flesh is a hard seed which can be removed if desired with a sharp knife.

Raspberries
Red and black varieties are available, although red is the most common. Look for firm, undamaged fruit in clean, unstained punnets with no mold. They are very delicate when fully ripe. Use in cakes, puddings, jams and sauces or simply eat on their own or in fruit salad with cream or smetana (see p. 47).

Preparation and cooking
Wash gently in a colander, picking over the fruit to remove any stems which may still be attached. To cook, simmer gently in a little water for 5-10 minutes and then strain if desired.

Recipe: Prune & Raspberry Whip (see p. 128).

Rhubarb
Rhubarb is the stem of a plant probably native to Tibet. It is in fact a vegetable but is always used as a fruit. Outdoor rhubarb has thick, succulent stalks, dark red or green in color. It has a sharp acid flavor. Hothouse rhubarb is smaller and pinker and usually sweeter.

Rhubarb is always eaten cooked. Use in puddings, pies, cakes, jams and pickles.

Preparation and cooking
Wash the rhubarb, trim and remove any strings. Cut into 1-inch pieces. Simmer in a little water until tender, about 10-15 minutes. Add sweetener and use as required.

Another way of cooking rhubarb which does not require additional liquid is to prepare it as above and then to place it in an ovenproof dish or on a baking tray and cook in a 400°F oven for 5 minutes or until tender. Be careful not to let it burn.

Recipe: Rhubarb & Almond Mousse (see p. 129).

Satsumas
Satsumas are a loose-skinned variety of citrus fruit, similar in appearance to a tangerine but seedless, with a sweeter flavor and thicker skin. Look for heavy, undamaged fruit and avoid any which look dry, withered or with soft spots.

Satsumas are delicious eaten by themselves or added to sweet and savory salads, puddings, cakes and marmalades.

Preparation
Peel off the skin, remove any pith, break into natural segments and use as desired.

Recipe: Use instead of oranges in Watercress & Orange Salad (see p. 96).

Strawberries
Strawberries are probably the most popular summer fruit. American in origin, they are now commercially produced all over the world.

Choose firm, undamaged fruit and eat on the day of purchase or refrigerate. Use in salads, soups, puddings, cakes, jams, jellies and juices.

Preparation and cooking
Wash carefully in a colander, and remove the stems; hull. To cook, simmer in a little water for 5-10 minutes until tender and then strain if desired.

Recipe: Strawberry Mousse (see p. 130).

Tangerines
Tangerines are another loose-skinned variety of citrus fruit, native to southern China and Laos. Similar in appearance to the satsuma, they have thinner skins and many seeds. Prepare and use as for satsumas (see above).

Recipe: Fresh Fruit Tart (see p. 125).

Ugli
The ugli fruit is a cross between the grapefruit and the tangerine, and is native to the East Indies. Uglis look like large, ugly grapefruit with thick, knobbly green and orange skins but the flesh is pink and sweet. They have very few seeds. Prepare and use as for grapefruit.

Recipe: Use instead of grapefruit in Spinach Salad (see p. 94).

DRIED FRUIT

Apples	Currants	Golden raisins	Pears
Apricots	Dates	Mangoes	Prunes
Bananas	Figs	Peaches and nectarines	Raisins

Drying is a useful way of storing perishable fruit and concentrating its nutritional value. The fruits are picked and either dried naturally in the sun or in dehydration units, which blast the fruit with hot air until all the moisture has evaporated.

Dried fruits are high in fiber, natural sugars, protein, vitamins A, B and C, iron, calcium and other minerals. They can be eaten raw as a snack or cooked in sweet and savory dishes, desserts, cakes and cookies. Dried fruits are an excellent source of natural sugar and sweeter than fresh fruit, so use them to help cut down on refined sugar.

Buying and storage

All dried fruit sold in retail stores should have a "for best results use before" stamp on the package. Although dried fruit can last for many months it is best to choose the freshest possible. Choose plump, unblemished fruit and check the labels for any additives (see below). Mixed dried fruit can be bought, but separate packages will usually be fresher.

All varieties of dried fruit should be stored in airtight containers, away from direct heat and sunlight. They are best eaten within 6 months.

Additives

There are two main additives used in the production of dried fruit; sulphur dioxide and a mineral spray.

To preserve some dried fruits and to prevent them from losing their bright colors, some manufacturers fumigate the fruit with sulphur dioxide. This gas is poisonous and in excess can cause severe alimentary problems and possibly genetic mutations. It also destroys vitamin B in the fruit. Since the whole fruit is thoroughly fumigated it is impossible to remove all of the additive by washing, so buy unsulphured fruits whenever possible, especially if you are giving them regularly to children. Figs and dates are not usually sulphured.

Mineral oils are sometimes sprayed on to the fruits after they have been dried, to give them a glossy appearance and to prevent them from sticking together. However, these oils can prevent the body's absorption of vitamins A, D, E and K, and also calcium and phosphorus. Some manufacturers are now using vegetable oils instead, but buy untreated fruit whenever possible. If mineral oils have been used, remove by careful washing in warm water.

Drying fruit

Fruit can be dried at home in a low oven. Apples, apricots, peaches and pears are some of the most successful to do. Either leave whole or peel, core and slice as required. Apples are usually peeled and cut into rings; peaches, nectarines and apricots are either left whole (with their pits removed) or halved; pears can be left whole (cored or uncored) or sliced.

Heat the oven to a low temperature, about 150°F. Leave the oven door open because there should be plenty of air; if you have a solid fuel cooker this is unnecessary. Spread the fruit on to racks or thread onto string (this is particularly suitable for apple rings). Leave for several hours until well dried.

Soaking and cooking

Currants, raisins and golden raisins are usually sold readywashed and need no soaking, although they can be plumped up before use by soaking for a few minutes in hot water. Other dried fruit should usually be washed before use.

If you wish to reconstitute dried fruit by soaking, simply cover with water in a bowl and leave for about 6 hours or until puffed up. Boiling gently will speed up this process.

To cook dried fruit, boil in the soaking liquid for about 30 minutes until soft. They can then be puréed in a blender or food processor if required.

DRIED FRUIT Per 4 oz	Water	Protein	Fat	Carbohydrate	Fiber	Vitamin A	Vitamin B₁	Vitamin B₂	Vitamin B₃	Vitamin B₆	Vitamin B₁₂	Vitamin C	Vitamin D	Vitamin E	Folic acid	Iron	Calcium	Magnesium	Sodium	Potassium	Phosphorus	Zinc
	g	g	g	g	g	µg	mg	mg	mg	mg	µg	mg	µg	mg	µg	mg	mg	mg	mg	mg	mg	mg
Recommended daily allowance	N	80M 60W	N	N	25-30	750	1.5	1.5	18	1.5	3	30	2.5	8	200	12	500	250	2500	1500	500	15
Apples	N	0	**1.4**	61	3.2	N	0.05	0.1	0.4	0.11	0	**9**	0	N	N	1.4	26	N	4	480	44	N
Apricots	15	**4.8**	Tr	43.4	**24**	**3600**	Tr	0.2	3	0.17	0	Tr	0	N	14	4.1	92	65	56	**1880**	**120**	0.2
Currants	22	1.7	Tr	63.1	6.5	220	**0.1**	0.03	0.5	**0.3**	0	0	0	N	11	1.8	95	36	20	70	40	0.1
Dates	15	2	Tr	63.9	8.7	50	0.07	0.04	2	0.15	0	0	0	N	**21**	1.6	68	59	5	750	65	0.3
Figs	17	3.6	Tr	52.9	18.5	50	**0.1**	0.08	1.7	0.18	0	0	0	N	9	4.2	**280**	**92**	**87**	1010	92	**0.9**
Golden raisins	18	1.8	Tr	**64.7**	7	30	**0.1**	0.08	0.5	**0.3**	0	0	0	**0.7**	4	1.8	52	35	53	860	95	0.1
Peaches	16	0.6	Tr	53	14.3	2000	Tr	0.19	**5.3**	0.1	0	Tr	0	N	14	**6.8**	36	54	6	1100	**120**	N
Prunes	**23**	2.4	Tr	40.3	16.1	1000	**0.1**	**0.2**	1.5	0.24	0	Tr	0	N	4	2.9	38	27	12	860	83	N
Raisins	22	1.1	Tr	64.4	6.8	30	**0.1**	0.08	0.5	**0.3**	0	0	0	N	4	1.6	61	42	52	860	33	0.1

KEY
All whole foods are uncooked unless otherwise stated. Some whole foods may not be included in the chart, as there is currently no nutritional data available.
g: grams **mg**: milligrams **µg**: micrograms **N**: no available data **Tr**: trace **M**: adult men **W**: adult women.   The recommended daily allowances are averages and vary depending on age, occupation and metabolism.   Figures in bold type indicate the whole food with the highest level of nutrient.

Apples

Available as rings and segments.

Dried apples are a good source of vitamin C, usually lost from other fruit in the drying process. They are often sold lightly sulphured.

To dry apple rings at home, peel, core and cut into rings. Then, heat in a 150°F oven for several hours until well dried.

Dried apples can be eaten as a snack or used soaked and cooked in soups, sauces, cakes, desserts and puddings.

Recipe: Couscous Cake (see p. 141).

Apricots

Available whole, halved, in pieces, sulphured and unsulphured. Hunza apricots can also be bought.

Apricots have the highest protein content of all dried fruit, and are also high in vitamins A and B_2. Both sulphured and unsulphured apricots can be bought. Hunza or wild apricots have been cultivated for centuries by the Hunza tribe in the Himalayas, and are thought to be the best variety. Hunza apricots are small, pale brown in color with an edible kernel. They are sold unsulphured.

Whole dried apricots can be eaten as they are, or soaked for a few hours until they expand. Halved apricots tend to be rather dirty and so wash well before eating or cooking. Apricot pieces cook quite quickly and are good for making jams and purées.

Use dried apricots as snacks or in soups, salads, curries, sweet and savory dishes, puddings, cakes, jams and chutneys.

Recipe: Apricot & Orange Sago Cream (see p. 121).

Bananas

Available whole, sliced lengthwise and as banana chips.

Dried whole or sliced bananas have a high sugar content and are deliciously sweet and chewy. They are nutritionally superior to banana chips, which are small pieces of unripe banana which have been deep-fried in an oily sugar mix.

Use dried bananas as snacks or in curries, savory dishes, puddings, cakes, jams, chutneys and pickles.

Recipe: Use 1 tbsp finely chopped dried banana instead of raisins in Fresh Vegetable Curry (see p. 106).

Currants

Available whole.

Currants are dried from a variety of black grape originating from Corinth. They are tiny, seedless, very sweet and are always sold unsulphured.

Currants can be eaten as a snack or used in salads, savory dishes, desserts, cakes and mincemeat.

Recipe: Fruit & Malt Bread (see p. 153).

Dates

Available whole, unpitted and pressed into slabs.

Dried dates are extremely high in sugar and also contain vitamin A and some B vitamins. Plump, soft whole dates taste best but the pressed slabs or blocks are good for cooking and for making purées. If using these, make sure that no pits have been left inside.

Dates are unsulphured but are often treated with mineral oils to give them glossy skins, so buy untreated dates if possible or ones which have been treated with vegetable oils.

Use dried dates as snacks or chopped in salads, savory dishes, puddings, cakes, jams, chutneys and pickles.

Recipe: Date & Oat Bars (see p. 141).

Figs

Available whole.

Figs have a high sugar content and are rich in protein, B vitamins and minerals, particularly calcium and magnesium. They are also a natural laxative. The best figs are dark brown with thin skins, often indicated by a sugary crusting on the surface.

Figs can be eaten as a snack or chopped in salads, savory dishes, puddings, cakes, jams, chutneys and pickles.

Recipe: Brandy Fruitcake (see p. 137).

Golden raisins
(White raisins/Sultanas)

Available whole.

Golden raisins are dried, seedless white grapes. Large, pale and succulent, they are sweeter than raisins and currants. Sultanas have often been sulphured and treated with mineral oils to give them a shiny appearance, but some (for instance Australian sultanas) are unsulphured and have been treated with vegetable oils instead, which are much better.

Use sultanas as you would currants and raisins, especially when the dish requires a sweeter taste.

Recipe: Barley, Fruit & Vegetable Pollo (see p. 99).

Mangoes

Available sliced.

Dried mangoes are usually available in long slices and are very sweet. They have often sulphured, so look for unsulphured mangoes if possible.

Use chopped in salads, sweet-and-sour dishes, curries, puddings, cakes, jams, chutneys and pickles.

Recipe: Use instead of apricots in Barley, Fruit & Vegetable Pollo (see p. 99).

Peaches and nectarines

Available whole and halved.

Dried peaches and nectarines have a similar appearance and use, although nectarines are rather smaller. Both perhaps lack the flavor and aroma of the fresh fruit, but they are an excellent source of iron and any unpleasant smell will disappear after soaking. They are often sulphured and some varieties (particularly from China) may have been preserved in sugar.

Use dried peaches and nectarines as you would apricots; as snacks and in soups, salads, savory dishes, puddings, cakes, jams, chutneys and pickles.

Recipe: Rich Muesli (see p. 70).

Pears

Available whole and halved.

Dried pear halves are tasty and retain much of the texture and flavor of the fresh fruit. If dried whole, the core and skin can be removed after soaking if liked. Dried pears are often sulphured, and some varieties (particularly from China) may even have been preserved in sugar.

To dry pears at home, first halve and core (there is no need to peel). Then, heat in a 150°F oven for several hours until well dried.

Dried pears can be eaten as a snack or used in compotes, savory dishes, puddings, desserts, cakes, jams and chutneys.

Recipe: Rich Muesli (see p. 70).

Prunes

Available whole, unpitted, pitted and tenderized.

Prunes are a dried variety of black-skinned plum, grown specifically for drying purposes. They are low in sugar and are also a natural laxative. Tenderized prunes have been partially cooked. Some prunes have been treated with mineral oils, so wash carefully or find untreated prunes if possible, or the cake may sink.

Prunes can be used whole or puréed, in compotes, stuffings, puddings, cakes, jams and confectionery.

Recipe: Prune & Raspberry Whip (see p. 128).

Raisins

Available whole.

Raisins are dried grapes, and are available in a number of varieties. Lexia raisins are from Australia, and are juicy and sweet with their seeds removed. Muscatel raisins are also large, pale in color and seedless. Small black seedless raisins are also available.

Raisins are usually unsulphured, although some may have been treated with mineral rather than vegetable oils. Generally, raisins should be washed and sorted before using, but dry carefully if they are to be used in a cake mixture, or the cake may sink.

Eat raisins raw or use in salads, sweet and savory dishes, curries, desserts, cakes, pickles and chutneys.

Recipe: Curried Coleslaw (see p. 90).

NUTS

Almonds	Coconuts	Pecans	Sesame seeds
Brazil nuts	Filberts	Pine nuts	Sunflower seeds
Cashew nuts	Macadamia nuts	Pistachio nuts	Tiger nuts
Chestnuts	Peanuts	Pumpkin seeds	Walnuts

The term nut is used to describe any seed or fruit with an edible kernel in a hard, usually brittle, shell. All the more common varieties of nuts are included in this section, as well as those seeds which are generally used in the same way as nuts: pumpkin, sesame and sunflower seeds.

Nutritional value

Nuts are extremely nutritious, providing large amounts of protein and many essential vitamins and minerals. Nuts are also high in carbohydrate, fats, oils and fiber, so should not be eaten in excess. However, most nuts (except coconut and pine nuts) contain a certain amount of linoleic acid, which is thought to help counteract the possible build-up of cholesterol from any saturated fats and oils.

Fortunately, shelled nuts from reputable whole food stores are not subjected to additives, although it is always best to check. Commercially packaged nuts are often treated with preservatives, inhibitors and dyes, however. You should also beware of snack-type nuts which are coated in saturated fats, roasted and often covered with large quantities of salt, thereby considerably reducing their nutritional value.

Storage

When buying nuts, you should check for freshness and only buy in small quantities. Because of their high fat and oil content they can turn rancid if left too long. Unshelled nuts will keep up to 6 months, but seeds and shelled nuts should be kept in an airtight container in a cool, dry and dark place. Chopped and ground nuts will go stale more quickly, and should ideally be eaten within 4-6 weeks.

Usage

Nuts can be eaten raw or added to all sorts of dishes, both savory and sweet. They can be used whole or chopped in salads, purées, casseroles, roasts, stuffings, cereals, bakes and confectionery. They are generally available in a variety of forms: in their shells, or shelled and whole, slivered, chopped, flaked or ground. Most are interchangeable, but the whole nuts are usually fresher.

You may wish to blanch whole nuts to remove the skins more easily. To do this, immerse in boiling water for a few minutes and then pop the nuts out of their skins. For grinding whole shelled nuts, use a small grater or mill.

Roasting nuts

Many recipes call for roasted nuts. This accentuates the flavor of the nut although it somewhat reduces the nutritional value. Vegetable oil, spices, honey or tamari can also be added to the roasting nuts to alter the flavor.

1 Preheat the oven to 375°F.

2 Spread the nuts evenly on a baking tray and bake for about 5 minutes, shaking occasionally until they are light golden-brown and crisp.

3 Remove from the oven and leave to cool.

NUTS Per 4 oz	Water	Protein	Fat	Carbohydrate	Fiber	Vitamin A	Vitamin B1	Vitamin B2	Vitamin B3	Vitamin B6	Vitamin B12	Vitamin C	Vitamin D	Vitamin E	Folic acid	Iron	Calcium	Magnesium	Sodium	Potassium	Phosphorus	Zinc
	g	g	g	g	g	µg	mg	mg	mg	mg	µg	mg	µg	mg	µg	mg	mg	mg	mg	mg	mg	mg
Recommended daily allowance	N	80M 60W	N	N	25-30	750	1.5	1.5	18	1.5	3	30	2.5	8	200	12	500	250	2500	2500	500	15
Almonds	5	16.9	53.5	4.3	14.3	0	0.24	**0.92**	2	0.1	0	Tr	0	20	96	4.2	**250**	260	6	860	440	3.1
Brazil nuts	9	12	61.5	4.1	9	0	1	0.1	1.6	0.17	0	Tr	0	6.5	N	2.8	180	**410**	2	760	590	4.2
Cashew nuts	5	17.2	45.7	27.9	1.5	60	0.43	0.25	1.8	N	0	Tr	0	N	N	3.8	38	267	15	464	390	N
Chestnuts	**52**	2	2.7	**36.6**	6.8	0	0.2	0.22	0.2	0.33	0	Tr	0	0.5	N	0.9	46	33	11	500	74	N
Coconuts – shredded	2.3	5.6	62	6.4	**23.5**	0	0.06	0.04	0.6	N	0	0	0	N	N	3.6	22	90	28	750	160	N
– fresh	42	3.2	36	3.7	13.6	0	0.03	0.02	0.3	0.04	0	**2**	0	0.7	9	2.1	13	52	17	440	94	0.5
Filberts	41	7.6	36	6.8	6.1	0	0.4	N	0.9	0.55	0	Tr	0	**21**	72	1.1	44	56	1	350	320	2.4
Macadamia nuts	N	7	55	8	2	0	0.15	0.1	1	N	0	0	N	N	N	1.5	40	N	N	200	180	N
Peanuts	5	24.3	49	8.6	8.1	0	0.9	0.1	16	0.5	0	Tr	0	8.1	**110**	2	61	180	6	680	370	3
Pecans	3	9.2	**71.2**	14.6	2.3	**130**	0.86	0.13	0.9	0.2	0	**2**	0	N	N	2.4	73	N	Tr	603	289	N
Pine nuts	6	**31.1**	47.4	11.6	0.9	N	0.62	N	N	N	0	N	0	N	N	N	N	N	N	N	N	N
Pistachio nuts	6	19.3	54	15	2.4	60	0.7	0.2	1.5	N	0	0	0	N	N	**14**	140	N	N	750	525	N
Pumpkin seeds	4	29	46.7	15	1.9	70	0.24	0.19	2.4	N	0	N	N	N	N	11.2	51	N	N	N	**1144**	N
Sesame seeds	5	26.4	54.8	6.4	9.1	40	0.72	0.09	**12.6**	N	0	N	0	N	N	7.8	131	347	**40**	407	890	**10.3**
Sunflower seeds	5	24	47.3	19.9	3.8	50	**1.96**	0.23	5.4	**1.2**	0	N	0	N	N	7.1	120	N	30	**920**	837	N
Walnuts	24	10.6	51.5	5	5.2	0	0.3	0.13	1	0.73	0	Tr	0	0.8	66	2.4	61	130	3	690	510	3

KEY

All whole foods are uncooked unless otherwise stated. Some whole foods may not be included in the chart, as there is currently no nutritional data available.
g: grams **mg**: milligrams **µg**: micrograms **N**: no available data **Tr**: trace **M**: adult men **W**: adult women. The recommended daily allowances are averages and vary depending on age, occupation and metabolism. Figures in bold type indicate the whole food with the highest level of nutrient.

Almonds

Available unshelled, shelled, blanched, slivered, flaked, roasted, chopped and ground.

Almond trees, with their beautiful pink and white blossom, are native to the Middle East. There are two types of almonds, bitter and sweet. Bitter almonds are broader and shorter than the sweet variety. Their bitter flavor is due to the presence of prussic acid, a highly volatile and poisonous substance which can only be removed by heating. You should therefore avoid eating raw bitter almonds. Their main use is in the production of almond oil (see p. 49) and almond extract (see p. 51).

Sweet almonds are extensively used in European and Eastern cookery. The nut has a thin, brown skin which can be eaten, but it is usually peeled away after roasting or blanching.

Almonds have the highest calcium content of all nuts, and are also high in protein and vitamin B_2. Use almonds whole and chopped in salads, dips, sweet and savory dishes, cakes, puddings and cookies. Flaked almonds can be tossed in butter and spices for a cocktail snack.

Recipe: Rhubarb & Almond Mousse (see p. 129).

Brazil nuts

Available unshelled, shelled, chopped and roasted.

Brazil nuts are native to the tropical regions of Bolivia, Brazil and Venezuela and grow along the banks of the Orinoko and Amazon rivers. The enormous wild Brazil trees grow to heights of 150-200 feet, producing large coconut-type shells inside which the seeds, or Brazil nuts, are wedged like segments of a fruit. Brazil nuts are rich and nutritious, but because of their high fat and oil content they can easily go rancid, so you should buy in small quantities.

Eat as a snack or use in nut rissoles, stuffings, cakes, some savory dishes and confectionery.

Cashew nuts

Available shelled, roasted, chopped and salted.

Cashew nuts originated in Brazil. A tree crop, the kidney-shaped nut grows underneath a false fruit or "cashew apple," which is often eaten in preference to the cashew itself. The nut has two shells, in between which is a caustic oil which can cause blisters and skin irritation if it touches the body. To render this oil harmless, the nuts are shelled and roasted before being sold.

They are usually eaten as a snack but are delicious in stuffings, Chinese dishes, cakes and desserts. The nuts can also be made into cashew nut butter (see p. 50).

Recipe: Cashew Cream (see p. 132).

Chestnuts
(Sweet chestnuts)

Available unshelled, shelled, peeled, dried, ground and puréed.

Edible chestnuts are sweet chestnuts, native to southern Europe. They should not be confused with the nuts of the buckeye or horse chestnut tree, which are inedible. Both the outer and inner skins should be removed before eating by boiling or roasting. They are always cooked before eating.

Sweet chestnuts can be eaten boiled, steamed, roasted or stewed in a variety of sweet and savory dishes, or they can be dried and ground to produce chestnut flour, which is delicious in bread or crêpes.

Recipe: Chestnut & Prune Roast (see p. 104).

Coconuts

Available unshelled, flaked, shredded and as creamed coconut.

The coconut is the fruit of the coconut palm, native to the Tropics.

Coconut meat can be eaten fresh or dried, and the "milk" inside the coconut makes a refreshing and nutritious drink. The dried flesh (often known as *copra*) may be shredded or compressed into hard cakes known as creamed coconut or coconut cream. Coconut can be used in curries, bakes and confectionery. It is extremely rich in oils and fats however, and should perhaps be eaten in moderation.

Recipe: Carrot & Coconut Cake (see p. 140).

Filberts
(Cobnuts/Hazelnuts)

Available unshelled, shelled, roasted, chopped and ground.

Filberts, cobnuts and hazelnuts all belong to the same family of plants. They originated in the Mediterranean and are now cultivated in most temperate areas of Europe, particularly Italy, France and Turkey.

The nuts grow in clusters, and are partially covered by a green helmet-shaped skin. They are particularly high in vitamins B_6 and E. Filberts can be eaten on their own or used in bakes and confectionery. The nuts can also be made into filbert butter (see p. 50).

Recipe: Banana Nut Cake (see p. 136).

Macadamia nuts
(Queensland nuts)

Available whole: unshelled, shelled, roasted and salted.

Macadamia nuts are native to Australia and are now also widely cultivated in Hawaii. Outside the country of origin, they are usually only available shelled and roasted. They look like pale filberts and have a very sweet, oily flavor. Like Brazil nuts, they have a very high fat and oil content, so go rancid quickly. They are usually eaten as a snack but are delicious in salads or sweet dishes.

Recipe: Fennel & Tomato Salad (see p. 91).

Peanuts
(Groundnuts/Monkey nuts)

Available unshelled, shelled, peeled, roasted and salted.

The peanut is actually a legume, the seed of an annual pod-bearing plant originating in South America. The nuts are encased in a dry, fibrous shell. Peanuts are highly nutritious, and can be eaten raw or roasted. They are used in peanut butter (see p. 50) and peanut oil (see p. 49).

Peanuts can be eaten as a snack or added to salads, sweet and savory dishes, cakes, puddings and cookies.

Recipe: Flapjacks (see p. 142).

Pecans

Available unshelled, shelled, roasted, chopped and salted.

Pecan nuts are indigenous to North America and were a staple food for Native Americans. They have a smooth reddy-brown or golden shell, and the nut inside resembles a walnut in appearance, although the taste is much milder.

Pecans are widely used in sweet and savory cooking, and can be added to salads, stuffings, cakes, cookies, pies and confectionery.

Recipe: Stuffed Eggplant with Tomato Sauce (see p. 115).

Pine nuts
(Pine kernels/Indian nuts/Pignolas)

Available raw, roasted and salted.

Pine nuts are the edible seeds of a number of pine trees, mainly the stone pine. They are native to the Mediterranean.

Pine nuts grow unshelled and the tiny, creamy-yellow oblong-shaped seeds have a rich, slightly turpentine flavor. They are eaten raw, like peanuts, or can be used in soups, sauces, salads, rice dishes, stews and stuffings. In Italy they are used in the traditional pesto sauce for pasta, and they are used in many Middle Eastern rice dishes.

Recipe: Add to Fennel & Tomato Salad (see p. 91).

Pistachio nuts

Available unshelled and shelled.

These green nuts in their semi-split shells are native to the Middle East and Central Asia. The naturally golden shell is sometimes dyed red for decorative effect.

Pistachio nuts are often eaten as a salted snack, served with or without their shells. They are often added to confectionery and halva (see p. 51) or used as a garnish for desserts.

Recipe: Brown Rice Risotto (see p. 100).

Pumpkin seeds

Available unhulled and hulled.

These small, flat green seeds are extremely nutritious, being high in protein, fats and minerals.

Pumpkin seeds can be eaten raw or cooked in both sweet and savory dishes, and can also be sprouted (see p. 23).

Recipe: Granola 2 (see p. 69).

Sesame seeds
(Benne seeds)

Available unhulled.

The sesame plant is probably African in origin and is now grown commercially in the Middle East, the Far East and Mexico. The tiny beige seeds are eaten whole (they do not need to be hulled), and are high in zinc, sodium and vitamin B_3.

Sesame seeds are most commonly processed into a fine, pale sesame oil (see p. 49). They are also often made into tahini, which is a thick cream-colored sesame paste (see p. 50), gomashio or sesame salt (see p. 50) and halva, a sweet sesame cake made with either sugar or honey (see p. 51).

Use whole sesame seeds in bread and cakes or in savory and sweet dishes. They have a delicious nutty flavor which blends well with most fruit, grains, vegetables and beans. Sesame seeds may also be sprouted successfully (see p. 23).

Recipe: Sesame Honey Bars (see p. 145).

Sunflower seeds

Available unhulled and hulled.

Sunflowers belong to the daisy family and probably originated in or around Mexico. The tall, erect plants with their large sun-like flowers were cultivated and worshipped by the Incas. They are now mainly grown for sunflower oil (see p. 49).

Sunflower seeds are very nutritious, being rich in protein, the vitamin B group and minerals, particularly potassium. They may also be sprouted (see p. 23).

The seeds can be bought ready-hulled in most whole food shops, and have a sweet nutty flavor. They are delicious in savory dishes, salads, breads, cakes and puddings or sprinkled over foods as a garnish.

Recipe: Sunflower Bars (see p. 145).

Tiger nuts
(Earth almonds)

Available whole or ground.

These are not in fact true nuts, but are rhizomes of a plant native to Africa. They are small, brown and knobbled in appearance, and have a flavor reminiscent of almonds. The chufa nut is similar to the tiger nut, and is more common in Europe. It is used in the Spanish drink *horchata de chufa*.

Eat tiger nuts raw as a snack or add to stuffings, cakes, sweet puddings, desserts and confectionery.

Walnuts

Available unshelled, shelled, chopped and ground.

Walnut trees are native to the Middle East and were taken to Europe by the Romans. There are many varieties but two main types of walnut, the English and the Black. English walnuts are sometimes called European or Persian walnuts. Black walnuts are native to America and are slightly larger, with a harder thicker shell and a stronger flavor.

Walnuts are used to make walnut oil (see p. 49), which has a pronounced flavor and is used for salad dressings. Immature green walnuts are available pickled in vinegar, and are used in the popular Mexican dish *chiles en nogada*. Walnuts contain some vitamin B_6 and folic acid, unusual in nuts.

Walnuts can be eaten as a snack or used in stuffings, salads, cakes, bakes, desserts and confectionery.

Recipe: Baked Avocado with Stilton & Walnuts (see p. 98).

SEAWEEDS

Agar-agar ☐   Dulse ☐   Laver   Nori ☐
Arame ☐   Hiziki ☐   Macrocystis porphyra   Wakame ☐
Carrageen ☐   Kombu ☐   Mekabu

☐ Pictured opposite page 48

Seaweeds grow abundantly in all the oceans and have been used as food, medicine and fertilizer for many thousands of years. They have a long tradition of use in Japan but have still to be fully appreciated in the West. If you are not familiar with their use, you can experiment with some of the recipes in this book and you should find the different varieties a valuable addition to your diet.

There are many varieties of seaweeds, with differing tastes and uses. Some have a strong sea flavor, while others are mild and sweet. Some seaweeds, such as agar-agar or carrageen, produce a clear tasteless jelly which can be used in place of animal gelatin for its setting properties.

Nutritional value

Nutritionally seaweeds rate highly. They are high in protein, containing essential amino acids, and are rich in minerals and trace elements, particularly iodine, calcium, potassium and iron. They also contain sizeable amounts of vitamins A, B, C and D, including vitamin B_{12}, which is only found in three other plant foods (alfalfa, comfrey and fermeted soybean products such as miso and tamari).

Seaweeds are also high in sodium, however, especially when cooked with shoyu or tamari, and they should not be eaten too frequently by people with high blood pressure.

Storage

Seaweeds are best bought ready-cleaned and dried from whole food shops. They will keep indefinitely unopened, but once open store in an airtight container and use within a few months.

Soaking

Most seaweeds need a preliminary soaking before use, unless they are going to be cooked in a stew or soup. In the preparation and cooking directions which follow it is suggested that the water used for soaking is thrown away. This is to reduce the strong, salty sea flavor of some seaweeds. However, this water does contain many useful nutrients, so do make use of it if you wish, either for cooking the seaweeds or in soups and broths.

SEAWEEDS Per 4 oz	Water	Protein	Fat	Carbohydrate	Fiber	Vitamin A	Vitamin B₁	Vitamin B₂	Vitamin B₃	Vitamin B₆	Vitamin B₁₂	Vitamin C	Vitamin D	Vitamin E	Folic acid	Iron	Calcium	Magnesium	Sodium	Potassium	Phosphorus	Zinc
	g	g	g	g	g	µg	mg	mg	mg	mg	µg	mg	µg	mg	µg	mg	mg	mg	mg	mg	mg	mg
Recommended daily allowance	N	80M 60W	N	N	25-30	750	1.5	1.5	18	1.5	3	30	2.5	8	200	12	500	250	2500	2500	500	15
Agar-agar	20	2.3	0.1	74.6	0	0	0	0	0	N	*	0	N	N	N	5	400	N	N	N	8	N
Arame	19	7.5	0.1	60.6	9.8	50	0.02	0.2	2.6	N	*	0	N	N	N	12	1170	N	N	N	150	N
Dulse	17	N	3	N	0.7	N	N	N	N	N	*	N	N	N	N	6.3	567	N	N	N	22	N
Hiziki	17	5.6	0.8	42.8	13	150	0.01	0.2	4	N	*	0	N	N	N	29	1400	N	N	N	56	N
Kombu	15	7.3	1.1	54.9	3	430	0.08	0.32	1.8	N	*	11	N	N	N	N	800	N	2500	N	150	N
Nori	11	35.6	0.7	44.3	4.7	11000	0.25	1.24	10	N	*	20	N	N	N	12	260	N	600	N	510	N
Wakame	16	12.7	1.5	51.4	3.6	140	0.11	0.14	10	N	*	15	N	N	N	13	1300	N	2500	N	260	N

KEY
All whole foods are uncooked unless otherwise stated. Some whole foods may not be included in the chart, as there is currently no nutritional data available. **g:** grams   **mg:** milligrams   **µg:** micrograms   **N:** no available data   **Tr:** trace   **M:** adult men   **W:** adult women. The recommended daily allowances are averages and vary depending on age, occupation and metabolism. Figures in bold type indicate the whole food with the highest level of nutrient. **✳** Exact figure unknown but thought to be very high.

Agar-agar
(Kanten)
Agar-agar is the Malay word for jelly. It is obtained from a variety of seaweeds and is mainly manufactured in Japan. Agar-agar is a natural, unflavored vegetable gelatin and is used as an alternative to animal gelatin. It is available in powder or flake form. The powdered varieties may be chemically processed, so the flakes are preferable.

Preparation and cooking
For a firm jelly, put 1 tbsp of agar-agar in a saucepan with 2½ cups of cold water, fruit juice or broth. Gently bring to a boil and simmer for 5 minutes. Remove from the heat, pour into a serving bowl and refrigerate for 4 hours or until set. Use 2 tsp for a delicate jelly.

Recipe: Rhubarb & Almond Mousse (see p. 129).

Arame
This is a good seaweed to begin with if you are not familiar with the taste and texture of seaweed, and it is particularly rich in calcium. Arame has a mild, sweet flavor and is grown abundantly in the seas around Japan. It is harvested in early spring and is parboiled, sun-dried and then shredded into thin strands to make it easier to cook and use.

Preparation and cooking
Put a handful of arame in a bowl and cover with boiling water. Leave to stand for 5 minutes and then strain.

Add soaked arame to soups, stews or savory dishes, and cook for a further 20-30 minutes. If you wish to cook it separately for salads or as a side vegetable, put it in a saucepan and cover with fresh cold water. Add 1 tbsp of shoyu or tamari for flavoring, bring to a boil and simmer gently for 20-30 minutes or until tender. A little garlic or grated ginger root can also be added during cooking, if liked. Eat hot or cold.

Recipe: Miso & Arame Soup (see p. 77).

Carrageen
(Irish moss)

Carrageen is grown in temperate North Atlantic coastal waters, in the seas around northern France, Ireland and New England. It is usually used for its gelling and setting properties, but the fan-like leaves can be cooked and eaten as a vegetable if desired.

The United States is the principal manufacturer of the by-product carrageenan, which is an emulsifying, thickening and gelling additive used widely in commercial ice creams, jellies, cookies, milk shakes, frozen desserts and some infant formulas. Although it is from a natural substance it can cause intestinal problems if eaten in excess.

Preparation and cooking

For use as a vegetable, prepare and cook as for arame (see p. 43).

For use as a setting agent in molds or blancmanges, first put 1 oz of carrageen in a bowl. Pour over boiling water and leave to stand for 15 minutes. Pour off the soaking liquid and put the seaweed in a saucepan. Add 2½ cups of fresh cold water, bring to a boil and simmer gently for 30 minutes.

Strain the cooking liquid off into a separate saucepan. Add your fruit, vegetables or flavoring as desired (depending on whether you require a sweet or savory mold) and heat for a further 10 minutes. Pour into a serving bowl and refrigerate for 4 hours or until set.

Dulse

This is another North Atlantic seaweed, grown and eaten in the coastal areas of Canada and North America, Iceland and Ireland. It has large, dark red flat leaves and no matter how long it is cooked it still remains tough and chewy with a strong, salty flavor. It is perhaps not a seaweed for beginners. It can be cooked as a vegetable or eaten raw.

Preparation and cooking

Put a handful of dulse in a bowl, cover with boiling water and leave to stand for 20 minutes. Pour off all the soaking liquid and put the seaweed in a saucepan. Cover again with cold fresh water and flavor with 1 tbsp shoyu or tamari, if liked. Bring to a boil and simmer for 40-50 minutes.

Recipe: Dulse Soup (see p. 75).

Hiziki

This seaweed is from Japan, and has been used there for many hundreds of years. It is hand-picked and allowed to dry in the sun before being coarsely shredded. Hiziki is extremely high in iron and calcium and has a sweet delicate flavor. It can be cooked with vegetables or by itself.

Preparation and cooking

Put a handful of hiziki in a bowl, pour over boiling water and leave to stand for 20 minutes. Pour off the soaking liquid.

Add the seaweed to soups, stews or savory dishes and cook for a further 30 minutes. If you wish to cook it separately as a side vegetable or for a salad, put in a saucepan and cover with fresh cold water. Add a little tamari, grated ginger or garlic for flavoring, bring to a boil and simmer for 30 minutes. Hiziki can be eaten hot or cold.

Recipe: Seitan with Hiziki (see p. 113).

Kombu

Kombu comes from Japan's northern seas, enjoying the cold Arctic currents. It has a strong sweet flavor and comes in thick black-green strips. Kombu is especially high in sodium but contains calcium and vitamins A and C, and makes a nutritious broth for soups and savory dishes. It is also used as a tea-like infusion in Japan.

Preparation and cooking

For use as a vegetable or to eat in soups, salads or savory dishes, first put 2 strips of kombu in a bowl. Pour over boiling water and leave to stand for 20 minutes. Strain off the soaking liquid and put the kombu in a saucepan. Cover with fresh cold water and add a little tamari and ginger root to flavor. Bring to a boil and simmer gently for 30 minutes.

For use as a broth, put 1 strip of kombu in a saucepan with about 2 cups of cold water. Bring to a boil and simmer gently for 30 minutes. Strain the liquid off and use it as a tasty, nourishing base for soups, stews and other savory dishes.

Recipe: Kombu Surprise (see p. 84).

Laver

Laver is a red seaweed grown in the waters around South Wales and Ireland. It grows close to the shore and can be gathered at low tide.

Laver has the appearance of spinach, and is a traditional breakfast food in South Wales, where it is rolled in old-fashioned oats, fried and served with bacon and eggs. It has a very strong seaweed flavor and is not recommended for those just beginning to experiment with seaweeds in their diet.

Prepare and use as for dulse.

Macrocystis porphyra

This is the variety of seaweed most often used in the preparation of kelp tablets and powders. Some people like to take these tablets as a daily nutritional supplement or to sprinkle a little of the powder onto savory dishes.

Mekabu

A Japanese seaweed, mekabu is a black-green seaweed similar to kombu. It is available in curled, dried strips. It is used mainly in soups, salads and as a garnish.

Prepare and use as for kombu.

Nori

Nori is a close relative of laver and is used extensively in Japanese cuisine. It is cultivated on bamboo frames in shallow bays and inlets around the coast of Japan. After harvesting, the broad leaves are spread out on bamboo racks, sun-dried and then hand-pressed to form thin sheets.

Nori is extremely high in protein and minerals, and is usually crumbled over vegetables and savory dishes as a garnish or wrapped in whole sheets around grains, vegetables and pickles. It can also be soaked and cooked.

Preparation and cooking

For use as a vegetable, cook as for arame.

For sprinkling purposes, take a sheet of nori between your fingers or with a pair of tongs and gently wave it over an open flame or a gas flame. In a matter of seconds the nori will turn a dark green and take on a crisp texture. Remove from the heat, leave to cool and then crumble with your hands.

For wrapping purposes, lightly toast the sheets of nori as above and mold around rice or a stuffing of your choice.

Recipe: Nori & Spinach Rolls (see p. 85).

Wakame

Wakame is another Japanese seaweed with an appearance and flavor very similar to kombu, though rather softer. It is especially high in protein, iron and calcium. Wakame is a good seaweed for beginners, as it is close in taste to a green vegetable.

Preparation and cooking

Put 2 strips of wakame in a bowl, pour over boiling water and leave to stand for 20 minutes. Pour off the soaking liquid and cut out the central veins. Cut into small pieces as a salad, or cook as a vegetable. To cook, put in a saucepan, cover with fresh cold water, bring to a boil and simmer for 10-15 minutes.

Recipe: Wakame (see p. 119).

DAIRY PRODUCE

Butter	Eggs	Sour cream
Buttermilk	Ghee	Soy milk
Cheese	Margarine	Yogurt
Cow's milk	Smetana	
Cream	Solid vegetable fat	

Milk, cream, butter, cheese and eggs have been consumed since animals were first domesticated, and in the West they form about one-third of our calorie intake. These animal products provide many nutrients, and are a highly concentrated form of energy. Milk, for instance, provides milk protein, calcium and vitamins; eggs supply complete protein, containing all the essential amino acids (see p. 8), and cheese is another good source of protein.

Dairy products can form a valuable part of a whole food vegetarian diet, particularly because of the complete protein and vitamin B_{12} which they contain, rare in plant foods. However, in recent years there has been strong evidence that for health reasons our intake of fats should be reduced, and of animal fats in particular, which are contained not only in meat but in dairy products.

Animal fats and disease

Fats provide over twice as much energy, weight for weight, as carbohydrates and proteins. Comparatively little fat is needed, therefore, to provide the necessary energy. Any excess fat can lead to obesity, which increases the likelihood of diabetes, high blood pressure, arthritis and gallbladder disease.

Excessive consumption of fat has also been linked with degenerative disease and heart disease, such as atherosclerosis, a restriction in the flow of blood to the heart caused by narrowing, or thickening, of the heart arteries. This narrowing is caused by the build-up of cholesterol deposits. Other arteries can be blocked in the same way, and may lead to other circulatory problems.

Cholesterol is contained in saturated fatty acids (see below). Although some cholesterol is needed by the body for the formation of certain hormones, any excess may build up in the arteries. Medical evidence suggests that reduction of fat intake would significantly reduce heart disease and that fat should form only about 30 per cent of energy intake.

Dairy products have sometimes been found to have other adverse effects. Cheese and other dairy foods are mucus-forming in some people, leading to sinus problems and migraine. Other people are allergic to milk protein, resulting in breathing problems, catarrh or eczema. Some are allergic to milk sugar (lactose), resulting in cramps and diarrhea.

Saturated and unsaturated fatty acids

Fats can be divided into three basic types: saturated, monounsaturated and polyunsaturated. Saturated fatty acids (or saturated fats) are mainly found in food from animal sources: fullfat milk, cheese, eggs, cream and butter. Cholesterol is contained in these saturated fatty acids.

Unsaturated fatty acids are of two types, monounsaturated and polyunsaturated. These are found mainly in liquid vegetable oils and soft margarines. Although they add to the daily fat intake, they contain no cholesterol.

Polyunsaturated fatty acids contain the essential acids linoleic acid and linolenic acid. Linoleic acid is of particular importance as it enables the body to synthesize other fatty acids from food. It is also thought actually to help lower the level of cholesterol in the blood. It is sometimes recommended therefore that saturated fat is eaten in conjunction with twice its amount of polyunsaturated fat.

Cutting down

There is no need to cut out dairy products altogether from your diet. If you are aware of the need to keep your intake down, and are aware of their presence in many processed foods (look at the labels), there are nutritional benefits to be gained from including some dairy products in your diet. However, because of all the medical information, many people are choosing to decrease their consumption of dairy products and/or look for substitutes.

Most dairy products have lowfat versions, such as lowfat or skim milk, lowfat cream cheese and lowfat cheese. Yogurt and smetana (a lowfat version of sour cream) can be used instead of fullfat cream in cooking and desserts.

There are also dairy alternatives made from plant or vegetable sources, which contain less saturated fat. Monounsaturated or polyunsaturated fatty acids are found in many vegetable oils, also used in the manufacture of margarines. However, it should be remembered that the process of hydrogenation, which is used to solidify fats and oils to make hard margarine, actually converts unsaturated fats into saturated fats.

Alternatives

As well as the lowfat substitutes such as lowfat milk, yogurt and lowfat cream cheese mentioned above, there are a number of non-dairy products which can be used successfully as dairy substitutes. Soy milk, included in this section because of its usage, is a nutritious and tasty cholesterol-free substitute for cow's milk, although it has a distinctive flavor which may seem strong at first. Also a product of the soybean, tofu (see p. 51) can be used in many dishes to replace both cheese and eggs. It comes in both a firm and soft form, the former being similar to cheese in consistency. Soft tofu can be beaten into ingredients as a binding agent instead of eggs, and it is often used in non-dairy cheesecakes instead of cream cheese. Another nondairy binding agent is tahini (see p. 50), which can be beaten into dishes mixed in a little water.

Smoked tofu and tempeh, another soybean product (see p. 51) have a stronger flavor and can be used instead of strong cheeses. Vegetable oils (see p. 49) can be used for cooking instead of butter or margarine.

Storage

Most dairy products and substitutes should be kept in the refrigerator. Pasteurized milk will keep for about 4-5 days; cream will keep for 2-3 days, but should be covered or it will harden. Margarines and butter keep well, and eggs will keep for 3-4 weeks in a cool place or the refrigerator. To store cheese, keep wrapped in foil or wax paper in a cool place or in a cheese compartment of the refrigerator (the salad box is also ideal). Take out the cheese and stand at room temperature for about 1 hour before serving.

DAIRY PRODUCE Per 4 oz	Water	Protein	Fat	Carbohydrate	Fiber	Vitamin A	Vitamin B1	Vitamin B2	Vitamin B3	Vitamin B6	Vitamin B12	Vitamin C	Vitamin D	Vitamin E	Folic acid	Iron	Calcium	Magnesium	Sodium	Potassium	Phosphorus	Zinc
	g	g	g	g	g	µg	mg	mg	mg	mg	µg	mg	µg	mg	µg	mg	mg	mg	mg	mg	mg	mg
Recommended daily allowance	N	80M 60W	N	N	25-30	750	1.5	1.5	18	1.5	3	30	2.5	8	200	12	500	250	2500	2500	500	15
Butter, salted	15	0.4	82	Tr	0	470	Tr	Tr	Tr	Tr	Tr	Tr	0.76	2	Tr	0.2	15	2	870	15	24	0.15
Buttermilk	N	3.5	0.08	4.8	0	4	0.04	0.18	0.08	0.4	0.22	0.2	N	N	N	0.04	120	N	128	136	92	N
Cheese – Cheddar	37	26	33.5	Tr	0	205	0.04	0.5	0.1	0.08	1.5	0	0.26	0.8	20	0.4	800	25	610	120	520	**4**
– cottage	79	13.6	4	1.4	0	18	0.02	0.19	0.08	0.01	0.5	0	0.02	N	9	0.1	60	6	450	54	140	0.47
– cream	46	3.1	47.4	Tr	0	220	0.02	0.14	0.08	0.01	0.3	0	0.03	1	5	0.1	98	10	300	160	100	0.5
– Edam	44	24.4	22.9	Tr	0	135	0.04	0.4	0.06	0.08	1.4	0	0.18	0.8	20	0.2	740	28	980	160	520	**4**
– Feta	56	16.8	19.9	Tr	0	20	0.03	0.11	0.2	N	1.4	0	Tr	N	15	0.2	384	20	**1260**	70	N	1.1
– Parmesan	28	**35.1**	29.7	Tr	0	195	0.02	0.5	0.3	0.1	1.5	0	0.27	0.9	20	0.4	**1220**	50	760	150	**770**	**4**
– Stilton	28	25.6	40	Tr	0	230	0.07	0.3	N	N	N	0	0.31	1	N	0.5	360.	27	1150	160	300	N
Cow's milk – skim	**91**	3.4	0.1	5	0	Tr	0.04	0.2	0.08	0.04	0.3	1.6	Tr	Tr	5	0.05	130	12	52	150	100	0.36
– fullfat	88	3.3	3.8	4.7	0	18	0.04	0.19	0.08	0.04	0.3	1.5	0.02	0.09	5	0.05	120	12	50	150	95	0.35
Cream – heavy	49	1.5	48.2	2	0	220	0.02	0.08	0.04	0.02	0.1	0.8	0.28	1	2	0.2	50	4	27	79	21	0.17
– light	72	2.4	21.2	3.2	0	98	0.03	0.12	0.07	0.03	0.2	1.2	0.12	0.4	4	0.3	79	6	42	120	44	0.26
Duck eggs	71	13.2	14.2	0.7	0	185	0.16	0.4	3.2	N	4.5	0	N	N	17	3.6	64	N	191	**258**	N	0.8
Goat's milk	87	3.3	4.5	4.6	0	0	0.04	0.15	0.19	0.04	Tr	1.5	0.06	N	1	0.04	130	20	40	180	110	0.3
Hen eggs – whites	88	9	Tr	Tr	0	0	0	0.43	2.7	Tr	0.1	0	0	0	1	0.1	5	11	190	150	33	0.03
– whole	75	12.3	10.9	Tr	0	Tr	0.09	0.47	3.7	**0.11**	1.7	0	1.75	1.6	2.5	2	52	12	140	140	220	1.5
– yolks	51	16.1	30.5	Tr	0	Tr	**0.3**	**0.54**	**4.8**	0.3	**4.9**	0	**5**	**4.6**	**52**	**6.1**	130	15	50	120	**500**	3.6
Margarine	16	0.7	**92**	1	0	**900**	0	0	0	Tr	Tr	0	7.94	8	Tr	0	23	N	1100	26	18	N
Sour cream	N	2.7	18	**32**	0	720	0.04	0.14	0.08	N	N	N	N	N	N	N	96	N	38	52	72	N
Soy milk	N	3.6	1.32	2	0	36	0.03	0.03	0.36	N	0	0	N	N	N	0.32	N	N	N	N	44	N
Yogurt	86	5	1	6.2	0	5	0.05	0.26	0.12	0.04	Tr	0.4	Tr	0.03	2	0.09	180	17	76	240	140	0.6

KEY
All whole foods are uncooked unless otherwise stated. Some whole foods may not be included in the chart, as there is currently no nutritional data available.
g: grams **mg:** milligrams **µg:** micrograms **N:** no available data **Tr:** trace **M:** adult men **W:** adult women.   The recommended daily allowances are averages and vary depending on age, occupation and metabolism.   Figures in bold type indicate the whole food with the highest level of nutrient.

Butter

Butter is made by separating the cream from fullfat milk and churning it until it coagulates. Like milk, it contains calcium, milk protein, milk sugar and minerals. Its fat content is 80 per cent, and it is twice as high in saturated fatty acids and cholesterol as milk. Most commercially produced butters have added salt and coloring; salt as a preservative to increase shelf life and coloring to make them more appealing to the eye. Buy unsalted (sweet) and untreated butters if possible.

Butter is usually used as a spread, but it has a wide range of culinary uses. It is used for sautéeing, sauces, bakes, flavored butters and many other dishes.
Recipe: Apple, Soy & Almond Pudding (see p. 120).

Buttermilk

Buttermilk was originally the sour residue left over from making butter, but most commercial buttermilk is now made from pasteurized lowfat milk with an added culture of bacteria to sour and thicken it. Easily digestible, buttermilk contains the protein and minerals of fullfat milk but hardly any of the fat. However, it also has a lower vitamin A content than fullfat milk.

Use buttermilk as a drink on its own, in baking and confectionery.

Cheese

Cheese is extremely nutritious, being rich in protein, fats, vitamins A and B, iron, calcium, phosphorus, potassium and sodium. However, cheese made from fullfat milk can be mucus-forming and is high in cholesterol, and so should be eaten in moderation or substituted with lowfat cheese when possible.

There are many types of cheese: natural, soft, semihard, hard, blue and smoked. Natural cheeses are made by coagulating milk and then separating the solid curds from the watery whey. The unripened curd is eaten shortly after it is made. These cheeses include ricotta, cottage cheese, Mozzarella, cream cheese, quark, fromage blanc and curd cheese. They have a high moisture content and are comparatively low in fat. Soft cheeses have been briefly ripened, and so are slightly firmer but still spreadable. They have a high moisture and fat content, though lower than hard cheese, and include such cheeses as Brie, Camembert and Feta.

Semihard and hard cheeses have been matured (aged) for a long time, often for many months, for their flavors to develop. These cheeses have a low moisture content and may contain up to 50 per cent fat. They include such cheeses as Cheddar and Parmesan.

Some cheeses contain an added substance called rennet, which is an enzyme found in calves' stomachs used to curdle and set the milk. Obviously, these cheeses are not acceptable to some vegetarians, but in recent years non-animal rennet has appeared and a wide range of vegetarian cheese is now available in most whole food shops.

Cheese can be used in soups, soufflés, sandwiches, salads, savory bakes and sweet dishes. Use according to type and requirement. Hard cheeses, such as Cheddar, are good for sauces or melting on toast; soft cheeses, such as Mozzarella and Gruyère, are good for fondues; natural cheeses such as curd or cream are good in cheesecakes. Feta, Roquefort and other crumbly cheeses can be used in salads.
Recipe: Stuffed Baked Mushrooms (see p. 86).

Cow's milk

Milk is an extremely nutritious food, full of easily assimilated animal protein, calcium, iron and some B vitamins. For those wishing to pursue a meatless diet, milk is particularly useful because it contains vitamin B_{12}.

However, fullfat milk can be mucus-forming and is high in saturated fatty acids (and therefore cholesterol), which can lead to thickening of the arteries and heart disease. It may also contain hormones and traces of spray chemicals ingested by the cows.

A variety of lowfat and skim milks are now available where all or most of the fat and cream have been removed.

Whereas fullfat milk contains not less than 3.25% milkfat, lowfat milk contains 0.5, 1, 1.5 or 2% milkfat. However, it should be remembered skim milk loses its fat-soluble vitamins, namely A, D and E. Fortified skim milk is available which has these important vitamins added.

Instant non-dairy dry milk is reconstituted with water.

Goat's milk is sometimes used by people allergic to cow's milk. It does contain more phosphorus, calcium and magnesium than cow's milk, but it is just as high in fats.
Recipe: Apricot & Orange Sago Cream (see p. 121).

Cream

As milk cools after milking, the fat rises to the surface. This is creamed off and either used as cream or churned to make butter.

Cream is extremely high in saturated fatty acids, although the fat content will vary depending on the type of cream. Light cream contains a minimum of 18 per cent fat; heavy whipping cream contains at least 36% milkfat. Half-and-half is a combination of cream and milk, which contains at least 10.5% milkfat.

Cream is usually used in sauces, soups, desserts and puddings. It can be substituted with smetana or Greek-style yogurt.
Recipe: Baked Bananas with Yogurt Sauce (see p. 121).

Eggs

Eggs are extremely nutritious, containing all the essential amino acids needed to form a complete protein (see p. 8), as well as iron, calcium, phosphorus, potassium and some B, E and K vitamins. However, eggs do have a very high cholesterol content, which in excess can lead to thickening of the arteries and heart disease. As a rough guide, 4 eggs per week is probably enough for the body to handle, although small children, invalids and older people may eat a few more.

Many vegetarians will only eat free-range eggs because of the cruelty of battery farming. Although nutritionally they are the same, the taste of free-range eggs is generally thought to be better. There is no difference between white and brown eggs, since the shell color relates only to the breed of hen. Duck eggs are slightly larger and richer than hen's eggs, and should be eaten very fresh if used.

Eggs are an extremely versatile food. They can be boiled, scrambled, poached, coddled, fried or made into omelets. Added to other ingredients, they act as a raising or setting agent for cakes, sauces, custards, soufflés, mousses or pastries. They can bind croquettes and burgers and can be used as a glaze for breads and pastries.

Egg yolks on their own add a rich creamy flavor to certain dishes and egg whites whipped separately add a delicious lightness to many desserts.
Recipe: Baked Eggs with Coriander (see p. 81).

Ghee

There are two types of ghee, real ghee made from clarified butter and vegetable ghee made from hydrogenated vegetable oils.

To make your own real ghee, simply melt butter and filter through cheesecloth. Vegetable ghee is made from coconut, sesame, peanut, or mustard oils. Because vegetable ghee is hydrogenated it is not much lower in cholesterol than ghee made from clarified butter. Both, however, are free from additives.

Unlike butter, ghee can be heated to a high temperature without burning, making it suitable for frying and cooking. It will leave food crisp, dry and light.
Recipe: Fresh Coriander Dhal (see p. 105).

Margarine

The commercial production of margarine as a cheap alternative to butter began in the 1870s. It was invented by a French chemist, Monsieur Mèga-Mouriés, and its popularity soon spread throughout Europe and America.

Margarines range from those containing significant amounts of animal fats, whey and other dairy products to pure varieties using only vegetable fats and oils. The former, like butter and lard, contain saturated fats and therefore cholesterol. The latter are high in polyunsaturated fatty acids and low in cholesterol. They contain linoleic acid, essential for the synthesis of fats from other fat-containing food in the body.

When buying margarine, look for the words "made from pure vegetable oils" (not just "oils and fats"), and buy unhydrogenated brands. Hydrogenation turns polyunsaturated fatty acids into saturated fatty acids in order to harden the product, so you may as well eat butter as far as cholesterol is concerned. Usually, the softer the margarine, the higher the polyunsaturated fat content.

Watch out also for additives in margarine, such as flavoring agents, yellow food pigments, emulsifiers, preservatives and salt. Margarine contains about 80% fat and 20% water; it is fortified with vitamin A and sometimes D.

Use margarine as you would use butter: for sauces, savories, desserts, cakes, adding to cooked vegetables and for spreading on bread.

Smetana

Smetana is made from a mixture of skimmed milk and light cream, and can be used as a lowfat substitute for cream or sour cream. Two types of smetana are available, smetana and creamed smetana.

Solid vegetable fat

This is the vegetarian alternative to lard or suet. It is made from hydrogenated vegetable oils, which does mean that it contains saturated fatty acids and therefore cholesterol.

Sour cream

Sour cream is cream which has been inoculated with a lactic acid culture. It is used in desserts, sauces, dressings and some savory dishes. For a lowfat alternative, use smetana or a mixture of cream and plain yogurt.

Soy milk

Soy milk looks very similar to cow's milk and has a slightly sweet, nutty flavor and creamy texture. Soy milk is made by soaking soybeans until they are thoroughly saturated and then grinding them up with boiling water. The liquid is strained off and heated before refrigeration.

Compared with cow's milk, soy milk has more protein, much more lecithin, less fats, no carbohydrates, no vitamin B_{12} and less calcium. It is easily digested and is useful for those allergic to cow's milk.

Some commercial soy milks taste rather bitter, but if you do not like the taste of one brand, try another because they all differ slightly. Some brands may contain added sugar, so check first.

Soy milk can be drunk on its own or used in soups, sauces, milk shakes, desserts and cakes.
Recipe: Strawberry Mousse (see p. 130).

Yogurt

Yogurt, a fermented milk product, has grown in popularity in the West over the past few years. In the Middle East, Far East and eastern Europe, the nutritional and medicinal properties of yogurt have been known for hundreds of years.

Nutritionally, yogurt is similar to milk, containing protein, calcium, iron and some A and B vitamins, including a little vitamin B_{12}. Yogurt bacteria breaks down the milk sugar to produce a lactic acid, which means that it is easier to digest than cow's milk and has a beneficial effect on the digestive system.

Commercial yogurts often contain additives, preservatives and coloring agents, so check first. Greek-style yogurt is strained through cheesecloth, and has a creamy, sweet taste. It is an excellent substitute for cream in most dishes.

Yogurt can be made from any milk, but goat's milk yogurt is even more digestible than cow's milk yogurt as it more closely resembles human milk. Eat yogurt on its own, plain or flavored, or use in dressings, soups, savory dishes and desserts.
Recipe: Cheesecake (see p. 122).

Home-made yogurt
Yogurt is simple, delicious and economical to make at home. There are many commercial yogurt-makers on the market but a wide-necked thermos flask will give as good a result. Fresh cow's or goat's milk can be used.

First, take $2\frac{1}{2}$ cups fresh milk and heat in a saucepan until just below boiling point. This is necessary because dairy herds are often given antibiotics, which then appear in the milk. These antibiotics can fight the yogurt bacteria and need to be killed by heating.

Let the milk cool until it is just above body temperature (it should feel just warm to the fingers). Mix in a large tablespoon of natural live yogurt and pour into a wide-necked flask. Secure the lid and leave for 12 hours. Then, refrigerate for a few hours and use as desired. Reserve a large spoonful of yogurt for the next batch.

NATURALLY PROCESSED PRODUCTS

OILS
Corn oil
Olive oil ☐
Peanut oil
Safflower oil ☐
Sesame oil ☐
Soy oil ☐
Sunflower oil
Walnut and almond oils
SAVORY PRODUCTS
Brewer's yeast ☐
Gomashio ☐
Kuzu

Miso ☐
Nut butters
Salt
Seitan
Tahini ☐
Tamari and shoyu ☐
Tempeh
Tofu ☐
Umeboshi plums ☐
Vegetable bouillon cubes ☐
Vinegars
Yeast extracts ☐

SWEET PRODUCTS
Carob powder ☐
Essences ☐
Fruit concentrates ☐
Halva
Honey ☐
Malt extract ☐
Maple syrup
Mirin
Molasses ☐
Sugar ☐
Sugar-free jams ☐

☐ Pictured opposite page 48

This section includes a range of familiar and less well known foods and flavorings which form part of the whole food diet. Naturally processed means that the products are obtained from whole foods without the use of harmful chemicals or additives and, as far as possible, retaining the full nutritional value of the original foods.

Oils

Unrefined cold pressed oils are useful in a whole food diet because they provide energy, contain some vitamins and minerals and are high in monounsaturated or polyunsaturated fatty acids. They can be used in cooking to replace butter and margarines, which are high in saturated fatty acids and therefore cholesterol.

Savory products

The products included in this section include the highly nutritious soybean products (tofu, tempeh, miso, tamari and shoyu) and yeast products (brewer's yeast and yeast extract). The protein, minerals and vitamins which these contain make them valuable additions to a whole food diet, and tofu can be used as a substitute for cheese and eggs if you are on a vegan

NATURALLY PROCESSED PRODUCTS Per 4 oz	Water	Protein	Fat	Carbohydrate	Fiber	Vitamin A	Vitamin B₁	Vitamin B₂	Vitamin B₃	Vitamin B₆	Vitamin B₁₂	Vitamin C	Vitamin D	Vitamin E	Folic acid	Iron	Calcium	Magnesium	Sodium	Potassium	Phosphorus	Zinc
	g	g	g	g	g	µg	mg	mg	mg	mg	µg	mg	µg	mg	µg	mg	mg	mg	mg	mg	mg	mg
Recommended daily allowance	N	80M 60W	N	N	25-30	750	1.5	1.5	18	1.5	3	30	2.5	8	200	12	500	250	2500	2500	500	15
Brewer's yeast	N	40.3	1.3	39	1.3	**0.1**	**15.6**	**4.42**	**39**	**2.6**	0	**0.1**	N	0	**83**	**18.2**	221	**234**	130	1950	**1820**	**5.2**
Carob powder	N	4.8	1.5	84	**8.1**	N	N	N	N	N	0	N	N	N	N	N	360	N	N	N	84	N
Honey – combs	20.2	0.6	N	74.4	N	0	Tr	0.05	0.2	N	0	Tr	0	N	N	0.2	8	2	7	35	32	N
– jars	23	0.4	N	76.4	N	0	Tr	0.05	0.2	N	N	Tr	0	N	N	0.4	5	2	11	51	17	N
Kuzu	17	0.2	0.1	82.1	0	0	0	0	0	N	N	0	N	N	N	2	17	N	2	N	10	N
Malt extract	N	6.8	N	100	Tr	N	0.4	0.52	11.2	N	0	N	N	N	N	10	56	N	92	260	372	N
Maple syrup	8	N	N	70	N	N	N	N	N	N	0	N	N	N	N	1.27	110	N	11	184	7	N
Miso – hacho	48	16.8	5.9	15.8	2.2	0	0.04	0.12	1.2	N	N	N	N	N	N	6.5	140	N	3800	N	240	N
– mugi	50	14	5	16.2	1.9	·0	0.03	0.1	1.5	N	N	N	N	N	N	4	115	N	4	N	190	N
– natto	63	16.9	7.4	11.5	3.2	0	0.07	0.5	1.1	N	N	N	N	N	N	3.7	103	N	N	249	182	N
Molasses – blackstrap	24	N	N	60	N	N	0.12	0.21	2.2	0.22	0	N	N	N	N	16.1	**733.3**	N	106.7	**2927**	93.3	N
Nut butter – peanut	N	36	**65**	22	2.5	N	0.17	0.17	20	0.43	0	0	0	**4.7**	53	2.6	80	180	800	850	500	3
Salt – block	0.2	0	0	0	0	0	0	0	0	0	0	0	0	0	0	0.3	230	140	38700	Tr	Tr	N
– table	Tr	0	0	0	0	0	0	0	0	0	0	0	0	0	0	0.2	29	290	**38850**	Tr	8	N
Seitan	N	**89**	5.4	N	N	0	N	N	2.4	N	0	N	N	N	N	0.6	N	N	N	N	N	N
Sugar – light brown	Tr	0.5	0	**104.5**	0	0	Tr	Tr	Tr	Tr	0	0	0	0	Tr	0.9	53	15	14	89	20	N
– white	Tr	Tr	0	105	0	0	0	0	0	0	0	0	0	0	0	Tr	2	Tr	Tr	2	Tr	N
Tamari and shoyu	63	5.6	1.3	9.5	0	0	0.02	0.25	0.4	N	0	0	N	N	N	4.8	82	N	7325	366	104	N
Tofu	85	7.4	4.2	2.4	0.1	0	0.06	0.03	0.1	N	N	0	N	N	N	1.9	128	N	7	42	128	N
Umeboshi plums	70	0.3	0.8	3.4	0.3	0	0.06	0.09	0.6	N	N	0	N	N	N	2	6.1	N	9400	N	26	N
Vinegar	**94**	Tr	0	5.9	N	N	N	N	N	N	N	N	N	N	N	9	6	N	1	100	9	N

KEY
All whole foods are uncooked unless otherwise stated. Some whole foods may not be included in the chart, as there is currently no nutritional data available.
g: grams **mg**: milligrams **µg**: micrograms **N**: no available data **Tr**: trace **M**: adult men **W**: adult women. The recommended daily allowances are averages and vary depending on age, occupation and metabolism. Figures in bold type indicate the whole food with the highest level of nutrient.

Seaweeds & Naturally Processed Products (See pp. 43 & 48)

Arame (see p. 43) is quite mild and sweet in flavor.

Dulse (see p. 44) is chewy with a strong salty taste.

Carrageen (see p. 44) is used for gelling.

Kombu (see p. 44) is a strong and salty seaweed.

Wakame (see p. 44) is like kombu, but rather milder.

Hiziki (see p. 44) has a sweet, delicate taste.

Agar-agar (see p. 43) is used as a setting agent.

Nori (see p. 44).

Olive oil (see p. 49) has a distinctive flavor.

Safflower oil (see p. 49) is very nutritious.

Sesame oil (see p. 49) has a slightly nutty taste.

Vegetable bouillon cubes (see p. 51) for flavoring liquids.

Gomashio (see p. 50) is salt and ground sesame seeds.

Tofu (see p. 51) is soy bean curd, rich in protein.

Tamari (see p. 51) is a type of strong soy sauce.

Brewer's yeast (see p. 50).

Yeast extract (see p. 51).

Umeboshi plums (see p. 51) are pickled Japanese plums.

Miso (see p. 50) is made from fermented soybeans.

Molasses (see p. 52) is a strong natural sweetener.

Dark brown sugar (see p. 52) contains some molasses.

Course light brown sugar (see p. 52) is cleaned raw brown sugar.

Tahini (see p. 50) is made from sesame seeds and oil.

Almond extract (see p. 51) is made from bitter almonds.

Pear and apple spread (see fruit concentrates, p. 51).

Raspberry fruit concentrate (see p. 51) for sweetening.

Pure honey (see p. 52).

Malt extract (see p. 52) is a natural sweetener.

Vanilla extract (see p. 51) is a useful flavoring.

Black currant reduced-sugar jelly (see p. 52).

Apple fruit concentrate (see p. 51) for sweetening.

Carob powder (see p. 51) is similar to cocoa in taste.

Herbs (See p. 53)

Bay leaves (see p. 53) are usually available whole, and are popular in broths.

Mint (see p. 54) has a distinctive, fresh taste and pleasant aroma.

Marjoram (see p. 54) is often used in stuffings.

Oregano (see p. 55) is very aromatic and is popular in Italian and tomato dishes.

Dill (see p. 54) is commonly used as a garnish and in Scandinavian dishes.

Parsley (see p. 55) is high in vitamins and minerals.

Coriander leaves (see p. 54) are used in many Eastern savory dishes.

Rosemary (see p. 55) is a very aromatic herb with a strong flavor.

Basil (see p. 53) is often used in tomato-based dishes.

Chervil (see p. 53) has a delicate, spicy taste popular in France.

Thyme (see p. 55) has a subtle, sweet flavor and is good with vegetables.

Chives (see p. 54) are best eaten raw and fresh, and have a mild onion flavor.

Sage (see p. 55) is quite strong in flavor and so should be used sparingly.

Tarragon (see p. 55) is delicious chopped and added to salads and soups.

diet. Salt is also included, but substitutes and alternatives are given if you wish to reduce your sodium intake.

Other savory products described in this section include kuzu, a natural thickener, nut butters, seitan, a highly nutritious form of wheat protein, and pickled plums from Japan.

Sweet products

Sweeteners add to the taste and appeal of many dishes, and are used in baking, sweet dishes, desserts, confectionery and drinks. The most commonly used sweetener is now sugar, but there are many alternative sweeteners available.

VEGETABLE OILS	SATURATED FATTY ACIDS	MONOUNSATURATED FATTY ACIDS	POLYUNSATURATED FATTY ACIDS
Corn oil	Low	Medium	High
Olive oil	Low	High	Low
Peanut oil	Low	High	Medium
Safflower oil	Low	Low	High
Sesame oil	Low	Medium	Medium
Soya oil	Low	Low	High
Sunflower oil	Low	Medium	High
Walnut and almond oils	Low	Medium	High

OILS

Oils are liquid fats extracted from plant or animal substances. There are many types of oil, with differing flavors, colors and uses. A large range of vegetable oils extracted from nuts, seeds and beans are described below.

Methods of oil extraction
The purest, finest oil is obtained by cold pressing. There may be three cold presses, the first being the superior. The first press of olive oil is often called "extra virgin or virgin oil." Cold pressed oils are unrefined and have the best taste and highest nutritional value.

Semirefined oils are usually oils made from secondary pressings under heat, to obtain larger quantities of oil. Nutritionally they are inferior to cold pressed oils.

Refined or "pure" oils have usually been highly processed. Some oil extraction methods may use chemical solvents such as hexane to break down the outer hull of the seed and thus obtain a higher extraction rate. These solvents also deodorize and bleach the oil. Some oils are also heated and treated with antioxidants, which help prevent the oil from becoming rancid. However, this process also converts any polyunsaturated fats into saturated fats. These extraction techniques decrease the nutritional value of the oils.

Storage
Cold pressed oils should be stored in cool, dark places and not bought in huge quantities unless you use them very fast. Once opened, oils may become rancid after a month, except for sesame oil (see below). Oils may go opaque and solidify in the refrigerator, but will quickly liquify if stood at room temperature. Refined oils will keep for longer, about 3 months.

Corn oil

Extracted from corn-on-the-cob, this is a good all-around oil with a mild flavor, suitable for all types of cooking and baking. It is a common ingredient in margarine. Cold pressed corn oil is high in polyunsaturated fatty acids.
Recipe: Mung Bean Casserole (see p. 109).

Olive oil

Olive oil is usually fairly thick with a golden or greenish-brown color and a very distinctive flavor, varying with the country of origin. Extra virgin olive oil is the best, and usually a golden color. Pure olive oil is from the second pressing and is usually a darker green color.

Olive oil is most often used for salad dressings although it can be used for general savory cooking. It is not suitable for deep-frying or for use in cakes and pastries. For optimum nutritional value, combine cold pressed olive oil with cold pressed safflower oil, because olive oil is relatively low in polyunsaturated fatty acids and safflower oil is high.
Recipe: Gazpacho (see p. 76).

Peanut oil

Peanut oil or groundnut oil is a good all-around oil. It has a mild flavor and is excellent for deep-frying as it can be heated to a high temperature without burning. It can be used in all sweet and savory dishes. Peanut oil is fairly low in polyunsaturates, however. It is frequently used in margarine manufacture and for canning purposes.
Recipe: Black Bean Chili (see p. 100).

Safflower oil

Safflower oil is often confused with sunflower oil, but they actually come from different plants belonging to the same botanical family. Cold pressed safflower oil is pale in color with a delicate, but distinctive flavor. It is extremely nutritious, being high in polyunsaturates and containing more linoleic acid than any other oil listed.

Safflower oil is particularly nutritious when combined with olive oil for salad dressings. It can be heated to a high temperature without burning, which makes it suitable for deep-frying and use in other savory dishes, although cold pressed safflower oil is not recommended for puddings, cakes and pastries because of its strong flavor.
Recipe: Brown Rice Salad (see p. 89).

Sesame oil

Sesame oil has a slightly nutty flavor and is made from toasted sesame seeds. There are two types, one rather dark, used in Chinese cooking, and a paler variety which is used in Indian cooking.

Sesame oil contains a substance called sesamol which prevents it from becoming rancid. It is also fairly high in polyunsaturates.

This is a good all-around oil which can be heated to a high temperature without burning, making it suitable for deep-frying. It can be used successfully in cooking most sweet and savory dishes.
Recipe: Smoked Tofu Appetizer (see p. 86).

Soy oil

Soy oil is pale with a very mild flavor and it is recommended for salads and all types of cooking. It keeps well if kept in a cool place, and is high in polyunsaturates. Soy oil is used for the majority of the cooking at the Neal's Yard Bakery.
Recipe: Basic Whole Wheat Sponge Cake (see p. 136).

Sunflower oil

Cold-pressed sunflower oil has a pale yellow color and a delicate flavor. It is a good substitute for safflower oil, being high in linoleic acid and monounsaturates. It is an all-around oil which can be used for salad dressings, frying and other savory uses, desserts and baking. Sunflower oil is often used in the manufacture of margarine.
Recipe: Mayonnaise (see p. 96).

Walnut and almond oils

These can occasionally be found in whole food stores. They each have a very distinctive, nutty flavor and are best used only in uncooked dressings. Both are high in polyunsaturates, walnut oil being the higher. Walnut oil is also rich in iodine.
Recipe: Corn & Mushroom Salad (see p. 95).

SAVORY PRODUCTS

Brewer's yeast
(Nutritional yeast)

Brewer's yeast is a by-product in the production of beers and spirits. It is dry and extremely nutritious, being high in protein and minerals, especially iron, potassium and phosphorus. It is also extremely rich in B vitamins, which is important as most foods are only high in one particular B vitamin. Brewer's yeast doesn't have any levening properties, so it is added to foods for its nutritional value.

Brewer's yeast may be sprinkled over soups and savory dishes, enjoyed on its own or used in drinks. Start using brewer's yeast in moderation, for example about $\frac{1}{2}$ tsp per day, and gradually build up to $\frac{1}{2}$-1 tbsp per day.
Recipe: Pep-Up Drink (see p. 61).

Gomashio
(Sesame salt)

Gomashio is made by grinding roasted sesame seeds very finely and adding sea salt, usually in a ratio of 10 parts sesame seeds to 1 part salt. It is widely used in Japan for sprinkling on top of food in preference to salt, and is useful for those wishing to reduce their salt intake. Gomashio has a light, nutty flavor and is a delicious addition to any savory dish.
Recipe: Seitan with Hiziki (see p. 113).

Kuzu

Kuzu comes from the roots of a plant which grows in the mountains of Japan. The deep roots are soaked in cold running water until only the starchy white "kuzu" remains. This is ground into a powder. In Japan, kuzu is used for preventing colds, strengthening weak constitutions, relaxing muscles and toning up the digestive system.

Kuzu can be used just as cornstarch or arrowroot: for thickening soups, sauces and gravies, or as a glaze for desserts.
Recipe: Cherry Pie
(see p. 123).

Miso

Miso is made by fermenting soybeans, rice, barley or wheat under pressure for 1-2 years, gradually adding sea salt until a thick paste has formed. It is extremely nutritious, being rich in complete protein (see p. 8), minerals and some B vitamins.

Hacho miso is made from soybeans, **genmai miso** from soybeans and brown rice, **mugi miso** from soybeans and barley, and **natto miso** from soybeans, barley, ginger and seaweed. Hacho and natto miso contain the most protein, although hacho is extremely high in sodium. All contain a fair amount of calcium. Genmai miso is lightest in color and contains slightly less salt than the others.

Use miso as a broth for soups and sauces, as a savory spread or in stews and casseroles as a flavoring. Because it contains living bacteria and enzymes from the fermentation, which are easily destroyed by boiling, miso is generally added at the end of cooking.
Recipe: Lettuce, Cucumber & Miso Soup (see p. 76).

Nut butters

Nut butters are blended mixtures of whole shelled nuts and oil, and have both savory and sweet uses. Peanut butter is probably the most well known, but filbert and cashew nut butters (sometimes called creams) are also available. Nutritious and tasty, nut butters can easily be made at home.

Put about $\frac{1}{2}$ pound shelled peanuts, filberts or cashew nuts in a blender, add 1 tbsp of vegetable, peanut or sesame oil and blend to a paste. The mixture can be blended until chunky or smooth, depending on your preference.

If buying nut butters or creams, check that they are not hydrogenated. This process prevents rancidity but also turns monounsaturated and polyunsaturated fatty acids into saturated fatty acids (see p. 45). Commercial nut butters also often contain added sugar, salt, and preservatives.

Use nut butters on toast and in sandwiches, or add to sweet and savory dishes, breads, sauces, cakes and cookies.
Recipe: Gado-Gado (see p. 106).

Salt
(Sodium chloride)

Salt is the mineral sodium chloride, either evaporated from the sea or mined from primeval sea deposits in the land. The three basic types of salt are described below.

Sodium, together with potassium, is essential for the healthy functioning of the human body. The kidneys monitor the amount of sodium in the blood and excrete or retain liquid as necessary to maintain the correct amount. However, we only need about 4 grams of salt a day and too much salt can be damaging. Excess salt will increase the volume of blood in the vessels and this overloading of the circulatory system causes the tiny arteries to constrict, in order to prevent themselves from being damaged. This leads to increased pressure in the larger vessels and hypertension or high blood pressure can occur, sometimes resulting in strokes and heart disease.

Many ethnic groups with a low sodium intake have no incidence of hypertension, whereas those with a high sodium intake, such as Japan, have a high incidence of hypertension. There are certain situations when additional salt in the diet is appropriate. Excessive sweating, through physical exertion or ill health, causes sodium to be lost through the urine and skin and pregnant women should also take rather more salt than usually necessary. However, as a general rule it is clear that our sodium intake is too high and should be reduced where possible.

All the salt we need can be obtained from fresh foods, but salt and other sodium-based additives are frequently added to a huge range of convenience foods, from salted snacks to sweet jellies and marmalades. The habit of heavily salting food at the table is also unnecessary, but our taste buds have become so accustomed to salt in food that we often find it difficult to appreciate flavors without it.

Reducing salt intake is only a matter of practice, however, and there are a number of low-salt flavorings which can be used instead. Gomashio, miso, tamari and shoyu are nutritious and although they contain salt, less is used. Salt substitutes, often consisting of potassium salt or a mixture of sodium and potassium salt, are also available for those wishing to cut down on sodium.

Table salt

Commercial table salt is made by pumping water into underground mines and vacuum-drying it to evaporate the water and thus obtain salt. This salt is then very finely ground and additives such as starch or phosphate of lime to prevent caking may be added. This processing removes all the trace elements.

Rock salt

Veins of salt from prehistoric seas are found deep in the ground, sandwiched between layers of ancient rock. This is rock salt, sold in varying degrees of coarseness. Refined rock salt is often called kitchen, lump or block salt, and contains no additives.

Sea salt (Kosher salt)

Sea or bay salt is formed by the evaporation of water from salt pans. Because it is from sea water it contains iodine, not found in land-mined salts. Usually sold in crystals, sea salt is thought by many to have the best flavor. Atlantic sun-dried sea salt is also considered superior to Mediterranean sea salt.

Iodized salt

Iodized salt is land-mined salt to which iodine has been added. Some leading food experts believe this is preferable to sea salt because of the increasing pollution of the seas.

Seitan

Seitan is wheat gluten, the sticky strands of protein contained in the starchy part of the kernel. It is obtained by first mixing wheat flour (any type) with water until a soft dough is formed. This is then kneaded to allow the strands of gluten to form. The dough is then washed under running water until only the shiny white gluten remains.

Seitan is very high in protein. It can be bought at most whole food stores and is generally a brown or beige color. This is because it is marinated with tamari, seaweed and ginger before packaging to make it more appetizing.

Use seitan in soups, pâtés or stews. It is especially good with grain and bean dishes. Chop into bite-sized pieces, or slice finely as required.
Recipe: Seitan with Hiziki (see p. 113).

Tahini

Tahini is a thick creamy paste made from finely ground sesame seeds and sesame oil. It has been popular in the Middle East for many hundreds of years and both dark and light tahinis are available. The dark variety is made from unhulled sesame seeds and has a slightly bitter flavor, but it is more nutritious than the light variety which is made from hulled sesame seeds.

Tahini can be used in sauces, pâtés or desserts, eaten with vegetables, beans or grains; or simply spread on bread for a delicious and nutritious snack. It can also be used as a

substitute for eggs if a binding agent is required. Use 2 tsp tahini in a little water for each egg used.
Recipe: Apple & Butter Bean Pâté (see p. 80).

Tamari and shoyu

These liquids are naturally fermented soy sauces, produced in the manufacture of miso. Japanese in origin, they are rich in protein, minerals, especially sodium, and some vitamins. They also improve circulation, aid digestion and promote the growth of healthy bacteria in the intestines.

Tamari has a stronger flavor than shoyu, and because it is only made from soybeans, salt and water, it is gluten-free. Shoyu is made from soybeans, wheat, salt and water and is less concentrated than tamari. Neither should contain any artificial additives. Beware, however, of some brands of manufactured soy sauce which contain caramel, artificial flavoring and refined salt.

Tamari and shoyu are delicious sprinkled over steamed vegetables, grains or beans. They can also be used in cooked savory dishes, as bases for marinades, or added to sauces and salad dressings.
Recipe: Carrot & Orange Soup (see p. 73).

Tempeh

Tempeh is another fermented soybean product. Soaked and boiled soybeans are treated with a fungus, wrapped in banana leaves and then left to ferment. It sounds unsavory but tempeh has a rich, cheese-like flavor and is a strong natural antibiotic.

Tempeh is usually cut into thin slices or cubes, shallow-fried in oil and eaten dipped in tamari flavored with grated ginger root and chopped garlic.
Recipe: Fried Tempeh with Orange Sesame Sauce (see p. 106).

Tofu
(Bean curd)

Tofu is soybean curd. It is made by crushing soaked and cooked soybeans into a smooth paste and adding a curdling or setting agent, usually nigari (which mainly consists of calcium sulphate). It is made in wooden presses and once set must be kept in clean water, (changed daily), and eaten within a week.

Tofu, like soy milk, is extremely nutritious, containing protein, iron, calcium and B vitamins. It also contains unsaturated fatty acids and is free from cholesterol. It is usually available in three forms, silken, soft and firm. Silken tofu has been lightly pressed, and is used for blending into other ingredients. Soft tofu is slightly firmer and firm tofu has been heavily pressed. Firm tofu has a consistency similar to cheese. Smoked tofu is also available and has a strong smoky flavor.

Tofu has a bland, subtle flavor and is extremely versatile. It can be used in sweet and savory dishes, dips and spreads, or can be eaten on its own with a sauce or marinade. It retains its setting property when cooked, so makes a perfect substitute for eggs when making cheesecakes.
Recipe: Marinated Tofu (see p. 84).

Umeboshi plums

These are salty pickled plums from Japan. They are usually pickled for at least two years before eating. Their sharp pungent flavor is due to the presence of lactic acid, produced by the microorganisms. This acid will help remove unwanted bacteria from the alimentary canal in the body and aids digestion.

Umeboshi plums can be cooked with grains, added to savory dishes or simply eaten on their own after a meal to help digestion.
Recipe: Seaweed Rolls (see p. 113).

Vegetable bouillon cubes

These are the vegetarian answer to meat bouillon cubes. They contain vegetable oils or fats, yeast extract, vegetable protein, starch, dehydrated vegetables, lactose, spices and salt. Vegetable concentrates are similar, but are solid in soft paste form.

Some brands can be extremely salty, although salt-free cubes are available in some stores. If you follow a vegan diet, check for the addition of lactose or milk sugar, which you may not want to include in your diet.

Vegetable cubes can be added to soups and savory dishes in place of water or broth to give extra flavor. Vegetable concentrates can be used in broths, hot drinks or for spreading on toast.
Recipe: Carrot & Rice Soup (see p. 73).

Vinegars

Vinegars are a neat solution of acetic acid produced by the fermentation and oxidation of natural carbohydrates. They are usually obtained from the fermentation of hard cider, wine and malt alcohols, hence the different cider, wine and malt vinegars. Wine vinegar is rather stronger than the other vinegars, and can be red or white depending on the color of the grape used in fermentation. A popular grain vinegar is brown rice vinegar, used widely in the Far East.

The vinegars often reflect the major raw product in each country of origin. If you wish, use rice vinegar in Oriental recipes, malt vinegar in traditional English recipes, wine vinegar in Mediterranean recipes and cider vinegar in American recipes.

Flavored vinegars are also available, with added herbs or spices such as tarragon, dill, rosemary, chili or peppercorns.

Use vinegars in salad dressings, sauces, sweet and sour dishes and dips. They are an essential ingredient in chutneys and pickles because of their preservative properties.
Recipe: Leeks Vinaigrette (see p. 84).

Yeast extracts

Yeast extracts are dark brown and are a mixture of brewer's yeast (see above) and salt. They have the same protein, minerals and vitamins as brewer's yeast with the addition of trace elements from the salt. They are therefore very nutritious but high in sodium, so should be used in moderation.

Yeast extracts are delicious spread on bread and toast, or they can be added to soups, broths and savory dishes as a flavoring.
Recipe: Millet Casserole (see p. 108).

SWEET PRODUCTS
Carob powder

Carob powder or flour is ground from carob beans, which are contained in the large pods of the Mediterranean carob tree.

The taste of carob is fairly similar to that of cocoa powder, and it can be used instead of cocoa or chocolate in recipes. Unlike cocoa and chocolate, carob has no caffeine, has a lower fat content and provides some calcium and phosphorus.

Carob can be used to flavor cakes, cookies, puddings and candies. Use sparingly as it is much sweeter than cocoa powder.
Recipe: Carob & Sunflower Mousse (see p. 122).

Extracts

These are highly concentrated extracts of fruit, nuts and plants. They are extracted by steam distillation or by maceration in water and alcohol. Extracts most commonly used for flavoring are vanilla, almond, orange blossom, rose, pear, peppermint and coffee.

Pure extracts are available at most whole food stores. Take care to buy a pure extract and not one containing preservatives, artificial colors or flavorings.

Extracts are very concentrated so only use 1 or 2 drops to flavor cakes, pastries, cookies, custards and drinks.
Recipe: Macaroon Cake (see p. 143).

Fruit concentrates

To make fruit concentrate, fresh fruit is first crushed to make fruit juice, which is concentrated at a low temperature to retain its flavor and nutritional value. A centrifugal process is then used to separate the juice from the flesh.

More and more natural fruit concentrates are now appearing on the market, the most common being apple concentrate. Other fruit concentrates available are cherry, black currant, pear and raspberry. All these are in fact mixed with some apple concentrate, but it does not interfere with their flavors. They are available in liquid form or in a highly concentrated spread, the most common being pear and apple spread.

Fruit concentrates are free from preservatives, coloring and artificial flavorings and will keep in a cool dark place or refrigerator.

Use as a sweetening agent in cakes, puddings, bread, cookies, salad dressings and popsicles or use simply as a refreshing drink diluted with filtered water. Fruit concentrates are very strong, so use in small amounts.
Recipe: Apple & Lima Bean Pâté (see p. 80).

Halva

Halva is a crumbly mixture made from crushed sesame seeds flavored with honey. It is popular in the Middle East and Mediterranean countries. Some halvas have pistachio nuts or chopped fruit added. Make sure that you do not buy halva sweetened with refined sugar.

Eat halva as a snack on its own (it is very sweet so eat in moderation), or sprinkle over desserts and puddings or add to ice cream.

Honey

Honey is made from the nectar of various flowers and plants taken into the bee's stomach where enzymic action converts the complex sugar molecules of the nectar into simple sugars. Once back in the hive this sugar solution is deposited in the honeycombs. Honey is extracted from the honeycombs by centrifugal force, and is then usually filtered before being packed.

Honey contains some protein, vitamins and most minerals, and is particularly good for invalids, athletes and children because the sugar can enter straight into the bloodstream, providing instant energy. Honey is sweet, nourishing and easy to digest, and has natural antiseptic, antibiotic and laxative properties.

There are many types of honey, each with a slightly different color and flavor depending on the flower or plant visited by the bee. Honeys are often available in both honeycomb and liquid form. The choice is a matter of personal preference, but choose pure, unfiltered honey rather than blended honey where possible. Make sure of the quality of the honey. In an attempt to produce cheap honey some manufacturers place white sugar solutions close to the hives, so the bees no longer fly any distance in search of plant nectars. The essential enzymic reactions do not take place and the honey is nutritionally inferior. Some manufacturers also heat the combs to obtain the maximum amount of honey, which decreases the nutritional value.

Honey may deepen in color and crystallize due to age or lowering of temperature. To make it runny again, put the jar in a bowl of warm water and store in a warm place.

Use honey instead of sugar in cakes, breads, puddings, pastries, biscuits, drinks and glazes. Remember that honey is sweeter than sugar, so use less if substituting in a recipe.
Recipe: Granola 2 (see p. 69).

Malt extract
(Barley syrup)
Malt extract is a natural sugar obtained from malted cereal grains, usually barley. The malted grains (see p. 11) are ground and soaked in water, which is then heated and reduced to a syrup. Malt extract is not as sweet as sugar, but does contain B vitamins and iron.

Malt extract can be used instead of sugar and honey in cakes, desserts and drinks and it is often given to children as a nutritional supplement.
Recipe: Date & Oat Bars (see p. 141).

Maple syrup

This delicious syrup is obtained from certain North American maple trees, chiefly the sugar maple and the black maple. The clear sap is extracted through small tapholes in the bark by vacuum pumping. It is then boiled in an open pan until only a thick dark syrup remains. Between 30-50 gallons of maple sap is needed to make 1 gallon of maple syrup.

Maple syrup is mainly sucrose but it does contain some potassium and calcium. Beware of products calling themselves maple syrup which are actually white sugar-based syrups with maple syrup flavoring added.

Apart from pouring over pancakes, waffles and ice cream, maple syrup can be used to sweeten cakes, puddings and pastries. It can even be used in savory sauces and vinaigrette salad dressings.
Recipe: Banana Frozen Yogurt (see p. 122).

Mirin

Mirin is a sweet brown liquid, a natural sweetener which has been used in Japan for centuries. To make it, a rice mold is added to *koji* (sweet brown rice). This mold breaks down the sugar in the grains over a period of 6 months or more. This resulting sweet liquid is then diluted with pure spring water to produce mirin.

Always boil mirin for 1 minute before use. Use it to sweeten vegetable dishes and sauces or as a marinade or glaze. A traditional Japanese marinade is made by boiling a little mirin for 1 minute and then adding shoyu, grated ginger root and brown rice vinegar or lemon juice.

Molasses

Molasses is a by-product of refined sugar and is sometimes known as black treacle. Molasses is a thick black syrup and is rich in minerals, particularly iron, calcium, phosphorus and potassium.

Blackstrap, or dark, molasses is thicker, richer and more nutritious than light molasses, as it is less refined. It is usually used in cooking. Light molasses has a milder flavor and is usually used as a table syrup.

Molasses can be used in place of sugar or honey to sweeten cakes, pastries, puddings or savory dishes and it is often an ingredient in nourishing pick-me-up drinks. It is not as sweet as refined sugar.
Recipe: Bran Muffins (see p. 137).

Sugar
(Sucrose)
Sugar, or sucrose, is extracted from two main sources; sugar cane and sugar beet, and three minor sources; maple trees, date palms and sorghum cane.

Separating the sucrose from the stems of the sugar cane is a complex process, involving crushing and grinding to release the sweet juice and treatment with chemicals or lime to clarify the liquid. This liquid is reduced by evaporating through boiling and then centrifugal force is used to separate out the crystallized raw brown sugar. The residue is molasses. The brown raw sugar is treated further with lime, carbon dioxide and sulfur dioxide to produce refined white sugar. Sugar from sugar beet is obtained in a similar way, although brown sugar cannot be produced from sugar beet.

Refined white sugar contains no nutrients, only calories. Consumption of refined sugar has rocketed in the last hundred years, to the detriment of our health. It is not only consumed in drinks, on cereals and in baking but is a hidden additive in many processed foods. Apart from the better-known physical effects of obesity, tooth decay and diabetes, too much refined sugar can actually reduce the level of nutrients in our body, in particular calcium and vitamin B. Hyperactivity in children and some kinds of mental depression in adults are also being linked with excessive sugar intake.

If you must use sugar, raw, unrefined sugars are better than white as they contain a little fiber. Light brown sugar contains approximately 2 per cent molasses. Muscovado sugar is much darker in color, being only partly refined, and is nutritionally superior as it contains approximately 13 per cent molasses; it is the molasses that adds the only nutrients to refined sugar.

Reduced-sugar jellies
Over the past few years various reduced-sugar jellies and marmalades have become available. By "reduced-sugar" the manufacturers mean that there is less refined sugar in the product. They are usually made from fruit concentrates, which are high in natural fruit sugars.

Reduced-sugar jellies tend not to be as sweet as traditional sugar jellies or jam and it may take a little while to get used to this. Once opened, they should be refrigerated. Use reduced-sugar jellies on bread, toast and biscuits or in puddings, cakes and custards.
Recipe: Bakewell Tart (see p. 134).

HERBS

Basil ☐
Bay leaves ☐
Bergamot
Borage
Bouquet garni
Burnet
Chervil ☐
Chives ☐

Comfrey
Coriander leaves ☐
Dill ☐
Fennel leaves
Fenugreek leaves
Fines herbes
Garlic
Lemon balm

Lemon verbena
Lovage
Marjoram ☐
Mint ☐
Mixed herbs
Nasturtiums
Oregano ☐
Parsley ☐

Rosemary ☐
Sage ☐
Tansy
Tarragon ☐
Thyme ☐
Winter savory

☐ Pictured opposite page 49

Herbs are the edible leaves, flowers, seeds, stems and roots of nonwoody plants which are used for flavoring and garnishing food. Garlic is included in this section because of its similar usage to many herbs, although it is strictly a bulb vegetable.

Each herb has a distinctive taste and aroma. It takes a little time (and possibly a few disasters) to learn the strengths and flavors of the different herbs, but it is well worth the effort. An understanding of herbs can greatly enhance your cooking and open up limitless creative possibilities in the kitchen.

There is little doubt that fresh herbs are far superior to dried. However, unless you have your own herb garden many herbs are often unavailable and in this case the dried versions are perfectly palatable if used correctly. If a recipe calls for 1 tsp of a fresh herb, use ½ tsp of the dried herb instead.

Drying herbs

Foliage herbs should be harvested just before flowering, when the leaves are most numerous and flavorful and before the spores have formed. Pick the stems early in the morning, after the dew has dried and before the hot summer sun evaporates the essential oils.

Either lay the herbs on wire screens or tie in loose bundles and place in large brown paper bags, fastening the mouth of the bag around the stems. Leave until the herbs are quite dry and will fall easily from their stems.

Crumble the herbs into small pieces by hand or through a coarse strainer. The herbs can then be finely ground with a mortar and pestle. Most fresh herbs will dry well except for parsley, chervil and chives, but these can be frozen (see p. 65).

Storage

Freshly cut herbs keep best if their stems are put in a glass of water. They can also be frozen if desired (see p. 65). Dried herbs should be kept in opaque, airtight jars away from direct sunlight and heat. If purchasing, buy a little at a time to ensure maximum freshness and flavor.

Basil

Basil originated in India and has large, rounded, bright green leaves. The herb has a sweet delicate flavor and aroma. It is especially popular in Italy where it is used in the traditional pesto sauce. It is best eaten fresh but retains its strength and flavor when dried.

Culinary uses
Basil is delicious in curries and spicy dishes as well as in soups, salads, casseroles and bakes. It combines particularly well with tomatoes, artichokes, peas, eggs and cheese.
Recipe: Minestrone (see p. 77).

Bay leaves

Bay leaves come from the sweet bay tree, a variety of laurel native to the Mediterranean.

Bay leaves are tough and leathery and can be used fresh or dried. They have a strong flavor which needs long cooking before it is released. Ground bay leaves are available but the whole leaves, fresh or dried, are preferable.

Culinary uses
Bay leaves can be used to flavor curries and spicy dishes, soups, casseroles, sauces and broths. Remove the leaves before serving, and be careful not to use too many. Bay leaves also make good garnishes for pâtés.
Recipe: Adzuki Bean Soup (see p. 72).

Bergamot
(Bee balm/Oswego)

Bergamot is a member of the mint family, and is native to America. It is now also widely grown in Europe. There are many varieties of bergamot, and both the flowers and the leaves can be used. It has a distinctive, strong flavor and can be used fresh or dried.

Culinary uses
Use chopped bergamot leaves in salads, soups, sauces and dressings. Fresh bergamot flowers, when in season, make a beautiful garnish. The leaves can also be used to make tea (see p. 59 for the method).

Borage

Borage is native to the Middle East and is now grown around the world. When in season, borage has bright blue flowers. Both the leaves and the flowers are used in cooking.

Culinary uses
Borage has a slightly cucumber-like taste. Chop finely and add to soups, dips, dressings, sauces, salads and drinks.

Bouquet garni

This is a ready-prepared mixture of herbs, either tied together in a bundle or chopped and tied into small cheesecloth bags. Packages of the loose-mixed herbs are also sometimes available. The herbs used in a bouquet garni are traditionally bay leaves, parsley and thyme, but other herbs may also be added depending on what is available.

Culinary uses
Bouquet garni is used widely in French cooking in many soups, casseroles and bakes. The herbs combine well with peppers, zucchini, eggplant, potatoes, leeks, onions and many other vegetables as well as most grains and beans. Remove the bunch or bag before serving the dish.
Recipe: Use instead of mixed herbs in Mung Bean Casserole (see p. 109).

Burnet
(Salad burnet)

Burnet is a small herb with tiny, scalloped leaves. Native to Europe, it is popular in French and Italian cooking. The leaves can be used fresh or dried, but the flavor is best when fresh and young.

Culinary uses
Burnet has a flavor similar to borage, and is also used in soups, dips, dressings, sauces, salads and drinks.

Chervil

Chervil originates from southern Russia and the Middle East. It is a very popular herb in Europe, particularly France, and grows well in temperate climates. It is similar in appearance to parsley and has a slightly spicy taste, rather like tarragon. It can be eaten fresh or dried but dried chervil does not retain its flavor as well as the fresh.

Culinary uses
Chervil can be used in soups, salads, stuffings, casseroles and other savory dishes. It is particularly delicious in milk-based sauces and with eggs, cheese, salad vegetables, spinach, potatoes, grains and beans.

Chives

Chives are native to Europe, and are a member of the onion, leek and garlic family. Their long, bright green, grass-like leaves have a mild oniony or garlicy flavor. Chinese chives have larger leaves and a slightly stronger flavor.

Chives are best eaten fresh, and ideally home-grown. They can be dried or frozen, the latter being preferable.

Culinary uses
Chopped chives are delicious in clear soups, salads and many savory dishes, and they can also be used as a garnish. They can be mixed with butter for spreading on potatoes or hot bread, and are often used in soups and egg and cheese dishes.

Recipe: Melon & Tomato Salad (see p. 91).

Comfrey

Native to Europe and Asia, comfrey is related to the borage plant. It has large, wide green leaves. Both the leaves and the roots can be used, fresh or dried.

Comfrey is extremely nutritious, due to the great length of its roots, which can grow as long as 10 feet. This enables the plant to draw up many minerals and nutrients usually only available to trees. Comfrey is high in the B vitamin group, including B_{12}, which is rare in plant foods.

Culinary uses
Use comfrey chopped fresh or dried in salads, soups, dips and savory dishes. It has a flavor rather like borage. The leaves can also be used to make tea (see p. 59).

Coriander leaves
(Cilantro/Chinese parsley)

A member of the carrot family, the coriander plant is Middle Eastern in origin and now grows in America, Europe and the Mediterranean. The soft, feathery leaves are sometimes known as cilentro or Chinese parsley. They have a distinctive aroma and a fresh, strong taste. (For coriander seeds, see p. 57.)

Culinary uses
Fresh coriander leaves may be chopped and used in salads and savory dishes, or sprinkled as a garnish over soups and appetizers. Use in dishes with an Oriental flavor.

Recipe: Baked Eggs with Coriander (see p. 81).

Dill

Dill is native to Europe and western Asia, and is now grown all over the world. It is very popular in Scandinavia. Dill has green, feathery leaves, which are often used as a garnish in the same way as parsley. Dill leaves or dill tops are best eaten fresh although dried dill, called dillweed, still retains a little of its distinctive flavor. Dill seeds are also available.

Culinary uses
Dill leaves are wonderful in salads or sprinkled over soups and other savory dishes. The flavor goes particularly well with mushrooms, leeks, cauliflower, tomatoes, zucchini and most grains and beans. Try adding fresh dill to cream sauces and mayonnaise.

Recipe: Stuffed Baked Mushrooms (see p. 86).

Fennel leaves

Fennel is native to Europe and is a tall, feathery herb with small dark green leaves. The large fennel root is eaten as vegetable (see p. 28). Fennel leaves have a slightly aniseed aroma and flavor.

Culinary uses
Use fennel leaves in soups, salads and stuffings, or as a garnish.

Fenugreek leaves
(Methi)

The leaves of the fenugreek plant, or methi, are often eaten as a vegetable in parts of the Far East and North Africa, although the fresh leaves are seldom found in Western countries. However, they are available in dried form. They have a milder flavor than the fenugreek seeds (see p. 57).

Culinary uses
Use fenugreek leaves in soups and savory dishes, particularly curries. They have a slightly bitter flavor.

Recipe: Use instead of cumin in Onion Bhajis with Yogurt Sauce (see p. 86).

Fines herbes

This is a ready-prepared mixture of chopped dried herbs, usually chervil, parsley, tarragon and chives.

Culinary uses
Fines herbes can be used in many savory dishes, such as soups, sauces and casseroles.

Garlic

Garlic is one of the oldest cultivated plants in the world, probably originating in Central Asia. It is an important ingredient in many great cuisines of the world. Choose firm, tightly packed "bulbs" of garlic, preferably with large cloves.

Garlic has a strong pungent flavor and can sometimes smell on the breath. Used in moderation, garlic can enhance many savory dishes and is extremely versatile. Fresh garlic is best, but dried flakes and powder are available.

Culinary uses
Garlic can be eaten raw or cooked. Peel and then crush or finely chop the raw cloves for use in salads, salad dressings, soups and sauces. When cooking garlic, add toward the end of cooking for the best results. Boiled garlic will have a milder flavor, but if fried in oil the flavor will become very pungent.

Garlic can be used in a number of Asian, Oriental and Mediterranean dishes, and it will blend well with most vegetables and grains.

Recipe: Garlic & Onion Soup (see p. 76).

Lemon balm
(Balm)

Lemon balm is native to the Mediterranean, and has oval-shaped, textured leaves. Available fresh or dried, it has a distinctive lemony aroma and flavor.

Culinary uses
Use lemon balm generously in soups, savory salads, sauces, drinks and fruit salads. The leaves can be used to make tea in the same way as lemon verbena (see p. 60).

Lemon verbena

This herb is native to South America, and is now also grown in parts of Europe. It is sometimes confused with lemon balm, but has longer, smoother leaves of a darker green. It is available fresh or dried.

Culinary uses
Lemon verbena has a fresh, lemony flavor and can be added to many light sauces, dressings, salads, soups, drinks and fruit dishes. It is also used to make tea (see p. 60).

Lovage
(Love parsley)

Lovage is a large, celery-like plant native to southern Europe. The whole plant is used, leaf, seed and root. It has a strong, aromatic flavor and is available as fresh leaves and root or as dried root.

Culinary uses
Lovage can be cooked whole, in the same way as celery (see p. 27). It can also be chopped and added to soups, sauces and salads.

Marjoram
(Sweet or pot marjoram)

Marjoram is native to the Mediterranean and has a sweet, delicate flavor when used in moderation. It has a high tannin content, so can taste slightly bitter if overused.

Marjoram is available fresh or dried. If using fresh marjoram, be sure to wash well because it grows very close to the ground and the downy leaves can easily pick up dust.

Culinary uses
The fresh herb is delicious chopped and sprinkled over salads or cooked vegetable dishes, and the dried herb can be added to any combination of vegetables, grains and beans. Marjoram combines particularly well with nut, egg and tomato dishes. A pinch of marjoram can also be added to salad dressings, sauces and mayonnaise.

Recipe: Cream Cheese Dip (see p. 82).

Mint

There are many varieties of mint, the most common being spearmint, applemint, peppermint and horsemint. They are native to the Mediterranean and western Asia, but are now grown worldwide. The dried herb can be used if fresh mint sprigs are not available.

Spearmint is common garden mint, and is used for culinary purposes. Applemint is a downy leaved variety with a fine flavor, also used in cooking. The peppermint is an offspring of spearmint and is usually used for the strong pungent oil which is extracted from the herb, but dried leaves are available.

Culinary uses
Common garden mint (spearmint) is used in sauces and drinks, and with potatoes, peas and other grains and vegetables. It is often used as a garnish and is extensively used in Middle Eastern dishes, such as Tabouleh (see p. 95).

Peppermint oil can be used in drinks and candy. The dried peppermint leaves can be used to make mint tea (see page 60).

Recipe: Citrus Cocktail (see p. 81).

Mixed herbs

This is a ready-prepared mixture of dried herbs, sometimes called Italian seasoning. Marjoram, thyme, parsley, basil and rosemary is one combination, others are for specific use with poultry, in salads or on barbecued foods.

Culinary uses

Mixed herbs can be used in many savory soups, broths and casseroles.

Nasturtiums

Native to Peru, nasturtiums are usually grown as a garden flower. Both the brilliant orange-red flowers and the large bright green leaves can be eaten, and have a peppery taste. Nasturtiums are usually eaten fresh.

Culinary uses

Leave the flowers and leaves whole or chop if desired and add to salads and sandwiches.

Oregano

(Wild marjoram)

Oregano is rather larger than marjoram, and has an aromatic flavor. Native to Asia, Europe and North Africa, it is used extensively in Italian and Greek cooking, and is usually the predominant herb in pizzas.

Culinary uses

Like marjoram, oregano can be used for almost any savory dish. It blends perfectly with tomatoes, raw or cooked, and is delicious with cheese dishes, pasta, grains, beans and most vegetables. Be careful not to use too much because it is quite strong.

Dried oregano has a stronger flavor than fresh and it can be used at any point during cooking, although a pinch added just before serving brings out the best flavor.

Recipe: Red Bean Salad (see p. 93).

Parsley

Parsley is Mediterranean in origin. There are several varieties, including broad-leaved Italian parsley, curly leaved parsley and Neapolitan parsley with thick stems. Best eaten fresh, parsley is extremely nutritious, being high in vitamins A, B, C and E as well as some minerals (see the nutritional chart on p. 26).

Culinary uses

Most of the nutrients are stored in the stems, so be sure not to discard all of these. Parsley can be chopped and sprinkled over salads or hot vegetable dishes, and its bright green color is very decorative.

Parsley can also be used in sauces, soups, stuffings and savory dishes. It combines very well with other herbs. If using in a hot dish, add towards the end of cooking.

Recipe: Creamed Cauliflower Soup (see p. 73).

Rosemary

Rosemary is native to the Mediterranean, and grows wild on many cliffs and shorelines there. The hard, spiky leaves contain oil of camphor, and fresh rosemary can have an intoxicating aroma and flavor.

Rosemary has a strong, pungent flavor and is best eaten fresh, although dried is still quite tasty. Dried is available as leaves.

Culinary uses

Rosemary needs a while to cook for its flavor to come through, so add it at the beginning of cooking. It is particularly good with root vegetables and grains, and can also be used to help counteract the oiliness of a dish. Use sparingly, however, as it can overpower the flavor of the other ingredients.

Recipe: Rye & Vegetable Broth (see p. 78).

Sage

Sage originated in the northern Mediterranean but now grows extensively in most temperate regions. There are several varieties. Sage is a welcome addition to a garden because it attracts honey bees, therefore helping the pollination of the other plants. The soft greeny-gray leaves can be used fresh or dried, but use cautiously because they have a very strong flavor and a high tannin content, which, when used in excess, causes a bitter taste.

Culinary uses

Sage is commonly used in stuffings, but it can also be used sparingly in spicy dishes and sauces. A few fresh leaves in a summer punch can be very refreshing.

Recipe: Chestnut & Prune Roast (see p. 104).

Tansy

Tansy is native to Europe, but is now also common in America. It has narrow, feathery leaves and a very distinctive flavor. Tansy is usually eaten fresh.

Culinary uses

Add chopped fresh tansy to dips, cottage or cream cheese, dressings, salads and fruit salads. It combines particularly well with eggs.

Tarragon

The tarragon plant is native to southern Europe. There are two main culinary varieties, the French and the Russian. French tarragon is superior and its pungent aniseed-like flavor is used extensively in French cooking.

French tarragon has to be grown from cuttings, since the plant itself produces no seed. It is not easy to grow and needs careful attention to begin with, but once established it will thrive. It can be used fresh or dried, the fresh being preferable.

Culinary uses

Fresh tarragon is delicious chopped and sprinkled over salads and mild-flavored vegetables, and is particularly good with tomatoes, eggs, asparagus or cream cheese. It can be added at any stage of cooking, as the longer it cooks the more flavorful it becomes. Tarragon is also a lovely addition to salad dressings, mayonnaise, and white and tomato-based sauces.

Recipe: Tiny Stuffed Tomatoes (see p. 87).

Thyme

This is another herb with Mediterranean origins which now grows successfully in all temperate areas. There are over 50 varieties, the main culinary herbs being garden thyme, wild thyme and lemon thyme. Lemon thyme is often preferred as its flavor is milder.

Thyme has a high tannin content, so should be used sparingly to avoid a bitter taste.

Culinary uses

The subtle, sweet flavor of thyme blends well with most vegetables, grains and beans. It is particularly good with zucchini, eggplant and peppers. If using the dried herb, add at the beginning of cooking. Fresh thyme should be added toward the end of cooking, or sprinkled on top of the dish before serving.

Winter savory

Winter savory is native to the Mediterranean, and has thin, small leaves and an aromatic, peppery flavor. Summer savory is similar and is thought by some to have an even better flavor. Savory is available fresh or dried.

Culinary uses

Use chopped winter savory as a seasoning or in vegetable, bean and grain dishes. It is a rather strong herb so should perhaps be used in moderation.

SPICES & SEEDS

Apple pie spice ☐   Cayenne pepper ☐   Curry powders ☐   Paprika ☐

Alfalfa seeds ☐   Celery seeds ☐   Fenugreek seeds ☐   Peppercorns ☐

Allspice ☐   Chili ☐   Garam masala ☐   Poppy seeds ☐

Anise-peppers   Chinese five-spice ☐   Ginger ☐   Saffron ☐

Anise seeds   Cinnamon ☐   Juniper berries ☐   Star anise ☐

Asafoetida ☐   Cloves ☐   Linseeds ☐   Turmeric ☐

Caraway seeds   Coriander seeds ☐   Mustard seeds ☐   Vanilla beans ☐

Cardamom ☐   Cumin seeds ☐   Nutmeg and mace ☐

☐ Pictured opposite page 64

Spices are basically the dried seeds, leaves, flowers, roots and barks of edible aromatic plants. Described in this section are many of the spices and seeds commonly used in cooking. As mentioned in the herb section, it may take you a little time to familiarize yourself with all the different flavors and usages, but once you master the art of spicing, a mere touch can transform a dish.

Grinding spices

Many spices and seeds can be bought ready-ground. This can be useful for the very hard spices but in general it is better to buy the whole spices or seeds and grind them yourself. A mortar and pestle is a good investment for this purpose. If you wish, the whole spices or seeds can be roasted or dry-fried before grinding, to release their aromatic oils and improve their flavor. Heat gently so as not to burn the delicate spice.

Storage

All whole or ground spices and seeds should be kept in opaque, airtight jars, away from direct sunlight or heat. Ready-ground spices do deteriorate and lose their flavors more quickly, so only buy in small quantities and use within 6 months.

Apple pie spice
(see Piespice, p. 58)

Alfalfa seeds
(Lucerne)

Alfalfa is an extremely important food supplement, being highly nutritious. It contains a high proportion of protein, vitamins and minerals, including vitamin B_{12}, which is essential to a healthy diet and usually only available in meat, fish and dairy products. Alfalfa seeds can also be sprouted (see p. 23).

Culinary uses

The tiny light brown seeds can be sprinkled over savory dishes or desserts.

Allspice
(Jamaica pepper/Pimento berries)

Allspice is the brown sun-dried berry from the pimento tree, indigenous to Central America and the West Indies. It is not a mixture of several spices, as is often thought, but is similar in flavor to cinnamon and cloves. Allspice is available as whole berries or ground.

Culinary uses

Allspice is widely used in Central and South American cooking and can be used in soups, savory dishes, pickles, cakes and puddings.

Recipe: Evelyn's German Potato Soup (see p. 75).

Anise-peppers
(Szechwan peppers)

Anise-peppers are the dried red berries of a tree native to China, and should not be confused with anise seeds. They are hot and aromatic, popular in Chinese cooking, and are an ingredient in Chinese five-spice powder.

Culinary uses

Use in savory Chinese and Oriental dishes, and in spicy soups, sauces and casseroles.

Anise seeds
(Aniseed/Sweet cumin)

The anise plant belongs to the carrot family, and originates from Greece and Egypt. Both the fresh leaves and the seeds are used as a spice, and they have a distinctive licorice flavor. The seeds are used whole or ground.

The oil extracted from anise seeds is used to make alcohol: *pastis* in France, *ouzo* in Greece and *raki* in Turkey. The oil is also used as a substitute for licorice extract in candy.

Culinary uses

Anise seeds can be used in curries, spicy dishes, desserts, cakes and pastries, confectionery and drinks. Use sparingly and add at the beginning of cooking.

Recipe: Black Bean Chili (see p. 100).

Asafoetida

Asafoetida is a sticky resin extracted from the stems of a plant native to Asia. It is used widely in Oriental and Eastern cookery, but is still quite hard to find in Western countries.

The resin is pale brown or yellow in color and extremely hard. You need a hammer or a very hard object to break off tiny chips, which should then be ground. It is easier to buy resin ready-ground, although some brands often contain artificial coloring.

Culinary uses

Use asafoetida sparingly in savory dishes. It is a very smelly spice, somewhat similar to strong garlic, and should be kept in an airtight container away from other spices. Asafoetida can also be used as a salt substitute.

Recipe: Fresh Coriander Dhal (see p. 105).

Caraway seeds

Caraway is a member of the carrot family and is native to Europe and Asia. The thin crescent-shaped seeds have a strong characteristic flavor which people tend to either love or hate. They are used whole.

Culinary uses

You can use caraway seeds in bread, curries, pastries and cakes. Use sparingly and add at the beginning of cooking.

Recipe: Unroasted Buckwheat Casserole (see p. 117).

Cardamom

Cardamom is a member of the ginger family, native to India and grown in most tropical countries. It is usually quite expensive because harvesting occurs sporadically, as the pods ripen at different times. The large green, black or white pods contain black seeds, and you can buy as whole pods, whole seeds or ground. Ground cardamom is one of the ingredients in garam masala (see p. 57).

Culinary uses

Cardamom has a very strong, aromatic flavor. It can be used whole or ground in curries, savory dishes, rice puddings and cakes.

Recipe: Eggplant & Potato Curry (see p. 98).

Cayenne pepper

Cayenne pepper is a variety of chili powder ground from certain hot red chili peppers native to Central America. Some commercial brands also contain added salt and spices.

Culinary uses

Cayenne pepper can be used in the same way as chili powder, although it is much hotter. Add sparingly to soups, white sauces, curries and spicy dishes.

Recipe: Fresh Vegetable Curry (see p. 106).

Celery seeds

These are the dried seeds of the celery plant, native to Italy. Celery seeds have a slightly sharp, bitter flavor, reminiscent of the vegetable. Celery salt is made by combining crushed celery seeds with refined salt, and is used as a seasoning.

Culinary uses

Use sparingly in savory soups, broths, casseroles and vegetable stews.

Chili

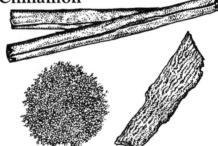

Chilies are an extremely pungent, fiery hot variety of pepper native to Mexico and South America. They are grown widely in all tropical regions of the world and can be eaten fresh or dried and used whole or ground. Dried flaked chilies are also available. Commercial chili powder is usually a blend of ground chili and other spices.

Culinary uses

Chili is used in Indian, Chinese, Mexican and West Indian dishes. Whole chilis can be finely minced (remove the seeds first) or used whole. Take great care to wash your hands well after preparation because they have a stinging action on the skin. If using whole chilies, remove them before serving. Add chili powder at the beginning of cooking.

Recipe: Black Bean Chili (see p. 100).

Chinese five-spice

This is a mixture of ground anise-peppers, star anise, cassia (a type of cinnamon), cloves and fennel seeds. It has a faint licorice flavor and is commonly used in Chinese cooking.

Culinary uses

Add a little Chinese five-spice to noodles or brown rice, or use in curries and Chinese-style cooked vegetables.

Cinnamon

Cinnamon is the aromatic bark of a variety of laurel tree native to Sri Lanka and southern India. Available as sticks, quills and ground.

Culinary uses

Cinnamon can be used in Oriental, African and Indian savory dishes. Ground cinnamon is commonly used in the West for flavoring sweet dishes, desserts and cakes. The sticks can be used to flavor drinks and syrups, and are removed before use.

Recipe: English Christmas Puddings (see p. 124).

Cloves

Cloves are the hard, dried flower buds of an evergreen tree of the myrtle family, native to Southeast Asia. Pink when they are picked, the buds turn reddy-brown after sun-drying. They are very aromatic and can be used whole or ground. Ground cloves are the powdered "heads" of the whole cloves.

Culinary uses

Cloves have a strong pungent flavor, so use sparingly. They can be used in spicy, sweet or savory dishes, mulled wines and punches, sauces, cakes, mincemeat, desserts, cookies and pastries.

Recipe: Baked Apples (see p. 121).

Coriander seeds

Coriander seeds are the dried, roasted fruit of a small annual plant originating from southern Europe and the Middle East. The mild, aromatic seeds can be bought whole or ground. Coriander leaves (see p. 54) have a quite different flavor.

Culinary uses

Coriander seeds are used in many Arabian and Eastern dishes, and can be added to a number of savory dishes, curries, desserts, puddings and pickles.

Recipe: Eggplant & Potato Curry (see p. 98).

Cumin seeds

Cumin is a member of the carrot family, originating from North Africa. The seeds resemble caraway seeds in appearance, but have a quite different flavor, being hot and pungent. They are widely used in Central American, North African and Asian cooking. Ground cumin is also available, and is a main ingredient in curry powder.

Culinary uses

Cumin has a strong, spicy flavor and is best added at the beginning of cooking. It is a common ingredient in curries and is also delicious in dips, yogurt relishes, soups, salads, savory and sweet dishes. Cumin is also used as a pickling spice.

Recipe: Potato & Beet Soup (see p. 78).

Curry powders

Curry powders are ready-prepared mixtures of ground coriander, turmeric, cumin, chili and other aromatic spices. Each manufacturer has an individual recipe. Curry powders can be mild, medium or hot, depending on how much chili is used. Curry pastes are also available, which usually contain fresh chilies, onion and ginger root as well as dry spices.

Culinary uses

Curry powder or paste can be added to soups, savory rice and bean dishes, curries, sauces and mayonnaise.

Recipe: Lima Bean Salad (see p. 90).

Fenugreek seeds

The fenugreek plant is native to the Middle East and western Asia and produces bittersweet, yellow rectangular seeds. Fenugreek seeds are available whole or ground and may also be sprouted (see p. 23). Fenugreek leaves are used as a herb (see p. 54).

Many Indian dishes call for fenugreek seeds and they can be used in chutneys and pickles. They should be added at the beginning of cooking and used in moderation.

Recipe: Add ground to Joey's Egg Curry (see p. 108).

Garam masala

Garam masala is a mixture of several spices ground together. Like curry powder, there is no standard recipe. Garam masala can be bought, but it is even better to make your own as described below:

1 tbsp cardamom seeds
1 tsp whole cloves
2-inch stick, or 2 tsp ground cinnamon
2 tsp cumin seeds
½ tsp black peppercorns
1 whole nutmeg, grated

If liked, first dry-fry the spices together in a dry skillet. Put all the ingredients through a fine spice mill or coffee grinder and store away from direct sunlight in an airtight jar. This will keep for a couple of months.

Culinary uses

Add to curries, spicy Indian dishes, vegetable, grain or bean dishes toward the end of cooking. Garam masala can also be added to sauces or mayonnaise.

Recipe: Onion Bhajis with Yogurt Sauce. (see p. 86).

Ginger

Fresh ginger is the knobbly, cream-colored root of a sturdy herbaceous plant, native to Southeast Asia and now common in most tropical areas. It is used extensively in Indian, Asian, Japanese, Caribbean, African and West Indian cooking.

The fresh ginger root should be scraped gently to help preserve the essential oils close to the surface and then cut into small pieces, thinly sliced or grated. The root is also available dried, whole or sliced, and needs to be soaked before using.

The dried root is also available ground, but only buy a little at a time as the strong pungent "gingery" flavor does not keep well. Stem ginger can also be found in crystallized form or preserved in syrup.

Culinary uses

Fresh or dried ginger can be added to soups, salad dressings, Chinese stir-fries, savory dishes, puddings, cakes, jams, chutneys and pickles. Stem ginger is often used in desserts and confectionery.

Recipe: Peach & Pear Crumble (see p. 127).

Juniper berries

Juniper is an evergreen shrub native to the northern hemisphere and found in many parts of America, Europe and Asia. The dried blue-black fruits or berries of the shrub are available whole.

Culinary uses

Juniper berries have a sharp, pungent flavor and can be used in pickles and chutneys. They are good for counteracting oily dishes.

Linseeds

Linseeds are the tiny, shiny brown oval-shaped seeds of the flax plant, itself grown for fiber in the production of linen.

Linseeds are mainly used in the production of oil, for industrial purposes as well as consumption. The whole seeds are also available however, and are nutritionally valuable as they are rich in three essential fatty acids. They have a distinctive smooth, nutty flavor.

Culinary uses
Linseeds may be added to bread dough, or sprinkled over the top of loaves before baking.
Recipe: Three-Seed Bread (see p. 156).

Mustard seeds

The mustard plant grows, both wild and cultivated, in the Mediterranean region. There are two types of mustard seeds generally available, black (brown) and white (yellow). Both have a characteristic hot, pungent flavor although the white seeds are milder than the black. They are both available whole. Ground mustard (dry mustard powder) is usually from a mixture of black and white seeds.

The commercial mustards bought as a relish are made from mustard seeds. Whole-grain mustard contains the whole seeds and is often flavored with herbs, spices, wines and sweeteners, such as tarragon, green peppercorns, allspice, white wine and honey.

Culinary uses
Mustard seeds are frequently added to Indian, African and Asian dishes, either whole or crushed. Fry them at the beginning of cooking in hot oil, to release their essential oil which carries the flavor. Ground mustard can be used for sauces, dressings and chutneys.
Recipe: Leeks Vinaigrette (see p. 84).

Nutmeg and mace

The evergreen nutmeg tree originated in Indonesia and is grown in most tropical areas.

Nutmeg is the dried kernel or seed of the plant and mace is its dried outer covering. Always buy whole nutmegs if you can and grate them yourself with a cheese grater, although ready-ground nutmeg is available.

Mace is available in pressed, flat "blade" form and ground. Mace has a brighter, more orange color than nutmeg.

Culinary uses
Nutmeg and mace make delicious and aromatic additions to soups, curries, sauces or pickles. They can also be used in desserts, cakes and pastries. Although similar in aroma and flavor, mace is slightly stronger.
Recipe: Cream of Mushroom Soup (see p. 74).

Paprika

Paprika is ground from a variety of peppers native to South America. Paprika can vary in taste from mild to hot, and in color from reddy-brown to bright red. It is a popular spice in Hungarian cooking. Buy ready-ground, but in small quantities so that it is as fresh as possible.

Culinary uses
Use paprika generously in dips, soups, savory dishes and white sauces. It should be added at the beginning of cooking to bring out its full flavor. Paprika can also be used uncooked, sprinkled over dishes as a garnish.
Recipe: Egg & Avocado Mayonnaise Dip (see p. 82).

Peppercorns

Peppercorns come from the pepper vine, native to Asia. They are available green, black and white. Green peppercorns are the unripe berries of the plant, usually sold in brine. Black peppercorns are sun-dried green peppercorns and have a strong, pungent flavor. White peppercorns are the fully ripened berries of the plant, sun-dried and with the red outer skin removed. They have a milder, more aromatic flavor. White pepper is relatively recent, only becoming fashionable when some great French chefs decided that tiny specks of black pepper ruined the aesthetic beauty of their creamy white sauces.

Both black and white peppercorns are available whole or ground. Freshly ground pepper will have the best flavor.

Culinary uses
Add whole or ground peppercorns to savory dishes, sauces, dressings, marinades and pickles. Ground pepper is used as a seasoning for most savory dishes.
Recipe: Hummus (see p. 83).

Pie spice

This spice is a ready-prepared mixture of nutmeg, cinnamon, ginger and allspice. It is sold as apple piespice.

Culinary uses
Mixed spice is commonly used in cakes, biscuits, desserts and pies but can also be added to savory dishes, especially curries.
Recipe: Baked Bananas with Yogurt Sauce (see p. 121).

Poppy seeds

These tiny blue-black or white seeds come from the opium poppy flower, but have no hallucinogenic properties. Native to the Middle East, the seeds are very popular in Russian, Jewish and Eastern cooking. They have a sweet, mild flavor and aroma.

Culinary uses
Poppy seeds are delicious added to sweet and savory dishes, either sprinkled on top or added at the beginning of cooking. They can also be added in baking to decorate bread.
Recipe: Joey's Egg Curry (see p. 108).

Saffron

Saffron is one of the most expensive spices available. The yellow-red strands are the dried stamens of an Asian crocus, and it can take 75,000 hand-harvested stamens to make just 1 pound of saffron. It is available in strands or as powder, but the latter is sometimes adulterated.

Culinary uses
Saffron has a delicate, aromatic flavor, and is used in soups, rice dishes, cakes, cookies and breads. A pinch of saffron added to a pan of cooking rice will turn it a vibrant yellow-orange. If using saffron for flavoring, add at the end of cooking, dissolved in a little water.
Recipe: Add to Brown Rice Risotto (see p. 100).

Star anise

This small, dried star-shaped pod is from an evergreen tree of the magnolia family, originating from China. The small oval seeds are contained in the pod, in the points of the star. Both the pods, whole or cracked, and the whole or ground seeds are available.

The flavor of star anise is reminiscent of licorice, and is similar to that of anise seeds. It is now used for the extraction of anise oil.

Culinary uses
Ground star anise is an ingredient of Chinese five-spice powder. It can be used in spicy dishes, curries, desserts, cakes and cookies or in recipes requiring anise seeds.
Recipe: Use in Black Bean Chili (see p. 100).

Turmeric

Turmeric is the ground root from a plant of the lily family, native to Southeast Asia, usually only found ground in a bright yellow powder. It has a mild aromatic flavor and will color food a bright yellow (it is sometimes known as "poor man's saffron"). Be careful not to use too much or the food may taste bitter.

Culinary uses
Turmeric is a basic ingredient in most curry powders. It can be cooked in many grain, bean or vegetable dishes and can be used in chutneys and pickles. Turmeric can also be used sparingly to add color to cakes and rice. Add at the beginning of cooking in small amounts.
Recipe: Onion Bhajis with Yogurt Sauce (see p. 86).

Vanilla beans

Vanilla beans come from a type of climbing orchid native to Central America. The bean is picked before the seeds inside mature, and then cured. It is used whole. To obtain the vanilla flavor from the bean, immerse it in the liquid to be used in the recipe. The longer the infusion, the stronger the flavor. Beans are reusable, so remove, rinse and pat dry, and store in an airtight jar.

Culinary uses
Vanilla beans can be used to flavor drinks, sweet sauces, puddings, cakes, custards, ice creams and confectionery.
Recipe: Add to Rice Pudding (see p. 130).

HERB TEAS

Bancha tea
Camomile tea ☐
Coltsfoot tea
Comfrey tea ☐

Fennel tea ☐
Lemon verbena tea
Linden tea ☐
Luaka tea

Mint tea
Mu tea ☐
Nettle tea ☐
Raspberry leaf tea ☐

Rose hip tea ☐
Twig tea ☐
Vervain tea ☐

☐ Pictured opposite page 65

Drink is an important part of the whole food diet and should not be overlooked. Many commercial drinks such as fruit and soda drinks contain high amounts of sugar as well as colorants, flavorings, preservatives and other additives. Alcohol is not only high in sugar but dehydrates the body, depleting it of B vitamins and, in excess, damaging the liver. Coffee and tea both contain caffeine, which can be damaging in large doses. Caffeine acts as an immediate stimulant, making the heart beat faster and more irregularly. It raises the blood pressure and insulin level, and is also thought to prevent the body's absorption of some vitamins and minerals, particularly B vitamins and iron. Tea also contains tannin, which can cause constipation in excess.

For all these reasons, it is recommended that you cut down your intake of sugared drinks, alcohol, coffee and tea. Herbal teas offer a wholesome alternative to the more commonly used tea and coffee, and have been drunk for their pleasant flavors and therapeutic effects for thousands of years. They can form a beneficial part of the daily diet, helping to calm, stimulate or cleanse the body in a gentle and natural way.

Listed here are a few of the most common herbal teas. Their therapeutic values are briefly mentioned. Some teas are taken only for their medicinal effects but most can be enjoyed purely for their pleasant and delicate flavors. Their therapeutic effects are not, of course, guaranteed, and should not be considered as a substitute for your doctor's advice. Other health drinks,

including fruit and vegetable juices and decaffeinated coffees, are described in the next chapter (see p. 61).

Herbal teas can be made from dried or fresh herbs. Many are now marketed in handy tea bags, which can be very convenient but also quite expensive. All herbal teas should be stored in opaque airtight containers.

Making herbal teas

As a general rule for an average strength of tea, use 1 tsp of dried herbs or 1 tbsp of crushed fresh herbs to each 1 cup of boiling water (preferably filtered). Pour over the boiling water and leave the tea to steep for 3-5 minutes before straining and drinking. If a stronger tea is desired, add more herbs to the pot or cup rather than increasing the steeping time. Over-steeping can ruin the delicate flavor and later the beneficial effect of the tea.

For herbal teas made from seeds rather than leaves, the proportions are 1 tsp of crushed seeds to each 1 cup of water. Put the seeds and water in a saucepan and boil together for 5 minutes before straining and drinking.

If you are making herb tea in a teapot, use a china pot rather than a metal one as the latter can affect the flavor of delicate teas. Do not leave for too long or the herb tea may stew.

All herbals teas can be drunk hot or cold. If drinking cold, be sure to strain before cooling. A little honey may be added as a sweetener, if desired.

Bancha tea

Bancha tea is a macrobiotic green tea from Japan. It is prepared from the leaves of the tea bush, picked after 3 years of growth.

Bancha tea has a slightly smoky flavor and is a soothing, relaxing tea. It is low in caffeine and tannin and high in calcium. Leftover bancha tea can be reheated and drunk later.

To prepare bancha tea, use 1-2 tsp of tea to 1 cup water. Put the tea and water in a saucepan, bring to a boil and simmer for 20 minutes. Strain and drink.

Camomile tea

Camomile is a daisy-like plant native to Europe, which can be found growing wild all over America and Europe. Only the flower-heads, either dried or fresh, are used.

Camomile tea is very good for soothing upset stomachs and relieving flatulence and indigestion. It is said to help regulate monthly periods for women and is good for fever and restlessness in children.

Externally, camomile tea is beneficial as a facewash to keep skin soft and supple, as a mouthwash to soothe inflamed gums or mouth ulcers, and as a hair rinse for fair hair.

Coltsfoot tea

The roots, leaves and flowers of coltsfoot may be used in the preparation of tea. It is sometimes known as "British tobacco," since the dried and crushed leaves are sometimes smoked or taken as snuff to relieve cold symptoms.

Coltsfoot is an excellent remedy for coughs, colds, phlegm, catarrh and associated bronchial diseases.

Externally, coltsfoot tea can be used for insect bites, leg ulcers, burns and swellings.

Comfrey tea

Comfrey tea is made from the dried, crushed leaves of the comfrey plant. It is a mild tea and is nutritionally valuable, being high in the B

vitamin group, including the rare vitamin B_{12}, and many minerals.

Comfrey tea is a powerful remedy for coughs, colds, catarrh, inflammation of the lungs and other associated bronchial diseases. It is also helpful for digestive and intestinal problems such as dysentery and diarrhea.

Externally, comfrey tea can be used for bruises, cuts and insect bites.

Fennel tea

The fennel plant is tall and feathery, with yellow seeds and a bulbous root eaten as a vegetable (see p. 28). Generally the fennel seeds are used to make fennel tea, although the leaves, roots and flowers may also be used.

Fennel tea is good for soothing upset stomachs, especially after food poisoning. It relieves abdominal cramps and flatulence, and is particularly good for children. It can also help expel mucus from the sinuses or lungs and is an effective soothing tea for those suffering from bronchitis or asthma. Fennel tea may also be taken for menstrual problems and is said to help stimulate the flow of milk in breast-feeding mothers.

Externally, warm fennel tea makes an excellent gargle for hoarseness, coughs or for sore throats.

Lemon verbena tea

Similar in flavor to vervain, lemon verbena is a larger plant with thick, bushy leaves and branches. It is indigenous to South America.

Lemon verbena tea has a powerful, stimulating effect and is useful in cases of depression, lethargy and mental exhaustion. It will help to sooth fevers, neuralgia and migraines and is also useful in reducing acid or wind in the stomach causing cramps or indigestion.

Linden tea
(Lime flower tea)

There are two varieties of linden plant, the American and the European. Infusions can be made from both the flowers and the leaves.

Linden tea is excellent for relaxing and encouraging sleep, especially for those suffering from chronic insomnia, anxiety attacks, nervous tension and irritability. It may also be taken for coughs, colds, sore throats and influenzas. Its diuretic properties make it useful for mild kidney and bladder problems, gout and rheumatism.

Externally, preparations made from the linden bark are soothing for skin irritations and burns.

Luaka tea

This tea comes from the high mountainous parts of Sri Lanka. It is not strictly a herbal tea, but contains significantly less caffeine and tannin than other "black" teas.

Mint tea

There are many varieties of mint (peppermint, spearmint, applemint, horsemint, etc.), native to the Mediterranean and western Asia and now growing prolifically in most parts of the world. It is commonly used as a herb (see mint, p. 54).

Mint tea is a tonic. It is often recommended as a substitute for "black" tea and coffee and it has a general stimulating and soothing effect on the nervous system. For these reasons it is particularly useful for children, old people and those recovering from illness or disease. It is also used to help heartburn, irritability, migraine, headaches, stomach cramps, nausea and vomiting.

Externally, an infusion of mint may be added to the bath to relieve itchy or irritating skin conditions. Gargling with mint tea can relieve toothache and helps freshen the breath.

Mu tea

Mu tea is a macrobiotic tea formulated in 1963 by George Ohsawa, a practitioner of Oriental medicine and philosophy who founded the macrobiotic movement.

There are two types of mu tea, one made from a combination of 9 natural herbs and the other from 16 natural herbs. It has a strong, aromatic flavor.

Mu tea is a natural tonic increasing vitality and strength. It is specifically good for wheezing coughs and other respiratory problems where there is difficulty in breathing.

To prepare mu tea, use 1-2 tsp of tea to 1 cup water. Put the tea and water in a saucepan, bring to a boil and simmer for 20 minutes. Strain and drink.

Nettle tea

Many people think of nettles as annoying weeds and do not realise their numerous culinary and medicinal uses. All parts of the plant may be used to prepare the tea.

Nettle tea can act as a gentle blood purifier and may be taken for rheumatism, gout, kidney and urinary problems. It is also helpful in stopping excessive bleeding or hemorrhaging. It can increase milk flow in nursing mothers and can help regulate monthly periods or bring them on when overdue.

Used externally, nettle is an ingredient in many beauty products helping to cleanse the skin and reduce acne and eczema. Nettle tea is also an excellent hair tonic.

Raspberry leaf tea

This tea is made from the leaves of a variety of mild raspberry.

The tea has a mild purgative effect and is useful for cases of dysentery and diarrhea, especially in children (although many children do not take readily to the taste and prefer fennel tea). Raspberry leaf tea can be taken by women to help regulate or decrease menstrual flow, or during pregnancy to help tone the uterus and prevent miscarriage. This tea has been taken by pregnant women in China for thousands of years.

Rose hip tea

Rose hips are the fruit of wild roses and are exceptionally high in vitamin C.

Rose hip tea is an excellent remedy for coughs, colds, sore throats, runny noses, influenzas and other bronchial infections. It may also be taken for chronic inflammation of the digestive tract, dysentery and diarrhea.

Twig tea
(Kukicha tea)

Twig tea is made from the same plant as bancha tea, but is prepared from the twigs rather than the leaves. The twigs are picked from the bottom of the tea bush after just 3 years of growth.

Prepare and use as for bancha tea.

Vervain tea

Although similar to lemon verbena, vervain is a different plant with thinner leaves and branches and smaller flowers. It is indigenous to Europe.

Vervain tea acts as a general tonic, helping to cleanse the system.

Externally, vervain tea may be used as a gargle for sore throats and tonsillitis. It is used in some medicinal concoctions for ulcers, burns, cuts and bruises.

HEALTH DRINKS

Described in this section are some of the caffeine-free coffees available, as well as a selection of nutritious fresh fruit and vegetable juices and delicious health drinks made from milk, yogurt and fruit.

CAFFEINE-FREE COFFEES

Dandelion coffee

Dandelion coffee is made from the ground, roasted roots of the dandelion plant. It can be bought ready-ground.

Preparation
Use 1 tsp of dandelion coffee for each 1 cup needed. Put the coffee in a saucepan and dry roast for 2-3 minutes. Add the water and simmer for 10 minutes. Strain and drink with or without milk.

Decaffeinated coffee

In recent years techniques have been developed which remove the caffeine from coffee with chemical solvents. Unfortunately, these chemicals are not totally removed from the coffee, and it is possible that they are harmful.

Grain coffees and coffee substitutes

There are grain coffees on the market. They are mixtures of ground and toasted whole grains, grain products, fruit, roots and natural sweeteners. Some common ingredients are barley, oats, millet, wheat, rye, bran, figs, malt and molasses.

Preparation
Put 1 tsp coffee into a cup, pour over boiling water and add milk if desired.

FRESH FRUIT AND VEGETABLE JUICES

As well as being delicious, fresh juices are extremely beneficial to the body, being highly concentrated in nutrients. Any fruit or vegetable can be juiced, and all have diuretic and laxative properties. Juices of particular value are described below. Of course, their therapeutic effects are not instantaneous or guaranteed, and should not be considered as a substitute for your doctor's advice.

Juices should not be drunk in huge quantities as they are so concentrated. About 1¼ cups or less a day will be plenty, particularly with some of the more acid fruit.

Citrus fruit can be squeezed by hand but you will need a special juicing machine (see p. 62) for most of the other fruit and vegetables. To use, wash the fruit or vegetables, top and tail, core and chop as necessary (there is no need to peel) and feed into the juicer.

Apple juice

Apple juice, like most fruit and vegetable juices, has diuretic and laxative properties. It is good for general cleansing of the system.

Beet juice

This is thought to build up red blood cells in the body, useful in cases of anemia. It also cleanses the liver, kidneys and gallbladder and may be helpful for women with menstrual problems or infertility.

Carrot juice

Carrot juice cleanses the digestive system, promoting vitality and a feeling of well being. It is a good skin cleanser and digestive aid, and is also believed by some to help break down ulcerous or cancerous growths. Carrot juice should not be taken in excess as it can be poisonous in large quantities.

Celery juice

This cleans away waste in the intestinal tract and is thought to be helpful in cases of arthritis, varicose veins and heart disease.

Cucumber juice

Cucumber juice has natural cleansing and diuretic properties. It is thought to promote hair growth, to regulate blood pressure and to alleviate arthritis and rheumatism.

Lettuce juice

Lettuce juice is high in iron, and is therefore helpful for women with heavy menstruation. It is also a natural relaxant and mild diuretic.

Orange juice

This juice is high in vitamin C, which is thought to help prevent coughs and colds. Orange juice can be fairly acid and should not be drunk in large quantities.

Parsley juice

Parsley juice is thought to stimulate the thyroid and adrenal glands and is helpful in urinogenital and kidney disorders.

Spinach juice

Spinach juice is a wonderful remedy for constipation. It is high in oxalic acid, which increases peristalsis.

Watercress juice

Watercress juice is a good general cleanser and purifier of the body.

MILK AND YOGURT DRINKS

Milk shakes

Commercial milk shakes are often filled with sugar synthetic coloring and even synthetic flavoring. However, milk shakes can be just as enticing and also nutritious if you make them yourself from natural ingredients.

1¼ cups fullfat milk, skim milk or soy milk
¼ pound fresh fruit, pitted and roughly chopped if necessary
a little sweetener, if liked

Blend all the ingredients until smooth.

Lassis

Lassis are similar to milk shakes but are made from yogurt instead of milk. They are a delightful alternative to milk shakes and are very quick and simple to make.

Plain lassis are usually made with an equal mixture of plain yogurt and water, beaten together with a hand beater or fork, and sweetened or salted as desired.

1¼ cups plain yogurt
¼ pound fresh fruit, pitted and roughly chopped if necessary
a little sweetener
a little grated citrus rind or grated nuts

Blend all the ingredients until smooth.

Pep-up drink

This is a wonderful way to start the day, giving you a good balance of protein, vitamins and minerals.

1¼ cups milk, fullfat, skim or soy
1¼ cups fruit or vegetable juice
1 tbsp brewer's yeast

Mix all the ingredients together in a glass.

KITCHEN EQUIPMENT

Although you do not need a wide range of kitchen equipment in whole food cooking, the following may be useful.

Baking pans

Baking pans are available in many shapes and sizes, and it is useful to have a selection. Cake pans can be round or square with varying depths and widths. The most commonly used size is 8-inches wide. Loose-bottomed or spring-form cake pans are particularly useful. Tart pans (for tarts and quiches) are shallow, round pans with removable bases.

A loaf pan can be used for both bread and cakes. The most commonly used sizes are 9- × 5- × 3-inches and 8½- × 4½- × 2½-inches; these are the sizes used for loaves in this book.

A jelly roll tin, patty tins and a baking tray are useful for cookies, small cakes and tarts.

Blender

An electric blender can be used to blend pâtés, purées, soups, sauces and drinks and also to grate nuts and bread crumbs. Vegetable purées are particularly beneficial because the vegetables only need to be be lightly cooked before blending, thus retaining most of their nutritional value. Only fill to about two-thirds from the top, as the contents will rise up.

Chopping boards

Wooden chopping boards are preferable as knives do not blunt so quickly. After use, a wooden board should be lightly washed and left to dry in a warm, dry place.

Food processor/mixer

A food processor or mixer is not really essential unless you are cooking with large quantities of food. However, it will enable you to mix cakes, bread and many other sweet and savory dishes in a very short time, leaving you free for other things. A good food processor should be able to chop, grind, shred and slice. Useful attachments for a food mixer are a shredder for vegetables and cheese, and a dough hook for breads and pastry.

Garlic press

For some recipes sliced or minced garlic is required, and a knife should be used, but for crushed garlic a press is a great help.

Grater

A small hand grater is invaluable for grating vegetables (especially the root varieties), cheese, hard fruit, nutmeg, ginger root and citrus rind. The shredding blade of a food processor is ideal for grating vegetables.

Juicer

A juicer is essential if you want to make your own fresh fruit and vegetable juices. It liquidizes the produce, separating the fresh juice from the pulp. It can be used for most fruit and vegetables, although citrus fruit can also be squeezed by hand or with a citrus juicer.

Knives

Good, sharp, well-weighted knives are a joy to work with. Sharpen them regularly with a knife sharpener for the best results. Stainless steel knives usually last longer than those made from carbon steel.

Longer knives are best for chopping and slicing; shorter knives for peeling. Serrated knives are useful for slicing soft produce and loaves of bread.

Pans

Pans should be made of stainless steel, stainless steel with copper bottoms, enamel, iron, or enameled iron. Glass or ceramic pans can cook unevenly. Avoid aluminum pans which leave a poisonous deposit on food. At the Neal's Yard Bakery stainless steel pans are preferred, but if using these, be careful not to scratch them as small amounts of metal can escape into the food.

The best pans are fairly heavy with tightly fitting lids and secure handles, preferably of a different, heat-resistant material.

Potato masher

This can be used for roughly puréeing any vegetable or soft fruit and for mixing up dips and sauces.

Pressure cooker

A pressure cooker is a good investment for whole food cooking, as it will cook dried beans, grains and root vegetables in a fraction of the time normally taken. It is particularly good for dried beans as it makes the initial fast boiling for some beans unnecessary. It can also be used for soups, stocks, stews and rice puddings. Pressure-cooking is not recommended for soft vegetables as they overcook.

Choose one made from stainless steel rather than aluminum if possible, as aluminum oxides can dissolve into the food.

Salad sprouter

Although it is very simple to sprout beans, grains and seeds in a jelly jar (see p. 23), a salad sprouter is well worth having if you are planning to sprout beans regularly. Because it has 3 layers it is possible to sprout 3 varieties of beans simultaneously.

Steamer

A steamer is important. Most vegetables retain more of their shape, flavor and nutritional value when steamed. There are quite a few good steamers on the market; the best are usually metal and "petal-shaped," expanding to fit the size of the saucepan. If you don't have a steamer, you can use a metal colander inside a saucepan with a tightly fitting lid.

Vegetable mill

This is used for puréeing vegetables. It is adjustable so that varying degrees of coarseness can be achieved.

Water filters

There are two basic types of water filter generally available. One can be attached to your fawcet, so all the water is filtered. The other is a jug through which you pour the water you wish to be filtered.

Filters will remove most of the chlorine (added intentionally) and most of the lead, mercury and cadmium (added unintentionally by water passing through old metal pipes). Use water filters for drinking water, making tea and for all water used in cooking.

Beaters

Hand beaters are basic kitchen utensils, used for stirring, mixing and beating. Use a wire balloon whisk for beating egg whites, stirring sauces and whipping cream, and a rotary beater for whipping cream, beating eggs and other light mixtures. For large quantities, such as cake batters, you may prefer to use a food processor or an electric mixer.

Wok

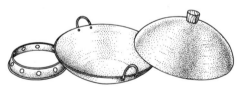

These are Chinese pans designed for quick stir-frying. Made of thin metal and rounded, the heat reaches all parts of the pan, cooking food quickly and evenly. They are usually made from carbon iron, and can have wooden or iron handles.

Woks are usually balanced on a stand over the heat. Some varieties are flat-bottomed and do not need a stand. These are particularly suitable if you are using an electric ring.

Miscellaneous

Other useful kitchen utensils are wooden spoons, a rolling pin, a vegetable brush, spatulas, a wire rack (for cooling cakes), a mortar and pestle (for grinding seeds), a rotary grater (for grinding nuts), a measuring jug, a colander, a strainer, a salad spinner, a zester (for citrus rind), an ice cream scoop, small brushes (for egg or oil glazes) and a clock.

FREEZING

Home freezing is a good way of storing surplus produce and ready-prepared dishes, and is particularly useful if you cook for a large family, lead a busy life or grow your own produce. Most fresh vegetables, fruit, raw foods and cooked dishes can be frozen successfully if you follow the guidelines given here.

The best freezer wrappings are heavy-duty or double-thickness plastic bags, plastic wrap or foil. If the wrappings are too thin, the food will deteriorate more quickly. Containers should be rigid, preferably plastic, and well-sealed. Label bags and containers before freezing for easy identification.

Fresh vegetables

All vegetables for freezing should be as young and tender as possible. If they are from your own garden or allotment, pick them first thing in the morning and blanch and freeze them immediately to preserve as much of their nutritional value as possible. If you are buying vegetables, choose the freshest available. Always prepare and blanch vegetables before freezing to preserve the color, flavor and texture.

Most vegetables freeze well, but there are some exceptions. Salad vegetables such as lettuce, cucumber, tomatoes, endive, chicory, avocados, watercress, radishes, peppers and celery do not freeze well, and also "wet" vegetables such as rutabagas and boiled potatoes. Too much water is lost during thawing and they will become limp and soft.

Preparation and blanching
Clean the vegetables well. Top and tail, break into flowerets, cut into small pieces or leave whole as appropriate.

Blanching destroys the enzyme which would otherwise spoil the color and flavor of the vegetable. There are two methods, water blanching and steam blanching.

Water blanching is the immersion of raw vegetables in fast boiling water for a given time (see the chart below). For blanching 1 pound of vegetables you will need about 5 quarts of fast boiling water. Put the prepared vegetables in a wire basket or strainer and lower into the water. The water should be brought back to a boil within 1 minute. Start timing when it begins to boil vigorously.

For steam blanching, put the prepared vegetables in a steamer with a tightly fitting lid and steam vigorously over boiling water for the given time (see the chart below).

When blanching is complete, remove the vegetables from the water and cool thoroughly in cold water. Drain well.

Freezing
Having prepared, blanched, cooled and drained your vegetables, pack in plastic bags or containers, in small or large quantities according to use. Take care to eliminate all the air.

Thawing and cooking
Most frozen vegetables can be cooked straight
Continued on page 65

VEGETABLE	WATER BLANCHING	STEAM BLANCHING	STORAGE TIME
Artichokes, French	8 minutes Add 1 tbsp lemon juice.	12 minutes	12 months
Asparagus	2-4 minutes, depending on size.	3-6 minutes	10 months
Beets: small **large**	5-10 minutes, until completely cooked.	5-10 minutes, until completely cooked.	6 months 6 months
Broccoli	3-5 minutes, depending on size.	4½ minutes, depending on size.	12 months
Brussels sprouts	4 minutes	6 minutes	12 months
Cabbages	1 minute Shred finely.	1½ minutes Shred finely.	6 months
Calabrese	As for broccoli.		
Carrots	3 minutes Leave whole if small or cut in 1-inch slices.	4½ minutes Leave whole if small or cut in 1-inch slices.	12 months
Cauliflowers	4 minutes Break into flowerets. Add 1 tbsp lemon juice.	6 minutes Break into flowerets.	6 months
Celery	3 minutes Cut in 1-inch pieces.	4½ minutes Cut in 1-inch pieces.	6 months
Celery root	3 minutes Cut in 1-inch pieces.	4½ minutes Cut in 1-inch pieces.	6 months
Corn-on-the-cob: small **large**	4 minutes 6 minutes	6 minutes 9 minutes	12 months 12 months
Eggplants	6 minutes Cut in 1-inch cubes.	9 minutes	10 months

VEGETABLE	WATER BLANCHING	STEAM BLANCHING	STORAGE TIME
English runner beans	2 minutes Cut in 1-inch pieces.	3 minutes Cut in 1-inch pieces.	12 months
Fava beans	3 minutes	4½ minutes	12 months
Fennel	3 minutes Cut in 1-inch pieces.	4½ minutes Cut in 1-inch pieces.	6 months
Green beans	2-3 minutes	4-5 minutes	12 months
Jerusalem artichokes	4 minutes Leave whole or cut in 1-inch pieces.	6 minutes Leave whole or cut in 1-inch pieces.	8 months
Kohlrabi	3 minutes Cut in 1-inch pieces.	4½ minutes Cut in 1-inch pieces.	12 months
Leeks	1 minute Cut in 1-inch slices.	1½ minutes Cut in 1-inch slices.	3 months
Mushrooms	These are best sautéed for 1 minute in a little butter or oil, whole if button mushrooms or in ½-inch slices if large. Cool and freeze.		3 months
Okra	2 minutes	3 minutes	6 months
Onions	2 minutes Chop, slice or leave whole as appropriate.	3 minutes Chop, slice or leave whole as appropriate.	2 months
Parsnips	2 minutes Cut in ½-inch slices.	3 minutes Cut in ½-inch slices.	12 months
Peas and snow peas	1 minute	1½ minutes	12 months
Peppers	2 minutes Cut in ½-inch slices.	3 minutes Cut in ½-inch slices.	12 months
Potatoes: new mashed	4 minutes —	6 minutes —	12 months 3 months
Pumpkins and squashes	3 minutes Cut in ½-inch slices.	4½ minutes Cut in ½-inch slices.	6 months
Salsify	2 minutes Cut in ½-inch pieces.	3 minutes Cut in ½-inch pieces.	12 months
Sea kale	1 minute	1½ minutes	6 months
Spinach	2 minutes	3 minutes	6 months
Sweet potatoes	3 minutes Cut in 1-inch pieces.	4½ minutes Cut in 1-inch pieces.	12 months
Swiss chard	2 minutes	3 minutes	12 months
Tomatoes	These are best frozen as tomato pulp. Peel and core the tomatoes and simmer in their own juice for 5 minutes. Cool and freeze.		12 months
Turnips	2 minutes Cut in ½-inch pieces.	3 minutes Cut in ½-inch pieces.	12 months
Yams	2 minutes Cut in 1-inch pieces.	3 minutes Cut in 1-inch pieces.	12 months
Zucchini	1 minute Cut in ½-inch slices.	1½ minutes Cut in ½-inch slices.	6 months

Spices & Seeds (See p. 56)

Alfalfa seeds (see p. 56) are very nutritious, containing protein, minerals and vitamins. Sprinkle them over sweet and savory dishes.

Pumpkin seeds (see p. 42) contain protein and minerals, particularly zinc and iron. Use raw or cooked as you would nuts, or as a garnish.

Poppy seeds (see p. 58) can be blue-black, as here, or white. Sweet and mild in flavor, they can be scattered over cakes and cookies.

Linseeds (see p. 58) are usually processed for their oil, but they can be used in baking and contain three essential fatty acids.

Curry powder (see p. 57) is a ready-prepared blend of spices, and can be mild or hot.

Paprika (see p. 58) can be mild or hot in taste, and is used in savory soups, stews and sauces.

Chilis (see p. 57) are available dried, as here, or fresh. They are extremely hot to taste.

Cayenne pepper (see p. 56) is ground from a variety of chili, and is very hot and pungent.

Juniper berries (see p. 57) are very pungent.

Allspice berries (see p. 56), also used ground.

Cinnamon sticks (see p. 57) can be used whole to flavor many drinks.

Mustard seeds (see p. 58) can be black or white. The white seeds are milder than the black.

Peppercorns (see p. 58) can be white or black. They are used whole or ground as a seasoning.

Whole nutmeg (see p. 58) is grated before use.

Mace (see p. 58) is the nutmeg's outer casing.

Ginger (see p. 57) is best if freshly grated.

Cloves (see p. 57) are very pungent and spicy.

Saffron (see p. 58) produces a lovely yellow color.

Garam masala (see p. 57) is a ready-prepared blend of ground spices.

Turmeric (see p. 58) is mild and aromatic and will turn food yellow.

Fenugreek seeds (see p. 57) have a slightly bitter-sweet flavor.

Asafoetida (see p. 56) is usually available ready-ground, as here.

Celery seeds (see p. 57) have a slightly bitter, savory flavor.

Chinese five-spice (see p. 57) is a ready-prepared blend of ground spices.

Black cardamom pods (see p. 56) are very aromatic, and are often used to flavor rice.

Green cardamom pods (see p. 56) are similar to the black, and can be used whole or ground.

Cracked star anise is the broken pods and seeds of whole star anise (see p. 58).

Star anise (see p. 58) is a star-shaped pod containing seeds with an aniseed-like taste.

Coriander seeds (see p. 57) have an aromatic subtle taste, popular in many Eastern dishes.

Cumin seeds (see p. 57) are hot and pungent, even bitter. They are often used in curries.

Rose hip tea (see p. 60) is made from ground rose hips and is high in vitamin C.

Linden tea (see p. 60) is a soothing herbal tea, clear and golden in color.

Lettuce juice (see p. 61) is a fairly strong, dark green juice, high in iron.

Parsley juice (see p. 61) has a delicate, distinctive flavor. It is high in vitamins.

Camomile tea (see p. 59) is a refreshing tea made from dried camomile flowers.

Nettle tea (see p. 60) is a dark green tea thought to have purifying effects.

Celery juice (see p. 61) is greeny-yellow in color and is believed to act as a cleanser.

Spinach juice (see p. 61) is a strongly flavored juice often used for constipation.

Comfrey tea (see p. 59) is particularly nutritious, containing vitamin B$_{12}$.

Fennel tea (see p. 59) is usually made from whole fennel seeds, as here.

Cucumber juice (see p. 61) is a refreshing, bright green juice, drunk as a cleanser.

Watercress juice (see p. 61) is believed to have general purifying effects on the body.

Twig tea (see p. 60) uses twigs from the tea bush, but it is tannin-free.

Raspberry leaf tea (see p. 60) has an unusual taste, acquired with practice.

Grain coffee (see p. 61) can be made from ground barley, as here, or from many other grains.

Lassis (see p. 61) can be plain, as here, or flavored with fruit and natural sweeteners.

Mu tea (see p. 60) is an aromatic, smoky tea made from a variety of herbs.

Vervain tea (see p. 60) is a fresh, golden tea often drunk as a general tonic.

Dandelion coffee (see p. 61) is made from ground dandelion roots and is caffeine-free.

Milk shakes (see p. 61) can be made with virtually any fruit. Here, banana is used.

Continued from page 63
from the freezer. Break them apart gently before boiling, steaming or baking. To calculate cooking times, simply deduct the blanching time from the time the fresh vegetables would usually take to cook, and start timing from when the water is boiling or when the vegetables are put in the oven.

If you wish to thaw the vegetables before cooking, 1 pound will take about 6 hours to thaw in a refrigerator and about 3 hours at room temperature. Fully thawed vegetables should be cooked immediately. Corn-on-the-cobs should be fully thawed before cooking.

Fresh fruit
Fast/open freezing
This method is particularly suitable for whole fruit, such as strawberries, raspberries and currants. Remove the stems or top and tail as appropriate. Spread in a single layer on a flat baking tray and freeze. If you have one, use the separate control on your freezer to lower the temperature a further 8°-10°. Transfer to plastic bags or rigid plastic containers and freeze at the usual temperature.
Sugar freezing
This method is useful for fruits which need peeling, coring or pitting and which discolor easily, such as apples, apricots, peaches, pears and nectarines. If sugar freezing, first blanch for 2 minutes in fast boiling water with a little lemon juice.

Prepare the blanched fruit by removing their skins, cores and seeds. Cut into slices and arrange in rigid plastic containers. Prepare a syrup made from 1 part honey or fruit concentrate and 3 parts water. A little lemon juice will help prevent browning. Pour the syrup over the fruit, leaving a $\frac{1}{2}$-inch space at the top. Cover securely and freeze.
Puréed fruit
Prepare, cook and purée the fruit (see p. 32). Sweeten to taste and pack in rigid containers, leaving a $\frac{1}{2}$-inch space at the top. Cover securely and freeze.
Storage and thawing
Most fruit, if frozen correctly, will last for about 12 months. Acid fruit that is frozen without any additional sweetener will deteriorate more rapidly than sweet fruit, because sugar acts as a preservative.

Fruit to be eaten raw should be defrosted in the refrigerator or at room temperature and eaten slightly chilled. To thaw 1 pound of frozen fruit, allow 6-8 hours in a refrigerator or 4-5 hours at room temperature. Do not leave thawed for too long as the fruit can lose its flavor.

Fruit to be cooked before eating can be heated gently from frozen.

Dairy produce
Some dairy products can be frozen, although there is usually no need as they are so readily available fresh.
Butter, margarine and vegetable fats
These should be double-wrapped in foil or plastic bags before freezing. They will keep for 3 months if salted, and up to 6 months if unsalted.

Cream
Fresh heavy or whipping cream can be frozen, and will keep for up to 3 months. It freezes more successfully if half-whipped first.
Eggs
Eggs do not freeze well as the egg yolks can harden. They can be separated and then frozen in waxed containers, but a little sugar or salt should first be mixed into the yolks.
Fresh and soft cheeses
These will keep for up to 6 months, although cottage cheese will only keep for 1-2 weeks. Wrap in foil or a plastic bag.

Thaw frozen cheese for 24 hours in the refrigerator and leave at room temperature before serving.
Hard cheeses
Hard cheese will go crumbly if frozen for more than a few weeks, but the flavor is not lost and the crumbly cheese is good for cooking. Either grate straight from frozen, or thaw for 24 hours in the refrigerator and leave at room temperature before serving. Thawed cheese should be eaten quickly as it will not keep very well.
Milk
Only homogenized milk should be frozen, or it will separate on thawing. Freeze in rigid plastic containers, not in glass bottles. It will keep for up to 1 month.

Herbs
Fresh herbs can be frozen successfully. Blanch the leaves for a few seconds in boiling water, plunge into cold water and then store in plastic bags, plastic containers or aluminum foil. To thaw the leaves, leave them at room temperature for a few minutes or crumble frozen over dishes as required. Alternatively, do not blanch but tie into bunches and freeze in rigid containers.

Soups, broths and sauces
Most soups, broths, sauces and similar liquids can be frozen successfully. The exceptions are egg-based sauces and mayonnaise, which can separate or curdle on thawing.

Chill the sauce or soup after cooking and pack into rigid containers, leaving a $\frac{1}{2}$-inch space at the top. Pack in small quantities; about $1\frac{1}{4}$-cups portions. Most sauces and soups will keep for 2-3 months. To thaw, either thaw in the refrigerator or reheat very gently from frozen in a heavy saucepan, stirring continuously.

Cooked meals
Freezing precooked meals has a number of advantages. You can save yourself time and money by cooking extra and freezing the leftovers for another time, and you can plan ahead for dinner parties or special occasions. Keep a supply of cooked meals in the freezer to cater for unexpected guests.

Cool the cooked food and then pack into rigid containers, leaving a $\frac{1}{2}$-inch space at the top. Ideally cooked dishes should not be kept longer than 1 month, although if frozen correctly they may last up to 3 months. Food which is left over after thawing and/or reheating must not be frozen again.

Cooked grains and beans
There is obviously no need to freeze uncooked beans or grains as they are dried and have a very long shelf life. However, it can be very useful to freeze precooked beans or grains as they will take only a few hours to thaw.

Cool after cooking and pack into rigid containers, leaving a $\frac{1}{2}$-inch space at the top, and seal tightly. They can be stored in the freezer for up to 3 months. To thaw 1 pound of frozen beans or grains, allow 6 hours in the refrigerator or 4 hours at room temperature. Use immediately after thawing.

Puddings and desserts
Most puddings can be frozen successfully, though they are extremely delicate. Mousses, whips and fools freeze well, but are best made in freezerproof serving dishes to avoid turning out. Cover securely with foil and keep for 2-3 months. Egg or cream-based desserts will tend to separate on thawing, however. Ice cream should be packed in rigid containers and frozen for up to 3 months.

Cakes, pastries, biscuits and cookies
These all freeze extremely well. Although raw cake and dough mixtures can be frozen for a few weeks, it is better to freeze the cakes, pastries and biscuits after cooking.

If undecorated, most cakes can be frozen for up to 6 months. Wrap in a double-thickness of plastic or foil and put in a rigid container. Thaw, in the bag or foil, at room temperature for 1-2 hours. If the cake is decorated or iced, it should only be frozen for up to 2 months. Thaw in its bag or foil at room temperature for about 4 hours.

For pastry dishes, pies and tarts, it is usually best to freeze the unfilled shell or base and then fill and decorate after thawing. Uncooked pie-crust dough is less delicate than cooked, and will keep for 3-4 months. Thaw at room temperature for 3-4 hours, or overnight in the refrigerator. Cooked pastry is best frozen in its tart or pie dish (if freezeproof) and wrapped in foil or plastic. It will keep for up to 6 months. Bake from frozen, adding about 5 minutes to the cooking time.

Cookies, muffins and biscuits can be frozen in bulk, in large plastic bags or well-sealed boxes. They will keep for up to 6 months. For loaf cakes or quick breads, wrap in foil and then a plastic bag. Thaw at room temperature: biscuits for about 1 hour and larger cakes in their bags for 2-3 hours. Alternatively, the biscuits can be thawed from frozen in a 400°F oven for 10 minutes.

Bread
Bread freezes very successfully, so it is often worth baking a couple of extra loaves and freezing them. They will keep for a few months, although are best eaten within 4 weeks. Crusty loaves and rolls will keep for rather less.

Freeze bread as fresh as possible, as soon as it is cool. Wrap loaves individually in polythene bags. To thaw, allow 4-8 hours at room temperature, depending on size.

How to use the recipes

Before using the recipes we recommend you read through the information in this section.

VEGETABLE PREPARATION

In the recipes assume that:

1 All vegetables are scrubbed or washed.

2 All vegetables, apart from onions and garlic, are NOT peeled unless otherwise specified. This is because many important vitamins and minerals lie just beneath the surface of the skin.

3 All vegetables have been topped and tailed, podded, seeded and have had their stems, roots and outer leaves removed where applicable.

4 All vegetables are medium-sized unless otherwise indicated.

FRUIT PREPARATION

In the recipes assume that:

1 All fruit are washed and/or picked over.

2 Fruit with edible skins, such as apples, peaches, plums, and so on, are NOT peeled unless otherwise specified.

3 Citrus fruit, tropical fruit and bananas DO have their skins removed.

4 All fruit have their cores, seeds and pits removed and are topped and tailed when applicable.

5 All fruit are medium-sized unless otherwise indicated.

Note: In general, it is preferable to use fresh vegetables and fruit, home-grown (i.e. local produce) whenever possible, and to make the maximum use of those in season.

INGREDIENTS

Where the following ingredients are mentioned, assume that:

Eggs are medium-sized and free-range.

Cheese is a hard Cheddar-style cheese, vegetarian if possible.

Butter is preferably unsalted (sweet).

Rice is short- or long-grain brown rice, preferably organic.

Honey is clear and runny.

Nuts are all shelled and unsalted.

Oil is vegetable oil. Use cold pressed oils whenever possible.

Yogurt is plain cow's milk yogurt, full- or lowfat. If a recipe calls for Greek--style yogurt, use a strained, thick yogurt.

Salt can be substituted with a low-sodium alternative if wished (see p. 50).

Quark is a German lowfat cheese made from skim milk available plain or flavored with herbs; look for it at health food stores or delicatessens.

ABBREVIATIONS

Ⓖ = gluten-free recipe.
Most recipes can be adapted to a gluten-free diet by substituting gluten-free grains, flours or baking powders when necessary (see p. 17, 133).

Ⓥ = vegan recipe (free from animal products).
Most recipes can be adapted to a vegan diet by substituting a vegetable oil or vegetable margarine for butter, unsweetened soya milk for cow's milk and a non-animal sweetener such as apple juice concentrate or maple syrup for honey.

Note: The Ⓖ and Ⓥ symbols refer to the recipes themselves and not necessarily to the serving suggestions.

tsp = level teaspoon	oz = ounce
tbsp = level tablespoon	fl oz = fluid ounce

Note on recipes

1 The recipes which follow vary in the size of servings. Some are suitable for large groups, others for smaller occasions. All recipes can be scaled up or down proportionately. If you wish to adjust the cake recipes, be aware that for smaller cakes, a greater proportion of baking powder to liquid will be required than for a larger cake.

2 Some recipes call for leftover cooked grains or beans. If you do not have enough left over, refer to the appropriate information section for cooking quantities and times.

3 For details on the kitchen equipment required for the recipes, see page 62.

CONVERSIONS

If you are ever shopping at Neal's Yard on a vacation in London, you will find all the products are sold according to their metric weights, a measurement rarely used in the United States but used throughout Europe. These charts should be useful.

If you are cooking while in London, there are several important points to remember. Most important, the British pint contains 20 fluid ounces, while the American pint contains only 16 fluid ounces.

Also, it is possible any stove you use will give temperatures in centigrade, not fahrenheit. Many of the stoves, however, are gas and in that case the oven temperature will be indicated by gas marks.

WEIGHTS

IMPERIAL Ounces		METRIC Grams to nearest 25 g
¼		8
½		15
¾		20
1		25
2		50
3		75
4	¼ lb	100
5		150
6		175
7		200
8	½ lb	225
9		250
10		275
11		300
12	¾ lb	350
13		375
14		400
15		425
16	1 lb	450
32	2 lb	900
35	2 lb 3 oz	1,000/1 kilo

Note: All dishes cooked in the oven are placed on the middle shelf unless otherwise specified.

In cases where greasing a container is mentioned, butter, margarine or oil may be used.

LIQUID MEASUREMENTS

IMPERIAL Fluid ounces/pints		METRIC Milliliters
1		25
2		50
3		75
4	½ American cup	100
5	¼ British pint	150
6		175
7		200
8	⅖ British pint (1 American cup)	225
9		250
10		275
15	¾ pt	425
16	1 American pint	450
20	1 British pint	570
25	1¼ pt	700
35	1¾ British pint	1,000/1 liter

1 tablespoon	15 ml
1 teaspoon	5 ml
1 cup	8 fl oz

OVEN TEMPERATURES

CENTIGRADE	FAHRENHEIT	GAS MARK
240	475	9
230	450	8
220	425	7
200	400	6
190	375	5
180	350	4
170 (160)	325	3
150	300	2
140	275	1
130 (120)	250	½
110	225	¼
100	200	Low
80	175	Very low
70	150	Extra low

BREAKFASTS

For additional breakfast ideas, see Bran Muffins (p. 137),
Cheese Biscuits (p. 140) and the Bread Section (p. 147).
For breakfast drinks, see Herb Teas (p. 59)
and Health Drinks (p. 61).

◆

Granola 1

½ cup soy oil
½ cup malt extract
4 cups old-fashioned oats
1 cup wheat flakes
2 cups rye flakes
4 tbsp sunflower seeds
⅓ cup chopped filberts
2 tbsp shredded coconut (optional)
⅔ cup raisins

Preparation 10 minutes
Cooking 1 hour
Makes 4-6 servings
Ⓥ

1 Preheat the oven to 275°F.

2 Melt the oil and malt in a large saucepan.

3 Add all the rest of the ingredients, except the raisins. Mix well.

4 Spread the mixture onto 2 large trays and bake for 1 hour until the flakes are brown and crispy. Stir frequently to prevent sticking.

5 Remove from the oven and leave to cool. Stir a couple of times while cooling to stop the flakes from sticking together. Add the raisins and store in an airtight container in a cool place.

Serve with milk, yogurt, soy milk or fruit juice. Add a little fresh fruit, if wished.

Granola 2

½ cup soy oil
⅓ cup honey
5⅓ cups old-fashioned oats
1 cup sunflower seeds
4 tbsp sesame seeds
2 tbsp pumpkin seeds
1 cup chopped mixed nuts
2 tbsp wheat germ
⅔ cup golden raisins

Preparation 10 minutes
Cooking 1 hour
Makes 4-6 servings

1 Preheat the oven to 275°F.

2 Melt the oil and honey in a large saucepan.

3 Add all the ingredients, except the wheat germ and golden raisins. Mix together well.

4 Spread the mixture onto 2 large trays and bake for 1 hour until the flakes are brown and crispy, stirring frequently to prevent sticking.

5 Remove from the oven and leave to cool. Stir a couple of times while cooling to stop the flakes from sticking together. Add the wheat germ and golden raisins and store in an airtight container in a cool place.

Serve with milk, yogurt, soy milk or fruit juice. Add a little fresh fruit, if wished.

Muesli Base

6 cups old-fashioned oats
2½ cups barley flakes
2¼ cups wheat flakes

Preparation 5 minutes
Makes 4-6 servings
Ⓥ

Unlike granola, muesli is not toasted. You can make this as rich or plain a muesli as you like, depending on the extra ingredients.

Combine the ingredients and store in an airtight jar in a cool place.

Add your own selection of dried or fresh fruit, nuts or seeds and serve with milk, yogurt, soy milk or fruit juice. Eat immediately or leave to soak overnight. Alternatively, cover with your choice of liquid, simmer gently for 5 minutes and eat warm.

Basic Muesli

3 cups old-fashioned oats
3 cups rye flakes
2¼ cups wheat flakes
2½ cups barley flakes
1½ cups raisins
1½ cups golden raisins
1½ cups filberts
3 cups sunflower seeds
1½ cups dried apricots
2½ cups bran (optional)

Preparation 10 minutes
Makes 8-12 servings
Ⓥ

Combine the ingredients and store in an airtight jar in a cool place.

Serve with milk, yogurt, soy milk or fruit juice and add a little fresh fruit, if wished. Eat immediately or leave to soak overnight. Alternatively, cover with your choice of liquid, simmer gently for 5 minutes and eat warm.

Gluten-Free Muesli

7½ cups rice flakes
7½ cups millet flakes
3 cups sunflower seeds
1½ cups raisins
1½ cups golden raisins
1½ cups filberts
1½ cups dried apricots
3 cups (6 tbsp) shredded coconut
4 cups soy bran (optional, for added
  fiber, see p. 14)

Preparation 10 minutes
Makes 8-12 servings
(GF) (V)

Combine the ingredients and store in an airtight jar in a cool place.

Serve with milk, yogurt, soy milk or fruit juice and add a little fresh fruit if wished. Eat immediately or leave to soak overnight. Alternatively, cover with your choice of liquid, simmer gently for 5 minutes and eat warm.

Rich Muesli

3 cups old-fashioned oats
3½ cups rye flakes
2¼ cups wheat flakes
2½ cups barley flakes
1½ cups raisins
1½ cups golden raisins
1½ cups filberts
3 cups sunflower seeds
1½ cups chopped almonds
1½ cups cashew nuts
1½ cups dried apricots
1½ cups dried pears
1½ cups dried peaches

Preparation 10 minutes
Makes 12-16 servings
(V)

Combine the ingredients and store in an airtight jar in a cool place.

Serve with milk, yogurt, soy milk or fruit juice and add a little fresh fruit if wished. Eat immediately or leave to soak overnight. Alternatively, cover with your choice of liquid, simmer gently for 5 minutes and eat warm.

Basic Oatmeal

2⅔ cups old-fashioned oats
2½ cups milk or water
a little salt (optional)

Preparation and cooking 15-20 minutes
Serves 2

To prevent sticking, soak the oats for 1 hour or overnight in the liquid in which they are to be cooked. This will also reduce the actual cooking time.
  For variety, replace the oats with any flaked grain, meal or flour.

1 Put the oats, milk and salt, if using, into a saucepan.

2 Bring to a boil, then lower the heat and simmer gently for 10-15 minutes until cooked, stirring frequently to prevent sticking.

Serve with a little milk or sweetener, if wished.

Steel-Cut Oatmeal

2⅔ cups steel-cut oats
4 cups milk or water or a mixture of
 both
a little salt (optional)

**Preparation and cooking 45 minutes
(allow 12 hours for soaking)
Serves 2**

1 Put the steel-cut oatmeal and milk in a saucepan. Leave to stand for 12 hours or overnight.

2 In the morning, bring to a boil, add the salt, if using, cover the pan and simmer over a low heat until the oats are tender and the liquid is absorbed. This will take about 45 minutes.

Serve immediately with a little milk or sweetener, if wished.

Soy & Oat Cereal

1⅓ cups old-fashioned oats
2 tbsp soy grits
pinch of salt
Scant 1 cup soy milk
Scant 1 cup water

**Preparation and cooking 15 minutes
(allow 12 hours for soaking)
Serves 2**
Ⓥ

1 Put the oats, soy grits and salt in a saucepan. Pour over the soy milk and water. Set aside for 12 hours or overnight.

2 Bring the cereal mixture to a boil and simmer gently for 8-10 minutes until cooked, stirring frequently to prevent sticking.

Serve immediately with a little milk or sweetener, if wished.

Toasted Mixed Cereal

¼ cup soy soil
2 cups old-fashioned oats
4 tbsp barley flakes
pinch of salt (optional)
2¼ cups water
Scant 1 cup milk

**Preparation and cooking 20 minutes
Serves 2**

1 Heat the oil in a saucepan. Add the oats and barley flakes. Toast gently, stirring frequently for 2-3 minutes.

2 Add the salt, water and milk and bring to a boil. Turn the heat down and simmer gently for 15 minutes until cooked, stirring frequently to prevent sticking.

Serve immediately with a little milk or sweetener, if wished.

SOUPS

Note: Many of these soup recipes require a blender or food processor. Alternatively, unless the recipe otherwise specifies, you can use a potato masher. This will produce a coarser-textured soup.

Adzuki Bean Soup

3 lb tomatoes
¼ cup soy oil
2 onions, chopped
2 celery stalks, chopped
2 carrots, chopped
2 garlic cloves, crushed
1 tbsp tomato paste
1 bay leaf
2 tsp finely chopped fresh thyme or
   1 tsp dried
1½ quarts vegetable broth or water
1 cup adzuki beans, soaked for 4 hours
salt and black pepper
finely chopped fresh parsley, to garnish

**Preparation 20-25 minutes
(allow 4 hours for soaking the beans)
Cooking 1 hour
Serves 6**
Ⓖ Ⓥ

This hearty soup is equally delicious with mung beans or split peas. Serve with a sprinkling of grated cheese for extra nutrition.

1 Put the tomatoes in a bowl and pour over boiling water. Set aside for 10-15 minutes to allow the skins to soften.

2 Heat the oil in a large heavy-bottomed saucepan and add the onion, celery, carrot and garlic.

3 Pour the water off the tomatoes. Drain, peel and coarsely chop.

4 Add the tomatoes, tomato paste, bay leaf and thyme to the celery and carrot mixture.

5 Add the broth and the presoaked adzuki beans and simmer for about 1 hour or until the beans are tender.

6 Adjust the seasoning and garnish with a sprinkling of fresh parsley.

Serve piping hot with whole wheat rolls.

Carrot & Orange Soup

3 tbsp soy oil
3 tbsp tamari
1 large onion, coarsely chopped
3 cups coarsely chopped carrots
juice and grated rind of 2 oranges
1½ cups finely chopped fresh parsley
about 2 quarts water
salt and black pepper

Preparation 10 minutes
Cooking 20 minutes
Serves 6-8
GF V

1 Heat the oil and tamari in a saucepan, add the onion and carrot and cook for 5 minutes until the onion is soft.

2 Add the orange juice and rind.

3 Reserve a little of the parsley for the garnish, and add the rest to the pan.

4 Pour over the water and simmer for 15 minutes. Put into a blender or food processor. Purée, then reheat.

5 Season to taste and garnish with the reserved fresh parsley sprinkled on top.

Carrot & Rice Soup

2 tbsp butter or soy oil
1 large onion, finely chopped
4 cups finely chopped carrots
4½ cups vegetable broth
1 tsp finely chopped fresh marjoram or
    ½ tsp dried
½ cup cooked brown rice
salt and black pepper

Preparation 15 minutes
Cooking 30 minutes
Serves 4
GF

This soup is ideal for using up leftover brown rice.

1 Melt the butter in a medium-sized saucepan and add the onion and carrot.

2 Add the broth, marjoram and cooked rice and simmer gently for 30 minutes, stirring occasionally to prevent sticking.

3 Transfer the soup to a blender or food processor. Blend until smooth and season to taste.

Creamed Cauliflower Soup

1 small cauliflower
1¼ cups water
2 tbsp butter
1 large onion, chopped
2 tbsp old-fashioned oats, ground
salt and black pepper
2½ cups milk
1 tbsp finely chopped fresh parsley

Preparation and cooking 25 minutes
Serves 4

1 Cut the cauliflower into small pieces, using as much of the stem and leaves as possible.

2 Put the water in a medium-sized saucepan with a tightly fitting lid. Add the cauliflower and bring to a boil. Lower the heat a little and simmer for 5 minutes.

3 Melt the butter in a saucepan. Add the onion and cook for 3-5 minutes until soft.

4 Stir in the oats and seasoning. Add the milk, a little at a time, taking care not to make any lumps.

5 Add the cauliflower and the water in which it was cooking and bring to a boil, stirring occasionally to prevent sticking. Cook for a further 5 minutes until tender.

6 Pour the mixture into a blender and blend until smooth. Return to the saucepan, add the parsley and warm through.

Cream of Mushroom Soup

1 large onion, finely chopped
¼ cup butter
8 cups finely chopped mushrooms
¼ tsp grated nutmeg
2 garlic cloves, crushed
4½ cups milk
salt and black pepper
finely chopped fresh parsley or
    mushroom slices, to garnish

Preparation 10 minutes
Cooking 20 minutes
Serves 4
(GF)

1 In a medium-sized saucepan, gently cook the onion in the butter until soft.

2 Add the mushrooms to the pan with the nutmeg and garlic.

3 Pour the milk over. Bring to a boil, then lower the heat and simmer gently for 20 minutes.

4 Transfer the soup to a blender or food processor and blend until smooth. Season to taste.

5 Garnish with a sprinkling of fresh parsley or finely chopped mushroom slices.

Serve immediately with fingers of cheese on toast and a fresh salad for a satisfying lunch.

◆

Cream of Watercress Soup

2 tbsp butter
1 large onion, finely chopped
3 potatoes, peeled and finely chopped
2 bunches watercress
2½ cups vegetable broth
2½ cups milk
salt and black pepper
½ cup sour or light cream, to serve
watercress sprig, to garnish

Preparation 15 minutes
Cooking 45 minutes
Serves 4
(GF)

This recipe uses potatoes to thicken the soup.

1 Melt the butter in a large heavy-based saucepan.

2 Add the onion and cook for 3-5 minutes until soft.

3 Add the potatoes, watercress, broth and milk.

4 Bring to a boil. Lower the heat and simmer for 45 minutes.

5 Transfer the soup to a blender or food processor and blend until smooth.

6 Season to taste. Pour into individual bowls and serve with a swirl of sour or light cream and a sprig of fresh watercress on top.

Serve with whole wheat rolls or slices of Three-Seed Bread (see p. 156).

Creamy Fava Bean Soup

½ pound young fava beans, shelled
2 tbsp butter
1 onion, finely chopped
2 garlic cloves, crushed
2 tbsp whole wheat flour
4½ cups milk or a mixture of equal parts
   of milk and broth
salt and black pepper
½ cup sour cream, to serve

Preparation 5 minutes
Cooking 20 minutes
Serves 4

Choose small, tender fava beans for this recipe, because the larger ones can be tough and floury.

1 Boil the fava beans for 6-8 minutes or steam for 8 minutes until cooked and tender.

2 In a medium-sized saucepan, melt the butter and sauté the onion and garlic for 5 minutes until the onion is soft.

3 Remove from the heat and mix in the flour. Gradually add the milk or milk and broth.

4 Pour this mixture into a blender or food processor with the cooked and well-drained fava beans and blend until smooth.

5 Return to the saucepan and heat gently, stirring constantly until the soup begins to thicken. Cook for a further 2-3 minutes. Adjust seasoning, pour into individual bowls and add a swirl of sour cream.

Serve piping hot with warm whole wheat or rye rolls.

◆

Dulse Soup

1 oz dulse (see p. 44)
4½ cups boiling water
1 tbsp soy oil
1 onion, thinly sliced
4 tbsp old-fashioned oats
salt and black pepper
2 tbsp shoyu (see p. 51)

Preparation 10 minutes
Cooking 30 minutes
Serves 6
Ⓥ

1 Rinse the dulse in cold water and put in a bowl. Pour over the boiling water.

2 Heat the oil in a medium-sized saucepan and add the onion. Cook for 5 minutes until soft.

3 Add the oats and cook for 1 minute. Add the dulse with its water and seasoning. Bring to a boil, lower the heat and simmer for 30 minutes until the soup thickens.

4 Add the shoyu and serve immediately.

Serve with whole wheat rolls.

◆

Evelyn's German Potato Soup

5¾ cups peeled and finely chopped
   potatoes
2 large onions, sliced into rings
12 allspice berries
4½ cups water
2½ cups Greek-style yogurt
salt and black pepper

Preparation 15 minutes
Cooking 20 minutes
Serves 6
ⒼⒻ

1 Put the potatoes, onions and allspice berries in a large saucepan and cover with the water. Boil for 20 minutes or until the potatoes are tender.

2 Remove from heat, mash the potato mixture with a fork or potato masher or in a blender or food processor until smooth.

3 Stir in the yogurt and season to taste.

Garlic & Onion Soup

2 tbsp butter
1 large onion, sliced into rings
4 cups shredded cabbage
3 garlic cloves, crushed
2 tbsp tamari
4½ cups water
1 cup grated cheese and a little finely
    chopped fresh parsley, to garnish

Preparation 10 minutes
Cooking 20 minutes
Serves 4
(GF)

This quick-and-easy soup can also be served with croutons fried in herb butter.

1 Melt the butter in a medium-sized saucepan.

2 Add the onion rings.

3 Add the shredded cabbage.

4 Add the garlic, tamari and water and simmer gently for 20 minutes or until the vegetables are cooked.

5 Pour into individual bowls and serve piping hot with a little grated cheese and chopped parsley sprinkled over the tops.

Gazpacho

3 cups tomato juice
¼ cup olive oil
¼ cup wine vinegar
3 garlic cloves
1 small cucumber, finely chopped
1 small red pepper, finely chopped
1 small fennel, finely chopped
1 onion, finely chopped
4 sprigs fresh parsley
2 slices whole wheat bread
salt and black pepper

Preparation 10 minutes
Chilling 20 minutes
Serves 4-6
(V)

A blender or food processor is essential for this quick-and-easy soup. Be sure to chill thoroughly before serving.

1 Blend half the tomato juice, with the olive oil, vinegar and garlic, into a blender or food processor until smooth.

2 Add half the vegetables and parsley and blend until smooth. Transfer to a serving bowl.

3 Put the other half of the tomato juice and the remaining vegetables and parsley into the blender with the whole wheat bread. Blend until smooth. Transfer to a serving bowl.

4 Mix well and season to taste. Chill for at least 20 minutes before serving.

Serve with crisp cheese croutons.

Lettuce, Cucumber & Miso Soup

1 tbsp soy oil
1 tbsp finely chopped scallions
3½ cups shredded lettuce
2 cups finely chopped cucumber
1 garlic clove
2 tsp miso (see p. 50)
1¼ cups water
salt and black pepper
sour cream or Greek-style yogurt, to
    serve (optional)

Preparation 10 minutes
Chilling 2 hours
Serves 4
(GF) (V)

You will need a blender or food processor for best results.

1 Heat the oil in a medium-sized saucepan and add the scallions.

2 Add the lettuce and cucumber to the saucepan and heat gently for 3-4 minutes until cooked.

3 Put the lettuce and cucumber into a blender or food processor with the garlic, miso and water and blend until thoroughly mixed. Season to taste.

4 Pour into a bowl and chill for about 2 hours or until quite cold. Top with a swirl of sour cream or Greek-style yogurt, if liked.

Serve with warm whole wheat bread.

Minestrone

4 tbsp olive oil
2 onions, finely chopped
2 carrots, finely chopped
2 celery stalks, finely chopped
1 cup finely chopped tomatoes
2 tbsp tomato paste
2 tsp finely chopped oregano or 1 tsp dried
1 tsp finely chopped fresh basil or ½ tsp dried
2 garlic cloves, crushed
4½ cups water
¾ cup cooked cannellini beans
¼ cup shelled fresh peas
1 cup mushrooms
salt and black pepper
grated cheese, to garnish (optional)

Preparation 15 minutes (allow extra time for cooking the beans)
Cooking 25 minutes
Serves 4-6
Ⓖ Ⓥ

Cannellini beans are traditionally added to this soup, but leftover black-eyed peas, navy or pinto beans taste just as good.

1 Heat the oil in a heavy-based saucepan and add the onions, carrots, celery and tomatoes.

2 Add the tomato paste, oregano, basil and garlic. Cook gently for a few minutes.

3 Add the water and cannellini beans, and simmer for 20 minutes.

4 Add the peas and mushrooms. Simmer a further 5 minutes, season to taste and garnish with grated cheese, if liked.

◆

Miso & Arame Soup

1 oz arame (see p. 43)
1 tbsp soy oil
1 onion, finely chopped
1 large carrot, finely chopped
1 celery stalk, finely chopped
1 tsp grated ginger root
6 tbsp tamari
4½ cups water
2 tbsp finely chopped fresh coriander leaves
1 tbsp miso (see p. 50)

Preparation 10 minutes
Cooking 30 minutes
Serves 4-6
Ⓖ Ⓥ

1 Put the arame in a bowl. Cover with boiling water and leave to stand for 5 minutes.

2 Meanwhile, heat the oil and onion in a medium-sized saucepan.

3 Add the carrot and celery.

4 Add the drained arame, ginger and tamari and simmer gently for 5 minutes.

5 Add the water and simmer gently for 15 minutes.

6 Add the chopped coriander leaves and cook for a further 5 minutes. Do not overcook.

7 Remove from the heat and stir in the miso. Return to the stove and heat to just below boiling.

Serve immediately with slices of Sunflower Seed Bread (see p. 155).

Parsnip Soup

2 tbsp butter
3-4 parsnips, finely chopped
1 large onion, finely chopped
2½ cups milk
1¼ cups water
½ tsp grated nutmeg
salt and black pepper

Preparation 10 minutes
Cooking 30 minutes
Serves 4
ⒼⒻ

Carrots, broccoli, cauliflower or leeks can be substituted for parsnips in this rich and healthy soup.

1 Melt the butter and gently sauté the parsnip and onion for 5 minutes until tender.

2 Add the milk, water, grated nutmeg and seasoning and simmer for 25 minutes.

3 Blend the soup in a blender or food processor until smooth.

Serve piping hot with warm crusty rolls.

♦

Potato & Beet Soup

¼ cup butter
1 large onion, finely chopped
3 potatoes, chopped
½ tsp ground cumin (optional)
1⅓ cups peeled and chopped cooked beets
3⅔ cups milk
salt and black pepper
finely chopped fresh parsley or coriander leaves, to garnish

Preparation 15 minutes
Cooking 20 minutes
Serves 4
ⒼⒻ

The bright pink color of this soup makes it especially popular with children.

1 Melt the butter in a large saucepan.

2 Add the onion and cook for 5 minutes until soft.

3 Add the potatoes to the pan, together with the cumin, if using.

4 Add the beets.

5 Pour the milk over and simmer for 20 minutes or until the potatoes are tender.

6 Blend until smooth. Season to taste.

7 Garnish with a sprinkling of parsley or fresh coriander leaves.

♦

Rye & Vegetable Broth

2 tbsp soy oil
1 large onion, coarsely chopped
3 carrots, coarsely chopped
1 small cauliflower, coarsely chopped
2 tsp coarsely chopped fresh sage or 1 tsp dried
3 bay leaves
2 tsp coarsely chopped fresh rosemary or 1 tsp dried
salt and black pepper
1⅓ cups rye berries
5 cups vegetable broth or water

Preparation 10 minutes
Cooking 2 hours
Serves 6
Ⓥ

This hearty soup makes an excellent lunch or supper meal if served with creamy mashed potatoes or rutabagas. For extra nutrition, stir in 1 tbsp miso (see p. 50) before serving.

1 Heat the oil in a large heavy-based saucepan. Add the chopped vegetables, sage, bay leaves, rosemary and seasoning. Cook gently for 2-3 minutes.

2 Add the rye berries and water. Mix together well. Bring to a boil, then lower the heat and simmer for 2 hours.

Serve with whole wheat rolls.

Sprouty Tofu Soup

2 tbsp olive oil
1 large onion, thinly sliced
2 garlic cloves, crushed
6 oz tofu (see p. 51), cubed
juice and grated rind of 1 lemon
¾-1 cup sprouted beans, grains or seeds
   (e.g. mung or lentil, or a mixture)
7½ cups water
salt and black pepper
5 tsp miso (see p. 50)

Preparation 5 minutes
Cooking 10 minutes
Serves 6
GF V

A very light and delicious soup. Use any type of sprouted bean, grain or seed, or a mixture of several.

1 Heat the oil in a saucepan. Add the onion and crushed garlic. Lightly cook for a few minutes.

2 Add the tofu, lemon juice and rind and sprouts.

3 Pour over the water and season. Bring to a boil, then lower the heat and simmer for 5 minutes.

4 Remove from heat, stir in the miso and serve immediately.

Tomato Soup

4 large tomatoes
2 tbsp butter
2 onions, finely chopped
2 tsp finely chopped fresh marjoram or
   1 tsp dried
2 tbsp tomato paste
2 tsp apple juice concentrate (see p. 51)
salt and black pepper
1 tbsp chicken flour
2 garlic cloves, crushed
up to 1¼ cups water or broth, if
   necessary
⅔ cup light cream

Preparation and cooking 30 minutes
Serves 6
GF

For variety, use different fresh herbs when in season or serve with a sprinkling of grated cheese on top.

1 Put the tomatoes in a bowl and pour over boiling water. Set aside for 10-15 minutes to allow the skins to soften.

2 Meanwhile, melt the butter in a saucepan and saute the onions.

3 Add the marjoram to the saucepan, together with the tomato paste, apple juice concentrate and seasoning. Stir well and continue cooking gently.

4 Pour the water off the tomatoes. Drain, peel and coarsely chop.

5 Sprinkle the chickpea flour over the onion mixture and stir in well. Add the tomatoes and crushed garlic and simmer gently for 2-3 minutes, stirring occasionally to prevent sticking.

6 Pour the mixture into a blender or food processor and blend until smooth. Return to the pan. If too thick, add the extra liquid as necessary. Pour in the light cream and heat through.

Vichyssoise

¼ cup butter
5 leeks, sliced into rings
1 large onion, sliced into rings
3 potatoes, chopped
4½ cups vegetable broth
salt and black pepper
⅔ cup light cream
fresh parsley and chives, to garnish

Preparation 15 minutes
Cooking 30 minutes
Serves 4-6
GF

This leek and potato soup can be eaten hot or cold.

1 Melt the butter in a large saucepan and add the leeks and onion. Sauté gently for 5 minutes. Add the potatoes.

2 Add the broth and simmer gently for 30 minutes, stirring occasionally.

3 Transfer the soup to a blender or food processor and blend until smooth. Season.

4 Add the cream just before serving and garnish with chopped parsley and chives.

APPETIZERS

Apple & Lima Bean Pâté

½ cup lima beans, soaked for 12 hours or overnight
2 tbsp grated tart apple or apple juice concentrate (see p. 51)
1 tbsp tahini (see p. 50)
2 tbsp finely chopped fresh parsley
juice of ½ lemon
salt and black pepper
sprigs of fresh parsley, to garnish

Preparation 5 minutes (allow 12 hours for soaking the beans)
Cooking 1½ hours
Chilling 1 hour
Serves 4
(GF) (V)

A blender or food processor is helpful for this recipe but not essential, as long as the lima beans are well cooked.

1 Transfer the soaked beans and their liquid to a saucepan. Top up with fresh water, if necessary, to cover the beans. Cover and bring to a boil. Lower the heat and simmer for about 1½ hours or until cooked. Drain and set aside.

2 Put the beans and the remaining intredients into a blender or food processor or large mixing bowl and mix thoroughly.

3 Season to taste and put in individual ramekins or a serving bowl.

4 Cover and chill for 1 hour to allow the flavors to mingle, then serve garnished with a few sprigs of fresh parsley.

Serve with fingers of whole wheat toast or warm whole wheat rolls.

Milk (see p. 46) can be full-fat or skim.

A range of delicious healthy drinks for breakfast. From the top, clockwise: **carrot juice** (see p. 61), **beetroot juice** (see p. 61), **Pep-Up Drink** (see p. 61), **orange juice** (see p. 61), **fruit lassis** (see p. 61) and **apple juice** (see p. 61).

Goat's milk yogurt (see p. 47) is very digestible.

Greek-style yogurt (see p. 47) is thick and creamy.

A nutritious selection of **mixed nuts** (see pp. 41-42).

Use **honey** (see p. 52) as an alternative to sugar.

Gluten-Free Muesli (see p. 70) for gluten allergy.

Rich Muesli (see p. 70) is high in dried fruit.

Soy & Oat Cereal (see p. 71) is tasty and unusual.

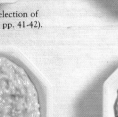

Toasted Mixed Cereal (see p. 71) has a nutty flavor.

Add your own ingredients to **Muesli Base** (see p. 69).

Basic Muesli (see p. 69) is simple and filling.

Basic Oatmeal (see p. 70) uses a standard recipe.

Steel-Cut Oatmeal (see p. 71) has a thicker texture.

Granola 1 (see p. 68) is a sweet, baked cereal.

Granola 2 (see p. 69) is a delicious variation.

A tasty selection of **dried fruit** (see pp. 38-39).

Delicious, seasonal **fresh fruit** (see pp. 32-37).

Soups (See p. 72)

Evelyn's German Potato
Soup (see p. 75) includes
pungent juniper berries.

Minestrone (see p. 77) is
a rich and filling soup,
almost a meal in itself.

Carrot & Rice Soup (see
p. 73) is high in fiber.

Marjoram adds interest to
this **Tomato Soup**
(see p. 79).

Dulse Soup (see p. 75) has
a strong seaweed flavor.

Potato & Beet Soup
(see p. 78) is attractive
to serve.

Creamed Cauliflower Soup
(see p. 73) is a mild soup.

Nourishing **Rye &
Vegetable Broth** (see p. 78).

Carrot & Orange Soup
(see p. 73) has a pleasant,
tangy flavor.

Miso & Arame Soup (see
p. 77) is quite strong.

Garlic & Onion Soup (see
p. 76) is tasty and mild.

Sprouty Tofu Soup (see
p. 79) is high in protein.

Gazpacho (see p. 76) is a
chilled soup from Spain.

Smooth-tasting **Creamy
Fava Bean Soup**
(see p. 75).

Cream of Mushroom Soup
(see p. 74) has a lovely
color.

Parsnip Soup (see p. 78)
includes a little nutmeg.

Unusual **Lettuce,
Cucumber & Miso Soup**
(see p. 76).

Vichyssoise (see p. 79) is
a leek and potato soup.

Adzuki Bean Soup (see
p. 72) could be eaten
as a stew.

Green, tangy **Cream of
Watercress Soup**
(see p. 74).

Eggplant Pâté

1 large eggplant
2 tbsp yogurt
2 tbsp olive oil
2 garlic cloves, crushed
juice of 1 lemon
½ tsp finely chopped fresh basil or
    ¼ tsp dried
salt and black pepper

Preparation 10 minutes
Cooking 40 minutes
Serves 4
(GF)

1 Preheat the oven to 400°F.

2 Cut the eggplant in half lengthwise and remove the fibrous core. Prepare as necessary (see p. 28).

3 Brush the eggplant halves all over with olive oil and bake in a greased baking tray for 40-45 minutes or until cooked through.

4 Peel off the skin and mash the flesh or blend in a blender or food processor.

5 Add the yogurt, olive oil and garlic and mix well.

6 Add the lemon juice and basil to the eggplant mixture. Season.

Serve hot or cold with whole wheat rolls or bread.

Baked Eggs with Coriander

a little butter or oil, for greasing
¾ cup light cream
¾ cup cream cheese
2 tbsp finely chopped fresh coriander
    leaves
salt and black pepper
8 eggs
finely chopped fresh parsley, to garnish

Preparation 5 minutes
Cooking 7-10 minutes
Serves 8
(GF)

1 Preheat the oven to 425°F.

2 Grease 8 ramekin dishes.

3 Mix together the light cream, cream cheese, coriander and seasoning.

4 Carefully break 1 egg into each ramekin dish.

5 Put 2 tbsp of the cream mixture on top of each egg.

6 Bake for 7-10 minutes or until the whites of the eggs are just set.

7 Sprinkle with a little chopped parsley and serve immediately.

Serve with hot crusty whole wheat rolls.

Citrus Cocktail

2 pink grapefruit
2 oranges
2 celery stalks, thinly sliced
½ tsp finely chopped fresh mint or
    ¼ tsp dried

Preparation 10 minutes
Standing 20 minutes
Serves 6
(GF) (V)

A light and refreshing start to a meal. Substitute other citrus fruit when in season.

1 Divide the grapefruit and oranges into separate segments over a bowl to catch any juice that might run out.

2 Cut the segments into bite-sized pieces and remove any seeds.

3 Add the celery to the citrus fruits.

4 Add the mint and stir thoroughly. Allow to stand for at least 20 minutes before serving.

Cottage Cheese Cooler

2 cups large curd cottage cheese
1 celery stalk, finely chopped
½ cucumber, finely chopped
1 small red pepper, finely chopped
1 carrot, grated
1 tbsp finely chopped fresh parsley
juice and grated rind of 1 lemon
1 tsp sesame seeds, to garnish

Preparation 10 minutes
Serves 4
(GF)

For this quick-and-simple recipe, you can use fresh lime juice instead of lemon and substitute sunflower for the sesame seeds.

1 Put the cottage cheese into a mixing bowl.

2 Add the celery, cucumber and red pepper.

3 Add the carrot and parsley.

4 Pour the lemon juice and rind over the cottage cheese mixture.

5 Mix everything together gently and turn into individual dishes. Sprinkle with sesame seeds.

Serve with hot Bran Muffins (see p. 137).

Cream Cheese Dip

1 lb cream cheese
1 small red pepper, finely chopped
¼ cucumber, finely chopped
1 tbsp finely chopped fresh parsley
1 tsp mixture of finely chopped fresh
   thyme, basil and marjoram or ½ tsp
   dried
2 garlic cloves, crushed
salt and black pepper

Preparation 10 minutes
Serves 6-8
(GF)

This rich appetizer also makes a good dip for buffets and parties.

1 Put the cream cheese into a mixing bowl.

2 Add the red pepper, cucumber and parsley.

3 Sprinkle the herbs and garlic over, mix well and season to taste.

Serve with hot whole wheat rolls or buttered fingers of toast and, if liked, a selection of cut, raw vegetables such as carrots, celery, cauliflower or cucumber.

Egg & Avocado Mayonnaise Dip

1 tbsp vinegar
juice of 1 lemon
2 eggs (or just the yolks for a thicker
   mixture)
1 tsp honey
1 tbsp finely chopped fresh parsley
6 tbsp olive oil
6 hard cooked eggs, shelled
2 ripe avocados
salt and black pepper
pinch of paprika, to garnish

Preparation 10 minutes
Serves 6-8
(GF)

A useful dip for buffets or parties, this recipe also makes a good sandwich filling. If you do not have a blender or food processor, a wire balloon whisk can be used.

1 Put the vinegar, lemon, eggs, honey and parsley into a blender or food processor and blend until smooth.

2 With the blender or food processor still running, slowly pour in the olive oil until a smooth mayonnaise is formed.

3 Add the eggs and avocados and blend until all the ingredients are well mixed.

4 Adjust seasoning and serve garnished with paprika.

Serve with wedges of toast or bread.

Guacamole

3 avocados
1 large tomato, finely chopped
juice and grated rind of 1 lemon
pinch of chili powder or cayenne
1 tbsp olive oil (optional)
salt and black pepper
black olives, to garnish

Preparation 10 minutes
Serves 6
(GF) (V)

This traditional Mexican dish needs really well-ripened avocados.

1 Put the avocado flesh into a mixing bowl and mash with a fork or a potato masher.

2 Add the tomato, lemon juice and rind.

3 Sprinkle over the chili and olive oil, if using, and season to taste.

4 Garnish with black olives.

Serve with corn chips or whole wheat pita bread.

Hummus

⅓ cup chickpeas, soaked for 12 hours
    or overnight
1 garlic clove, crushed
2 tbsp lemon juice
good pinch of salt
black pepper
¼ cup olive oil
½ cup water or orange juice
1 tbsp tahini (see p. 50)

Preparation 10 minutes (allow 12 hours for soaking the chickpeas)
Cooking 2 hours
Serves 2-4
(GF) (V)

A blender or food processor is essential for this recipe. Make sure the chickpeas are thoroughly cooked before blending.

1 Transfer the soaked chickpeas and their liquid to a saucepan. Top up with fresh water, if necessary, to cover the chickpeas. Cover and bring to a boil. Lower the heat and simmer for about 2 hours or until cooked. Drain.

2 Place the garlic, lemon juice, seasoning, oil and water in a blender or food processor. Blend, then gradually add the chickpeas, blending until smooth.

3 Add the tahini and blend, adding a little extra liquid if the mixture is too dry.

Serve as a dip, with a crisp salad and whole wheat rolls.

Kombu Surprise

1 oz kombu (see p. 44)
2 tsp soy oil
2¼ cups water
5 tsp honey
½ cup tamari

Preparation 5 minutes
Standing 20 minutes
Cooking 35 minutes
Serves 4-6
(GF)

This traditional kombu dish is served in Japan as a light snack before dinner with *sake* or rice wine.

1 Put the kombu in a bowl, cover with boiling water and leave to stand for 20 minutes. Pour off the water and cut the kombu into small pieces.

2 Heat the oil in a saucepan. Add the kombu and cook gently for 1-2 minutes.

3 Add the water, honey and tamari and simmer, uncovered, for about 35 minutes or until the liquid has reduced to a few tablespoons.

Serve with warm Three-Seed Bread (see p. 156).

Leeks Vinaigrette

4 small leeks, halved lengthwise

Vinaigrette
1 tsp whole-grain mustard
½ tsp apple juice concentrate (see p. 51)
   (optional)
scant ½ cup apple cider vinegar
¾ cup olive oil
salt and black pepper

Preparation 15 minutes
Chilling 2 hours
Serves 4
(GF) (V)

Long, thin leeks are best for this recipe. If unobtainable, cut larger, thicker leeks into ½-inch thick rounds.

1 Steam the leeks for 5-10 minutes or until tender.

2 Meanwhile, make the dressing: put the ingredients for the vinaigrette in a screw-top jar and shake vigorously.

3 When the leeks are ready, drain well. Transfer to a serving dish and pour the vinaigrette over, while the leeks are still hot (this will help them absorb the dressing more easily).

4 Cover and chill for at least 2 hours before serving.

Serve with crusty bread or rolls.

Marinated Tofu

1 lb 2 oz tofu (see p. 51), cubed
⅔ cup shoyu (see p. 51)
generous cup orange juice
1 tbsp soy oil
1 garlic clove, crushed
½ tsp grated ginger root
finely chopped fresh basil, to garnish

Preparation 10 minutes
Chilling 30 minutes
Serves 6
(GF) (V)

This is a delicious way to eat tofu. The dish is best if prepared well in advance to allow the marinade to soak into the tofu.

1 Put the tofu into a serving bowl.

2 In a separate bowl, mix together the shoyu, orange juice, soy oil, garlic and grated ginger.

3 Pour the mixture over the tofu and chill for at least 30 minutes.

4 Sprinkle a little chopped basil over the top before serving.

Serve with hot Sunflower Seed Bread (see p. 155).

Nori & Spinach Rolls

water
salt
½ lb fresh spinach
1 tsp soy oil
2 eggs, beaten
2 sheets nori (see p. 44)
tamari

Sauce
½ cup tamari
3 scallions, finely chopped
¼ tsp grated ginger root

Preparation and cooking 35 minutes
Serves 4

(GF)

Not an easy recipe to attempt first time around, but it is well worth the effort to learn.

1 Put the water and salt into a large saucepan and bring to a boil.

2 Wash the spinach thoroughly without cutting off the stems. Put into the boiling water and cook for 3 minutes. Drain and cover with cold water.

3 Pour off the water and squeeze any remaining excess water from the spinach by hand. Divide in halves. Take half the spinach, squeeze again and cut off the stem ends so that the spinach measures the same length as the short side of the nori. Follow the same procedure for the rest of the spinach. Set aside.

4 Heat the oil in a small skillet and cook the eggs like a small omelet. Set aside.

5 Take the corners of a sheet of nori in your fingertips. Wave the smooth side of the seaweed over an open flame or electric ring until it turns green.

6 Place the nori on a flat surface, and place on top of it, in turn, half the egg, a sprinkling of tamari and half the spinach. Roll up as tightly as possible. Follow the same procedure for the other spinach roll.

7 Make the sauce: put the sauce ingredients in a screw-top jar and shake vigorously.

8 Cut each of the 2 spinach rolls into 4 pieces with a very sharp knife, and leave to cool before serving on individual plates. Serve with sauce handed separately.

Making the nori and spinach rolls

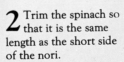
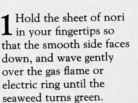

1 Hold the sheet of nori in your fingertips so that the smooth side faces down, and wave gently over the gas flame or electric ring until the seaweed turns green.

2 Trim the spinach so that it is the same length as the short side of the nori.

3 After placing the egg, tamari and spinach on the nori, roll up carefully.

Onion Bhajis with Yogurt Sauce

2¼ cups chickpea flour
1¼ cups semolina
1 tbsp garam masala (see p. 57)
¼ tsp chili powder
2 tsp ground turmeric
2 tbsp finely chopped fresh coriander
    leaves
salt and black pepper
2¼ cups water
oil for frying
3 large onions, very thinly sliced

Yogurt sauce
1¼ cups yogurt
2 tbsp finely chopped scallions
1 tbsp finely chopped fresh coriander
    leaves
½ tsp ground cumin
salt and black pepper

Preparation 10 minutes
Standing 30 minutes (for the sauce)
Cooking 15 minutes
Serves 6

This yogurt sauce is delicious with hot, spicy dishes or with rice balls, rissoles or savory loaves. You can also use sheep's or goat's milk yogurt, or fresh mint and parsley instead of the fresh coriander leaves.

1 Make the batter: in a large bowl mix together the chickpea flour, semolina, garam masala, chili powder, turmeric, coriander leaves and seasoning.

2 Add the water gradually, beating well until the mixture is stiff.

3 Heat the oil in a large skillet.

4 Mix the slices of onion into the batter. Drop 1 tbsp of the mixture into the very hot oil and cook on both sides until golden brown. Drain on paper towels to absorb any excess oil. Repeat with the remaining batter.

5 Make the yogurt sauce: put all the sauce ingredients into a bowl and mix well.

Serve with the yogurt sauce handed separately.

Smoked Tofu Appetizer

½ lb smoked tofu (see p. 51), cubed
1 orange, chopped
4 scallions, finely chopped
1 tsp brown rice vinegar
1 tbsp sesame oil
1 tsp tamari
2 cups alfalfa sprouts
finely chopped fresh parsley or coriander
    leaves, to garnish

Preparation 10 minutes
Serves 4
Ⓖ Ⓥ

1 Put the tofu into a mixing bowl.

2 Add the orange and scallions.

3 Pour over the vinegar, sesame oil and tamari.

4 Finally, add the alfalfa sprouts (separate them with your fingers to prevent them from sticking together) and mix well together.

5 Garnish with a little fresh parsley or coriander and serve in individual bowls.

Stuffed Baked Mushrooms

8 field mushrooms

Stuffing
1 cup filberts, finely chopped
½ cup grated vegetarian gouda cheese
1½ cups fresh whole wheat bread crumbs
1 garlic clove, crushed
2 tsp finely chopped fresh dill or 1 tsp
    dried

Any nuts can be used for this recipe. Buy them whole if you have a blender or food processor; otherwise buy chopped or ground.

1 Preheat the oven to 375°F.

2 Remove stems from mushrooms. Mince or finely chop the stems.

3 Combine all the ingredients for the stuffing in a bowl with the minced mushroom stems. Mix thoroughly.

2 tbsp lemon juice
salt and black pepper

Preparation 10 minutes
Cooking 30-40 minutes
Serves 8

4 Divide into 8 portions and stuff into the mushroom caps.

5 Brush the mushrooms all over with a little olive oil and put them on an oiled baking tray. Cover tightly with aluminum foil.

6 Bake for 30-40 minutes until the mushrooms are tender.

Tiny Stuffed Tomatoes

8 small tomatoes
¼ cucumber, finely chopped
2 large dill pickles, finely chopped
1 tsp finely chopped fresh tarragon or
 ½ tsp dried
1 tbsp finely chopped fresh parsley
1 small dessert apple
2 garlic cloves, crushed
1 tbsp light cream (optional)
½ cup cottage cheese
salt and black pepper
shredded lettuce, to serve

Preparation 15 minutes
Serves 4
(GF)

Tiny sweet-flavored tomatoes are best for this recipe. The filling may also be used as a party dip or for stuffing celery or mushrooms.

1 Cut the bottoms off the tomatoes and keep to one side to use as "lids" for the stuffed tomatoes. (They tend to sit better on their stem ends, so fill them upside down.) Scoop out the centers and keep for another recipe.

2 Place the tomato shells cut side down, to help drain out any excess moisture, and set aside until needed.

3 Combine the cucumber, pickles, tarragon and parsley in a bowl.

4 Grate the apple and add to the bowl.

5 Add the garlic, cream, if using, and cottage cheese. Season.

6 Fill the tomato shells with the stuffing, replace the "lids" and serve.

Vegetable Pâté

1 tbsp soy oil
1 onion, chopped
½ tsp grated ginger root
1 tsp ground coriander
pinch of chili powder
2 carrots, finely chopped
¼ cauliflower, finely chopped
2 cups thinly sliced mushrooms
2 tbsp tamari
salt and black pepper
1½ cups cooked beans or grains (for
 gluten-free grains, see p. 17)
1 garlic clove, crushed
2 tbsp water
finely chopped fresh parsley or lemon
 wedges, to garnish

Preparation 15 minutes (allow extra time if cooking the beans or grains)
Chilling 1 hour
Serves 6

You will need a blender or food processor for this recipe.

1 Heat the oil in a saucepan and add the chopped onion, grated ginger, ground coriander and chili powder.

2 Add the carrot and cauliflower.

3 Add the mushrooms to the saucepan with the tamari and seasoning and simmer for 5-10 minutes or until the vegetables are tender.

4 Pour the cooked vegetables into a blender or food processor with the beans, garlic and water and blend until smooth.

5 Put the pâté into a serving bowl or into individual ramekins. Cover and chill for at least 1 hour before serving, then garnish with a little parsley or lemon wedges.

Serve with buttered toast or whole wheat rolls.

SALADS

◆

Beet, Cheese & Peach Salad

3 cooked beets, peeled
½ lb soft goat's cheese
3 peaches, sliced
sprigs of fresh tarragon, to garnish

Dressing
2 tbsp lemon juice
4 tbsp soy oil
½ tsp finely chopped fresh tarragon or
  ¼ tsp dried
½ tsp apple juice concentrate (see p. 51)
salt and black pepper

Preparation 10 minutes
Serves 6
Ⓖ Ⓕ

A delicious and decorative summer salad. Cottage cheese can be substituted for the goat's cheese, and oranges or pears can be used instead of peaches.

1 Cut the beets into circular slices.

2 Cut the cheese into similar-sized pieces.

3 Arrange the beets, cheese and peaches on a plate.

4 Make the dressing: put all the ingredients for the dressing into a screw-top jar and shake vigorously.

5 Pour over the salad and garnish with fresh tarragon.

Beet & Zucchini Salad

8 cups peeled and finely chopped
  cooked beets
3 zucchini, thinly sliced
1 small onion or shallot, finely chopped

Dressing
6 tbsp goat's milk yogurt
3 tbsp olive oil
1 tbsp cider vinegar
½ tsp mustard powder
2 garlic cloves
juice of ½ lemon
salt and black pepper

Preparation 10 minutes
Standing 1 hour
Serves 6
(GF)

**See page 27 for notes on cooking beets and on buying
ready-cooked.**

1 Put the cooked beets into a salad bowl.

2 Add the zucchini and onion.

3 Make the dressing: put all the dressing ingredients into a screw-
top jar and shake vigorously.

4 Pour over the vegetables and leave to marinate for at least 1 hour
before serving. Chill, if preferred.

Serve garnished with garden cress.

Brown Rice Salad

1⅓ cups brown rice
2 cups water
1 large carrot, finely chopped
1 small cauliflower, finely chopped
1 green pepper, finely chopped
1 tbsp finely chopped fresh parsley
1 tbsp finely chopped fresh dill or
  ½ tbsp dried

Dressing
½ tsp mustard powder
½ tsp apple juice concentrate (see p. 51)
1 tbsp brown rice vinegar
4 tbsp safflower oil
salt and black pepper

Preparation 10 minutes
Cooking 40-45 minutes
Chilling 1 hour
Serves 6
(GF) (V)

You can substitute whole wheat or barley for the brown rice.

1 Put the rice and water in a large saucepan. Bring to a boil. Lower
the heat and simmer, covered, for 45 minutes. Remove from the
heat and set aside to cool.

2 Prepare the dressing: put all the dressing ingredients in a screw-
top jar and shake vigorously.

3 When the rice has cooled a little, add the vegetables. Pour the
dressing over and stir thoroughly. Cover and chill for at least 1 hour
before serving.

Buckwheat & Coconut Salad

1½ cups roasted buckwheat
2½ cups water
1 large tomato, finely chopped
1 tbsp chopped fresh parsley
2 tbsp shredded coconut
1 tbsp tamari
1 tsp brown rice vinegar
2 garlic cloves, crushed
salt and black pepper

Preparation 10 minutes
Cooking 20 minutes
Chilling 1 hour
Serves 6
(GF) (V)

1 Put the buckwheat in a medium-sized saucepan. Pour the water over. Bring to a boil, cover and simmer for 20 minutes or until cooked (by this time all the water should be absorbed). Put the cooked buckwheat into a salad bowl.

2 Add the remaining ingredients to the warm buckwheat. Stir together and chill for at least 1 hour before serving the salad.

Lima Bean Salad

1 cup lima beans, soaked for 12 hours
  or overnight
2 corn-on-the-cobs
1 carrot, finely grated
6 scallions, thinly sliced
2 tbsp finely chopped fresh parsley

Dressing
1 tsp curry powder (optional)
⅔ cup mayonnaise (see p. 96)
salt and black pepper

Preparation 10 minutes (allow 12 hours
for soaking the beans)
Cooking 1½ hours
Serves 4-6
(GF) (V)

This delicious salad tastes just as good with a vinaigrette dressing.

1 Transfer the soaked beans and their liquid to a saucepan. Top up with fresh water, if necessary, to cover the beans. Cover and bring to a boil. Lower the heat and simmer for about 1½ hours or until cooked. Drain and set aside.

2 Put the corn cobs into a large saucepan of boiling water and cook for 10 minutes until tender. Remove from the heat and leave to cool.

3 Carefully remove the kernels from the cob, using a sharp knife.

4 Put the carrot, onion and parsley into a salad bowl with the beans and corn.

5 Make the dressing: mix the curry powder, if liked, into the mayonnaise, season to taste and pour over the salad. Mix well.

Curried Coleslaw

4⅔ cups shredded white cabbage
4 carrots, finely grated
1 small green pepper, finely chopped
2 celery stalks, finely chopped
¼ cucumber, finely chopped
1 dessert apple
juice and grated rind of 1 lemon
⅓ cup walnut halves
2 tbsp raisins

Dressing
scant 1 cup mayonnaise (see p. 96)
1 tsp curry powder

Preparation and Standing 45 minutes
Serves 6
(GF) (V)

1 Put the shredded cabbage into a salad bowl.

2 Add the carrots.

3 Add the green pepper, celery and cucumber.

4 Cut the apple into small pieces and soak in the lemon juice and rind to prevent browning. Add it all to the salad.

5 Add the walnuts and raisins and mix well.

6 Make the dressing: combine the mayonnaise and the curry powder and pour over the salad. Mix thoroughly and leave to stand for 30 minutes before serving to allow the flavors to mingle.

Fennel & Tomato Salad

1 large fennel, sliced into strips
1 large tomato, finely chopped
4 large scallions, thinly sliced
2 tbsp shelled macadamia nuts

Dressing
1 tsp Dijon mustard
1 tbsp cider vinegar
½ tsp apple juice concentrate
4 tbsp olive oil
salt and black pepper

Preparation 10 minutes
Standing 30 minutes
Serves 6
Ⓖ︎Ⓕ︎ Ⓥ︎

Crisp and crunchy salad ingredients go well with the richness of the macadamia nuts. Try almonds, filberts or cashew nuts if you cannot find macadamias.

1 Put the fennel into a salad bowl.

2 Add the tomatoes, scallions and nuts.

3 Make the dressing: put all the ingredients for the dressing into a screw-top jar and shake vigorously.

4 Pour the dressing over the salad and mix well. Leave to stand for 30 minutes before serving to allow the flavors to mingle.

Green Salad with Dill Dressing

1 small iceberg lettuce, thinly sliced
½ cucumber, sliced
½ green pepper, sliced
2 celery stalks
1 cup garden cress
1 tbsp chopped fresh parsley
1 tbsp pumpkin seeds

Dressing
½ tsp mustard powder
½ tsp honey
1 tbsp vinegar
4 tbsp olive oil
2 garlic cloves, crushed
1 tsp finely chopped fresh dill or ½ tsp dried
salt and black pepper

Preparation 10 minutes
Serves 6
Ⓖ︎Ⓕ︎

You can also use zucchini or any other green vegetable in season for this salad.

1 Put the lettuce strips into a salad bowl.

2 Add the cucumber, green pepper and celery.

3 Add the cress and chopped parsley and mix gently.

4 Make the dressing: put all the ingredients for the dressing in a screw-top jar and shake vigorously.

5 Pour the dressing over the salad just before serving and garnish with the pumpkin seeds.

Melon & Tomato Salad

1 large honeydew melon
2 large tomatoes
1 tbsp finely chopped fresh mint or ½ tbsp dried
1 tbsp snipped fresh chives
juice of 1 lemon
1 tbsp soy oil
salt and black pepper

Preparation 10 minutes
Serves 6
Ⓖ︎Ⓕ︎ Ⓥ︎

1 Slice the melon open and remove the seeds. Cut in quarters over the salad bowl to catch the juice, peel and cut into small cubes.

2 Cut the tomatoes into pieces of a similar size. Add to the melon.

3 Add the mint and chives.

4 Pour the lemon juice and soy oil over the salad. Season to taste and cover and chill until ready to serve.

Mushroom, Apricot & Endive Salad

4 cups thinly sliced button mushrooms
2 large fresh apricots, pitted and
    quartered
2 cups finely sliced endive

Dressing
⅔ cup sour cream
1 tbsp finely snipped fresh chives
1 tsp apple juice concentrate (see p. 51)
salt and black pepper

Preparation 10 minutes
Serves 6

A good summer salad when fresh apricots are in season. Soaked, dried apricots may also be used.

1 Put the mushrooms, apricots and endive in a salad bowl and mix.

2 Make the dressing: put all the dressing ingredients into a screw-top jar and shake vigorously.

3 Pour over the salad and mix well.

Pineapple Salad

½ cup brown rice
¾ cup water
1 small pineapple, finely chopped
⅔ cup cooked peas
2 celery stalks, finely chopped
6 tbsp roasted sunflower seeds, to
    garnish

Dressing
juice and grated rind of 1 lime
¼ cup soy oil
2 tbsp finely chopped fresh tarragon or
    1 tbsp dried
1 tsp whole-grain mustard
salt and black pepper

Preparation 10 minutes
Cooking 45 minutes
Serves 6
(GF) (V)

You can substitute whole wheat or barley for the brown rice. It is preferable to use fresh pineapple, although cans of pineapple in natural juices are now available.

1 Put the rice and water into a large saucepan. Cover and bring to a boil. Lower the heat, simmer for 45 minutes, then leave to cool.

2 Combine the rice and all the salad ingredients in a bowl.

3 Make the dressing: put all the dressing ingredients into a screw-top jar and shake vigorously.

4 Pour the dressing over the salad, mix well and leave to stand for a few minutes.

5 Sprinkle with roasted sunflower seeds before serving.

Red Bean Salad

⅔ cup kidney beans, soaked for 12 hours
  or overnight
1½ cups finely chopped red cabbage
1 small shallot, finely chopped
4 tomatoes, sliced
1 small yellow pepper, sliced
8 radishes, sliced
1 tbsp finely chopped fresh parsley

Dressing
1 tsp whole-grain mustard
1 tbsp red wine vinegar
¼ cup olive oil
2 garlic cloves, crushed
1 tsp finely chopped fresh oregano or
  ½ tsp dried
salt and black pepper

**Preparation 15 minutes (allow 12 hours
for soaking the beans)
Cooking 1½ hours
Chilling 1 hour
Serves 6**
ⒼⒻ Ⓥ

1 Transfer the soaked beans and their liquid to a saucepan. Top up with fresh water, if necessary, to cover the beans. Cover and bring to a boil. Cool briskly for 20 minutes, then lower the heat and simmer for about 1 hour until cooked. Drain and leave to cool.

2 Put the cooked and cooled kidney beans in a salad bowl.

3 Add the red cabbage and shallot.

4 Add the tomatoes, pepper and radishes and gently mix into the salad, along with the parsley.

5 Make the dressing: combine all the ingredients in a screw-top jar and shake vigorously.

6 Pour the dressing over the salad and marinate in the refrigerator for about 1 hour before serving.

◆

Soy Bean Salad

½ cup soybeans, soaked for 12 hours or
  overnight
2 tangerines or 1 orange (optional)
1 cooked beet, peeled and cubed
¼ cucumber, cubed
4 scallions, thinly sliced
2 tbsp finely chopped fresh coriander
  leaves, to garnish

Dressing
½ tsp whole-grain mustard
1 tsp apple juice concentrate (see p. 51)
1 tsp miso (see p. 50)
2 tbsp tahini (see p. 50)
juice and grated rind of 1 lime
1 tbsp brown rice vinegar
pinch of chili powder

**Preparation 10 minutes (allow 12 hours
for soaking the beans)
Cooking 2 hours
Serves 6**
ⒼⒻ Ⓥ

1 Transfer the soaked beans and their liquid to a saucepan. Top up with fresh water, if necessary, to cover the beans. Cover and bring to a boil. Lower the heat and simmer for about 2 hours or until cooked. Drain.

2 Divide the tangerines into segments, if using.

3 Combine all the ingredients in a serving bowl.

4 Make the dressing: put all the dressing ingredients into a small bowl and mix thoroughly together.

5 Pour the dressing over the salad, mix well and garnish with the chopped coriander before serving.

Spinach Salad

¼ lb spinach, torn into small pieces
2 cups finely chopped red cabbage
1 small yellow pepper, finely chopped
¼ cucumber, finely chopped
1 grapefruit, finely chopped
1 dessert apple
pumpkin seeds and sliced kiwi, to
   garnish

Dressing
scant 1 cup medium-fat skim-milk cheese
2 tsp finely chopped fresh dill or 1 tsp
   dried
1 tbsp olive oil
½ tsp apple juice concentrate (see p. 51)
1 garlic clove, crushed
salt and black pepper

Preparation 15 minutes
Serves 6
(GF)

1 Put the spinach in a salad bowl.

2 Add the remaining vegetables and the grapefruit.

3 Finely chop the apple and add to the salad.

4 Make the dressing: put all the ingredients for the dressing into a screw-top jar and shake vigorously.

5 Pour over the salad vegetables and stir well. Garnish with pumpkin seeds and sliced kiwi.

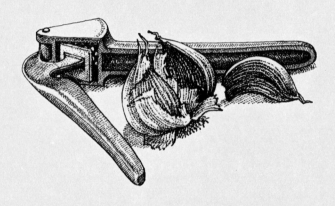

Sprouty Salad

2 cups mung bean sprouts
1 small red pepper, finely chopped
½ cucumber, finely chopped
2 cups finely chopped Chinese cabbage
   leaves
3 celery stalks, finely chopped
4 unsulphured dried apricots (see p. 39),
   soaked for at least 3 hours, then finely
   chopped
⅓ cup cashew nuts, to garnish

Dressing
1 tbsp brown rice vinegar
¼ cup soy oil
¼ tsp grated ginger root
1 tsp tamari
salt and black pepper

Preparation 10 minutes (allow 3 hours
for soaking the apricots)
Serves 4
(GF) (V)

The grated ginger root and brown rice vinegar give this salad an Oriental flavor. Any grain, seed or bean sprouts may be used.

1 Put the bean sprouts into a salad bowl.

2 Add the red pepper, cucumber, Chinese cabbage and celery.

3 Add the apricots.

4 Make the dressing: put all the ingredients for the dressing into a screw-top jar and shake vigorously.

5 Pour the dressing over the salad, mix well and garnish with the cashew nuts.

Sweetcorn & Mushroom Salad

2 corn-on-the-cobs
2 cups chopped button mushrooms
½ romaine lettuce
3 tomatoes, chopped
6 radishes, chopped

Dressing
1 tsp whole-grain mustard
1 tbsp white wine vinegar
¼ cup walnut oil
2 garlic cloves, crushed
½ tsp finely chopped fresh basil or
  ¼ tsp dried
salt and black pepper

Preparation 20 minutes
Chilling 20 minutes
Serves 4
(GF) (V)

Fresh corn is best for this salad. However, you can use fast-frozen kernels which do not contain added salt or sugar.

1 Put the corn cobs in a large saucepan of boiling water. Lower the heat and simmer for 10 minutes until tender. Remove from the heat and leave to cool.

2 When cool, carefully remove the kernels from the cobs, using a sharp knife.

3 Put the corn in a salad bowl.

4 Add the mushrooms, lettuce, tomatoes and radishes.

5 Make the dressing: put all the ingredients for the dressing into a screw-top jar and shake vigorously.

6 Pour the dressing over the salad and allow to marinate for 20 minutes in the refrigerator before serving.

◆

Tabouleh

1½ cups bulgur
6 tbsp olive oil
juice and grated rind of 3 lemons
3 garlic cloves, crushed
4 tsp finely chopped fresh mint or 2 tsp
  dried
4 tomatoes, finely chopped
1 cucumber, finely chopped
1 green pepper, finely chopped
1 small onion, finely chopped
salt and black pepper
romaine lettuce, to serve
12 ripe olives and a few lemon wedges,
  to garnish

Preparation 10 minutes
Chilling 2 hours
Serves 6
(V)

This traditional Middle Eastern salad can also be made with couscous. However, bulgur is more nutritious.

1 Put the bulgur in a large bowl, cover with boiling water and leave for 5 minutes until it absorbs the water and puffs up.

2 Add the olive oil, lemon juice, rind, garlic and mint and mix well.

3 Add the tomatoes, cucumber, green pepper and onion. Adjust seasoning to taste.

4 Set aside to cool a little or chill for at least 2 hours.

5 Serve on a bed of romaine lettuce. Garnish with olives and a few lemon wedges.

Tabouleh is delicious served with whole wheat pita bread and Hummus (see p. 83).

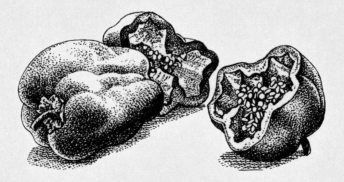

Watercress & Orange Salad

1 bunch watercress
4 carrots, grated
2 cups chopped endive
2 oranges
1 tbsp finely chopped fresh parsley
1 tbsp sunflower seeds, to garnish

Dressing
1 tsp honey-spiced mustard
1 tbsp cider vinegar
¼ cup sunflower oil
salt and black pepper

Preparation 10 minutes
Serves 4-6

A nutritious salad that is high in vitamin C. Choose bright, crisp green watercress and avoid any with yellowing or wilting leaves.

1 Break the watercress into small pieces into a salad bowl.

2 Add the carrots.

3 Add the endive.

4 Using a fine grater, grate the rind off the oranges and set aside for the dressing.

5 Peel off the remaining pith and cut the orange segments into small pieces, adding them to the salad bowl.

6 Mix in the chopped parsley.

7 Make the dressing: put all the ingredients for the dressing into a screw-top jar. Add the orange rind and shake vigorously.

8 Pour the dressing over and garnish with sunflower seeds.

Mayonnaise

1 egg
1 tbsp lemon juice
1 tsp vinegar
1 tsp mustard powder
2 tsp finely chopped mixed fresh herbs
  or 1 tsp dried
salt and black pepper
1¼-1½ cups sunflower oil

Preparation 10 minutes
Makes 2 cups
(GF)

This recipe uses dairy products, while the next recipe is suitable for a vegan diet. Both recipes may be kept for 4-5 days in an airtight container in the refrigerator. If you do not have a blender or food processor, use a wire balloon whisk.

1 Blend the egg, lemon juice, vinegar, mustard powder, herbs and seasoning in a blender or food processor until smooth.

2 Gradually add the oil with the motor still running until you have a thick consistency. If you add the oil too quickly the mayonnaise may curdle.

Vegan Mayonnaise

½ cup soy milk
¼ cup lemon juice
2 tsp mustard powder
2 tsp finely chopped mixed herbs or
  1 tsp dried
salt and black pepper
scant ½-1¼ cups soy oil

Preparation 10 minutes
Makes 2 cups

See Mayonnaise recipe above for usage, equipment and storage.

1 Blend the soy milk, lemon juice, mustard powder, herbs and seasoning in a blender or food processor until smooth.

2 Gradually add the oil with the motor still running until you have a thick consistency.

Vegetable Pâté (see p. 87) has a soft, spreading consistency. Serve with fingers of warm toast.

Stuffed Baked Mushrooms (see p. 86) are a filling appetizer with a smoky taste.

Cream Cheese Dip (see p. 82) is flavored with fresh thyme, basil and marjoram.

Smoked Tofu Appetizer (see p. 86) contains alfalfa and tofu, both very nutritious.

Cottage Cheese Cooler (see p. 82) is a pleasant, light appetizer with a fresh lemon tang, ideal in summer.

Citrus Cocktail (see p. 81) is a mixture of grapefruit, oranges, celery and mint.

Leeks Vinaigrette (see p. 84) is particularly delicious if made with tender baby leeks.

Tiny Stuffed Tomatoes (see p. 87) make a decorative appetizer for a dinner party.

Hummus (see p. 83) is rich in flavor but not heavy.

Egg & Avocado Mayonnaise Dip (see p. 82) also makes a soft and tasty sandwich filling.

Apple & Lima Bean Pâté (see p. 80) has a delicate, slightly sweet flavor.

Guacamole (see p. 83) is a milder version of the traditional Mexican dish.

Eggplant Pâté (see p. 81) has a rich, smoky taste.

Marinated Tofu (see p. 84) is an unusual appetizer.

Nori & Spinach Rolls (see p. 85) look exciting and yet are easy to prepare.

Onion Bhajis with Yogurt Sauce (see p. 86) are a delicious, spicy appetizer.

Baked Eggs with Coriander (see p. 81) have a smooth, creamy taste with a bite of fresh coriander.

Kombu Surprise (see p. 84) is a simple seaweed recipe.

Salads (See p. 88)

Spinach Salad (see p. 94) is nutritious with a sharp, interesting flavor.

Lima Bean Salad (see p. 90) is a fresh, summery salad which is quite light.

Tabouleh (see p. 95) is a Middle Eastern dish, made here with bulgur wheat.

Curried Coleslaw (see p. 90) is a colorful salad with fruit, nuts and raisins.

Mushroom, Apricot & Endive Salad (see p. 92) has a fresh, fruity flavor.

Fennel & Tomato Salad (see p. 91) is very refreshing.

Crisp and fresh **Green Salad with Dill Dressing** (see p. 91).

Sprouty Salad (see p. 94) includes mung bean sprouts, dried apricots and cashew nuts.

Beet, Cheese & Peach Salad (see p. 88) uses goat's cheese for a strong flavor.

Melon & Tomato Salad (see p. 91) is light, sweet and crisp, ideal in summer.

Pineapple Salad (see p. 92) has a tarragon dressing for extra flavor.

Buckwheat & Coconut Salad (see p. 90) is an unusual and delicious combination.

Red Bean Salad (see p. 93) has bright splashes of radish and yellow pepper.

Soybean Salad (see p. 93) is a substantial, highly nutritious salad.

Corn & Mushroom Salad (see p. 95) has a delicious walnut oil dressing.

Beet & Zucchini Salad (see p. 89) has a vivid color and an intriguing taste.

Watercress & Orange Salad (see p. 96) has a lovely, slightly tangy flavor.

Brown Rice Salad (see p. 89) is quite filling, with a good contrast of textures.

MAIN COURSES

◆

Artichokes & Tomatoes with Basil

2 large tomatoes
¼ cup butter
1 large onion, chopped
2 garlic cloves, crushed
1 tsp finely chopped fresh basil, or
   ½ tsp dried
1 lb Jerusalem artichokes, chopped
salt and black pepper
finely chopped fresh parsley, to garnish

Preparation 20 minutes
Cooking 10 minutes
Serves 6
(GF)

This quick-and-simple dish can be made in advance and reheated.

1 Put the tomatoes in a bowl and pour over boiling water. Set aside for 10-15 minutes to allow the skins to soften.

2 Meanwhile, melt the butter in a medium-sized saucepan over a low heat and add the onion, garlic and basil.

3 Add the artichokes, and continue cooking gently.

4 Pour the water off the tomatoes. Drain, peel and break them up with a fork. Add to the artichokes. Season.

5 Simmer for about 10 minutes or until the artichokes are cooked.

6 Serve hot, garnished with the chopped parsley.

Serve with a cooked grain dish and a side salad.

Eggplant & Potato Curry

1 large tomato
1 large eggplant, cubed
¼ cup soy oil
1 tsp cumin seeds
2 tsp coriander seeds
1 large onion, finely chopped
½ tsp ground mace
½ tsp ground cardamom
½ tsp chili powder
1 tbsp tomato paste
1½ cups finely cubed potatoes

Preparation and cooking 30 minutes
Serves 4
(GF) (V)

This is a dry curry, so make sure you stir frequently to prevent the mixture sticking.

1 Put the tomatoes in a bowl. Pour over boiling water and set aside for 10-15 minutes to allow the skins to soften.

2 Meanwhile, prepare the eggplant as necessary (see p. 28).

3 Heat the oil in a medium-sized saucepan. Add the cumin and coriander seeds and cook gently for a few minutes until the cumin seeds pop.

4 Add the onion, mace, cardamom, chili powder and tomato paste. Cook gently for a further 5 minutes.

5 Add the potatoes and stir well to prevent sticking.

6 Add the eggplant.

7 Pour the water off the tomatoes, drain and peel them and add to the saucepan.

8 Cook gently for a further 10-15 minutes, stirring frequently, until the vegetables are cooked.

Serve with brown rice, a slightly "wetter" vegetable dish and a selection of chutneys and other traditional curry accompaniments.

◆

Baked Avocado with Stilton & Walnuts

2 tbsp soy oil or 2 tbsp butter
1 onion, thinly sliced
2 cups thinly sliced mushrooms
2 tbsp lowfat skim-milk cheese
½ cup crumbled Stilton cheese
scant ⅓ cup walnut halves
salt and black pepper
2 large avocados

Preparation 15 minutes
Cooking 10 minutes
Serves 4
(GF)

This is included as a main course as it is both substantial and rich. Any combination of nuts and cheese can be used. For a vegan diet substitute tofu (see p. 51) for the cheese. Danish blue cheese can also be substituted for the Stilton.

1 Preheat the oven to 300°F.

2 Heat the oil in a medium-sized saucepan, and sauté the onion and mushrooms for about 5 minutes until soft.

3 Add the lowfat cheese, the Stilton, walnuts and seasoning. Stir well and remove from heat.

4 Halve the avocados and scoop out most of the flesh, leaving a small amount close to the skins.

5 Mash the avocado flesh, add it to the onion mixture and adjust the seasoning to taste.

6 Pile the mixture into the avocado shells and bake for 10 minutes, or until warmed through.

Serve with a light salad or steamed vegetables.

Barley, Fruit & Vegetable Pollo

generous 1 cup whole pot barley
3 cups water
2 tbsp tahini (see p. 50)
¼ cup butter or ¼ cup soy oil
1 large onion, chopped
1 green pepper, chopped
2 carrots, chopped
⅔ cup shelled peas
2 tbsp finely chopped fresh coriander
  leaves
salt and black pepper
2 tbsp golden raisins
2 oz unsulphured dried apricots (see
  p. 39)
⅓ cup cashew nuts
2 tbsp orange juice
1 tbsp tamari
½ cup boiling water

Preparation 15 minutes
Cooking 1 hour 10 minutes
Serves 4

1 Put the whole barley in a saucepan, add the water and bring to a boil. Lower the heat and simmer, covered, for 45 minutes or until cooked and tender.

2 Preheat the oven to 350°F.

3 Remove barley from heat and mix in the tahini.

4 Melt half the butter in a large pan. Add the onion, pepper and carrots and cook gently for 5 minutes until soft.

5 Add the peas and coriander and mix well. Season and put aside.

6 Melt the remaining butter in a small pan. Add the golden raisins, apricots and cashews. Cook for a few minutes.

7 Stir in the orange juice and tamari and set aside.

8 Spread half the barley over the bottom of an ovenproof dish.

9 Cover with the vegetable mixture.

10 Spread over half the remaining barley and then the fruit mixture.

11 Put the rest of the barley on top. Pour over the boiling water and cover with a tightly fitting lid.

12 Bake for 20-25 minutes or until the vegetables are cooked.

Serve with leafy green vegetables and a fresh salad.

Beanburgers

⅔ cup black-eyed peas, soaked for 12
  hours or overnight.
scant 1 cup brown rice
1¼ cups water
1 small onion, finely chopped
½ red pepper, finely chopped
1 tbsp chopped fresh parsley
1 tsp ground cumin
½ tsp ground coriander
¼ tsp chili powder
2 tsp finely chopped fresh basil or 1 tsp
  dried
1 tbsp tomato paste
1 tbsp tamari
2 tsp shredded coconut
¼ cup raisins (optional)
salt and black pepper
mixture of whole wheat flour and a few
  sesame seeds, for rolling
a little oil, for shallow- or deep-frying

**Preparation 10 minutes (allow 12 hours
for soaking the beans)**
Cooking 1 hour 20 minutes
Makes 8 burgers
Ⓥ

1 Transfer the soaked black-eyed peas and their liquid to a saucepan. Top up with fresh water, if necessary, to cover the beans. Cover and bring to a boil. Lower the heat and simmer, covered, for 1 hour or until cooked and tender.

2 Meanwhile, put the rice in a saucepan with the water. Bring to a boil. Lower the heat and simmer for 45 minutes or until cooked.

3 Combine the beans, rice and remaining ingredients, except the flour, sesame seeds and oil, in a blender or food processor or large bowl and mix thoroughly until the mixture holds together well.

4 Using an ice cream scoop or your hands, form the rice and bean mixture into smaller burger shapes. Roll them in the flour and sesame seeds until well covered.

5 Heat enough oil for deep- or shallow-frying and when very hot gently lower the beanburgers into the oil and fry for 3-4 minutes on each side till golden brown. Drain on paper towels.

Serve warm or cold or sandwiched between a whole wheat hamburger bun with mayonnaise, tomato and cucumber.

Black Bean Chili

generous cup black kidney beans, soaked
    for 12 hours or overnight
2 lb tomatoes
2 tbsp peanut oil
1 large onion, thinly sliced
1 large green pepper, thinly sliced
¼ tsp ground cinnamon
1 tsp ground coriander
¼-½ tsp chili powder
¼ tsp ground anise (optional)
4 zucchini, grated
4 tbsp tomato paste
salt and black pepper
1 cup grated sharp cheese

**Preparation 15 minutes (allow 12 hours
for soaking the beans)
Cooking 1 hour 45 minutes
Serves 6**
(GF)

**This chili dish is traditionally made with red kidney beans but
black beans make an attractive change.**

1 Transfer the soaked beans and their liquid to a saucepan. Top up
with fresh water, if necessary, to cover the beans. Cover and bring to
a boil. Lower the heat and simmer, covered, for 1½ hours until
tender. Drain and set aside and leave to cool.

2 Meanwhile, put the tomatoes in a bowl. Pour boiling water over
them and set aside for 10-15 minutes to allow the skins to soften.

3 Heat the oil in a large saucepan. Add the onion, green pepper and
spices. Cook gently for 5 minutes or until the onion is soft.

4 Add the zucchini to the saucepan. Stir well and continue cooking
gently.

5 By now the tomatoes should be ready to peel. Pour off the water,
drain, peel and chop the tomatoes coarsely, taking care not to lose
their juices.

6 Add the chopped tomatoes, their juices and the tomato paste to
the mixture in the saucepan, stir well and continue cooking.

7 Add the beans, season to taste and cook for a further 5-10
minutes or until the beans are heated through.

8 Stir the cheese into the chili just before serving.

Serve on a bed of brown rice or other grain if preferred.

Brown Rice Risotto

2 onions, sliced into rings
¼ cup butter or soy oil
3 carrots, chopped
4 celery stalks, chopped
1 cup chopped broccoli
2 tsp finely chopped fresh basil or 1 tsp
    dried
1 tbsp ground turmeric
salt and black pepper
1⅓ cups brown rice
¼ cup tamari
3¾ cups vegetable broth or water
1 cup shelled pistachio nuts, to garnish

**Preparation 15 minutes
Cooking 1½ hours
Serves 6-8**
(GF) (V)

**You can also use a mixture of brown rice and rye grain in this
delicious risotto.**

1 Preheat the oven to 400°F.

2 Sauté the onions in the butter in a saucepan for 5 minutes until
soft and tender.

3 Add the carrots, celery and broccoli to the onions, together with
the basil, turmeric and seasoning.

4 Stir in the brown rice and mix well. Simmer for 3-4 minutes,
stirring occasionally.

5 Pour the tamari and stock over the mixture and transfer to an
ovenproof dish.

6 Bake, covered, for 1½ hours or until the rice is completely cooked.

7 Sprinkle with the pistachio nuts before serving.

Serve with Ratatouille (see p. 110) and a crisp salad.

Buckwheat Crêpes with Tomato Sauce

Crepes
1 cup plus 2 tbsp buckwheat flour
1 cup plus 2 tbsp whole wheat flour
2 tsp baking powder
1 tsp finely chopped fresh dill or $\frac{1}{2}$ tsp
  dried
1 cup milk
$\frac{1}{2}$ cup water
$\frac{1}{2}$ cup Greek-style yogurt
3 eggs, beaten
salt and black pepper (optional)
a little butter or oil for frying

Sauce
3 large tomatoes
2 tbsp soy oil
1 large onion, finely chopped
1 large red pepper, finely chopped
3 bay leaves
2 tsp finely chopped fresh marjoram or
  1 tsp dried
$\frac{1}{2}$ tsp grated nutmeg
pinch of chili powder (optional)
3 tbsp tomato paste
2 tsp apple juice concentrate (see p. 51)
salt and black pepper
finely chopped fresh parsley and grated
  cheese, to garnish

Preparation 20 minutes
Cooking 15 minutes
Makes 16-20 crepes

To prepare the batter in advance, make up as directed but do not add the baking powder until just before cooking. The sauce can also be made in advance and reheated when needed. If you do not have a blender or food processor, use a potato masher.

1 First make the crêpe batter: combine all the dry ingredients in a bowl. Then, in a pitcher, mix the milk, water, yogurt and eggs.

2 Pour the liquid into the flour and mix together gently, stirring, until there are no lumps. Add a little salt and pepper, if wished, and set aside.

3 Next, make the sauce: put the tomatoes in a bowl and pour over boiling water. Leave to stand for 10-15 minutes to allow the skins to soften.

4 Meanwhile, heat the oil in a medium-sized saucepan and add the onion, red pepper, bay leaves, marjoram, nutmeg and chili, if using. Cook gently for 5 minutes or until the vegetables are soft.

5 Pour the water off the tomatoes and peel off their skins. Chop coarsely and add to the saucepan with the tomato paste and apple juice concentrate. Simmer for a further 2-3 minutes.

6 Blend the mixture into a blender or food processor until smooth. Pour back into the saucepan. Season to taste and set aside.

7 Now you are ready to make the crêpes: put about 2 tsp oil into a small skillet over a high heat. When the oil is hot, carefully spoon 2 tbsp of the batter into the skillet. (The crêpe should be about 6 inches in diameter.)

8 Turn the heat down a little and cook for 3-4 minutes until little bubbles appear on the surface. Turn the crêpe over and cook the other side.

9 Remove the crêpe from the pan, drain on paper towels and keep warm while you are cooking the remaining crêpes. Repeat the process until all the crêpes are cooked.

10 Before serving, reheat the tomato sauce and serve either separately or poured over the crêpes. Decorate with a sprinkling of chopped parsley and grated cheese.

Serve with a green salad or a green leafy vegetable.

Buckwheat Spaghetti with Mushrooms, Dill & Sour Cream

about 4½ cups water
9 oz buckwheat spaghetti (soba)
¼ cup butter
2 large onions, sliced
2 garlic cloves, crushed
2 tsp finely chopped fresh dill or 1 tsp dried
6 cups sliced mushrooms
⅔ cup sour cream or Greek-style yogurt
salt and black pepper
a little fresh parsley, to garnish

Preparation and cooking 30 minutes
Serves 4
(GF)

Pour the water into a medium-sized saucepan and bring to a boil. Add the spaghetti. Stir a few times to prevent sticking and simmer for about 20 minutes or until cooked.

2 Meanwhile, melt the butter in a large skillet and add the sliced onions, garlic and dill. Cook for 5 minutes, stirring occasionally, until the onions are soft.

3 Add the mushrooms and cook for a further 5 minutes.

4 Finally, add the sour cream, a little salt, if liked, and a generous helping of freshly ground black pepper.

5 By now the spaghetti should be ready. Drain well, put in a serving dish, pour over the mushroom sauce and sprinkle liberally with the freshly chopped parsley.

Try serving with a fresh salad, baby carrots or peas.

Caribbean Stew

2 tbsp peanut oil
1 large onion, finely chopped
1 red pepper, finely chopped
1 tsp grated ginger root
4 garlic cloves, crushed
1 small rutabaga, cubed
1 small parsnip, cubed
1 large sweet potato, cubed
2½ cups pineapple juice
2 tbsp tomato paste
4 tbsp creamed coconut
½-1 tsp chili powder
salt and black pepper

Preparation 15 minutes
Cooking 20 minutes
Serves 6-8
(GF) (V)

Quick and simple to make, the creamed coconut, sweet potato and ginger root give this stew a truly Caribbean flavor.

1 Heat the oil in a medium-sized saucepan. Add the onion, red pepper, grated ginger and crushed garlic. Sauté for 5 minutes, stirring occasionally, until the onion is soft.

2 Add the rutabaga, parsnip and sweet potato to the saucepan and sauté for a further 3 minutes to seal in the flavors.

3 Add the pineapple juice, tomato paste, coconut, chili powder and seasoning and simmer for 20 minutes or until the vegetables are cooked and tender.

Serve on a bed of brown rice with Red Bean Salad (see p. 93).

Cauliflower & Carrots with Spicy Filbert Sauce

1 large cauliflower
2 carrots, sliced
¼ cup butter, ghee (see p. 47) or
   vegetable oil
1 red pepper, finely chopped
½ tsp grated ginger root
¼ tsp chili powder
1 bunch scallions, finely chopped
½ cup filbert butter (see p. 50)
scant 1 cup boiling water
2 tbsp shoyu (see p. 51)

Preparation and cooking 15 minutes
Serves 4-6
(GF) (V)

You can substitute peanut, cashew or almond butter for the filbert butter.

1 Break the cauliflower into flowerets and cut the stem and leaves into similar-sized pieces.

2 Steam the cauliflower and carrots for 5-10 minutes or until tender.

3 Meanwhile, melt the butter in a saucepan. Add the red pepper, ginger and chili and cook gently. Add the scallions.

4 Put the filbert butter into a bowl. Pour on the boiling water and shoyu and mix to a smooth paste.

5 Add to the red pepper mixture, mix well and season.

6 By now the cauliflower and carrots will be cooked. Transfer to a serving dish, pour over the filbert sauce and serve immediately.

Serve with cooked grains and a side salad.

Cheesy Stuffed Peppers with Creamed Mushroom Sauce

2 large red peppers

Stuffing
2 cups fresh whole wheat
   breadcrumbs
1 cup grated cheese
1 parsnip, finely grated
⅓ cup cashew nuts
1 tbsp sugar-free tomato sauce
pinch of chili powder
generous ½ cup vegetable broth or the
   same quantity of water plus 1 tbsp
   tamari
salt and pepper

Sauce
1 large onion, sliced
¼ cup butter
2 garlic cloves, crushed
¼ tsp grated nutmeg
4 cups mushrooms
½ cup light cream
salt and black pepper

Preparation 20 minutes
Cooking 40 minutes
Serves 4

For a vegan diet, substitute tofu (see p. 51) for the cheese and serve with tomato sauce (see p. 115).

1 Preheat the oven to 375°F.

2 Cut the peppers in half lengthwise. Remove the core and seeds. Put the pepper halves in a large saucepan, and cover with cold water. Cover and bring to a boil, then remove from heat, pour off the water and turn face down to drain away any excess liquid.

3 Prepare the stuffing: in a large mixing bowl, put the bread crumbs, grated cheese, grated parsnip, cashew nuts, tomato sauce, chili powder and broth.

4 Mix together until you have a soft pliable mixture, adding more liquid if necessary. Season to taste.

5 Fill the peppers with the stuffing, place in an ovenproof dish and cook for 30 minutes or until the peppers are cooked.

6 Meanwhile, make the sauce: sauté the sliced onion in the butter.

7 Next, add the garlic, nutmeg and mushrooms. Cook for a further 5 minutes and remove from heat. Add the cream. Mix and season.

8 Remove the peppers from the oven when cooked. Pour the mushroom sauce over the top, return to the oven for 10 minutes and serve immediately.

Serve with a salad, grain or potato dish.

Chestnut & Prune Roast

1⅓ cups dried chestnuts, soaked for 12
  hours or overnight
1½ cups dried prunes, soaked for 12
hours or overnight
2 cups whole wheat bread crumbs
½ cup curd cheese
1 egg, beaten
2 tsp finely chopped fresh tarragon or
  1 tsp dried
2 tsp finely chopped fresh sage or 1 tsp
  dried
salt and black pepper

**Preparation 15 minutes (allow 12 hours
for soaking the chestnuts and prunes)
Cooking 2 hours
Serves 6**

**For a vegan diet, substitute crumbled tofu (see p. 51) for the
curd cheese and 1 tbsp of tahini for the egg.**

1 Top up the water on the chestnuts to cover, if necessary, and boil
in a saucepan for about 1½ hours or until tender.

2 Reserve a little of the cooking liquid and set aside.

3 Preheat the oven to 350°F.

4 Purée the chestnuts in a blender or food processor.

5 Remove the pits from the prunes and purée in a blender or food
processor. Retain a little of the soaking liquid.

6 In a large bowl, combine the chestnut and prune purées and add
the bread crumbs, curd cheese, egg, tarragon, sage and seasoning.
(You want a fairly moist mixture so add a little of the reserved
liquid if necessary.)

7 Spoon the mixture into an ovenproof casserole dish and bake,
covered, for 35-40 minutes until the roast is set and browned on top.

Serve with buttered Brussels sprouts, carrots or a crisp green salad.

Chestnut Roast

1½ cups dried chestnuts, soaked for 12
  hours or overnight
2 tbsp cider vinegar
1 cup finely chopped parsnips
1 cup finely chopped rutabaga
¾ cup finely chopped Brussels sprouts
1 tbsp sesame oil
1 onion, chopped
3 garlic cloves, crushed
2 tbsp tamari
2 cups mushrooms
juice and grated rind of 1 orange
7 cups whole wheat bread crumbs
about 1¼ cups vegetable broth or water
sprigs of fresh parsley and orange slices,
  to garnish

**Preparation 15 minutes (allow 12 hours
for soaking the chestnuts)
Cooking 2 hours
Serves 6**
Ⓥ

This is a delicious dish for a vegetarian Christmas dinner.

1 Top up the water on the chestnuts to cover, if necessary, and boil
in a saucepan with the cider vinegar for about 1½ hours or until tender.

2 Preheat the oven to 325°F.

3 Meanwhile, steam the parsnips, rutabagas and sprouts for 8-10
minutes until tender. Leave to cool and set aside.

4 When the chestnuts are cooked, pour off the water and chop
coarsely. Put into a large mixing bowl.

5 Put the oil in a small saucepan and add the chopped onion and
garlic. Cook gently.

6 Add the tamari and mushrooms and continue cooking for a
further 5 minutes.

7 Remove from heat and add to the chestnuts. Add the vegetables.

8 Add the orange juice and rind, together with the bread crumbs.

9 Mix vigorously and gradually add the broth or water until the
mixture has the consistency of a thick paste.

10 Press into a well-greased ovenproof dish and bake for 30 minutes
or until cooked through. Cool and turn out on to a board.

11 Garnish with parsley and thin slices of orange.

Country Vegetable Pie

3 cups finely chopped parsnips
4 cups grated carrots
2 tbsp sunflower oil
1 large onion, sliced
2 leeks, sliced
1 red pepper, thinly sliced
2 tsp finely chopped fresh herbs of
  your choice or 1 tsp dried
2 garlic cloves, crushed
4 cups sliced mushrooms
salt and black pepper
¼ cup butter
¼ tsp grated nutmeg

Preparation 30 minutes
Cooking 20 minutes
Serves 6
(GF)

Parsnips and carrots make an interesting change from potatoes as a topping. Sweet potatoes and turnips can also be used.

1 Preheat the oven to 350°F.

2 In a saucepan, boil the parsnips and carrots for 10-15 minutes or until tender.

3 Meanwhile, heat the oil in a medium-sized saucepan. Add the sliced onion and cook gently.

4 Add the leeks and red pepper.

5 Add the mixed herbs and garlic. Stir well.

6 Add the sliced mushrooms, simmer for 2-3 minutes, season to taste and remove from the heat.

7 By now the parsnips and carrots should be ready. Drain well and set aside.

8 Add the butter and grated nutmeg to the leek mixture. Blend to a smooth puree in a blender or food processor. Season with salt and pepper to taste.

9 Put the vegetable mixture into an ovenproof dish and spread the parsnips and carrots over the top.

10 Cook in the oven for 20 minutes.

Serve immediately with steamed green vegetables or a crisp salad.

◆

Fresh Coriander Dhal

2 tbsp ghee (see p. 47) or butter
2 large onions, thinly sliced
4 garlic cloves, thinly sliced
14-oz can tomatoes
2 tbsp garam masala (see p. 57)
1 tbsp grated ginger root
pinch of grated asafoetida (see p. 56)
pinch of grated nutmeg
5 tbsp finely chopped fresh coriander
  leaves
½-1 tsp chili powder
2¼ cups lentils or split peas
10 cups water

Garnish
1 large onion, sliced into rings
finely chopped fresh coriander leaves
lemon slices

Preparation 10 minutes
Cooking 35 minutes
Serves 6-8
(GF)

1 Heat the ghee in a large saucepan and sauté the onions and garlic for 5 minutes until soft.

2 Add the rest of the ingredients, except the water, and stir-fry for a few minutes.

3 Add the water, bring to a boil and simmer for 35 minutes or until cooked.

4 Prepare the garnish: in a skillet, cook the onion for the garnish in a little ghee until crispy brown.

5 When the dhal is cooked, pour into a serving dish and garnish with the fried onion, coriander and lemon slices.

Serve with brown rice and steamed vegetables.

Fresh Vegetable Curry

4 tbsp peanut oil
2 tsp grated ginger root
3 garlic cloves, crushed
1 tsp coriander seeds
1 tsp ground cumin
½ tsp ground cardamom
2 tsp cayenne
½ tsp chili powder
1 large onion, finely chopped
1 kohlrabi, finely chopped
1 large green pepper, finely chopped
2 large carrots, finely chopped
1 large parsnip, finely chopped
scant 1 cup orange juice
1 large tart apple
1 tbsp raisins (optional)
salt and black pepper

Preparation and cooking 30 minutes
Serves 6
(GF)(V)

This quick-and-simple curry can be made in advance and reheated later without spoiling its flavor.

1 Heat the oil in a large skillet and add the spices and onion.

2 Add the kohlrabi.

3 Add the green pepper, carrots and parsnip.

4 Pour over the orange juice. Finely chop the apple, and add to the pan with the raisins, if using, and cook for about 15 minutes or until the vegetables are tender. Season to taste.

Serve with brown rice, tamari, roasted peanuts and a selection of chutneys and other traditional curry accompaniments.

◆

Fried Tempeh with Orange Sesame Sauce

2 tbsp peanut or sesame oil
8 oz tempeh (see p. 51), thawed if
   frozen, cubed
¼ tsp grated ginger root

Sauce
1 tbsp miso (see p. 50)
3 tbsp tahini (see p. 50)
juice and grated rind of 1 orange or
   1 lemon
⅔ cup water

Preparation and cooking 10 minutes
Serves 4
(GF)(V)

1 Heat the oil gently in a small skillet.

2 Add the tempeh and ginger and shallow-fry for about 5 minutes, turning occasionally, until the pieces are evenly browned. Place onto paper towels to drain.

3 Make the sauce: put the miso and tahini into a bowl and add the grated orange or lemon rind and squeezed juice.

4 Now add the water and mix the sauce ingredients together into a smooth paste.

Serve with the sauce handed separately, and with brown rice and stir-fried vegetables.

◆

Gado-Gado

1½ potatoes
2 carrots
2 cups green beans
1 tbsp peanut oil
1 large onion, finely sliced
4 oz tempeh (see p. 51), cubed
1 cucumber, coarsely chopped
1 small Chinese cabbage, shredded
1 cup bean sprouts
4 oz tofu (see p. 51), cubed
2 eggs, hard-cooked and sliced

1 Boil the potatoes for about 20 minutes until tender. Drain and leave to cool, then cut into bite-sized pieces and set aside.

2 Meanwhile, steam the carrots and green beans together for 8-10 minutes and drain. Slice into bite-sized pieces and set aside.

3 Make the sauce: heat the oil in a small saucepan and add the onion, chili and garlic. Cook for 5 minutes, stirring occasionally, until the onion is soft.

4 Add the peanut butter, coconut, honey, lemon juice, rind and water. Simmer gently until the sauce is smooth and thick. Set aside.

5 Heat the peanut oil in a skillet and add the onion and tempeh. Cook for 5 minutes, turning the tempeh until golden brown. Drain on paper towels.

6 Arrange the cooked vegetables together with the remaining, raw, vegetables and tofu on a serving platter. Top with the sliced hard-cooked eggs, and serve with the peanut sauce handed separately.

Serve with a tomato salad.

Sauce
2 tbsp peanut oil
1 onion, chopped
2 green chili peppers, chopped, or 1 tsp chili powder
3 garlic cloves, crushed
1⅓ cups peanut butter
¼ cup grated creamed coconut
1 tsp honey
juice and grated rind of 1 lemon
2½ cups water

Preparation 10 minutes
Cooking 25 minutes
Serves 6
(GF)

Home-Style Baked Beans

⅔ cup navy beans, soaked for 12 hours or overnight

Sauce
2 large tomatoes
2 tbsp soy oil or butter
1 large onion, chopped
2 tsp finely chopped fresh marjoram or 1 tsp dried
3 tbsp tomato paste
salt and black pepper
1 tbsp apple juice concentrate (see p. 51)

Preparation 20 minutes (allow 12 hours for soaking the beans)
Cooking 2½ hours
Serves 4
(GF) (V)

This is a healthier alternative to the canned varieties: a good recipe for young children.

1 Transfer the soaked beans and their liquid to a saucepan. Top up with fresh water, if necessary, to cover the beans. Cover and bring to a boil. Lower the heat and simmer for 1½ hours or until tender.

2 While the beans are cooking, make the sauce: first put the tomatoes in a bowl and pour over boiling water. Cover and set aside for 10-15 minutes to allow the skins to soften.

3 Meanwhile, heat the oil in a saucepan. Add the onion and marjoram, and cook gently for 5 minutes.

4 Pour the water off the tomatoes. Drain, peel and chop coarsely, and add to the saucepan.

5 Add the tomato paste, seasoning and apple juice concentrate. Bring to a boil and simmer for 5 minutes.

6 Blend the mixture in a blender or food processor until smooth, or mix together well, using a potato masher.

7 Preheat the oven to 350°F.

8 When the beans are cooked, drain well, reserving ½ cup of the cooking liquid. Add the beans and the liquid to the tomato sauce.

9 Mix well and pour into an ovenproof casserole dish.

10 Put the bean mixture in the oven and bake, covered, for 1 hour. Serve on toast and with steamed vegetables.

Joey's Egg Curry

2 tbsp soy oil
1 tbsp poppy seeds
¼ tsp fennel seeds
1 large onion, chopped
1 tbsp Madras curry powder
1 green pepper, chopped
2 garlic cloves, crushed
2¾ cups Greek-style yogurt
¼ cup creamed coconut
½ cup orange juice
4 eggs, hard-cooked and shelled
salt and black pepper

Preparation and cooking 20 minutes
Serves 4-6
(GF)

1 Put the oil in a medium-sized saucepan. Add the poppy seeds and fennel seeds and cook over a medium heat, stirring occasionally.

2 Add the onion and curry powder. Stir well.

3 Add the green pepper and garlic and continue cooking for a further 5 minutes.

4 Mix in the yogurt, coconut and orange juice. Simmer gently for 5 minutes until the coconut has melted and you have a smooth sauce.

5 Add the eggs to the curry sauce. Season and serve immediately.

Serve with brown rice and a selection of chutneys and other traditional curry accompaniments.

Macaroni & Cheese

2 tbsp butter
1 onion, finely chopped
1 red pepper, thinly sliced
2 tbsp whole wheat flour
1¼ cups milk
1½ cups grated sharp cheese
¼ tsp grated nutmeg
salt and black pepper
1½ cups whole wheat macaroni
1 tbsp coarsely chopped fresh parsley

Preparation and cooking 20 minutes
Serves 4

1 Melt the butter in a medium-sized saucepan and sauté the onion.

2 Add the red pepper and cook for 3-4 minutes.

3 Remove from the heat and stir in the whole wheat flour. Gradually add the milk, a little at a time.

4 Return to the stove and bring to a boil, stirring continuously. When the sauce begins to thicken, add the grated cheese, nutmeg and seasoning. Set aside.

5 Bring a saucepan half-full of water to the boil, add the macaroni and simmer for 10 minutes or until tender. Drain well.

6 Reheat the sauce till it bubbles. Add the macaroni and the chopped parsley. Stir through and serve immediately.

Millet Casserole

2 tbsp soy oil
1 small onion, chopped
⅓ cup chopped celery root
1 carrot, chopped
1 small green pepper, thinly sliced
1 leek, cut into rings
⅔ cup whole millet
4½ cups water
1 tsp yeast extract
salt and black pepper
1 cup grated cheese
3 eggs, separated

Preparation 20 minutes
Cooking 30 minutes
Serves 4
(GF)

1 Preheat the oven to 350°F.

2 Heat the oil in a medium-sized saucepan and sauté the onion, celery root and carrots. Add the pepper and leeks.

3 Add the millet and stir-fry for 1 minute. Pour the water over and add the yeast extract and seasoning. Bring to a boil.

4 Add half the grated cheese and the egg yolks to the saucepan. Stir well.

5 Stiffly whip the egg whites and fold into the millet mixture.

7 Transfer to an ovenproof dish. Sprinkle the remaining cheese on top and bake for 30 minutes or until browned.

Mung Bean Casserole

⅔ cup mung beans, soaked for 4 hours
1 tbsp corn oil
1 large onion, chopped
1 red pepper, chopped
½ tsp mixed herbs
generous 2 cups coarsely chopped
    broccoli
1¼ cups carrot juice
salt and black pepper
1 tbsp cashew nuts, to garnish

**Preparation 15 minutes (allow 4 hours
for soaking the beans)
Cooking 1 hour 5 minutes
Serves 4**
ⒼⒻ Ⓥ

**If you have a juicer, make your own carrot juice. Otherwise,
bottled juice is fine.**

1 Transfer the soaked beans and their liquid to a saucepan. Top up
with fresh water, if necessary, to cover the beans. Cover, bring to a
boil and then lower the heat and simmer for 45 minutes.

2 Meanwhile, heat the oil in a medium-sized saucepan, and add the
chopped onion and red pepper. Add the mixed herbs and cook
gently for 5 minutes.

3 Add the broccoli.

4 Pour the carrot juice over and simmer for 15 minutes.

5 Add the drained and cooked beans and seasoning to taste.

6 Serve immediately, garnished with cashews.

Serve on a bed of bulgur, brown rice or couscous.

Pinto, Zucchini & Mushroom Bake

½ cup pinto beans, soaked for 12 hours
    or overnight
¼ cup butter
1 large onion, finely chopped
1 tbsp tomato paste
2 tsp finely chopped fresh basil or
    1 tsp dried
2 zucchini, thinly sliced
4 cups finely chopped mushrooms
2 garlic cloves, crushed
salt and black pepper
4 tomatoes, sliced

Sauce
¼ cup butter
2 tbsp whole wheat flour
2½ cups milk
1¼ cups grated cheese
salt and black pepper
½ tsp grated nutmeg
1 egg, beaten
1 tbsp finely chopped fresh parsley,
    to garnish

**Preparation 30 minutes (allow 12 hours
for soaking the beans)
Cooking 2 hours 20 minutes
Serves 6**

Flageolet or cannellini beans can be used instead of pinto beans.

1 Transfer the soaked beans and their liquid to a saucepan. Top up
with fresh water, if necessary, to cover the beans. Cover and bring
to a boil. Lower the heat and simmer for 1½ hours until tender.
Drain and set aside.

2 Meanwhile, melt the first ¼ cup butter in a saucepan.

3 Add the onion and cook gently.

4 Stir in the tomato paste and basil.

5 Add the zucchini and mushrooms.

6 Add the garlic. Mix well and leave the vegetables to simmer on a
low heat, covered, for 20 minutes.

7 Meanwhile, make the white sauce: melt ¼ cup butter. Remove
from heat and stir in the whole wheat flour.

8 Gradually add the milk and return to the stove.

9 Heat gently, stirring continuously until the sauce thickens.

10 Pour half of the sauce into a pitcher and add the grated cheese
to the remaining half in the saucepan. Cook for 1 minute, remove
from heat and season if liked.

11 Preheat the oven to 375°F.

12 Add the cooked pinto beans, mix thoroughly and pour into a
large heatproof serving dish.

13 Season the vegetables and pour over the beans.

Continued, page 110.

Pinto, Zucchini & Mushroom Bake, continued from page 109.

14 Lay the tomatoes down the two longest sides of the dish, leaving a space so that the vegetables show in the middle.

15 To the remaining white sauce, add the nutmeg and a good sprinkling of black pepper.

16 Add the beaten egg to the sauce and carefully pour it over the vegetables, trying not to cover the tomatoes.

17 Bake for about 50 minutes or until the top is golden brown.

18 Serve garnished with chopped parsley.

Serve with a grain dish and a salad.

Ratatouille

1 large eggplant, chopped
2 tbsp olive oil
1 large onion, sliced
1 red pepper, thinly sliced
4 zucchini, thinly sliced
3 tbsp tomato paste
2 large tomatoes, peeled and coarsely chopped
2 cups thinly sliced mushrooms
3 garlic cloves, crushed
salt and black pepper
finely chopped fresh parsley or coriander, to garnish

Preparation 30 minutes
Cooking 45 minutes-1 hour
Serves 4
(GF) (V)

1 Prepare the eggplant as necessary (see p. 28).

2 Heat the olive oil in a large saucepan. Add the onion and red pepper. Cook gently for 4-5 minutes.

3 Add the zucchini.

4 Add the eggplant with the tomato paste. Stir well.

5 Add the tomatoes and mushrooms.

6 Finally, add the garlic, season to taste, turn the heat down low and simmer gently for 45 minutes-1 hour, stirring occasionally, but taking care not to break up the vegetables too much. (You should not have to add any extra liquid if the vegetables are cooked gently.)

7 Before serving, sprinkle liberally with a garnish of chopped fresh parsley or coriander.

Serve with brown rice.

Red Pepper & Broccoli Quiche

Pastry
2 cups plus 2 tbsp whole wheat flour
½ tsp salt
¼ cup soy oil
scant 1 cup cold water

Filling
¼ cup butter
1 large onion, chopped
1 large red pepper, chopped
3 cups chopped broccoli
salt and black pepper
8 eggs
3¾ cups milk
1½ tsp grated nutmeg
salt and black pepper
2 cups grated cheese

Preparation 30 minutes
Cooking 45 minutes
Serves 8-10

1 Preheat the oven to 400°F.

2 Grease a 12 × 10 inch ovenproof dish. Sprinkle with a little of the whole wheat flour.

3 Make the pastry: put the flour and salt in a large mixing bowl or blender or food processor. Add the oil and mix in thoroughly.

4 Slowly add the water. Stop mixing in the water as soon as the pastry holds together. Do not overbeat the mixture, or it will become rubbery.

5 Put the pastry dough on a flat floured surface and roll out to a thickness of ¼ inch. Line the dish and flute the edges of the pastry. Prick the bottom and sides of the dough with a fork and put in the oven for 10-15 minutes. Remove from the oven and put to one side.

6 Meanwhile, prepare the filling: melt the butter in a medium-sized saucepan and sauté the onion and pepper.

7 Add the broccoli to the other vegetables with some salt and pepper. Simmer gently for 10 minutes.

8 Break the eggs into a mixing bowl and beat them vigorously. Add the milk, grated nutmeg and seasoning.

9 Put the cooked vegetables in the bottom of the cooked pastry case. Sprinkle over the grated cheese, then pour over the sauce.

10 Bake for 45 minutes until golden brown on top. Remove from oven and leave to stand for 5 minutes before cutting.

Serve with steamed vegetables and a bean salad.

Preparing the quiche pastry

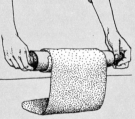 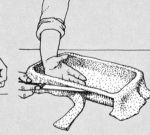  

1 To line the quiche dish: roll the pastry on to the floured rolling pin so that it can be moved easily on to the dish.

2 Trim the excess pastry away with a sharp knife, just under the rim of the quiche dish.

3 Flute the edges of the pastry for decoration, squeezing between your forefinger and thumb.

4 Prick the base of the pastry with a fork before putting in the oven.

Rice Balls

1⅓ cups brown rice
2 cups water
1 small onion, finely chopped
1 tbsp finely chopped fresh parsley
1 tsp grated ginger root
1 tbsp tahini (see p. 50)
1 tbsp tamari
1 tbsp sunflower seeds
1-2 garlic cloves, crushed
½ tsp coriander seeds (optional)
salt and black pepper
a little whole wheat flour and a few
    sesame seeds for rolling
a little oil for frying

Preparation 5-10 minutes
Cooking 50 minutes
Makes 8 rice balls
Ⓥ

1 Put the rice and water in a large saucepan. Bring to a boil. Lower the heat and simmer, covered, for 45 minutes until the rice is cooked. Leave to cool and set aside.

2 Combine all the ingredients, except the flour, sesame seeds and oil, in a large bowl or food processor and mix together thoroughly for 3-4 minutes until the mixture holds together easily.

3 Sprinkle the whole wheat flour and sesame seeds onto a plate and mix together with your fingertips.

4 Using an ice cream scoop or your hands, form the rice mixture into small balls. Roll the balls in the flour and sesame seeds until well covered.

5 Heat enough oil for deep- or shallow-frying and when very hot gently lower the rice balls into the oil and fry for 2-3 minutes until golden brown.

6 Drain on paper towels.

Serve warm or cold with a vegetable dish or salad.

Savory Kombu & Carrots

½ oz kombu (see p. 44)
1 tbsp peanut oil
1 onion, sliced into rings
1 large carrot, cut in thin matchsticks
1¼ cups water
2 tbsp tamari

Preparation 20-30 minutes
Cooking 20 minutes
Serves 4
ⒼⒻ Ⓥ

This seaweed has a strong flavor. Try serving with a sprinkling of gomashio (see p. 50).

1 Put the kombu into a bowl and cover with boiling water. Leave for 20 minutes.

2 Heat the oil in a saucepan. Add the onion and carrots and sauté for 5 minutes or until the onion is soft.

3 Drain the kombu, cut into thin strips and add to the saucepan.

4 Pour over the water and tamari and simmer, without a cover, for 20 minutes.

Serve with a cooked grain and steamed vegetables.

Seaweed Rolls

1⅓ cups brown rice
2 cups water
¼ tsp grated ginger root
1 tsp tahini (see p. 50)
salt and black pepper
3 sheets of nori (see p. 44)
a little tamari
1 large carrot, cut into long thin strips
¼ cucumber, cut into long thin strips
3 umeboshi plums (see p. 51)

Preparation 15-20 minutes
Cooking 40-45 minutes
Chilling 1 hour
Serves 6
(GF) (V)

1 Put the rice and water in a large saucepan. Bring to a boil, lower the heat and simmer, covered, for 40-45 minutes until cooked.

2 Transfer the cooked and drained rice to a mixing bowl. Add the grated ginger, tahini and seasoning and mix well.

3 Wave the smooth side of the nori over a gas flame or electric ring until it turns green.

4 Now you are ready to make the rolls: lay 1 slice of the nori on a dry, flat surface. Brush with a little tamari.

5 Divide the rice mixture into 3. Take one third of the rice in damp hands, squeeze together and roll into a sausage shape to fit the length of the seaweed. Press it down securely along the short side of the seaweed, flattening it with your hand.

6 Lay a strip of carrot and cucumber in the middle of the rice. Put an umeboshi plum in the middle. Roll up the seaweed. Make up the other seaweed rolls in a similar way.

7 Cut each roll in half. Refrigerate for about 1 hour before serving.

Serve with shoyu (see p. 51) or tamari.

Making the seaweed rolls

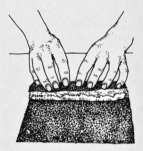

1 Wave the sheet of nori over the heat until the seaweed turns green.

2 Place the rice mixture, carrot, cucumber and umeboshi on the nori.

3 Roll up the nori carefully, starting from the side nearest to you.

Seitan with Hiziki

½ oz hiziki (see p. 44)
2 tbsp soy oil
1 onion, finely chopped
1 tsp grated ginger root
1 zucchini, finely chopped
1 tbsp tamari
1 garlic clove, crushed
1¼ cups water
½ lb seitan (see p. 50)
1 tsp gomashio (see p. 50)

Preparation 20 minutes
Cooking 30 minutes
Serves 4-6
(V)

1 Pour boiling water over the hiziki and soak for 20 minutes.

2 Meanwhile, put the oil into a medium-sized saucepan and add the onion and ginger. Cook gently for about 5 minutes.

3 Add the zucchini to the saucepan with the tamari and garlic.

4 Drain the hiziki, squeezing out excess water, and add to the pan.

5 Pour the 1¼ cups water over, then break the seitan into small pieces and add to the saucepan.

6 Simmer, covered, for 30 minutes. Garnish with gomashio.

Serve on a bed of brown rice with steamed vegetables.

Sesame Roast Parsnips

1 cup soy oil
4 tbsp sesame seeds
¼ cup tamari
4 parsnips, sliced into strips

Preparation 5 minutes
Cooking 10 minutes
Serves 4
(GF) (V)

1 Preheat the oven to 425°F.

2 Pour the oil into a baking dish and heat for a few minutes in the oven.

3 Add the sesame seeds and tamari and mix well.

4 Finally, add the parsnips and roast for about 10 minutes until brown on the outside and soft inside.

Serve with cooked grains and steamed vegetables.

Spinach & Mushroom Lasagne

1¼ lb fresh spinach
¼ tsp grated nutmeg
salt and black pepper
½ lb spinach whole wheat lasagne
grated cheese, to garnish

Mushroom sauce
2 tbsp butter
2 large onions, thinly sliced
4 cups thinly sliced mushrooms
4 garlic cloves, crushed
2 tsp finely chopped fresh oregano or
    1 tsp dried
1 tsp finely chopped fresh basil or ½ tsp
    dried
4 tbsp tomato paste
14-oz can tomatoes
1 tbsp tamari
1 tsp honey
salt and black pepper

Cheese sauce
6 tbsp butter
4 tbsp fine whole wheat flour
2½ cups milk
2 cups sharp grated cheese
salt and black pepper

Preparation 30 minutes
Cooking 40 minutes
Serves 6-8

Use fresh spinach where possible. If not available, you can substitute frozen spinach.

1 Preheat the oven to 350°F.

2 First make the mushroom sauce: melt the butter in a saucepan. Add the onions and sauté.

3 Add the mushrooms to the onions with the crushed garlic, oregano, basil and tomato paste.

4 Put the canned tomatoes in a bowl and roughly break them up with a fork. Add to the sauce with the tamari, honey and seasoning and simmer for 10 minutes.

5 Now make the cheese sauce: melt the butter in another saucepan. Add the flour and cook over a high heat, stirring continuously for about 3 minutes.

6 Add the milk slowly, keeping the pan on a low heat and stirring throughout. Bring to a boil and simmer for 3 minutes. Remove from the heat and add the grated cheese and seasoning. Set aside.

7 Pack the spinach into a pan without any water. Place over a high heat for 1-2 minutes. Add the nutmeg and seasoning. Lower the heat and simmer for another 5 minutes.

8 Put a large pan of water on to boil and parboil the spinach lasagne by boiling for 8 minutes. Drain well.

9 Grease a large ovenproof dish. Line the bottom and sides with some of the parboiled lasagne. Proceed with alternate layers of cheese sauce, spinach, mushroom sauce and lasagne, finishing with a layer of cheese sauce. Sprinkle a little grated cheese on top.

10 Bake for 40 minutes or until browned on top.

Serve immediately with assorted steamed vegetables and salad.

Stir-Fried Swiss Chard & Mushrooms

2 tbsp soy oil or butter
4 cups shredded Swiss chard
4 cups thinly sliced mushrooms
¼ tsp grated nutmeg
2 tsp tamari
1 tsp roasted sesame seeds, to garnish

Preparation 5 minutes
Cooking 10 minutes
Serves 4

Any green leafy vegetable such as spinach or sea kale can be used instead of the Swiss chard.

1 Heat the oil in a wok or large saucepan. Add the chard and cook over a high heat, stirring continuously for 3-4 minutes or until the chard begins to shrink in size.

2 Add the mushrooms, grated nutmeg and tamari and stir-fry for a further 5 minutes or until the mushrooms and chard are cooked.

3 Sprinkle over roasted sesame seeds and serve immediately.

Serve with brown rice, buckwheat or millet.

Stuffed Eggplant with Tomato Sauce

3 large eggplants
olive oil for brushing
1 tbsp finely chopped fresh parsley or
   pecans, to garnish

Sauce
2 large tomatoes
¼ cup butter
1 large onion, finely chopped
2 tsp finely chopped fresh oregano or
   1 tsp dried
3 garlic cloves, crushed
salt and black pepper

Stuffing
½ cup dried chestnuts, soaked for 12
   hours or overnight
⅔ cup pecans
½ cup fresh orange juice
2 cups fresh whole wheat bread crumbs

**Preparation 20 minutes (allow 12 hours
for soaking the chestnuts)**
Cooking 2 hours 15 minutes
Serves 6

You will need a blender or food processor for this recipe.

1 Begin to prepare the stuffing: put the chestnuts in a saucepan and cover with water. Bring to a boil, then lower the heat and simmer for 1½ hours or until tender.

2 Meanwhile, cut the eggplants in half lengthwise, and scoop out the middles, leaving about ¼ inch all the way around. (Keep flesh for another recipe.) Salt inside of shell as necessary (see p. 28).

3 Make the sauce: put the tomatoes in a bowl, cover with boiling water and leave to stand for 10-15 minutes for the skins to soften.

4 Melt the butter in a saucepan and add the onion, oregano and garlic. Continue cooking for 5 minutes or until the onion is soft.

5 Pour the water off the tomatoes. Drain and peel the tomatoes, break them up and add to the onion. Cook for a further 5 minutes, season with black pepper and salt and set aside.

6 Preheat the oven to 350°F.

7 Now you are ready to make the stuffing: blend the pecans, orange juice and drained chestnuts in a blender or food processor until smooth.

8 Put the mixture into a bowl, add the bread crumbs and mix well.

9 Divide the stuffing into 6 equal portions and fill the centers of the eggplants. Brush with olive oil and put in a heatproof dish, covered with foil.

10 Bake for 45 minutes or until the eggplants are cooked.

11 Just before the eggplants are ready, reheat the tomato sauce and pour over the top. Garnish with chopped parsley or a sprinkling of pecans.

Serve with a fresh salad and a grain dish.

Summer Okra Casserole

6 tbsp soy oil
2 onions, finely chopped
2⅔ cups cubed potatoes
6 cups topped, tailed and thinly sliced
  okra
14-oz can tomatoes
2 green peppers, thinly sliced
salt and black pepper
2 tbsp finely chopped fresh oregano or
  1 tsp dried
4 garlic cloves, crushed

Preparation 20 minutes
Cooking 20 minutes
Serves 6
(GF) (V)

Buy young, tender okra, as the large ones can be very tough and stringy. Okra can also have a rather slimy texture, which can be reduced by soaking the cut pieces in water beforehand.

1 Heat 3 tbsp of the oil in a large saucepan and sauté the onions for 5 minutes until soft.

2 Add the potatoes and cook for about 10 minutes until browned, stirring frequently to prevent sticking.

3 Heat the remaining oil in another large saucepan and add the okra. Sauté gently, stirring occasionally, for about 5 minutes, or until the okra is tender but still firm.

4 Add the tomatoes and green peppers and cook for a further 5 minutes.

5 When the potatoes are browned, add to the okra and mix well. Simmer gently for 10 minutes over a low heat. Season to taste.

6 A few minutes before serving, add the fresh oregano and crushed garlic.

Serve with brown rice, bulgar or any other grain.

◆

Rutabaga & Orange Pie

2 tbsp soy oil
1 large onion, finely chopped
1 large red pepper, finely chopped
2 small turnips, finely chopped
½ tsp ground cinnamon
1 tbsp tomato paste
1 tbsp tamari
4 zucchini, finely chopped
2 cups finely chopped mushrooms
salt and black pepper

Topping
7 cups chopped rutabaga
¼ cup soy oil or butter
juice and grated rind of 1 orange
¼ cup shredded coconut
salt and black pepper

Preparation 15 minutes
Cooking 20 minutes
Serves 6
(GF) (V)

Puréed rutabagas with a hint of orange and coconut make this an unusual dish.

1 Preheat the oven to 400°F.

2 First boil the rutabagas for the topping for 10 minutes or steam them for 15 minutes until tender.

3 Meanwhile, heat 2 tbsp oil in a medium-sized saucepan and add the onion, red pepper and turnips.

4 Add the cinnamon, tomato paste and tamari and cook gently.

5 Add the zucchini and mushrooms to the saucepan. Cook for a further 8-10 minutes or until the vegetables are tender. Season to taste.

6 By now the rutabagas should be ready. Drain well.

7 Make the rest of the topping: add the oil, orange juice and rind and coconut to the rutabagas and blend to a smooth paste in a blender or food processor. Season to taste.

8 Put the vegetables into an ovenproof dish and spread the rutabasas over the top.

9 Bake for 20 minutes until cooked through.

Serve immediately with a crisp green salad.

Tofu & Mushroom Tart

Pastry
1½ cups plus 2 tbsp fine whole wheat flour
¼ tsp salt
1 tsp chopped fresh dill
¼ cup soy oil
⅔ cup cold water

Filling
1 tbsp olive oil
1 onion, finely chopped
1 garlic clove, crushed
4 cups thinly sliced mushrooms
2 tbsp shoyu (see p. 51)
¼ tsp black pepper
9 oz tofu (see p. 51)
juice of 1 lemon

Preparation 20 minutes
Cooking 40 minutes
Serves 4-6
Ⓥ

1 Preheat the oven to 400°F.

2 Grease a 9-inch pie plate.

3 Put the whole wheat flour, salt and dill into a mixing bowl or food processor. Thoroughly mix in the soy oil.

4 Slowly mix in the water. Stop mixing in the water as soon as the pastry holds together. Do not overbeat, or the pastry will become tough and rubbery.

5 Put the pastry dough on a flat, floured surface. Roll out to a thickness of ¼ inch and line the pie plate. Cut off the excess pastry around the edge, prick the bottom and the sides of the dough with a fork and bake for 10 minutes or until the bottom is cooked. Remove from oven and set aside.

6 Meanwhile, make the filling: heat the olive oil in a skillet and sauté the onion and garlic.

7 Add the mushrooms to the onion with the shoyu and black pepper. Cook gently for 5 minutes or until the onion is soft.

8 Meanwhile, put the tofu in a bowl. Add the lemon juice and mash well with a potato masher.

9 When the mushroom mixture is ready, remove from heat and stir in the tofu mixture.

10 Spoon the mushroom and tofu mixture into the precooked pastry shell, return to the oven and bake for 30 minutes until the topping has set.

Serve warm or cold with a grain and salad dish.

◆

Unroasted Buckwheat Casserole

2 tbsp peanut oil
1 cup whole raw buckwheat
1 large onion, thinly sliced
1 green pepper, thinly sliced
2 carrots, thinly sliced
½ tsp caraway seeds
2 cups thinly sliced mushrooms
salt and black pepper
1¾ cups water
1 tbsp tamari
finely chopped fresh parsley, to garnish

Preparation 10 minutes
Cooking 20 minutes
Serves 4
ⒼⒻ Ⓥ

1 Heat the oil in a medium-sized saucepan. Add the buckwheat and gently sauté for 2-3 minutes until slightly browned. Add the green pepper, carrots and caraway seeds. Cook gently for 2-3 minutes.

2 Add the mushrooms to the saucepan and season.

3 Add the water and tamari. Bring to a boil. Lower heat and simmer for 20 minutes until the buckwheat is cooked. Remove from heat and serve, garnished with a sprinkling of parsley.

Serve with some steamed vegetables with a cheese sauce (see p. 114).

Vegetable Loaf with Couscous

scant 1 cup couscous
1 tsp soy grits (optional)
1 tbsp sesame oil
1 onion, thinly sliced into rings
4 celery stalks, thinly sliced
2 tsp finely chopped fresh basil or 1 tsp
   dried
1 tbsp tomato paste
2 cups thinly sliced mushrooms
1 tbsp tamari
salt and black pepper
6 slices of tomato
1 tsp gomashio (see p. 50)

Preparation 25 minutes
Chilling 4 hours (minimum)
Serves 4-6
(v)

This easy dish can look quite spectacular if the top and sides are decorated with slices of vegetables and/or nuts.

1 Put the couscous and soy grits, if using, in separate bowls. Cover both with boiling water and set aside for about 10 minutes until they puff up.

2 Meanwhile, heat the oil in a skillet and sauté the onion and celery with the basil and tomato paste. Cook gently for 5 minutes.

3 Add the mushrooms, tamari and drained soy grits, if using. Cook for a further 5 minutes or until the vegetables are tender.

4 Add the drained couscous to the vegetables. Mix well and season to taste.

5 Grease an $8\frac{1}{2}$- $\times$ $4\frac{1}{2}$- $\times$ $2\frac{1}{2}$-inch loaf pan and line with a layer of wax paper.

6 Put the tomato slices on the bottom of the loaf pan. Sprinkle with gomashio.

7 Pour the vegetables and couscous mixture into the loaf pan and press down well.

8 Cover and chill for at least 4 hours or overnight. Remove from refrigerator just before serving.

9 To serve, gently slide a knife between the sides of the pan and the paper. Turn out on to a serving dish and cut into slices.

Try serving with a tomato sauce (see p. 115) or yogurt sauce (see p. 86).

Preparing the pan and turning out the vegetable loaf

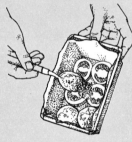

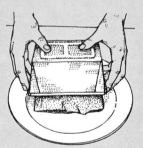

1 Place 6 tomato slices in the lined loaf pan and sprinkle gomashio over the top.

2 To turn out the cooked loaf, turn upside-down on a plate, tap firmly and gently pull off the pan.

3 Peel off the wax paper and the loaf is ready for slicing.

Wakame

1½ oz wakame (see p. 44)
1 cucumber, thinly sliced

Dressing
4 tbsp sesame seeds
1 tbsp soy oil
1 tsp mustard powder
6 tbsp brown rice vinegar
½ cup shoyu (see p. 51)

Preparation 20 minutes
Cooking 30 minutes
Serves 6-8
(GF) (V)

1 Put the wakame in a saucepan. Cover with boiling water and leave to stand for 20 minutes. Bring back to a boil and simmer for 30 minutes until the wakame is cooked.

2 Meanwhile, prepare the dressing: put the sesame seeds on a chopping board and chop them roughly with a large sharp knife to bring out their flavor.

3 Heat the oil in a small skillet and add the sesame seeds. Stir-fry for 5-8 minutes or until the seeds are a golden brown color. Remove from heat.

4 Mix together the mustard powder, rice vinegar and shoyu in a bowl.

5 By now the wakame will be ready. Drain well and cut into small pieces. Arrange on a serving plate.

6 Add the cucumber.

7 Pour the dressing over the top and sprinkle with the sesame seeds.

Serve with brown rice and a side dish of vegetables.

Whole Wheat Pizza

Dough
1 oz compressed yeast
1¼ cups warm water
4 cups plus 2 tbsp whole wheat flour
½ tsp salt

Sauce
14-oz can tomatoes
2 tsp finely chopped fresh oregano or
    1 tsp dried
3 garlic cloves
pinch of chili powder
salt and black pepper

Topping
1 onion, thinly sliced
3 cups sliced mushrooms
1½ cups grated cheese
1 green pepper, sliced
3 tomatoes, sliced in rings
12 ripe olives

Preparation 20 minutes (allow 1 hour proving time)
Cooking 15 minutes
Serves 6

1 Make the dough: crumble the yeast into the warm water and stir in a scant 2½ cups of the flour to make a thick batter. Cover and leave in a warm place to rise for about 30 minutes.

2 Add the salt and work in the remaining flour until the dough holds together. Turn onto a lightly floured surface and knead. The dough should be strong and elastic and not stick to your hands. Return to the bowl when smooth and leave in a warm place to rise for another 30 minutes.

3 Punch down, divide into 2 and roll out each piece on a lightly floured board.

4 Grease two 12- × 8-inch baking trays and line with the dough, pushing it well into the sides.

5 Preheat the oven to 500°F.

6 Make the sauce: put all the ingredients into a blender or food processor and mix thoroughly. Alternatively, mash thoroughly with a potato masher. Spread the sauce over the dough.

7 Make the topping: sprinkle over the chopped onion and mushrooms. Cover with cheese and decorate with the green pepper, tomatoes and olives.

8 Bake for about 15 minutes or until the base is cooked and the cheese and vegetables are slightly browned.

Serve with a selection of salads.

DESSERTS

☐ Pictured opposite page 129

Note: Cashew Cream is a delicious substitute for whipped cream or yogurt to serve with desserts.

Apple, Soy & Almond Pudding

4 tart apples, finely chopped
⅔ cup boiling water
½ cup butter
4 tbsp honey
1 egg, beaten
juice and grated rind of 1 lemon
½ cup ground almonds
2 tbsp soy flour
¼ tsp vanilla extract
½ tsp taking powder (use appropriate baking powder for recipe, see p. 133)

Preparation 15 minutes
Cooking 30-40 minutes
Serves 4
(GF)

You can substitute fresh plums or peaches for the apples, when they are in season.

1 Preheat the oven to 350°F.

2 Put the apples into a medium-sized saucepan, add the water and stew gently for 5 minutes.

3 In a bowl, cream together the butter and honey. Add the egg to the creamed mixture and mix well.

4 Add the lemon juice and rind.

5 Add the almonds, soy flour, vanilla extract and baking powder and beat together until you have a smooth mixture.

6 Put the apples in an ovenproof dish.

7 Spread the cake mixture over the top and bake for 30-40 minutes or until golden brown on top.

Serve immediately with yogurt or cream.

Apricot & Orange Sago Cream

1⅓ cups dried apricots, soaked for 12
  hours or overnight
juice and grated rind of 1 orange
2½ cups milk
generous ⅔ cup sago
2 eggs, separated

**Preparation 20 minutes (allow 12 hours
for soaking the apricots)**
Cooking 20 minutes
Chilling 2 hours minimum
Serves 4
(GF)

You will need a blender for this recipe.

1 Drain the apricots and reserve 4 for decoration. Purée the rest, together with the orange juice, then set aside.

2 Put the milk, sago and orange rind in a medium-sized saucepan and simmer gently for 15 minutes or until the sago is cooked. Stir occasionally to prevent sticking.

3 Add the egg yolks and heat gently for a further 5 minutes.

4 Remove from the heat and stir in the puréed apricots. Cool.

5 Whip the egg whites stiffly and fold into the cooled sago mixture.

6 Pour into 4 individual dishes and chill in the refrigerator for at least 2 hours before serving. Decorate with the reserved apricots.

Baked Apples

6 large tart apples, cored

Stuffing
1 cup finely chopped mixed dried fruit
2 tbsp honey or apple juice concentrate
  (see p. 51)
1 tsp apple pie spice
½ tsp ground cloves
1 cup old-fashioned oats

Preparation 10 minutes
Cooking 30 minutes
Serves 6
(V)

The dried fruit needs to be chopped very finely, to ensure thorough cooking.

1 Preheat the oven to 425°F.

2 Place the apples on a greased baking tray.

3 Make the stuffing: mix together the mixed dried fruit, honey, piespice, cloves and oats.

4 Using a teaspoon, fill the centers of the apples with the stuffing.

5 Bake for 30 minutes or until the apples are soft.

Serve warm with whipped cream, yogurt or custard.

Baked Bananas with Yogurt Sauce

1 tbsp honey
6 tbsp butter
1 tsp apple pie spice
6 bananas

Sauce
2 cups Greek-style yogurt
6 tbsp light cream
¼ tsp ground cardamom
1 tsp grated nutmeg
1 tbsp honey
juice and grated rind of 1 orange or
  1 lemon

Preparation 10 minutes
Cooking 20 minutes
Serves 6
(GF)

1 Preheat the oven to 350°F.

2 Gently melt the honey and butter in a small saucepan and add the spice.

3 Coat the bananas in the mixture and place on a greased baking tray.

4 Bake for 20 minutes or until the bananas are soft.

5 Meanwhile, make the yogurt sauce: mix all the sauce ingredients together. Pour over the hot bananas and serve immediately.

Banana Frozen Yogurt

3 bananas
1¼ cups Greek-style yogurt
2 tbsp maple syrup
juice and grated rind of ½ lemon
  (optional)

Preparation 5 minutes
Freezing 5 hours minimum
Chilling 45 minutes
Serves 4
(GF)

You will need a blender or food processor for this recipe.

1 Blend all the ingredients in a blender or food processor until smooth.

2 Pour into a serving bowl or freezer container and put in the freezer for about 3 hours or until almost set.

3 Remove from the freezer and beat again.

4 Return to the freezer for about 2 hours or until completely set.

5 Refrigerate for about 45 minutes to soften slightly before serving.

Carob & Sunflower Mousse

3 cups sunflower seeds
scant 1½ cups water
2 tbsp carob powder
1 tbsp pear and apple spread (see p. 51)
1 tbsp brandy (optional)

Preparation 5 minutes
Chilling 1 hour minimum
Serves 6
(GF) (V)

This very rich mousse should be served in small quantities. For a lighter, non-vegan mousse, fold in 2 whipped egg whites.
  You will need a blender or food processor for this recipe.

1 Blend all the ingredients in a blender or food processor until smooth.

2 Pour into 6 individual dishes and chill for 1 hour before serving.

Cheesecake

Crust
2 tbsp honey
2 tbsp butter
6 tbsp fine whole wheat flour
½ tsp baking powder

Topping
⅛ cup honey
½ cup butter
4 tbsp potato flour
4 eggs, separated
juice and grated rind of 1 lemon or
  1 orange
2¼ cups yogurt
2¼ cups lowfat skim-milk cheese

Preparation 20 minutes
Cooking 1½ hours
Cooling 1 hour
Serves 8

1 Preheat the oven to 325°F.

2 Grease and line a 9-inch pie dish or shallow cake pan.

3 Make the crust: cream together the honey and butter in a bowl.

4 Add the flour and baking powder, to make a fairly crumbly dough.

5 Place the mixture in the prepared pan, press down well and bake for 15 minutes or until lightly browned. Remove from the oven. Turn the oven down to 300°F.

6 Make the topping: cream together the honey and butter.

7 Add the potato flour and mix it in.

8 Add the rest of the ingredients, except the egg whites, and mix thoroughly.

9 Beat the egg whites until stiff and carefully fold into the mixture. Pour over the crust.

10 Bake for 1¼ hours or until set.

11 Turn the oven off and leave for another hour so it can cool down slowly. Remove from the oven and serve chilled, if wished.

Cherry Pie

Piecrust dough
1½ cups plus 2 tbsp whole wheat flour
½ cup butter or margarine
2 tbsp water
1 tbsp apple juice concentrate (see p. 51)

Filling
5 cups fresh cherries, unpitted
2½ cups water
1 tbsp apple juice concentrate (see p. 51)
4 tsp kuzu (see p. 50), crushed
grated rind of 1 lemon

Preparation 30 minutes
Cooking 10 minutes
Serves 8
Ⓥ

This pie is delicious hot or cold. A little vegetable oil can be substituted for the butter, if preferred.

1 Preheat the oven to 400°F.

2 Grease a 9-inch pie dish.

3 Put the cherries in a medium-sized saucepan and add the water. Bring to a boil and simmer for about 30 minutes or until tender.

4 Meanwhile, prepare the dough: put the whole wheat flour in a large mixing bowl. Cut in the butter until the mixture resembles fine bread crumbs.

5 Add the 2 tbsp water and 1 tbsp apple juice concentrate, and mix in with a knife or metal spoon until the pastry sticks together.

6 Roll out the dough as thinly as possible on a lightly floured surface and line the prepared pie dish. Prick the bottom and sides of the dough with a fork.

7 Bake for 10-15 minutes or until the dough is cooked and crisp.

8 While the dough is cooking, remove the cherries from the heat, reserving the cooking liquid. Set the cherries aside to cool for a few minutes, then take out the pits. Put the cherries in a bowl and set aside.

9 Pour the reserved cooking liquid into a measuring jug. Add 1 tbsp apple juice concentrate and top up with water to make 1¼ cups liquid.

10 Sprinkle the crushed kuzu into the saucepan in which the cherries were cooked and gradually add the liquid, taking care not to form any lumps.

11 Heat gently, stirring continuously, and cook for about 2 minutes until the sauce thickens. Remove from heat.

12 Stir in the lemon rind and cherries.

13 By now the piecrust will be cooked. Pour the cherry mixture into the piecrust shell and set aside until needed.

Serve hot or cold. To reheat, cover with aluminum foil and heat gently at 325°F.

English Christmas Puddings

1 cup plus 2 tbsp soy oil
1½ tsp apple pie spice
½ tsp grated nutmeg
1 tsp cinnamon
1 cup plus 2 tbsp whole wheat flour
2⅓ cups honey
2 cups sultanas
2 cups raisins
2½ cups currants
2 cups chopped almonds
juice and grated rind of 2 oranges
juice and grated rind of 2 lemons
1 large cooking apple, grated
6 eggs, beaten
generous 1 cup stout
½ cup brandy

Preparation 30 minutes
Cooking 5 hours
Makes 4 × 2 lb puddings

This recipe makes 4 good-sized puddings. Do not make more than 2 months in advance.

1 Mix all the ingredients together in a large bowl.

2 Grease four 2 lb pudding bowls. Cut out 4 circles of wax paper to fit the tops.

3 Place one-quarter of the mixture into each of the prepared pudding bowls and cover with wax paper.

4 Steam each pudding for 3 hours or pressure-cook for 1 hour according to manufacturer's directions.

5 Leave to cool. Wrap each pudding in cloth, then store in a cool place for between 2 weeks and 2 months.

6 To serve, steam for 2 hours or pressure-cook for 45 minutes to 1 hour.

Serve with hard sauce and whipped cream or Cashew Cream (see p. 132).

Crustless Cheesecake

½ cup butter
⅓ cup honey
2 eggs, beaten
2¼ cups mediumfat skim-milk cheese
juice and grated rind of 1 large lemon
⅔ cup semolina
2 tsp baking powder
lemon or fresh fruit slices, to decorate

Preparation 10 minutes
Cooking 1 hour
Serves 6-8

1 Preheat the oven to 350°F.

2 Grease an 8-inch spring form pan.

3 Cream together the butter and honey.

4 Gradually add the eggs and cheese, mixing in alternately.

5 Mix in the lemon juice and rind.

6 Carefully mix in the semolina and baking powder. Pour the mixture into the prepared pan and bake on the bottom shelf of the oven for 1 hour or until set.

7 Remove from oven and leave to cool completely before removing from the pan. Decorate with slices of lemon or other fresh fruit.

Fresh Fruit Tart

Crust
¼ cup butter
⅓ cup honey
1 cup whole wheat flour
1 tsp baking powder

Topping
a mixture of fresh fruit (i.e. strawberries, peaches, apricots, etc.), sliced
½ cup black grape juice
2 tsp potato flour

Preparation 15 minutes
Cooking 25 minutes
Cooling 1 hour minimum
Serves 6-8

This tart is ideal for a dinner party, as it can be made in advance.

1 Preheat the oven to 325°F.

2 Grease a 9-inch tart pan and line with greased wax paper.

3 Make the crust: cream together the butter and honey in a bowl.

4 Add the flour and the baking powder and mix in. Press the dough into the bottom of the prepared pan and prick with a fork.

5 Bake for 20-25 minutes or until golden brown. Remove from the oven and leave to cool.

6 Prepare the topping: arrange the fresh fruit over the crust.

7 Put the grape juice and potato flour into a small saucepan. Bring to a boil, stirring continuously, and simmer for 30 seconds.

8 Remove from heat and carefully spread over the top of the flan with a tablespoon.

9 Leave to cool for at least 1 hour before serving.

◆

Gooseberry Fool

6½ cups gooseberries
1¼ cups water
2 tbsp honey
2 tsp kuzu (see p. 50)
⅔ cup heavy cream
2 egg whites (optional)

Preparation 30 minutes
Chilling 2 hours
Serves 4
Ⓖ Ⓕ

1 Put the gooseberries in a medium-sized saucepan with the water. Boil gently for 5 minutes or until the gooseberries are soft.

2 Add the honey and kuzu and cook for a further 5 minutes. Cool.

3 Meanwhile, whip the cream and egg whites (if using) until stiff, in separate bowls.

4 Mix the cream into the gooseberry mixture, then gently fold in the egg white.

5 Put into individual serving glasses and chill for 2 hours before serving.

◆

Hunza Cream

1½ cups hunza apricots (see p. 39), soaked for 12 hours or overnight
generous 1 cup Greek-style sheep's milk yogurt
2 egg whites
grated rind of 1 lemon

Preparation 10 minutes (allow 12 hours for soaking the apricots)
Chilling 30 minutes minimum
Serves 4-5
Ⓖ Ⓕ

You will need a blender or food processor for this recipe.

1 Take the pits out of the apricots and put the diced flesh into a blender or food processor.

2 Add the yogurt and blend until smooth. Pour into a bowl.

3 Whip the egg whites until stiff and fold them into the apricot and yogurt mixture.

4 Add the grated lemon rind and pour the mixture into a serving bowl or individual dishes and chill for at least 30 minutes before serving.

Peach & Brandy Ice Cream

1½ lb fresh peaches
4 egg yolks
1¼ cups light cream
2 tbsp acacia honey
2 tbsp brandy

Preparation 20 minutes
Freezing 5 hours
Chilling 45 minutes
ⒼⒻ

You will need a blender or food processor for this recipe.

1 Put the peaches into a large bowl and pour over boiling water. Set aside for about 10 minutes to allow the skins to soften.

2 Put the egg yolks and cream into the top of a double boiler, or into a bowl over a pan of boiling water and cook gently until the mixture thickens.

3 Pour the water off the peaches. Drain, peel and pit the peaches.

4 Blend the peach flesh, honey and brandy in a blender or food processor until smooth.

5 Add the cream and egg yolks, blend and check for sweetness. (Remember, the mixture will not taste as sweet when frozen.)

6 Pour into a bowl or freezer container and put into the freezer for about 3 hours or until almost set.

7 Remove from the freezer and beat thoroughly.

8 Return to the freezer for about 2 hours or until set.

9 Chill for about 45 minutes to soften slightly before serving.

◆

Peach Custard Tart

Crust
generous 3 cups cake crumbs
3 tbsp brandy or water

Custard
2 peaches
1 tsp vanilla extract
1¼ cups light cream
1 tbsp maple syrup
3 eggs

Topping
4 peaches
2 tsp maple syrup
1 tsp kuzu (see p. 50)

Preparation 25 minutes
Cooking 55 minutes
Chilling 3 hours minimum
Serves 6

1 Preheat the oven to 425°F.

2 Grease a 9-inch cake pan.

3 Put the peaches for the custard and the topping in a large bowl. Pour over boiling water. Set aside for about 10 minutes to allow the skins to soften.

4 Meanwhile, in another bowl, combine the cake crumbs and brandy. Press the mixture on to the base of the prepared cake pan.

5 Bake for 10 minutes until the base is firm.

6 While the crust is cooking, prepare the custard: remove the skins and pits from 2 of the peaches and put the flesh into a blender or food processor.

7 Add the vanilla extract, cream, maple syrup and eggs and blend until the custard is smooth.

8 When the base is ready, remove from oven and turn the heat down to 400°F.

9 Pour the custard over the crust and put the tart in the oven. Cook for another 40-45 minutes or until the custard has set.

10 While the custard is cooking, make the topping: remove the skins and pits from 2 more peaches and blend to a purée. Transfer the purée into a small saucepan.

11 Add the maple syrup to the peach purée and heat the mixture gently. Sprinkle the kuzu on top and cook gently until thickened. Set aside.

12 Cut the remaining 2 peaches into thin slices.

13 When the custard has set, remove base from oven and set aside for at least 10 minutes to allow the cake to cool a little. When cooled, arrange the peach slices along the edges on top and pour the peach purée into the space in the middle. Using a small pastry brush, lightly coat the outsides of the peach slices with the purée.

Chill for at least 3 hours before serving.

Peach & Pear Crumble

4 peaches
2 pears
2 tbsp apple juice concentrate (see p. 51)

Crumble topping
1⅓ cups old-fashioned oats
scant 1 cup whole wheat flour
½ tsp ground ginger
2 tbsp soy oil
2 tbsp apple juice concentrate (see p. 51)

Preparation 15 minutes
Cooking 1 hour
Serves 4
(v)

A few sesame or sunflower seeds can be added to the crumble for a nuttier flavor and texture.

1 Preheat the oven to 350°F.

2 Put the peaches in a bowl and pour over boiling water. Set aside for about 10 minutes to allow the skins to soften.

3 Meanwhile, cut the pears into quarters. Remove the cores, and peel if tough. Cut into slices and put in a heatproof dish.

4 To make the crumble: put the oats, flour and ginger in a mixing bowl.

5 Add the oil and 2 tbsp apple juice concentrate and mix in with a spoon or your fingertips.

6 Pour the water off the peaches. Drain, peel and remove the pits. Cut into slices and add to the heatproof dish with the pears and 2 tbsp apple juice concentrate.

7 Sprinkle the crumble mixture over the top and bake on the bottom shelf of the oven for 1 hour or until the topping is golden brown.

Serve with whipped cream, custard or yogurt.

Polenta Pudding with Seasonal Fruit

2½ cups milk
1 cup polenta
⅔ cup raisins
1 tsp vanilla extract
2 tbsp butter
1 tbsp honey
juice and grated rind of 1 lemon
   (optional)
½ cup pecans, broken into small pieces
sliced fresh seasonal fruit, to decorate

Preparation 10 minutes
Chilling 2 hours minimum
Serves 8
(GF)

Instead of seasonal fruit, try spreading a fruit purée over the top. Dried apricots are particularly delicious, or puréed rhubarb or apple thickened and sweetened with a little kuzu (see p. 50) and honey.

1 Put the milk in a medium-sized saucepan and warm till just below boiling. Put the polenta into a bowl. Pour over the warm milk slowly. Mix thoroughly and return to saucepan.

2 Bring to a boil, stirring all the time. Simmer for 5 minutes: the mixture should be rather stiff.

3 Remove from heat. Add the raisins, vanilla extract, butter and honey. Mix in well.

4 Add the lemon juice and rind to the mixture.

5 Stir in the pecans. Set aside.

6 Grease and line a 12- × 8-inch baking tray. Press the mixture into the tray, smoothing down the surface with a flat spatula. Leave to cool for at least 2 hours. The polenta will have set hard by this time.

7 Cut the polenta into slices and decorate each with the fresh fruit.

Serve with fresh whipped cream or yogurt.

Prune & Raspberry Whip

1⅓ cups dried prunes, soaked for 12
   hours or overnight
1¼ cups prune juice (water from soaked
   prunes)
9 oz tofu (see p. 51)
2 tbsp maple syrup
juice and grated rind of 1 lemon
1½ cups fresh raspberries or strawberries

Preparation 5 minutes (allow 12 hours
for soaking the prunes)
Chilling 1 hour minimum
Serves 4-6
(V)

You will need a blender or food processor for this recipe.

1 Remove the pits from the prunes.

2 Put the prune flesh, prune juice, tofu, maple syrup, lemon juice and rind into a blender or food processor. Reserve a few raspberries for decoration and add the rest to the blender.

3 Blend until smooth. Pour into a serving bowl or individual dishes and chill for at least 1 hour before serving. Decorate with the reserved raspberries.

From top, clockwise: **Tofu & Mushroom Tart** (see p. 117), **Rutabaga & Orange Pie** (see p. 116), **Red Pepper & Broccoli Quiche** (see p. 111), **Whole Wheat Pizza** (see p. 119).

Rice Balls (see p. 112) on a bed of watercress leaves.

Wakame (see p. 119) combines seaweed and sesame seeds.

Joey's Egg Curry (see p. 108) on rice and chickpeas.

Deliciously spicy **Eggplant & Potato Curry** (see p. 98).

Savory Kombu & Carrots (see p. 112) is light and tasty.

Cauliflower & Carrots with Spicy Filbert Sauce (see p. 103).

Baked Avocado with Stilton & Walnuts (see p. 98).

Summer Okra Casserole (see p. 116) includes oregano.

Seitan with Hiziki (see p. 113) is high in protein.

Black Bean Chili (see p. 100) is succulent and very spicy.

English Christmas Pudding (see p. 124) is packed with fruit, nuts and spices.

Cashew Cream (see p. 132) is a delicious topping.

Use plain yogurt (see p. 47) instead of cream.

Rhubarb & Banana Crumble (see p. 129) is a crunchy, high-fiber pudding.

Exotic Fruit Salad (see p. 132) is a lovely combination of flavors.

Apricot & Orange Sago Cream (see p. 121) is a rich but sugar-free dessert.

Rice Pudding (see p. 130) is made with brown rice for texture and flavor.

Peach & Brandy Ice Cream (see p. 126) has a smooth, luxurious taste.

Baked Bananas with Yogurt Sauce (see p. 121) has a coating of rich caramel.

You can use any fruit to top **Polenta Pudding with Seasonal Fruit** (see p. 128).

Gooseberry Fool (see p. 125) is a light dessert, sweet with a hint of sharpness.

Hunza Cream (see p. 125) is a low-fat dessert made from dried hunza apricots.

Strawberries and lychees are the topping for **Fresh Fruit Tart** (see p. 125).

Apple, Soy & Almond Pudding (see p. 120) is a warming winter pudding.

Strawberry Mousse (see p. 130) uses soy milk for an unusual, creamy flavor.

Carob & Sunflower Mousse (see p. 122) uses carob as a substitute for chocolate.

Prune & Raspberry Whip (see p. 128) is sweetened naturally with maple syrup.

Rhubarb & Almond Mousse (see p. 129) is light and fluffy, with a nutty taste.

Red Currant & Raspberry
Summer Pudding

2⅔ cups red currants
3 cups raspberries
3 tbsp agar-agar flakes (see p. 43)
1-2 tbsp honey or maple syrup
6-8 slices whole wheat bread, crusts
   removed

Preparation 20 minutes
Chilling 3 hours minimum
Serves 6
Ⓥ

This traditional recipe uses red currants and raspberries, but any combination of berry fruits can be used, as available.

1 Put the red currants and raspberries in a heavy-bottomed saucepan with no added water. Heat gently and simmer for 5 minutes.

2 Sprinkle on the agar-agar and simmer for another 5 minutes.

3 Remove from heat and stir in the honey to taste.

4 Line a 2-pound pudding bowl with slices of whole wheat bread, making sure there are no gaps between the slices.

5 Pour the fruit mixture into the lined bowl and chill for at least 3 hours, or preferably overnight.

6 Just before serving, loosen the pudding around the edges with a knife and turn it out onto a plate.

Serve with whipped cream or yogurt.

Rhubarb & Almond Mousse

2½ cups unsweetened soy milk
1 tbsp agar-agar flakes (see p. 43)
1 cup stewed rhubarb
2 tbsp apple juice concentrate (see p. 51)
⅓ cup ground almonds
1 small banana (optional)

Preparation 15 minutes
Chilling 2 hours minimum
Serves 4
ⒼⒻ Ⓥ

You will need a blender or food processor for this recipe.

1 Pour the soy milk into a saucepan and add the agar-agar flakes.

2 Bring to a boil and simmer for 5 minutes, stirring occasionally.

3 Remove the milk from the heat and pour into a blender or food processor.

4 Add the stewed rhubarb, apple juice concentrate, ground almonds and banana, if using. Blend for 2-3 minutes until smooth.

5 Pour the mousse into a serving dish or individual dishes and chill for at least 2 hours.

Rhubarb & Banana Crumble

8 cups finely chopped rhubarb
3 bananas
juice and grated rind of 1 orange
3 tbsp honey
1 cup millet flakes
1 cup plus 2 tbsp whole wheat flour
1 tsp baking powder
1 tbsp sunflower seeds
1 tsp ground ginger
6 tbsp butter

Millet flakes are used in this crumble topping, but any other grain could be added.

1 Preheat the oven to 375°F.

2 Put the rhubarb in an ovenproof dish. Slice the bananas and put on top.

3 Pour the orange juice over the rhubarb and bananas.

Continued, page 130

Rhubarb & Banana Crumble, continued from page 129.

Preparation 15 minutes
Cooking 40 minutes
Serves 6

4 Pour 2 tbsp honey over the top. If your honey is set and not runny, first heat gently in a pan until soft.

5 Put the millet flakes, whole wheat flour, baking powder, sunflower seeds, ginger and orange rind in a mixing bowl.

6 Melt the butter and remaining honey together. Pour over the dry ingredients and mix thoroughly.

7 Cover the rhubarb with the crumble and bake for 40 minutes or until golden brown.

Serve with yogurt or cream.

Rice Pudding

generous 1 cup brown rice
good pinch of salt
4 tbsp honey
¼ cup butter
scant 1 cup water
4½ cups milk

Preparation 10 minutes
Cooking 3-3½ hours
Serves 6
(GF)

1 Preheat the oven to 300°F.

2 Wash the rice and put in a large ovenproof dish with the salt, honey and butter.

3 Boil the water and pour over the rice. Heat the milk to just below boiling and pour over the rice. Mix together well.

4 Bake, uncovered, for 3-3½ hours, stirring the skin in every 30 minutes. When cooked, the grains of the rice should be soft and the texture of the pudding thick but moist.

Serve warm or cold on its own, with cream or yogurt.

Strawberry Mousse

2½ cups unsweetened soy milk
1 tbsp agar-agar flakes (see p. 43)
1½ cups hulled strawberries
1 tbsp maple syrup

Preparation 10 minutes
Chilling 4 hours minimum
Serves 4
(GF) (V)

This mousse is made without eggs or dairy products, but is wonderfully rich and creamy.

You will need a blender or food processor for this recipe.

1 Pour the soy milk into a saucepan and add the agar-agar flakes.

2 Bring to a boil and simmer for 5 minutes, stirring occasionally.

3 Pour the soy milk and agar-agar into a blender or food processor. Add the strawberries and the maple syrup and blend for 2-3 minutes until smooth.

4 Pour the mousse into a serving bowl or individual dishes and chill for at least 4 hours.

5 Decorate with fresh strawberries before serving.

Sweet Potato Pie

Piecrust dough
generous 1½ cups whole wheat flour
½ cup butter
2 tbsp water
1 tbsp apple juice concentrate
  (see p. 51)

Filling
3 sweet potatoes, peeled and cut into
  small pieces
2 tbsp butter
2 tbsp honey
½ tsp ground cinnamon
¼ tsp ground ginger
pinch of salt

Glaze
juice and grated rind of ½ lemon
1 tbsp honey

Preparation 25 minutes
Cooking 15 minutes
Chilling 1 hour
Serves 6-8

For a special occasion, lay slices of fresh fruit over the sweet potato mixture before adding the glaze. Peaches or nectarines are particularly delicious when in season.

1 Preheat the oven to 400°F.

2 Boil or steam the potatoes for 10-15 minutes until soft.

3 Grease a 9-inch pie plate.

4 Make the piecrust dough: put the whole wheat flour into a mixing bowl. Cut in the butter until the mixture resembles fine bread crumbs.

5 Add the water and apple juice concentrate. Mix in with a knife or metal spoon until the mixture holds together.

6 Roll the dough out on a lightly floured board as thinly as possible and line the prepared pie dish. Prick the sides and bottom of the dough with a fork.

7 Bake for about 15 minutes or until the piecrust is cooked.

8 When the sweet potatoes are cooked, drain well and add the butter, honey, cinnamon, ginger and salt. Mash well with a potato masher or in a food processor.

9 Remove the cooked piecrust shell from the oven and spoon in the sweet potato mixture. Smooth down evenly.

10 Make the glaze: mix the lemon juice and rind with the honey. Then, using a pastry brush or the back of a spoon, spread the glaze over the pie and chill for 1 hour before serving.

Serve with whipped cream or yogurt.

◆

Tapioca & Lime Soufflés

scant ½ cup tapioca
2½ cups milk
5 tsp honey
½ tsp vanilla extract
grated rind of 1-2 small limes
2 egg whites
1½ tbsp butter

Preparation 20 minutes
Cooking 15 minutes
Makes 8
(GF)

These individual soufflés need to be served as soon as they are cooked.

1 Preheat the oven to 350°F.

2 Put the tapioca, milk, honey, vanilla extract and grated lime rind into a saucepan. Bring to a boil and simmer gently for 15 minutes, stirring occasionally.

3 Whip the egg whites until stiff. Set aside.

4 Remove the tapioca from the stove and mix in the butter.

5 Fold in the whipped egg whites and pour the mixture into 8 buttered ramekin dishes.

6 Bake for 10-15 minutes or until soufflés are well risen and browned on top. Serve immediately.

Traditional Apple Crumble

3 tart apples
⅔ cup water
¼ cup apple juice concentrate
  (see p. 51)
1 tsp ground cinnamon
scant 1½ cups fine whole wheat flour
½ cup butter
4 tbsp honey
1 tsp grated lemon rind

Preparation 15 minutes
Cooking 45-50 minutes
Serves 6

1 Preheat the oven to 350°F.

2 Cut the apples into very small pieces. Put into an ovenproof dish.

3 Pour the water, apple juice concentrate and cinnamon into a measuring jug. Mix together and pour over the apples.

4 Put the flour in a mixing bowl. Gently cut in the butter until the mixture resembles bread crumbs.

5 Add the honey and grated lemon rind: stir in carefully with a metal spoon.

6 Pour the crumble topping over the apple and bake at the bottom of the oven for 45-50 minutes or until the topping is browned. Serve immediately with whipped cream or yogurt.

Exotic Fruit Salad

1 large mango
1 papaya
1 pineapple
2 ripe bananas
1 ripe avocado
2 granadillas (see p. 36)
juice and grated rind of 1 lime
1 tbsp shredded coconut
2 kiwi, sliced, to decorate

Preparation 10 minutes
Serves 4
(GF) (V)

1 Cut the mango, papaya, pineapple, bananas and avocado into small pieces in a large serving bowl.

2 Scoop out the granadillas and add to the bowl.

3 Add the lime juice and rind to the salad together with the shredded coconut. Mix well.

4 Decorate the top with sliced kiwi.

Serve with a creamy Greek-style yogurt or Cashew Cream (see below).

Cashew Cream

1½ cups cashew nuts
generous 1¼ cups water
1 tbsp apple juice concentrate
  (see p. 51)

Preparation 5 minutes
Serves 10
(GF) (V)

This makes a delicious substitute for whipped cream on cakes, puddings and pastries.
  You will need a blender or food processor for this recipe.

1 Put all the ingredients into a blender or processor.

2 Blend for 3-4 minutes until a smooth thick paste is formed. Transfer to a serving bowl.

CAKES, PASTRIES, BISCUITS & COOKIES

Introduction to making cakes

The light, delicate texture which characterises a sponge cake is achieved by techniques that are in many ways opposite to those used when making bread (see p. 147). Unlike bread, once the flour has been added to the wet ingredients, the barest mixing is sufficient or else the cake will have a tough, bread-like consistency. For the best results, you can use a hand beater. Again, cakes are generally risen with a swiftly acting chemical rising agent, usually baking powder, rather than with yeast which requires time to work.

Baking powder is a mixture of an alkali (baking soda) and an acid (cream of tartar) in a base of wheat flour. When the liquid is added, the alkali and acid elements form a chemical reaction which releases gases that aerate the sponge. Baking powder only works until this reaction is exhausted, so it is vital to get a cake into the oven as quickly as possible once the liquid ingredients have been added. Some recipes include acid ingredients such as sour milk or lemon and therefore only require the use of baking soda; however as a general rule baking powder and baking soda are not interchangeable.

Rather than adding baking powder to all-purpose flour, many people prefer to use self-rising flour, where a proportion of baking powder has been premixed with the flour. The main advantages are convenience and a consistent rise for cakes and biscuits. But, different cake recipes call for different proportions of baking powder to flour, so you will probably get better results if you buy all-purpose flour and add your own baking powder. Baking powder usually consists of baking soda and wheat flour. Low-sodium, gluten-free baking powder is available, consisting of potassium bicarbonate and potato flour.

Cake pans

Cake pans with a non-stick finish do not as a rule need greasing, but you should follow manufacturer's instructions where applicable. All other pans will need greasing: vegetable shortening, margarine or butter may be used.

For some recipes, you should line the cake pans; lightly grease the surface with vegetable shortening then cover with a piece of wax paper, cut to fit. If not using wax paper, the greased pans should be sprinkled with flour to avoid sticking. Jelly-roll pans are traditionally lined with wax paper.

To line a deep cake pan, you will need to cut a circle of wax paper for the bottom and a long strip to go around the sides. Cut the strip of paper about 2 inches longer than the circumference of the cake pan, and about 1 inch wider for an overlap. To fit it into the pan, make a few small cuts along the length of one side, so that the paper can bend at the bottom.

To test if a cake is cooked

To test if a cake is fully cooked, insert a skewer or toothpick which should come out clean, or press the top of the cake gently with your finger – the sponge should spring back up when pressure is released. Always remove a cake from the oven gently and carefully: if you bang it down, it is likely to sink. After removing the cake from the oven, leave it in the pan for 10 minutes on a wire rack. By leaving cakes to cool in this way they will shrink from the sides of the pan, making them easier to turn out. A palette knife can be used to ease the cake out if necessary. Turn it out onto a wire rack and peel off the wax paper, if used.

Applesauce Cake

½ cup soy oil
⅓ cup honey or maple syrup
⅔ cup applesauce (not too runny)
½ cup raisins or golden raisins
scant 1½ cups whole wheat flour
1 tsp ground cinnamon
¼ tsp ground allspice
1 tsp baking soda
pinch of salt (optional)
water or fruit juice, if necessary

Preparation 10 minutes
Cooking 1-1¼ hours
Makes an 8-inch round cake
Ⓥ

1 Preheat the oven to 325°F.

2 Grease an 8-inch deep round cake tin and line with wax paper.

3 In a blender or food processor or large mixing bowl combine the oil, honey and applesauce.

4 In another bowl, combine all the dry ingredients, mixing well.

5 Add the dry ingredients to the oil, honey and applesauce. Mix in gently but thoroughly. (You should be able to pour the mixture into the cake pan: if it is too stiff, add a little water or fruit juice.)

6 Pour the mixture into the prepared cake pan and bake for about 1 hour until golden brown, or until a skewer inserted into the cake comes out clean.

7 Remove from the oven and leave to cool before turning out.

Bakewell Tart

Crust
2 tbsp honey
2 tbsp butter
generous ½ cup whole wheat flour
½ tsp baking powder
½ cup reduced-sugar raspberry jelly
  (see p. 52)

Topping
½ cup butter
⅓ cup honey
2 eggs, beaten
1 tsp almond extract
scant 1 cup soy flour, sifted
2 tsp baking powder, sifted

Preparation 20 minutes
Cooking 1 hour 50 minutes
Makes a 9-inch round cake

1 Preheat the oven to 325°F.

2 Grease a 9-inch shallow round cake pan and line with wax paper.

3 For the crust: cream together the honey and butter in a bowl.

4 Add the flour and baking powder, to make a fairly crumbly dough. Line the bottom of the prepared pan with the dough and bake for 15 minutes or until lightly browned. Turn the oven down to 300°F.

5 Spread the jelly over the precooked crust.

6 For the topping: cream together the butter, honey and eggs in a bowl.

7 Add the almond extract. Mix in the soy flour and baking powder.

8 Spread the topping over the jam, taking care not to squeeze all the jam to the outside. (To counteract this, try putting little dots of topping on the jam, spreading each very carefully.)

9 Bake in the center of the oven for 1-1½ hours, until set and golden brown or until a skewer inserted into the cake comes out clean. Remove from oven and leave to cool before carefully removing from pan. Peel off the paper.

Making the Bakewell Tart

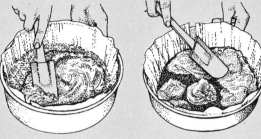

1 Press the crust mixture into the lined cake pan with a spatula.

2 After the jelly has been spooned over the crust, spoon the topping over the jelly in large blobs, then spread into each other with a spatula.

Banana Cream Cake

Crust
7 cups cake crumbs
scant 1 cup fruit juice

Topping
2½ bananas
4 tbsp honey
¼ tsp grated nutmeg
6 eggs
juice and grated rind of 1 lemon
2½ cups milk

Preparation 15 minutes
Cooking 20 minutes
Serves 12

1 Preheat the oven to 350°F.

2 Grease a 9- × 12-inch cake pan and line with wax paper.

3 Make the crust: put the cake crumbs and fruit juice into a large bowl and beat together thoroughly. Press into the bottom of the pan, making sure the mixture reaches right into the corners. Bake for about 10 minutes while you make the topping.

4 Make the topping: put the bananas into a mixing bowl and beat until smooth.

5 Add the honey, nutmeg, eggs, juice and rind and beat again.

6 Add the milk and mix thoroughly.

7 Remove the crumb crust from the oven and pour the banana cream mixture over.

8 Return to the middle of the oven and bake for 20 minutes or until the banana cream has set.

9 Remove from oven and leave to cool before cutting.

Banana Nut Cake

1 large banana
6 tbsp soy oil
¼ cup honey
2 eggs, beaten
juice and grated rind of 1 lemon
⅔ cup raisins
⅓ cup filberts
scant 2½ cups whole wheat flour
½ tsp baking soda
2 tbsp chopped cashew nuts

Preparation 10 minutes
Cooking 1 hour 20 minutes
Makes one loaf cake

1 Preheat the oven to 325°F.

2 Grease an 8½- × 4½- × 2½-inch loaf pan. Line with wax paper.

3 Put the banana into a large bowl and beat until smooth.

4 Mix in the oil, honey, eggs, lemon juice and rind.

5 Add the raisins and filberts and mix in gently.

6 Fold in the flour and baking soda carefully, taking care not to overbeat the mixture.

7 Pour into the loaf pan, sprinkle the cashew nuts on top, and bake for about 1 hour and 20 minutes until golden brown, or until a skewer inserted into the cake comes out clean.

8 Remove from oven and leave to cool.

Basic Whole Wheat Sponge Cake

½ cup plus 2 tbsp soy or other oil
½ cup honey
2 eggs
pinch of salt
1 tsp baking powder
1 cup whole wheat flour

Preparation 10 minutes
Cooking 35-40 minutes
Makes an 8-inch round cake

This is an easy and extremely versatile recipe. To vary the recipe, add fresh or cooked fruit, nuts and spices, and sherry or custard. If dry ingredients are added, you may need to use less flour; if wet, add slightly more flour. For a richer sponge, substitute butter or milk for the oil.

1 Preheat the oven to 325°F. Grease and lightly flour an 8-inch round cake pan.

2 Put the oil, honey and eggs into a large bowl and beat them all together till smooth.

3 Mix the salt and baking powder with the flour before adding to the liquid ingredients. Beat the mix just enough to achieve a smooth consistency.

4 Pour the mixture into the pan and bake for 35-40 minutes until a skewer inserted into the center of the cake comes out clean.

Note: For a layer cake, you can double the quantities and use 2 pans.

Brandy Fruitcake

¼ cup butter
4 tbsp honey
2 tbsp soy oil
2 eggs, separated
scant 1 cup whole wheat flour

Fruit mix
1⅓ cups raisins
1 cup currants
⅓ cup finely chopped dried figs
⅓ cup finely chopped dried apricots
juice and grated rind of 1 orange
juice and grated rind of 1 lemon
¼ cup brandy
cider

**Preparation 10 minutes (allow 12
hours for soaking the fruit mix)
Cooking 1 hour 45 minutes
Makes one loaf cake**

**If hard cider is unavailable, substitute apple juice or an additional
½ cup brandy.**

1 First prepare the fruit mix. Mix all the ingredients together well
and marinate for 12 hours or overnight in a container with a tightly
fitting lid.

2 Preheat the oven to 300°F.

3 Grease an 8½- × 4½- × 2½-inch loaf pan. Line with wax paper.

4 In a large bowl or blender or food processor, combine the butter
and honey. Add the oil and mix well.

5 Add the egg yolks. Pour in the prepared fruit mix and mix
thoroughly but gently.

6 Gradually mix in the flour, taking care not to break up the fruit.
The batter should have a soft consistency: neither too stiff nor too
runny. Add a little extra liquid or flour, if necessary.

7 Beat the egg whites until stiff and fold into the cake batter.

8 Pour into the prepared cake pan and smooth down the surface
with the back of your hand, dipped in water.

9 Put on the bottom shelf of the oven and bake for 1 hour and 45
minutes until brown, or until a skewer inserted into the center of
the cake comes out clean.

10 Remove from oven and leave to cool before removing from pan.

Bran Muffins

1 cup bran
1 cup whole wheat flour
1 tsp baking soda
pinch of salt
⅔ cup raisins
1 egg, beaten
¼ cup soy oil
2 tbsp molasses
2 tbsp honey
generous 1 cup milk
juice and grated rind of 1 orange
orange slices, to decorate
mixture of 1 tsp honey and 1 tsp
    lemon juice, to glaze (optional)

**Preparation 10 minutes
Cooking 10-15 minutes
Makes 12 muffins**

1 Preheat the oven to 350°F.

2 Put the bran, whole wheat flour, baking soda, salt and raisins into
a mixing bowl. Mix together with a wooden spoon.

3 In another bowl or a measuring jug, mix together the egg, oil,
molasses, honey, milk, orange juice and rind.

4 Make a well in the center of the dry ingredients and pour in the
liquid mixture.

5 Mix together gently, taking care not to overbeat the batter.

6 Place 12 fluted paper cups into a muffin tin. Put about a
dessertspoonful of the mixture into each case and press a small slice
of orange on top of each. Bake at the top of the oven for 10-15
minutes or until brown. Remove from oven.

7 Spoon the glaze over, if liked, and leave to cool.

Brioche Whirls

Filling
3 cups puréed dates or other
  dried fruit
scant 1 cup dried apricots, soaked
  for 12 hours or overnight
⅓ cup raisins, soaked for 12 hours
  or overnight
⅓ cup chopped mixed nuts
1 tsp ground cinnamon

Dough
1 tbsp honey
1¼ cups milk
¾ oz compressed yeast or 1 tsp
  active dried
2 cups plus 4 tbsp fine whole wheat
  flour
¼ cup butter
pinch of salt
1 egg
mixture of 1 tsp honey and 1 tsp
  lemon juice, to glaze

**Preparation 2 hours (allow 12 hours for
soaking the fruit)
Cooking 15 minutes
Makes 12 brioches**

**These delicious pastries will reward the little extra time and effort
required to make them.**

1 Prepare the dough: stir the honey with the milk and then crumble
in the yeast and allow it to dissolve. If using dried yeast, cover and
put in a warm place for about 15 minutes.

2 Put all but a handful of the flour into a large mixing bowl. Cut
the butter into the flour. Mix in the salt.

3 Make a well in the center of the flour and break the egg into it.
With a spoon, work the flour from around the edges into the center,
gradually adding the yeasted milk and honey until you have a
sticky dough.

4 With your hands work in the remaining flour and set aside. The
dough should be slack but not wet.

5 Cover the bowl and set aside for 30 minutes in a warm place to
rise.

6 Remove the dough from the bowl and place on a flat, lightly
floured surface. Scrape the bowl clean, grease and set aside.

7 Gently knead the dough into a smooth, compact mass and replace
in the oiled bowl. Cover and set aside for another 30 minutes in a
warm place until the dough has almost doubled in size.

8 Meanwhile, make the filling: put the ingredients, except the
apricots, into a bowl and mix well.

9 Knead the dough again, flour it on both sides and carefully roll it
out into a sheet measuring 18 × 12 inches.

10 Spread the filling thinly and evenly over the entire surface
except for a strip 1-inch wide along the side nearest to you.

11 Arrange a row of the soaked apricots along the side away from
you. Then, reaching to the far side of the dough, with both hands
roll it up toward you, using the row of apricots as a core. Keep the
roll as tight as you can, taking care not to let it tear.

12 Just before you finish rolling, brush the bare strip of dough with
milk and seal the end of the brioche.

13 Gently smooth out the sausage of dough and cut off the ends.

14 Preheat the oven to 450°F.

15 Line 2 large baking trays with wax paper.

16 Cut the dough into approximately 12 slices about 1½-inches
wide. Carefully lay the flat slices on the trays. Gently press them
down and shape them into circles about 4-inches across. Leave at
least 1-inch between each brioche.

17 Brush with milk and leave to rise for about 10 minutes.

18 Bake for 12-15 minutes or until golden brown.

19 Remove from oven and brush with the honey and lemon glaze. Leave to cool before eating.

Making Brioche Whirls.

1 Spread the filling over the rolled-out oblong of dough and place the soaked apricots in a neat line along the edge of the dough away from you. Press down gently.

2 Starting from the far edge, and using the line of soaked apricots as a core, roll up the brioche tightly toward you.

3 Holding the brioche roll tightly in one hand, carefully cut off thick slices. These can then be slightly flattened with your hand to make them larger and rounder.

Carob Brownies

1¼ cups soy oil
⅔ cup honey
4 eggs, beaten
6 tbsp carob powder (see p. 51), sifted
1½ cups plus 2 tbsp whole wheat flour
1 tsp baking powder

Frosting (optional)
1 tbsp carob powder (see p. 51)
11 oz cream cheese
1 tsp vanilla extract
1 tbsp honey

Preparation 10 minutes
Cooking 25 minutes
Makes 12 brownies

These delicious cakes can be served plain or frosted. Decorate with nuts for special occasions.

1 Preheat the oven to 350°F.

2 Grease and flour a 12- × 9-inch shallow cake pan.

3 In a bowl or blender or food processor, combine the oil, honey and eggs.

4 Carefully add the carob powder, whole wheat flour and baking powder and mix in thoroughly but gently.

5 Pour the cake mixture into the prepared pan and bake for 25 minutes until dark brown or until a skewer inserted into the cake comes out clean. Remove from oven and leave to cool before cutting.

6 If making the frosting, sift the carob powder into the cream cheese. Add the vanilla extract and honey. Mix thoroughly and spread over top of cake before cutting.

Carrot & Coconut Cake

½ cup plus 2 tbsp soy oil
⅓ cup honey
2 large eggs
2 cups grated carrots
½ cup raisins
⅔ cup shredded coconut
scant 1½ cups whole wheat flour
1 tsp baking powder
1 tsp ground cinnamon
¼ tsp grated nutmeg
¼ tsp apple pie spice

Preparation 10 minutes
Cooking 1 hour 20 minutes
Makes one loaf cake

1 Preheat the oven to 325°F.

2 Grease and flour an 8½- × 4½- × 2½-inch loaf pan.

3 Put the oil, honey and eggs into a large bowl or blender or food processor and beat together until smooth.

4 Add the grated carrot, raisins and coconut and mix in gently.

5 Fold in the flour, baking powder, cinnamon, nutmeg and spice, taking care not to overbeat the batter. (This hinders the action of the baking powder and breaks up the fruit.)

6 Pour into the loaf pan and bake for 1 hour and 20 minutes until brown, or until a skewer inserted into the cake comes out clean.

7 Remove from oven and leave to cool before removing from tin.

Cheese Biscuits

½ cup butter
3 cups plus 2 tbsp whole wheat flour
1 tbsp baking powder
1 tsp salt
1 tsp mustard powder
2 tsp finely chopped fresh herbs
    or 1 tsp dried
½ tsp black pepper or pinch of
    chili powder
2¼ cups grated cheese
½ cup milk
mixture of 1 beaten egg and a little
    milk, to glaze
grated cheese, to garnish

Preparation 15 minutes
Cooking 15 minutes
Makes 12 biscuits

Fresh dill or basil is particularly delicious in these biscuits.

1 Preheat the oven to 425°F.

2 In a large mixing bowl, cut the butter into the flour.

3 Add the rest of the dry ingredients.

4 Pour in the milk and mix together gently to form a soft dough.

5 On a lightly floured surface, roll out the dough to a thickness of about 1½ inch and cut out biscuits with a 2-inch cutter.

6 Brush each biscuit with the egg glaze and top with a little grated cheese to garnish.

7 Set the biscuits on a floured baking tray and bake for about 15 minutes or until golden brown.

8 Remove from oven and leave to cool before serving.

Couscous Cake

1½ cups mixed dried fruit
scant 3 cups couscous
4 tbsp sesame seeds
juice and grated rind of 1 lemon
4 tbsp maple syrup or apple
 juice concentrate (see p. 51)
 (optional)

Preparation 15 minutes (allow 1 hour for soaking the fruit)
Chilling 6 hours minimum
Makes a 6-inch round cake
Ⓥ

This unusual cake requires thorough chilling before serving.

1 Cover the dried fruit with boiling water and leave to stand for at least 1 hour until the fruit has absorbed some of the liquid.

2 Grease and lightly flour a 6-inch round cake pan.

3 Gently squeeze the fruit and pour off the liquid into a separate jug. Top up the liquid with boiling water to make 3 cups plus 2 tbsp.

4 Cut the fruit into small pieces.

5 Put the couscous in a bowl and pour over the liquid made up from the reserved fruit juice and boiling water.

6 Add the chopped fruit, sesame seeds, juice and rind of the lemon and maple syrup, if using, and leave to stand for 15 minutes or until the couscous absorbs some of the liquid and puffs up.

7 Press the mixture down into the pan and chill for at least 6 hours until the mixture has set.

◆

Date & Oat Bars

3 cups pitted dried dates
3⅔ cups old-fashioned oats
scant 1½ cups whole wheat flour
½ tsp salt
¾ cup malt extract
¾ cup soy oil
4 tbsp shredded coconut

Preparation 10 minutes (allow extra time for soaking and cooking the dates, if necessary)
Cooking 30-40 minutes
Makes 16 bars
Ⓥ

1 Preheat the oven to 350°F.

2 Grease and lightly flour a 9- × 12-inch cake pan.

3 Put the dates in a medium-sized saucepan. Cover with water. Bring to a boil, then lower the heat and simmer, covered, for 10-15 minutes until the dates have softened. Stir well when cooked and leave to cool.

4 Put the old-fashioned oats, flour and salt into a bowl or blender or food processor.

5 Pour the malt into the dry mixture and mix as fast as possible for 2-3 minutes.

6 Mixing more slowly, gradually pour in the oil, to end up with a light crumbly mixture.

7 Spread three-quarters of this mixture into the bottom of the prepared cake pan, packing it down well with your hands.

8 Spread the dates over the top.

9 Add the coconut to the remaining oat mixture and sprinkle this on top of the dates.

10 Bake for 30-40 minutes until golden brown.

11 Remove from oven and leave to cool before cutting.

Flapjacks

scant 1 cup whole wheat flour
1 cup old-fashioned oats
$\frac{2}{3}$ cup peanuts
$\frac{2}{3}$ cup chopped mixed nuts
$\frac{2}{3}$ cup raisins
$\frac{1}{2}$ cup butter, melted
$\frac{1}{3}$ cup molasses
$\frac{1}{4}$ cup honey
$\frac{1}{2}$ cup plus 2 tbsp soy oil

Preparation 10 minutes
Cooking 45 minutes
Serves 12

1 Preheat the oven to 350°F.

2 Grease a 9- × 12-inch cake pan and line with wax paper.

3 Put all the ingredients into a large bowl and mix thoroughly with a wooden spoon.

4 Pour into the cake pan, making sure the mixture reaches right into the corners and the surface is smooth.

5 Bake for 45 minutes or until dark brown.

6 Remove from oven and leave to cool before cutting.

Fruit Biscuits

3 cups plus 2 tbsp whole wheat flour
$\frac{1}{2}$ cup butter
2 tsp apple pie spice
1 tbsp baking powder
$\frac{2}{3}$ cup raisins
$\frac{1}{3}$ cup honey
$\frac{1}{2}$ cup milk
1 egg, beaten
nuts, to decorate

Preparation 10 minutes
Cooking 15-20 minutes
Makes 20 biscuits

These can be served plain or with butter, jelly and/or honey.

1 Preheat the oven to 450°F.

2 Mix the flour and the butter together in a large bowl or blender or food processor.

3 Add the spice, baking powder and raisins.

4 Mix the honey and milk together and pour onto the dry ingredients. Mix to form a soft dough.

5 On a lightly floured surface, roll out the dough to a $\frac{1}{2}$-inch thickness and cut the biscuits into squares or circles as desired.

6 Brush the top with beaten egg and decorate each biscuit with a nut.

7 Cook on a baking tray for about 15 minutes or until browned.

Ginger Cake

$1\frac{1}{2}$ cups plus 2 tbsp whole wheat flour
2 tbsp ground ginger
1 tbsp mustard powder
1 tbsp ground cinnamon
1 tbsp baking powder
scant 1 cup soy oil
$\frac{1}{4}$ cup molasses
$\frac{1}{4}$ cup malt extract
4 tbsp honey
2 eggs
$\frac{1}{2}$ cup milk or water

Preparation 10 minutes
Cooking $1\frac{1}{4}$-$1\frac{1}{2}$ hours
Makes a $1\frac{3}{4}$ lb loaf cake

A rich, spicy but not too sweet loaf.

1 Preheat the oven to 300°F.

2 Grease an $8\frac{1}{2}$- × $4\frac{1}{2}$- × $2\frac{1}{2}$-inch loaf pan.

3 Mix together the flour, ginger, mustard powder, ground cinnamon and baking powder. Set aside.

4 In another bowl, beat together the oil, molasses, malt, honey, eggs and milk.

5 Fold the oil mixture into the dry ingredients.

6 Pour into the prepared loaf pan. Bake on the bottom shelf of the oven for $1\frac{1}{4}$-$1\frac{1}{2}$ hours or until a skewer inserted into the cake comes out clean. Remove from oven and leave to cool before serving.

Macaroon Cake

1 cup soy oil
scant ⅔ cup honey
3 eggs
1 tsp vanilla extract
2 cups whole wheat flour
2 tsp baking powder

Topping
5 eggs, separated
generous 3 cups shredded coconut
⅓ cup honey
½ tsp almond extract
½ cup low-sugar jelly (see p. 52), or
  fruit purée

Preparation 30 minutes
Cooking 45 minutes
Makes a 9- × 12-inch cake

This cake can also be eaten warm with custard as a pudding.

1 Preheat the oven to 350°F.

2 Grease and flour a 9- × 12-inch cake pan and line with wax paper.

3 In a blender or food processor, combine the oil, honey, eggs and vanilla extract.

4 Add the whole wheat flour and baking powder and mix in thoroughly but gently.

5 Pour the cake mixture into the prepared pan and bake for about 25-30 minutes or until cooked through.

6 Meanwhile, make the topping: put the egg yolks in a bowl with the coconut, honey and almond extract. Mix well.

7 Beat the egg whites until stiff and gently fold into the coconut mixture. Set aside.

8 When the cake is cooked, remove from the oven and leave to cool for a few minutes.

9 Spread the jelly or fruit purée over the cake, then spread the coconut mixture on top.

10 Return to the oven and cook for a further 30 minutes or until the top is golden brown.

11 Remove from the oven and leave to cool before cutting.

Oat & Raisin Cookies

1 cup raisins
scant 1½ cups boiling water
5⅓ cups old-fashioned oats
scant 1 cup whole wheat flour
2 tbsp sunflower seeds
good pinch of salt
generous ½ cup soy oil

Preparation 10 minutes (allow 30 minutes for soaking the raisins)
Cooking 20 minutes
Makes 24 cookies
Ⓥ

1 Put the raisins in a bowl, pour over the boiling water and leave to stand for 20-30 minutes until the fruit has absorbed some of the liquid. Strain and reserve the soaking liquid.

2 Preheat the oven to 375¼F.

3 In a food processor or large bowl, mix the dry ingredients.

4 Add the oil. Then add the raisins and ¾ cup plus 2 tbsp of their soaking liquid. Mix together well and add a little more liquid if necessary, to form a soft, pliable dough.

5 On a lightly floured surface, roll out the dough to a thickness of about ½ inch. Cut the cookies out with a 3-inch cutter.

6 Place on a floured baking tray and cook for 20 minutes or until golden brown.

7 Remove from the oven and leave to cool. (The cookies will harden a little as they cool.)

Orange Sesame Cake

½ cup soy oil
⅓ cup plus 2 tbsp honey
2 eggs, beaten
juice and grated rind of 1 large orange
¼ cup water
scant 1 cup sesame seeds
5½ cups whole wheat flour
1 tbsp baking powder

Filling
11 oz cream cheese
1 tbsp honey
1 orange

Preparation 20 minutes
Cooking 35 minutes
Makes an 8-inch round cake

1 Preheat the oven to 350°F.

2 Grease two 8-inch round cake pans.

3 Put the oil and honey in a blender or food processor and mix together until smooth. Stir the eggs into the mixture.

4 Add the orange juice and rind to the mixing bowl with the water and sesame seeds.

5 Add the flour and baking powder. Mix thoroughly and divide the mixture between the 2 cake tins.

6 Bake for 30-35 minutes until golden brown or until a skewer inserted into the cake comes out clean. Remove from oven and leave to cool before turning out.

7 For the filling: mix the cream cheese and honey together in a bowl. Grate the orange, using the finest part of the grater, and add to the cream cheese mixture. Cut the orange into decorative strips.

8 Spread half the mixture over one cake and put the other cake on top. Put the rest of the cream cheese icing on top and decorate with slices of orange.

Peanut Butter Cookies

½ cup soy oil
⅓ cup honey or maple syrup
1½ cups peanut butter
generous 1½ cups old-fashioned oats
2 cups plus 2 tbsp whole wheat flour
1 tsp baking powder
½ tsp ground cinnamon
¼ tsp ground cloves
¼ tsp ground nutmeg
½ tsp salt
½ cup raisins

Preparation 15 minutes
Cooking 8-10 minutes
Makes 25 cookies
Ⓥ

1 Preheat the oven to 450°F.

2 In a blender or food processor or large bowl, beat together the oil, honey and peanut butter.

3 In a separate bowl, combine all the remaining dry ingredients and mix thoroughly.

4 Mix the dry ingredients with the peanut butter mixture to make a fairly stiff dough.

5 On a lightly floured surface, roll out the dough to a thickness of ½ inch and cut into 3-inch circles.

6 Bake the cookies on a lightly floured baking tray for 8-10 minutes or until golden brown.

7 Remove from oven and leave to cool before eating.

Cakes, Pastries, Biscuits & Cookies (See p. 133)

Ginger Cake (see p. 142) is rich and succulent, with a spicy flavor.

Banana Nut Cake (see p. 136) is a delicious mixture of nuts, banana, honey and raisins.

Carrot & Coconut Cake (see p. 140) is moist and chewy, a delicious cake for any time.

Brandy Fruitcake (see p. 137) is packed with dried fruit, nutritious and tasty.

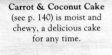

Vegan Fruit Bars (see p. 146) are made without animal or dairy products.

Date & Oat Bars (see p. 141) contain coconut and malt extract for added flavor.

These **Flapjacks** (see p. 142) are dark and rich because of the molasses and honey.

Orange Sesame Cake (see p. 144) has a sponge base flavored with sesame seeds and orange, topped with honey cream cheese.

Sesame Honey Bars (see p. 145) have a deliciously sweet, nutty taste.

Carob Brownies (see p. 139) use carob as a nutritious alternative to chocolate.

Banana Cream Cake (see p. 135) is succulent and moist, good as a dessert.

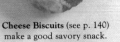

Cheese Biscuits (see p. 140) make a good savory snack.

Unusual **Tofu Cake** (see p. 146) consists of a spicy tofu cream on a malted oat base.

Sunflower Bars (see p. 145) are rich and chewy, with a nutty texture.

Macaroon Cake (see p. 143) is a honey sponge with a melt-in-the-mouth topping.

Brioche Whirls (see p. 138) are rich fruity pastries.

Fruit Biscuits (see p. 142) have a moist, chewy texture.

Bran Muffins (see p. 137) contain orange rind and juice for an extra tang.

Peanut Butter Cookies (see p. 144) are nutty biscuits popular with children.

Oat & Raisin Biscuits (see p. 143) have sunflower seeds for crunch and taste.

Breads (See p. 147)

The standard **Basic Whole Wheat Bread** (see p. 149).

Cheese & Herb Bread (see p. 152) is full of flavor.

Three-Seed Bread (see p. 156), unusual and rich.

Nutritious **Sunflower Seed Bread** (see p. 155).

Sourdough Bread (see p. 147) has a sharp flavor.

Rye Bread (see p. 154) is dark and moist.

Whole Wheat Rolls (see p. 149).

Rolls with sesame seeds.

Dervish Barley Bread (see p. 152) is unleavened.

Whole wheat bread dough can be shaped in many ways. Here, it is patted into a large round before baking.

A **Whole Wheat Cottage Loaf** is easily made with basic whole wheat dough (see the diagrams on p. 149).

Fruit & Malt Bread (see p. 153) is rich and sweet.

A whole wheat French loaf made with whole wheat dough (see p. 149).

A whole wheat braid is an interesting variation (see p. 149 for method).

Basic White Bread (see p. 150) is a lighter loaf.

Sesame Honey Bars

Crust
1 cup butter
½ cup honey
2 cups plus 2 tbsp whole wheat flour

Topping
3 eggs, beaten
¾ cup honey
generous 1 cup shredded coconut
1 cup sesame seeds
1 tsp baking powder

Preparation 10 minutes
Cooking 30-40 minutes
Makes 20 bars

1 Preheat the oven to 350¼F.

2 Grease a 9- × 12-inch cake pan and line with wax paper.

3 Make the crust in a blender or food processor or large bowl, combine the butter, honey and whole wheat flour.

4 Spread this mixture over the bottom of the prepared cake pan. Smooth down with a damp spatula or the dampened back of your hand and prick the surface all over with a fork.

5 Bake for 15-20 minutes or until golden brown.

6 While the crust is cooking, make the topping: in a large bowl combine the beaten eggs, honey, coconut and sesame seeds and mix thoroughly. Set aside. Just before you take the cake pan out of the oven, add the baking powder and mix well.

7 Pour the topping over the cooked base and return to the oven for a further 15 minutes or until the top is golden brown.

8 Remove from oven. Cut into pieces while still hot and leave to cool before removing from the cake pan.

Sunflower Bars

6 tbsp filbert or cashew nut butter
  (see p. 50)
6 tbsp apple juice concentrate
  (see p. 51) or maple syrup
½ tsp vanilla extract
½ tsp salt
3 cups sunflower seeds
1½ cups shredded coconut

Preparation 10 minutes
Cooking 35 minutes
Makes 10-12 bars
ⒼⒻ Ⓥ

1 Preheat the oven to 350°F.

2 Grease a 12- × 9-inch baking tray.

3 In a blender or food processor, combine all the ingredients.

4 Press down into the prepared pan and bake for 35 minutes or until golden brown.

5 Remove from oven. Cut while still warm and leave to cool completely before removing from baking tray.

Tofu Cake

Crust
scant 1 cup whole wheat flour
1⅓ cups old-fashioned oats
pinch of salt
4 tbsp malt extract
¼ cup soy oil

Topping
12 oz tofu (see p. 51)
6 tbsp apple juice concentrate
   (see p. 51)
scant 1 cup water
3 tbsp puréed dates
1 tsp tahini (see p. 50)
juice and grated rind of 1 lemon
pinch each of grated nutmeg, ground
   cinnamon and apple pie spice
fresh fruit slices, to decorate

Preparation 15 minutes
Cooking 35 minutes
Makes an 8-inch round cake
Ⓥ

Similar to a cheesecake, this recipe substitutes tofu for the more fattening and less nutritious cream cheese.
   You will need a blender or food processor for this recipe.

1 Preheat the oven to 325°F.

2 Make the crust: put the flour, oats and salt into a blender or food processor. Add the malt and mix thoroughly until evenly distributed. Add the oil and mix again.

3 Grease an 8-inch springform cake pan. Press the oat mixture firmly into the bottom of the pan and bake for 10-15 minutes or until browned.

4 Make the topping: blend all the ingredients for the topping in a blender or food processor until smooth.

5 Pour the mixture over the partially cooked base and bake for 25 minutes until the tofu is set. Remove from oven and cool.

6 Carefully remove from the cake pan and decorate with slices of fresh fruit before serving.

Vegan Fruit Bars

scant 2 cups dried whole apricots,
   soaked for 12 hours or overnight
⅔ cup dried apricot halves,
   soaked for 12 hours or overnight
generous 1 cup raisins, soaked for
   12 hours or overnight
1 cup mixed nuts
1½ cups shredded coconut
scant 1 cup whole wheat flour
1⅓ cups old-fashioned oats
6 tbsp soy oil
6 tbsp apple juice concentrate
   (see p. 51)
1 tsp almond extract
4 tbsp pumpkin seeds

Preparation 10 minutes (allow 12 hours
for soaking the fruit)
Cooking 30-40 minutes
Makes 18 slices
Ⓥ

1 Preheat oven to 300°F.

2 Grease a 9- × 12-inch cake pan and line with wax paper.

3 Mix all the ingredients together by hand in a large mixing bowl until you have a soft pliable mixture. You may need to add a little more liquid because some brands of oats and flours are more absorbent than others.

4 Pour into the cake pan, making sure that the mixture reaches right into the corners. Flatten with the back of your dampened hand or with a damp spatula and bake in the bottom of the oven for 30-40 minutes, or until browned.

5 Remove from oven and leave to cool before cutting.

BREADS

Introduction to bread making

Making good bread is as much an art as a science and strict adherence to a recipe will therefore not always produce the best results. There are many factors to take into account, such as the temperature in your kitchen, the type of oven you use, and so on. So do not give up if your first attempt is disappointing. The following notes may be useful.

Using yeast

Yeasts are not chemicals, but living organisms that are all around us in different forms: in the air, on the leaves and fruit of plants and even on our own skins. In moist, warm conditions, such as in a mass of dough, yeast cells will reproduce rapidly, feeding on the sugary starch from the grain and releasing carbon dioxide and alcohol.

Compressed yeast for baking is usually gray and crumbly in texture. It is increasingly available in health food stores, or even from supermarkets or a local baker. It will keep for 6 months in the freezer or 6 weeks in the refrigerator. Active dried yeast is also available and can be kept for as long as 3 years. It acts exactly like fresh yeast when dissolved in water and produces the same results. The nutritional supplement, Brewer's Yeast, however, is not suitable for making bread rise.

Compressed yeast is available in various size cakes up to 1 pound. It can easily be divided into 1-ounce portions, but for greater accuracy it is a good idea to invest in a small set of kitchen scales, available from gourmet kitchen stores.

Dried yeast is available as active dried or quick rise. All the recipes in this book use active dry. In particularly cold weather, you may need to use slightly more yeast, but in general you should not try to hurry bread making by using extra yeast. A dough that has not had time to mature and strengthen will tend to collapse, however much yeast is used.

In order to scale a recipe up or down, you need to alter the proportion of yeast to other ingredients. If quantities of flour and water are doubled, then only one and a half times the amount of yeast is required. If the quantities of flour and water are halved, then two-thirds the amount of yeast should be used.

Spontaneous leaven and sourdough

Although compressed baker's yeast is now most commonly used, you can make your own yeast leaveners. Natural or "spontaneous" leavens are made by mixing a thick cereal of whole wheat flour and warm water, about $2\frac{1}{2}$ cups water to every 3 cups plus 2 tbsp flour. Leave the mixture to stand in a warm place at least 12 and up to 20 hours, during which time the yeasts in the atmosphere and in the flour itself start a spontaneous ferment. Loaves made with this dough will rise less and more slowly than those made from a normal yeasted dough. Salt is not normally added, since this inhibits the action of the leaven.

The sourdough method provides a stronger rise. Here, a naturally leavened dough is made as above and part of it is kept back as a starter, about $\frac{3}{4}$ cup. For a couple of days before baking the starter is kept at room temperature and fed once every 24-48 hours with about $\frac{1}{2}$ cup water and a handful of flour. Then, it is put in a plastic bag and refrigerated until needed. To make the bread, work another 3 cups plus 2 tbsp flour and 1 cup warm water into the dough, knead gently and bake as for Basic Whole Wheat Bread (see p. 149). Keep a lump of this dough back as a starter for the next batch. It should get stronger with each batch.

Proving or rising

It is important to have a warm, draft-free place in which to rise or "prove" a yeasted dough. On top of a hot oven or near a warm radiator are ideal places. An old-fashioned kitchen range with a warming compartment is also ideal. In summer, a draft-free spot inside a sunny window works well.

Kneading

Unlike cakes and biscuits, bread dough has to be mixed and kneaded over a period of several hours. The moistened flour needs time to release its gluten (see p. 17) and must be kneaded vigorously to bind the strands of gluten into a strong dough to obtain the elasticity which enables bread to rise and hold together successfully.

The dough should be kneaded on a smooth, lightly floured surface such as Formica, marble or stainless steel, although any kitchen tabletop will do. Start to knead as soon as you can remove the dough from the bowl without it sticking to your hands. Push the dough down and away from you with the heels of your hands, and fold it back toward you with your fingers. Do this a few times, then turn the dough through 90 degrees and repeat. Turn and repeat, turn and repeat. If the dough sticks, scrape the surface clean and lightly flour it again. Try not to work in more flour than the dough can easily absorb, or it will become dry and hard. Try not to tear the dough: steady pressure in the kneading action is better than fierce strength. For the final kneading and molding of the loaves, you may find it better to oil the surface and your hands slightly, rather than flouring them.

Finishing the loaves

For a neater finish, always make sure that the last fold in the molded dough is at the bottom of your loaf. To prevent the top crust from drying out in the final rising, brush it with warm water. Make a cut in the top of the loaf to help prevent the crust from cracking as the bread rises.

After the final rising, be gentle when transferring the pans to the oven: just a knock can cause the bread to subside and become heavy.

Bread pans

Bread pans are available in a variety of sizes and shapes, but for standard loaves it is best to have loaf pans in these sizes: $8\frac{1}{2} \times 4\frac{1}{2} \times 2\frac{1}{2}$ inches, and $9 \times 5 \times 3$ inches. Good quality double-thickness bread pans with reinforced corners can be bought fairly cheaply.

All bread pans should be very thoroughly greased the first couple of times they are used, and should not be used for other types of baking. Your bread pans should last a lifetime, and will gradually season to give you evenly baked loaves which slip easily from the pan every time with only the lightest oiling. Avoid non-stick pans: they are more expensive and the surface will eventually break up, leaving bits of the "magic" coating in the crusts of the loaves.

Ovens

Modern domestic ovens (except in old-fashioned kitchen ranges) generally bake by heating and circulating the air inside the oven, rather than by all-around heat from floor, walls and roof which is better for bread making. To improve results, you should stand the pans on a metal tray preheated in the oven, rather than on the rails of the oven shelves, and place an ovenproof dish of water on the bottom of the oven to create a moist atmosphere. Loaves should always be baked in the middle of the oven; rolls are better at the top where the oven is hottest. To brown off the bottom of your loaves, you may need to turn them upside down in their pans for the last 5 minutes of baking.

One final point: you should never open the oven door until just before you expect bread (or cakes) to be done. The longer the oven temperature is maintained, the better bread will bake. If cooked, the bread will sound hollow when gently tapped on the bottom.

Measurements

It is particularly important in baking to follow the exact measurements given in the recipes. Be sure to measure carefully and use level cup, tablespoon and teaspoon measures. Different brands of flour have different degrees of absorbency so it is a good idea to have extra liquid available to use if needed.

Making bread

1 In a bowl, thoroughly mix a little over half the flour into the water and dissolved yeast with a hand whisk. It should have a smooth, soupy or oatmeal-like consistency.

2 After proving, work in the salt and the remaining flour with your hand to form a dough.

3 It is easiest to knead the dough while still in the bowl. Use one hand to knead and the other to turn the bowl. The first movement involves pulling the dough up and over toward you with your fingers so that it folds over.

4 The second kneading movement involves pushing the folded dough down into the bowl with your fist. Then, push the dough away from you, pick up the edge and begin the movements again. The process is a smooth continuous one, and the bowl should be rotated all the time to ensure even kneading of the dough.

5 Divide the dough into 2 halves and pat each into a loaf shape. Place into the prepared loaf pans.

Basic Whole Wheat Bread

1 oz compressed yeast or 1½ tsp active dried

2½ cups warm water

7 cups whole wheat flour

2 tsp salt

Preparation 20 minutes (allow 2 hours rising time)

Cooking 40-45 minutes

Makes one 9- × 5- × 3-inch loaf or two 8½- × 4½- × 2½-inch loaves

1 In a large bowl, dissolve the yeast in the water.

2 Stir in a little over half the flour until the mixture has an oatmeal-like consistency.

3 Mix thoroughly with a hand whisk, then cover and stand to prove in a warm, draft-free place for 30-45 minutes until the mixture has risen visibly.

4 Stir in the salt with a wooden spoon, then gradually work in more flour until you have a dough that you can knead.

5 Knead thoroughly and methodically until a smooth texture is achieved.

6 Cover and stand to rise in a warm, draft-free place for 30-45 minutes until the dough has doubled in size.

7 Knead again, then divide and mold into individual loaves.

8 Oil one 9- × 5- × 3-inch loaf pan or two 8½- × 4½- × 2½-inch loaf pans. Place the loaves in the pans. Stand to rise for a further 30 minutes or until they have doubled in size, rising to fill the pans.

9 Meanwhile, preheat the oven to 425°F.

10 Bake for 40-45 minutes until the loaves sound hollow when tapped. Remove from pans and stand on a rack to cool.

Shaping different loaves

Making a cottage loaf
1 Pat the dough into shape, cut off one-third and roll into 2 balls.

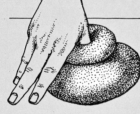

2 Press the small ball into the large ball with your thumb.

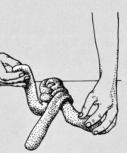

Making a braid
1 Roll out 3 long tubes, press together at one end and braid.

2 Tuck the ends under the loaf and securely press together.

Making French bread
1 Roll out the dough into a long thick tube with your hands.

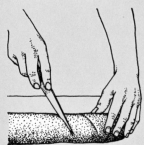

2 Round the edges and make evenly spaced diagonal cuts with a sharp knife for decoration.

Making rolls
1 To make 8 rolls, cut the dough into even segments. Pull apart and pat each into a ball.

2 Knead each roll with the palm of your hand on a flat surface, rolling and folding.

Making a mouse
1 You need: an egg-shaped body, 2 ears, a tail, a nose and 2 raisins for eyes.

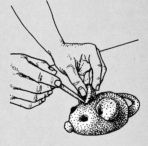

2 Put the pieces together, using a little water to seal. Press the ears on to the body with a chopstick.

Basic White Bread

¾ oz compressed yeast or 1 tsp active
   dried
scant 2 cups warm water
4 cups plus 4 tbsp flour
1½ tsp salt

**Preparation 20 minutes (allow 1½
   hours rising time)**
Cooking 40-45 minutes
Makes three 6 × 3½ × 3-inch loaves

1 In a large bowl, dissolve the yeast in the water.

2 Stir in a little over half the flour until the mixture has an oatmeal-like consistency.

3 Mix thoroughly with a hand whisk, then cover and stand to rise in a warm draft-free place for 30 minutes until the mixture has risen visibly.

4 Stir in the salt with a wooden spoon, then gradually work in more flour until you have a dough you can knead.

5 Knead the dough thoroughly and methodically until a smooth texture is achieved.

6 Cover and stand to rise in a warm, draft-free place for 30-45 minutes until the mixture has doubled in size.

7 Knead again, then divide and mold into loaves.

8 Oil three 6 in × 3½ in × 3 in loaf pans. Place the loaves in the pans. Stand for a further 20 minutes until they have approximately doubled in size, rising to fill the pans.

9 Meanwhile, preheat the oven to 425°F.

10 Bake for 40 minutes until the loaves sound hollow when tapped.

11 Remove from pans and leave to cool on a rack.

◆

Cheese Croissants with Mushrooms

Filling
¼ cup butter
4 cups thinly sliced mushrooms
1 tbsp tamari
3 garlic cloves, crushed
½ tsp grated root ginger
1 tsp finely chopped fresh basil or
   ½ tsp dried
2¼ cups grated cheese

Dough
1 oz compressed yeast or 1½ tsp active
   dried
1¼ cups milk
4 cups plus 2 tbsp whole wheat flour
½ cup butter
½ tsp salt
2 eggs
extra milk for glazing

**Preparation 20 minutes (allow 1¼
   hours rising time)**
Cooking 15 minutes
Makes 12 croissants

These delicious croissants are surprisingly easy to make.

1 Make the filling: melt the butter in a pan. Sauté the mushrooms in the butter. Cover and cook over a low heat for 2-3 minutes.

2 Add the tamari, garlic, ginger and basil and cook for a further 1-2 minutes until the mushrooms are cooked.

3 Remove from the heat. Stir in 1¾ cups of cheese, reserving the remainder for putting on top of the croissants. Leave to cool.

4 Make the dough: in a bowl, dissolve the yeast in the milk.

5 Put all but 2 handfuls of the flour into a large mixing bowl. Cut the butter into the flour. Mix in the salt.

6 Make a well in the center of the flour and break the eggs into it. Beat the eggs roughly with a fork and begin to mix gently with a wooden spoon.

7 Gradually add the milk and yeast and mix together until you have a sticky dough.

8 Using your hands, work in the remainder of the flour and set aside. The dough should be slack but not wet.

9 Cover the bowl and set aside in a warm, draft-free place for 30-45 minutes until the mixture has risen visibly.

10 Gently knead the dough into a smooth, compact mass. Cover and set aside in a warm, draft-free place for 30-45 minutes until the dough has doubled in size.

11 Knead the dough again. Flour it on both sides and carefully roll it out into a sheet measuring 36 × 12 inches. Divide this into twelve 6-inch squares. (You may find it easier to halve the dough and roll out 2 sheets, each measuring 18 × 12 inches and divide these into six 6-inch squares each.)

12 Divide the filling into 12 portions: it may still be warm but it should not be hot. Place in a diagonal strip along each square.

13 Starting from one corner, roll up each croissant, taking care not to tear the dough. Pinch the ends together. Bend them around into crescent shapes, giving each a twist as you do it.

14 Preheat the oven to 475°F.

15 Place the finished croissants on a greased baking tray at least 1-inch apart. Brush the top of each croissant with milk and sprinkle a little grated cheese on top. Set the croissants aside in a warm place for another 15 minutes to rise.

16 Bake the croissants for 12-15 minutes until the tops are a rich golden brown. Serve warm.

Making the croissants

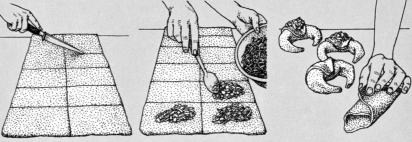
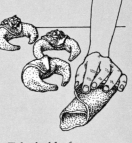

1 Divide the rolled-out sheet of dough into 12 squares.

2 Place a spoonful of the filling onto each square, and spread out so that it stretches diagonally across the pastry.

3 Take hold of one corner of the pastry square and fold it diagonally over the filling. Take hold of the opposite corner of pastry and fold it over the first corner. Press down securely, then pinch the two ends together firmly and bend into a croissant shape.

Cheese & Herb Bread

¾ oz compressed yeast or 1 tsp active
dried
1¼ cups warm water
1 tsp salt
3½ cups plus 2 tbsp whole wheat flour

Filling
4 cups grated cheese
1 tsp paprika
2 tsp finely chopped fresh basil
or 1tsp dried
2 tsp finely chopped fresh oregano
or 1 tsp dried
1 tbsp finely chopped fresh parsley

**Preparation 20 minutes (allow 2 hours
rising time)
Cooking 40-45 minutes
Makes two 6 × 3½ × 3-inch loaves**

**Great care should be taken in handling the freshly baked loaf, as
the cooked cheese inside it will make it softer than a regular loaf.**

1 In a large bowl, dissolve the yeast in the water.

2 Stir in a little over half the flour until the mixture has an oatmeal-like consistency.

3 Mix thoroughly with a hand whisk, then cover and stand to rise in a warm, draft-free place for 30-45 minutes until the mixture has risen visibly.

4 Stir in the salt with a wooden spoon, then gradually work in more flour until you have a dough that you can knead.

5 Knead the dough thoroughly and methodically until a smooth texture is achieved.

6 Cover and stand to rise in a warm, draft-free place for 30-45 minutes until the dough has doubled in size.

7 Knead again, then divide and mold into 2 pieces.

8 Prepare the filling: mix the cheese and paprika with the herbs.

9 On a lightly oiled surface, roll out the 2 pieces of dough into strips about 4 × 12 inches. Spread with the cheese and herb mixture, reserving about a quarter of the mixture for the topping. Roll up the 2 strips as tightly as possible.

10 Oil two 6 in × 3½ in × 3 in loaf pans. Press the roll firmly down into the pans and top with the remaining cheese and herb mixture.

11 Stand to rise in a warm, draft-free place for 30-45 minutes, until the loaves have almost doubled in size, rising to fill the pans.

12 Meanwhile, preheat the oven to 425°F.

13 Bake for 40-45 minutes until the loaves sound hollow if tapped.

◆

Dervish Barley Bread

1 tbsp honey
1½ cups water
scant 2 cups fine oatmeal
good pinch of salt
scant 2 cups barley flour

**Preparation 10 minutes (allow 30
minutes standing time)
Cooking 15 minutes
Makes 8 breads**

1 Mix together the honey, water, oatmeal and salt in a large mixing bowl. Beat into a smooth batter with a hand whisk. Leave to stand for 10 minutes until the oatmeal has absorbed some of the liquid.

2 Gradually add the barley flour and work into a wet sticky dough with a spoon; you should need slightly less than 2 cups. Allow to stand for another 20 minutes until the dough is soft but workable.

3 Divide into 8 roughly equal pieces. Mold each piece carefully into a compact flat oval shape and place on a lightly greased surface.

4 Preheat the oven to 400°F.

5 Roll each piece of dough out into a strip approximately 7 × 1½ inches. Arrange the strips on a lightly floured baking tray and put straight into the oven.

6 Bake for 15 minutes or until a golden crust has formed. Cool on a rack before serving.

Fruit & Malt Bread

¾ oz compressed yeast or 1 tsp active dried
1 cup plus 2 tbsp warm water
3½ cups plus 2 tbsp whole wheat flour
1 tsp salt
1 tbsp soy oil
3 tbsp malt extract
1½ cups raisins, currants or other dried fruit

Preparation 20 minutes (allow 2 hours rising time)
Cooking 45 minutes
Makes two 6 × 3½ × 3-inch loaves

1 In a large bowl, dissolve the yeast in the water.

2 Stir in a little over half the flour until the mixture has an oatmeal-like consistency.

3 Mix thoroughly with a hand whisk, then cover and stand to rise in a warm, draft-free place for 30-45 minutes until the mixture has risen visibly.

4 Add the salt, oil, malt and dried fruit and stir together, then gradually work in more flour until you have a dough that you can knead.

5 Knead the dough thoroughly and methodically until a smooth texture is achieved.

6 Cover and stand to rise in a warm, draft-free place for 30-45 minutes until the dough has doubled in size.

7 Knead again on a lightly greased surface, then divide and mold into 2 individual loaves.

8 Oil two 6 in × 3½ in × 3 in loaf pans. Place the loaves in the pans. Stand to rise for a further 30-45 minutes or until they have approximately doubled in size, rising to fill the pans.

9 Meanwhile, preheat the oven to 400°F.

10 Bake for 40-45 minutes until the loaves have a dark, even crust.

11 Remove from pans and stand on rack to cool.

Rye Bread

3½ cups plus 2 tbsp medium rye flour
2½ cups warm water
1 oz compressed yeast or 1½ tsp active
   dried
2 tsp salt
1 tbsp soy or other oil
1 tbsp molasses
1 tsp caraway seeds (optional)
about 3½ cups plus 2 tbsp whole wheat
   flour

**Preparation 20 minutes (allow
12 hours standing time and 1½ hours
rising time)
Cooking 45 minutes
Makes one 9½- × 5- × 3-inch loaf or
two 8½- × 4½- × 2½-inch loaves**

Rye bread can be given an attractive striped finish by dusting the tops of the loaves with rye flour just before they are put into the pans, and then giving them a series of diagonal cuts, which open as the loaves rise.

1 In a large bowl, mix the rye flour with the water. Beat together with a hand whisk until the mixture has an oatmeal-like consistency and leave to stand overnight.

2 After overnight standing, thoroughly stir in the yeast to dissolve. Cover and stand to rise in a warm, draft-free place for 30 minutes until the mixture has risen visibly.

3 Add the salt, oil, molasses, and the caraway seeds, if liked, and then gradually work in the whole wheat flour until you have a dough that you can knead.

4 Knead the dough thoroughly and methodically until a smooth texture is achieved.

5 Cover and stand to prove for 30-45 minutes. (The dough may not have quite doubled in size, but should have risen visibly.)

6 Knead again, then divide and mold into a loaf shape.

7 Lightly grease a 9½- × 5- × 3-inch pan or two 8½- × 4½- × 2½-inch loaf pans. Place the dough in the pan. Stand to rise for a further 30 minutes, or until approximately double in size, rising to fill the pan(s).

8 Meanwhile, preheat the oven to 425°F.

9 Bake for 40-45 minutes until the loaves sound hollow if tapped.

10 Remove from pans and stand on a rack to cool.

Note: This method may also be followed using entirely rye flour: about 7 cups. The bread will not rise quite as much, of course, but can be delicious, and provided you do not omit the stage of leaving an oatmeal-like mixture of rye flour and water to stand overnight, you should be able to achieve an acceptable result. Some cracked rye, or soaked or partially cooked whole rye kernels may also be used. They should be added at the first stage, and allowed to steep overnight in the oatmeal-like mixture.

Sunflower Seed Bread

¾ oz compressed yeast or 1 tsp active dried
1¼ cups warm water
3½ cups plus 2 tbsp whole wheat flour
1 tsp salt
1 tbsp soy oil
1 tbsp honey
1 cup sunflower seeds

Preparation 20 minutes (allow 2 hours rising time)
Cooking 45 minutes
Makes two 6 × 3½ × 3-inch loaves

1 In a large bowl, dissolve the yeast in the water.

2 Stir in a little over half the flour until the mixture has an oatmeal-like consistency.

3 Mix thoroughly with a hand whisk, then cover and stand to rise in a warm, draft-free place for 30-45 minutes until the dough has risen visibly.

4 Add the salt, oil, honey and sunflower seeds and stir in, then gradually work in more flour until you have a dough that you can knead easily.

5 Knead the dough thoroughly and methodically until a smooth texture is achieved.

6 Cover and stand to rise in a warm, draft-free place for 30-45 minutes, until the dough has doubled in size.

7 Knead again on a lightly oiled surface, then divide and mold into 2 individual loaves.

8 Lightly grease two 6 in × 3½ in × 3 in loaf pans. Place the loaves in the pans. Stand to rise for a further 30-45 minutes or until they have approximately doubled in size, rising to fill the pans.

9 Preheat the oven to 400°F.

10 Bake for 45 minutes until the loaves sound hollow when tapped.

11 Remove from pans and stand on a rack to cool.

Three-Seed Bread

¾ oz compressed yeast or 1 tsp active
   dried
1¼ cups warm water
3½ cups plus 2 tbsp whole wheat flour
1 tsp salt
1 tbsp soy oil
1 tbsp malt extract
4 tbsp sesame seeds
4 tbsp poppy seeds
4 tbsp linseeds

**Preparation 20 minutes (allow 2 hours
rising time)**
Cooking 45 minutes
Makes two 6 × 3½ × 3-inch loaves

1 In a large bowl, dissolve the yeast in the water.

2 Mix in a little over half of the flour until the mixture has an oatmeal-like consistency.

3 Mix thoroughly with a hand whisk, then cover and stand to rise in a warm, draft-free place for 30-45 minutes until the dough has risen visibly.

4 Add the salt, oil, malt extract and seeds and stir together, then gradually work in the rest of the flour until you have a dough that you can knead.

5 Knead the dough thoroughly and methodically until a smooth texture is achieved.

6 Cover and stand to rise in a warm, draft-free place for 30-45 minutes until the dough has doubled in size.

7 Knead again on a lightly oiled surface, then divide and mold into 2 individual loaves.

8 Lightly grease two 6 in × 3½ in × 3 in loaf pans. Place the loaves in the pans. Stand to rise for a further 30-45 minutes until they have approximately doubled in size, rising to fill the pans.

9 Preheat the oven to 400°F.

10 Bake for 45 minutes, until the loaves sound hollow when tapped.

11 Remove from pans and stand on a rack to cool.

INDEX

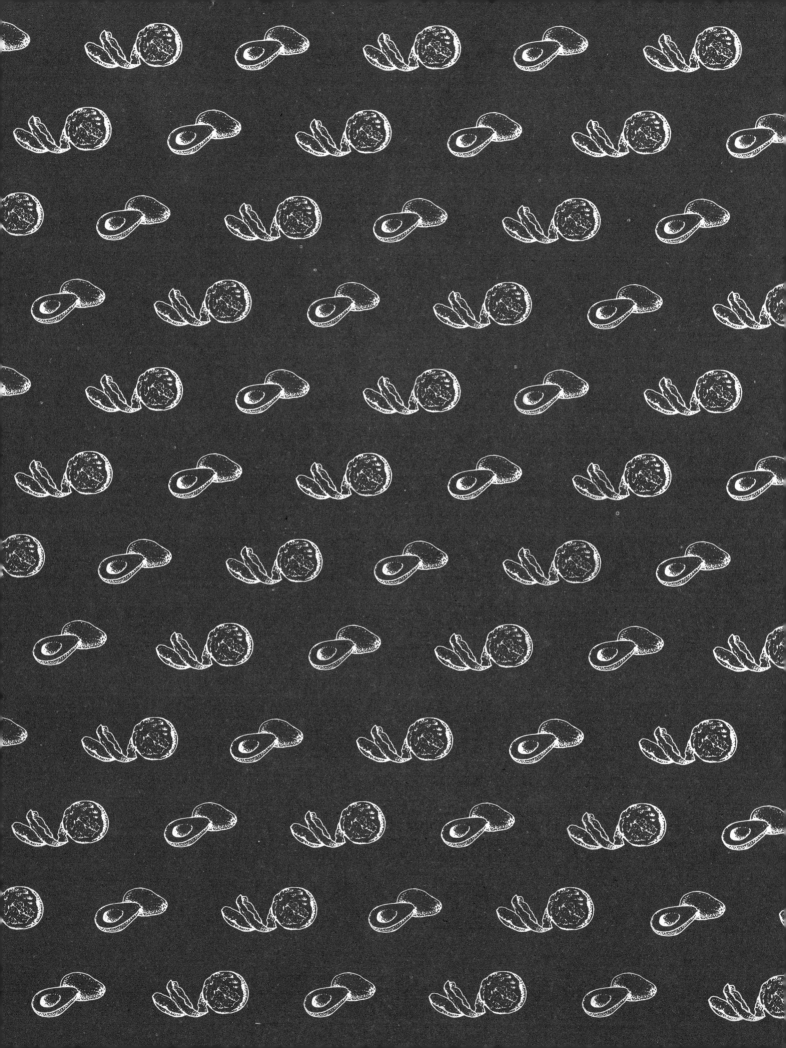